Subversive Habits

Subversive Habits

Black Catholic Nuns in the Long
African American Freedom Struggle

SHANNEN DEE WILLIAMS

Duke University Press *Durham and London* 2022

© 2022 DUKE UNIVERSITY PRESS. *All rights reserved*
Typeset in Helvetica and Arno Pro.

Library of Congress Cataloging-in-Publication Data
Names: Williams, Shannen Dee, [date] author.
Title: Subversive habits : Black Catholic nuns in the long African American
freedom struggle / Shannen Dee Williams.
Description: Durham : Duke University Press, 2022. |
Includes bibliographical references and index.
Identifiers: LCCN 2021032231 (print)
LCCN 2021032232 (ebook)
ISBN 9781478015574 (hardcover)
ISBN 9781478018209 (paperback)
ISBN 9781478022817 (ebook)
Subjects: LCSH: African American nuns—History—20th century. | African
American Catholics—History—20th century. | Women in the Catholic
Church—UnitedStates— History—20th century.|Segregation— Religious
aspects—CatholicChurch— History—20th century.| BISAC: SOCIAL
SCIENCE / Black Studies (Global) | RELIGION / Christianity / Catholic
Classification: LCC BX1407.B63 W55 2022 (print) | LCC BX1407.B63 (ebook) |
DDC 277.30089/96073—dc23
LC recordavailableatHTTps:// lccn.loc.gov/2021032231
LC ebook recordavailableatHTTps:// lccn.loc.gov/2021032232

Cover art: Sister Mary Antona Ebo, FSM, addresses the crowd in Selma,
Alabama, March 10, 1965. Courtesy BeTTmann/GeTTy Images.

For my mother,
Vidonia Williams,

and
Dr. Patricia Grey

In loving memory of my father,
U. D. Williams Jr.

CONTENTS

AUS	Association of Urban Sisters
BVM	Sisters of Charity of the Blessed Virgin Mary
CBMWCP	Catholic Board for Mission Work among the Colored People
CDP	Congregation of Divine Providence, also known as the Sisters of Divine Providence
CSFN	Sisters of the Holy Family of Nazareth (Latin: Congregatio Sororum Sacrae Familiae de Nazaret)
CSJ	Congregation of the Sisters of Saint Joseph, also known as the Sisters of Saint Joseph; and the Sisters of Saint Joseph of Carondelet
CSSF	Congregation of Sisters of Saint Felix of Cantalice, also known as the Felician Sisters
CUA	Catholic University of America
DC	Daughters of Charity of Saint Vincent de Paul, also known as the Sisters of Charity of Saint Vincent de Paul (SC)
DD	Doctor of Divinity (Latin: Doctor Divinitatis)

DES	Department of Educational Services of the National Catholic Conference for Interracial Justice
DHM	Daughters of the Heart of Mary
FCC	Federated Colored Catholics of the United States
FCSP	Daughters of Charity, Servants of the Poor, later known as the Sisters of Providence (French: Filles de la Charité, Servantes des Pauvres)
FHM	Franciscan Handmaids of the Most Pure Heart of Mary, originally the Handmaids of the Most Pure Heart of Mary
FMI	Daughters of Mary Immaculate, also known as the Marianist Sisters (French: Filles de Marie Immaculée)
FSM	Franciscan Sisters of Mary (formerly the Sisters of St. Mary, SSM)
FSP	Daughters of St. Paul (Latin: Filiarum Sancti Pauli)
FSPA	Franciscan Sisters of Perpetual Adoration
HDR	Handmaids of the Divine Redeemer
HM	Sisters of the Humility of Mary
HVM	Sisters, Home Visitors of Mary
IC	Immaculate Conception (School), Charleston, SC
IHM	Sisters, Servants of Immaculate Heart of Mary, also known as the Immaculate Heart of Mary Sisters
LCWR	Leadership Conference of Women Religious
MFIC	Missionary Franciscans of the Immaculate Conception
MM	Maryknoll Missionaries, also known as the Catholic Foreign Mission Society of America
MSBT	Missionary Servants of the Most Blessed Trinity, also known as the Trinitarians
MSOLA	Missionary Sisters of Our Lady of Africa, also known as the White Sisters of Africa

NAACP	National Association for the Advancement of Colored People
NBCCC	National Black Catholic Clergy Caucus, originally the Black Catholic Clergy Caucus
NBSC	National Black Sisters' Conference
NCCIJ	National Catholic Conference for Interracial Justice
NCEA	National Catholic Educational Association
NCWC	National Catholic Welfare Conference
NOBC	National Office for Black Catholics
OCD	Order of Discalced Carmelites (Latin: Ordo Carmelitarum Discalceatorum)
OP	Order of Preachers, also known as the Dominicans (Latin: Ordo Praedicatorum)
OSA	Order of Saint Augustine
OSB	Order of Saint Benedict
OSF	Order of Saint Francis and Order of the Third Order of Saint Francis
OSP	Oblate Sisters of Providence
RGS	Religious of Our Lady of Charity of the Good Shepherd, also known as the Good Shepherd Sisters
RSCJ	Religious of the Sacred Heart of Jesus, also known as the Society of the Sacred Heart and the Sacred Heart Sisters (Latin: Religiosae Sanctissimi Cordis Jesu)
RSM	Religious Sisters of Mercy, or the Sisters of Mercy
SBS	Sisters of the Blessed Sacrament, formerly the Sisters of the Blessed Sacrament for Indians and Colored People
SC	Sisters of Charity of St. Joseph and the Sisters of Charity of Saint Vincent de Paul
SCA	Sisters of Charity of Saint Augustine
SCN	Sisters of Charity of Nazareth

SCNY	Sisters of Charity of New York
SCSH	Sisters of Charity of Seton Hill
SJ	Society of Jesus, also known as the Jesuit Fathers
SL	Sisters of Loretto at the Foot of the Cross
SLU	Saint Louis University
SND	Sisters of Notre Dame
SNDdeN	Sisters of Notre Dame de Namur
SNJM	Sisters of the Holy Names of Jesus and Mary
SP	Sisters of Providence and Sisters of Providence of Saint Mary-of-the-Woods
SSE	Society of Saint Edmund
SSF	Sisters of the Holy Family (French: Soeurs de Sainte Famille)
SSH	Sisters of the Sacred Heart (in Benin City, Nigeria)
SSJ	Sisters of Saint Joseph
SSJ	Society of Saint Joseph of the Sacred Heart, also known as the Josephite Fathers
SSM	Sisters of Saint Mary, later the Franciscan Sisters of Mary (FSM)
SSND	School Sisters of Notre Dame
SSpS	Missionary Sisters, Servants of the Holy Spirit, formerly the Missionary Sisters, Servants of the Holy Ghost (Latin: Servae Spiritus Sancti)
SSSF	School Sisters of Saint Francis
SVD	Society of the Divine Word, also known as the Divine Word Missionaries (Latin: Societas Verbi Divini)
UAS	Urban Apostolate of Sisters
USCCB	United States Conference of Catholic Bishops
VSC	Vincentian Sisters of Charity

NOTE ON TERMINOLOGY

Throughout this study, I use the terms *sister* and *nun* interchangeably. However, there are important differences between the two. A Roman Catholic nun is a woman who has professed the vows and lives in a cloistered setting with minimal contact with the secular world. A sister, in contrast, is a woman who has professed the vows but engages in public works such as teaching, nursing, and other social service ministries. Because sisters and nuns participate in the religious life of the Church, they are both women religious. The overwhelming majority of the women discussed in this study are sisters. However, nuns and sisters both use the title Sister, and many sisters engaged in public ministries refer to themselves as nuns. So I have followed their lead. At the end of this book, there is a glossary from the Leadership Conference of Women Religious with a few additional terms for those unfamiliar with religious life and the Catholic Church more broadly.[1]

Prior to the Second Vatican Council, or Vatican II, most women and girls who entered communities and professed vows took religious names to signify their consecrated status and stopped using their baptismal and family names. Most sisters' religious names included "Mary" or "Marie" in some fashion to honor Mary, Jesus's mother. After the reforms of Vatican II, many congregations granted their members the option of reverting back to their baptismal names, and many sisters did so. Some, though, legally assumed their religious names.

This book includes the names of scores of women religious. When available, I have included a sister's religious, baptismal, and family name. Baptismal names are provided in parentheses. For example, in the case of Mother Mary Lange, the chief foundress of the Oblate Sisters of Providence, her name will appear as Mother Mary (Elizabeth Clarisse) Lange at first mention. Elizabeth Clarisse is her baptismal name; Lange is her family name. Because sisters identified themselves, and/or were referred to by others, using varying versions of their names at different points in religious life, I have followed the lead of the sister or the source in which she is identified and cross-referenced her name for clarity in the endnotes. Finally, in several instances, I have included the stories of ex-sisters and laywomen who later married and changed their surnames. In a few of those cases, I have used only the women's maiden names to avoid confusion.

PREFACE. BEARING WITNESS TO A SILENCED PAST

I regard my responsibilities as a Black writer as someone who must bear witness, someone who must record the way it used to be. —TONI MORRISON, 1977 interview on WTTW's *Chicago Tonight*

This book began as an attempt to make sense of an extraordinary news story and photograph that I stumbled on in early 2007. At the time, I was perusing microfilmed editions of Black-owned newspapers in search of a little-known dimension of the American past. While scanning through a roll of the *Pittsburgh Courier*, I finally encountered a 1968 article announcing the formation of a Black power federation of Catholic nuns called the National Black Sisters' Conference (NBSC). The article's title alone, "Black Sisters Weigh Contradictions in Christian and Secular Community: 200 Negro Nuns Attend First Nat'l Meet," immediately piqued my interest. However, it was the accompanying photograph of four smiling Black Catholic sisters that steadied my hand on the microfilm reader that day.[2] Until that moment, I, a lifelong Catholic, had never seen a Black nun except in a Hollywood film. In fact, the only Black sister that I knew of at the time was Sister Mary Clarence, the fictional character played by Whoopi Goldberg in the critically acclaimed *Sister Act* film franchise. Deeply ashamed of my ignorance, I soon learned that I was not alone. Even my mother—who attended Catholic schools for the entirety of her formal education and who in 1974 became one of the first three Black women to graduate from the University of Notre Dame—was unaware of the existence of Black nuns in our church. "No, only white nuns taught us in our schools," my mother relayed to me on the telephone later that evening. "But I wish I had known. I wish we'd had Black nuns in Savannah[, Georgia,] when I was growing up."

Stunned by my mother's revelation, I set out to learn as much as I could about the NBSC and understand the roots of the invisibility of Black Catholic sisters in our lives. From Cyprian Davis's landmark study of the US Black Catholic community, I discovered that there had been Black nuns in my mother's hometown in the late nineteenth and early twentieth centuries. Before anti-Black prejudice and violent threats pushed these consecrated women out, members of two all-Black sisterhoods helped to lay the foundation for and ensure the survival of the city's Black Catholic educational system. Their heroic efforts made my mother's—and by extension my own—journey into Catholicism possible.[3] Yet the white nuns and priests who taught my mother and hundreds of other Black children in Savannah during America's civil rights and Black power years never once alluded to Black sisters in their lessons. According to my mother, her white instructors did not teach any Black history or art either. After calling and writing a host of Catholic institutions to track down some of the sisters and ex-sisters who established the NBSC, I finally began to understand why.

"The saga of America's black women who have dared to be poor, chaste, and obedient is largely untold," wrote Sister Mary Shawn Copeland in 1975. "It is an uneasy story, not only because it is rooted in the American dilemma—racism—but also because the position of [a] woman in an oppressed group is traditionally delicate and strategic."[4] By the time I interviewed her, Copeland was a distinguished professor at Boston College and the first Black president of the Catholic Theological Society of America. She had also been out of religious life for thirteen years. In the 1960s and 1970s, however, Copeland—the first African American Felician Sister in Detroit, Michigan, and later an Adrian Dominican Sister—had been one of the NBSC's most visible leaders.[5] She had also done more than anyone to preserve the organization's memory in the face of marginalization and erasure.[6] In addition to publishing the first scholarly article on the NBSC, Copeland in the early 2000s arranged for the deposit of the organization's papers at Marquette University.[7] "I am so glad that you are interested in the Black Sisters' Conference," Copeland expressed during our first conversation. "We've been waiting on someone to tell this story."[8]

While Copeland's willingness to share her experiences with me proved pivotal, it was Dr. Patricia Grey, the NBSC's founding president and one of the four nuns featured in the *Pittsburgh Courier* photograph, who radically changed this book's focus. Routinely described by her female and male peers as one of the most intellectually talented and charismatic Catholic sisters of her generation, Grey, known in religion as Sister M. Martin de Porres, had been the NBSC's heart and soul in its formative years.[9] As Pittsburgh's first Black Religious Sister of Mercy and the conference's leading public voice, Grey was also the face and force of the "new Black nun." However, in 1974, Grey abruptly departed religious life and stopped giving interviews related to the NBSC.[10]

"I don't like to look back," Grey frequently repeated during the first of our many conversations over the years.[11] However, after I presented Grey with a recently published book on Catholic sisters' activism in the Black freedom struggle of the 1960s and 1970s, she quickly changed her mind. Visibly frustrated by the book's erasure of Black sisters' vanguard activism in the Catholic fight for racial justice, its cursory mention of white sisters' long-standing practices of white supremacy and exclusion, and its glaring omissions about the one Black nun briefly discussed in its pages, the sixty-five-year-old ex-nun quietly stood and departed the room.[12] Several minutes later, Grey returned with a treasure trove: her personal archive from her tenure in religious life. In handing over the materials, Grey revealed that in the 1970s, the NBSC executive board had desired to publish a book documenting Black sisters' history in the United States. She also lamented the enduring invisibility of Black sisters' lives and labors in church and wider American history. Then, in her great wisdom, Grey gently encouraged me to consider expanding my attention to the mostly unsung and underresearched history of the nation's Black sisterhoods. "We [the NBSC] were not the first Black sisters to revolt in the Church," she quietly declared. "If you can, try to tell all of our stories."[13]

In the pages ahead, I recover the voices of a group of Black American churchwomen whose lives, labors, and struggles have been systematically ignored, routinely dismissed as insignificant, and too often reduced to myth. For thirteen years, I sought the untold stories of the nation's Black Catholic sisters, and I found no accounts bearing any resemblance to the fabled Hollywood tale of Sister Mary Clarence. I also failed to encounter Black sisters whose lived experiences confirmed many of the existing narratives of American Catholicism or the master story of Catholic sisters in the United States. Instead—from a host of widely ignored archival sources, previously sealed Church records, out-of-print books, periodicals, and over a hundred oral interviews—I bore witness to a profoundly unfamiliar history that disrupts and revises much of what has been said and written about the US Catholic Church and the place of Black people within it. Because it is impossible to narrate Black sisters' journey in the United States—accurately and honestly—without confronting the Church's largely unacknowledged and unreconciled histories of colonialism, slavery, and segregation, I address these violent systems of power and their perpetrators—male and female—directly. In so doing, this book also recovers an overlooked chapter in the history of the long African American freedom struggle—a tradition of sustained Black Catholic resistance to white supremacy and exclusion that most scholars argue does not exist.

When confronted with a silenced past, the greatest responsibility of the historian—and the most radical thing any person can do—is to tell the story that was never meant to be told. *Subversive Habits*, then, marks a new starting point in historical truth telling in the Catholic Church and wider American society. For far too long, scholars of the American, Catholic, and Black pasts have unconsciously or consciously declared—by virtue of misrepresentation, marginalization, and outright erasure—that the history of Black Catholic nuns does not matter. In offering the first full survey of Black sisters' lives and struggles in the United States, this book unequivocally demonstrates that their history does matter—and has always mattered.

ACKNOWLEDGMENTS

Subversive Habits would not have come to fruition without the generosity and support of many people and institutions. I would be remiss, however, if I did not begin by acknowledging and praising the sure and ever-present hand of God, which guided me to this project. I never intended to pursue research in Black Catholic history, yet telling stories of the Church's Black faithful has become my life's work. I thank Sisters Mary Aloysius Becraft, Mary Ursula Wallace, and Thea Bowman and Mothers Mary Lange, Henriette Delille, Josephine Charles, Mathilda Beasley, M. Theresa Jacques, and Mary Theodore Williams for lighting the way.

I owe a tremendous debt to the many individuals who shared their stories with me over the years. They include a host of sisters, former sisters, priests, lay Catholics, and others whose lives intersected with African American sisters in some way. Without their contributions, it would have been impossible to write this book. I am grateful for every interview given, every photo and document shared, and every friendship cultivated. To those who were unable to discuss their tenures in religious life on the record but still sent their prayers for this book's success, thank you also. *Subversive Habits* is first and foremost a labor of love written for the nation's Black Catholic sisters and all those who have witnessed and benefited from their efforts.

The Leadership Conference of Women Religious (LCWR) also deserves special mention. In my early research, I encountered a host of restrictive archival policies limiting access to documents essential to reconstructing the history of racial segregation and exclusion in female religious life. During an invited keynote address at the annual LCWR meeting in 2016, I outlined these challenges and asked the nation's women congregational leaders for assistance. In response, several pledged their support. I received a research grant from Region IV of the LCWR to continue my research, and several leaders invited me to deliver talks to their communities and the regional LCWR meetings. Conversations following these presentations and expanded archival access proved invaluable. A special thanks to Sisters Mary Greta Jupiter, Mary Pellegrino, Sally Witt, and Anita Baird. My gratitude also extends to all the congregations that invited me to speak and/or welcomed me into their archives over the years, especially the Sisters of Mercy of America, the Sisters of Charity of New York, the Sisters of Notre Dame de Namur, the Sisters of Loretto at the Foot of the Cross, the Dominican Sisters of Peace, and the Sisters of St. Joseph of Carondelet.

Subventions for research, travel, and writing from several foundations also aided in this book's completion. The Postdoctoral Fellowship in African-American Studies at Case Western Reserve University, the Scholar-in-Residence Fellowship at the Schomburg Center for Research in Black Culture in New York City, and a research leave from the University of Tennessee, Knoxville, provided critical time and space to conduct additional research and work on this manuscript. Other institutional support includes the Albert K. LePage Endowed Assistant Professorship, Villanova University; Catholicism and the Common Good Research Grant, Henry Luce Foundation; Charlotte W. Newcombe Doctoral Fellowship for Religion and Ethics, Woodrow Wilson National Foundation; Benjamin L. Hooks Institute for Social Change Visiting Fellowship, University of Memphis; Huggins-Quarles Award, Organization of American Historians; John Tracy Ellis Dissertation Award, American Catholic Historical Association; Cushwa Center for the Study of American Catholicism Research Travel Grant, University of Notre Dame; Dorothy Mohler Research Grant, Catholic University of America; Rutgers Center for Historical Analysis Graduate Research Fellowship, Rutgers University; and Andrew W. Mellon Foundation Research Grant, Rutgers Graduate School of Arts and Sciences.

Without the labor and efficiency of an army of archivists and librarians, conducting the research for this book would have been much more difficult. Tremendous thanks are due to the staffs of the libraries and archives consulted for this project, especially Sharon Knecht, Elizabeth S. Johnson, and Sisters Carolyn Leslie, Louise Grundish, and Celia Struck. Special thanks are also due to the Oblate Sisters of Providence and the Sisters of the Holy Family for providing me extensive access to their congregational archives. In the case of the Franciscan Handmaids of the Most Pure Heart of Mary, I am indebted to former congregational leader Sister Loretta Theresa Richards for granting me access to her personal archive. Critical research assistance was also provided at various stages by Kevin Fox, Tessa Evans, Ermithe Maurancy, Naomi Lorrain, and Nicholas Kovach.

The formal intellectual journey that culminated in this book began in the former Memphis City School System and reached important new plateaus at Agnes Scott College. For being models of excellence and putting me on the path to earning a PhD, I especially thank Sandra Jowers, Lala Ball Cooper, Nalini Ayer, Ollie J. Allen, Violet Showers Johnson, Mary Cain, and Willie Tolliver Jr. In graduate school, I was also taught and mentored by the best of the best. At the University of Wisconsin–Madison, special thanks are due to Christina Greene, Brenda Gayle Plummer, and the late Nellie Y. McKay. At Rutgers, I especially thank the incomparable Deborah Gray White, Nancy A. Hewitt, Donna Y. Murch, Carolyn Brown, Ann Gordon, David Foglesong, and James Livingston.

While writing this book, I benefited greatly from debates and discussions with colleagues at a host of scholarly conferences and seminars. For their meaningful questions and suggestions, I especially thank the late Rev. Cyprian Davis, OSB, Diane Batts Morrow, and Tia Noelle Pratt. For reading and providing crucial feedback on various sections of the manuscript over the years, I thank Barbara D. Savage, Bettye Collier-Thomas, Tiffany Gill, Rhonda Y. Williams, Laura Ann Twagira, Brent Edwards, Timothy Giffiths, Mela Araya, Candacy Taylor, Kim Hall, Mignon Moore, Philip Misevich, Anthony Di Lorenzo, Darlene Weaver, Michael Moreland, Jeremy Cruz, Bryan Massingale, Kristin Heyer, Linh Hoang, Jennifer Beste, and Tricia Bruce.

Having supportive colleagues is a gift when writing a book. For their kindness and generosity at the University of Tennessee, Knoxville, I especially thank Brandon K. Winford, Cynthia Griggs Fleming, Rickey Hall, Dawn Duke, Kristen Block, Julie Reed, Tore Olsson, Luke Harlow, Monica Black, Margaret Andersen, Sara Ritchey, Denise Phillips, Chad Black, Charles Sanft, Viejas Liulevicius, and Ernest Freeberg. For warmly welcoming me into the fold and making Villanova University a special place to work, I thank all my former colleagues in the history department. I especially thank Marc Gallicchio, Maghan Keita, Elizabeth Kolsky, Paul Steege, Whitney Martinko, Hibba Abugideiri, Paul Rosier, Catherine Kerrison, Judy Giesberg, Craig Bailey, Andrew Liu, Cristina Soriano, and Eliza Gettel for their feedback on various sections of this book. In the greater

Villanova community, I also thank Camille Burge, Crystal Lucky, Adele Lidenmeyr, Terry Nance, Chiji Akoma, Barbara Wall, Vincent Lloyd, Patricia Hampson-Eget, and the Rev. Peter M. Donohue, OSA.

The editorial staff at Duke University Press are the best in the business. Gisela Fosado's enthusiastic support of this project and her steady assurance as we brought *Subversive Habits* to print was a godsend. I am also grateful to the readers and editors who provided feedback on earlier drafts of the manuscript. Their insightful comments, hard questions, and meaningful suggestions made this book so much better.

I am fortunate to have a community of friends who have encouraged and cheered me on over the years. For making Agnes Scott a transformative experience, I thank Jakil Hill-Turner, Anya Wallace, Shawnte and Monique Rogers, Jameda Hugh, Whitney Peoples, Nicole Pace, Shayla Thomas, Brandi Collins-Dexter, Shakeh Grady, Shikina Reid, Rosemary Lokko, and Linda Githiora. For making graduate school at the University of Wisconsin and Rutgers enjoyable and intellectually stimulating, I especially thank Eric Pritchard, Matthew Blanton, Tanisha C. Ford, Crystal Moten, William Sturkey, Marsha E. Barrett, Melissa L. Cooper, Laura Ann Twagira, and Stephanie Jones-Rogers. For their longtime friendship and support, I thank Kendra Bell, Gadson William Perry, Marshetta Brazley, and Larmarques Smith.

Family members of scholars make tremendous sacrifices of time and togetherness to support the research and writing process. Without the loving support and patience of my immediate and extended families, I would never have finished this book. Over the years, my sister, Cantrice, and nephew, Cameron, made trips to wherever I was living to keep me company and when necessary pull me away from my office to go on sightseeing adventures. I am grateful for their unwavering support and reminders to never forget life's most important treasures. This book is dedicated to my parents, U. D. (Jr.) and Vidonia Williams. Their unyielding love, support, and sacrifices provided me a life filled with choices. My father was the first historian I ever knew. I like to think I inherited his knack for recalling obscure facts and dramatic storytelling. Although he did not live to see me earn my PhD, my father never doubted that I would succeed. I thank him every day for instilling in me the pride of our history and the joy of life. In many ways, this book's origins lie in the 1950s when my seven-year-old mother asked her Protestant parents for permission to convert to Catholicism and they said yes. Without my mother's self-determination and my grandparents' support, I doubt I would have become the person to write this book. My mother's fearlessness and faithfulness have sustained me through life's great challenges. I thank her with all my heart.

Many years into this project, I became the member of another family. I thank my in-laws for their loving support and generosity. Whenever my husband and I needed to move or simply come home to restore ourselves, Derrick and Shirley were there with wide smiles, kind encouragement, and helping hands. My husband, Kenon, is my biggest champion and best friend. During the inevitable bouts with writer's block or when I felt over-whelmed by the weight of the stories I was entrusted to tell, he always knew what to say and do to bring me down from the metaphorical ledge. Thank you, Love, for all that you are. We did it!

Introduction

AMERICA'S FORGOTTEN

BLACK FREEDOM FIGHTERS

There is no agony like bearing an untold story inside you.
—ZORA NEALE HURSTON, *Dust Tracks on a Road*

In June 1968, Sister Mary Antona Ebo had every reason to be fed up. One month earlier, a twenty-five-year-old Black nun in Pittsburgh, Pennsylvania, backed by her local bishop and the leader of the Conference of Major Superiors of Women, had called for a weeklong gathering of the nation's Black Catholic sisters to discuss their role in solving America's "racial problem."[1] The invitation—made in the wake of the assassination of the Reverend Dr. Martin Luther King Jr. and the historic organization of the nation's Black Catholic priests soon thereafter—had been extended to Black sisters through their female congregational leaders (then called superiors). Yet Ebo—pronounced Ēbo like the West African ethnic group to which her enslaved ancestors belonged—learned about the meeting only by chance from a white priest.[2] One year earlier, the leaders of Ebo's nearly all-white order of nursing sisters had run similar interference. In 1967, Ebo, then forty-three years old, had been unable to accept an assignment with the National Catholic Conference for Interracial Justice, the nation's most prominent Catholic civil rights organization, because her congregational superiors had refused to grant her a short-term release from her regular duties.[3] When she wrote Sister Mary Peter (Margaret) Traxler, the highest-ranking nun in the conference, in May 1967, Ebo bluntly criticized how the long-standing culture and practices of white supremacy in US female religious life had circumscribed the opportunities of Black sisters seeking to become more active in the secular fight for Black freedom. "Perhaps you can use this as a reply to some of the people who criticize you for not having Negro sisters on the team," Ebo wrote, "not only the lack of generosity of those orders who may have a sister to contribute . . . but also the orders who have for so long taken a 'lily white' attitude toward God-given vocations. Per-haps, some of the rest would have Negro sisters to contribute if the attitude would have been different."[4] In an act of protest, Ebo also sent a copy of her response to Traxler to her superior general to make known her willingness to expose the congregation's hypocrisy on racial issues and their desire to silence *her* voice. Thus, Ebo did not hesitate to confront her congregational leaders again in 1968. Nor did the forty-four-year-old African American nun fail to secure a place as a speaker at the inaugural meeting of the Na-tional Black Sisters' Conference (NBSC) that August.[5]

In 1965, Ebo shocked the world when she arrived in Selma, Alabama, with five other nuns from St. Louis, Missouri, to protest the police violence of Bloody Sunday and rally national support for Black voting rights. As the only African American member in the inaugural delegation of Catholic sisters to join the Selma protests, Ebo not only garnered the lion's share of attention from civil rights leaders but also explained to reporters why she took the risk to join the march. "I am here today because I am a Negro, a nun, a Catholic, and because I want to bear witness," Ebo proclaimed. She also declared that she had voted in the previous day's election in St. Louis and that she believed every person should have the right to vote.[6] On the following morning, images of Ebo, whom local leaders strategically placed on the front lines of an interracial group of marchers, graced the front pages of newspapers across the country (figure Intro.1).[7] In the days and weeks that followed, that image and the participation of hundreds of ad-ditional nuns in the Selma protests helped to awaken hundreds of white Catholic sisters to the moral righteousness of the African American fight for racial justice. As National Catholic Conference for Interracial Justice leader Sister Mary Peter Traxler (who traveled to Selma after Ebo) wrote in an editorial in June 1965, "Like the faithful women of the Gospel, Sisters must follow Christ into the world ministering to His needs in the person of the poor, the sick, the persecuted. When people are in crisis, they are par-ticularly disposed to look inward to evaluate themselves in relation to God. This is one reason why Sisters have a place at the other Selmas."[8] Yet many

FIGURE INTRO.1. Sister Mary Antona (Elizabeth Louise) Ebo led voting rights marchers in Selma, Alabama, on March 10, 1965. Courtesy of the Associated Press.

of the white sisters who publicly marched for civil rights on the streets were not as committed to principles of racial justice and desegregation as they proclaimed they were, especially when it came to confronting anti-Black racism in the Church. And no one knew this better than African American Catholic sisters.

Indeed, in the decades before Selma, the battles that Sister Ebo had waged to gain access to a Catholic education and enter religious life had revealed that her church and its most visible labor force—white Catholic nuns—were among the most dedicated practitioners of racial segregation and exclusion. For example, in 1942, shortly after her conversion to Catholicism, eighteen-year-old Elizabeth Louise Ebo had to desegregate Holy Trinity High School in her hometown of Bloomington, Illinois, in order to secure a Catholic education.[9] In 1944, after being denied admission to Catholic nursing schools in Illinois, which were led by white sisters, solely on the basis of race, Ebo moved to St. Louis, Missouri, to enroll as a US nurse cadet in St. Mary's Infirmary School, the nation's only Black Catholic nursing school.[10] Two years later, she made headlines when she became one of the first three Black women admitted into the historically German

Sisters of St. Mary (SSM), the order of her nursing educators, later known as the Franciscan Sisters of Mary.[11] Two more Black candidates were admitted later in the year. While Catholic proponents of racial equality heralded the SSM's admission of five Black women as a monumental step against racial segregation and exclusion in the Church, Ebo and her Black counterparts quickly learned that their congregational leaders' commitment to racial equality literally stopped at the doors of their motherhouse.[12] White SSM leaders not only initially barred the first five Black postulants from entering the order's administrative headquarters but also enforced strict segregation in dining, training, and social interactions. In 1947, white SSM leaders even forced the new Black members to profess their first vows in a segregated ceremony.[13]

While Ebo opted to remain in religious life and push back against the order's most egregious mandates of segregation, the depths of the SSM's commitment to white supremacy forever changed her. Shortly after Ebo took her first vows, a white member of her order denied her father admission to the community's all-white St. Mary's Hospital in the St. Louis suburbs. Although the order allowed the immediate family members of any sister to be treated at their hospitals, a white nun invoked segregation to refuse the ambulance carrying Ebo's father, Daniel. Ebo later learned that her dying father even pleaded with the nun, proclaiming that his daughter was also a Sister of St. Mary. The death of her father shortly thereafter and her superiors' unwillingness to rebuke the offending white sister almost proved too much for Ebo to bear.[14] As she later explained, "I made up my mind at that time that nobody is ever going to forget I'm a black woman . . . my father's daughter."[15]

Ebo's example of "uncommon faithfulness" and unyielding resistance to anti-Black racism is not exceptional in the history of the US Catholic Church.[16] Neither are instances in which white Catholics proved willing to put race before faith in order to maintain white supremacy and exclusion in American society and a church that considered itself universal. The Catholic Church not only inaugurated African slavery in the sixteenth century in the land area that became the United States but also served as the nation's largest Christian practitioner of racial segregation through the Jim Crow era. Minimal attention, however, has been paid to the leading roles that white Catholics played in the sociocultural, political, and spiritual propagation of white supremacy.[17] Histories of Black Catholic resistance to white racism are also rare. This is especially true of battles waged in women's religious life.

In recent decades, scholars have brought the lives and labors of white Catholic sisters from the margins to the center of both US and Catholic history. As a result, few would deny the visible and often essential roles that white nuns played in expanding and sustaining the Church from the colonial era through its greatest decades of growth.[18] Yet few have considered what it meant that most of the sisters to minister in the United States before 1850, including the nation's earliest female saints and sainthood candidates, were slaveholders or people who relied on the labor, sale, and brutal mistreatment of enslaved people—and the economic benefits of whiteness and racial segregation—to establish and secure the financial futures of their orders and celebrated social service institutions.[19] Historians have paid even less attention to the fact that most white sisterhoods—including those led by saints and others under consideration for canonization—enforced racial exclusion and institutionalized ideas of white superiority and Black and Brown inferiority in their ranks and social service ministries for most of their histories in the United States.[20]

The few narratives that acknowledge sisters' slaveholding and/or segregated pasts have usually presented these realities as inconsequential to white sisters' ministries and as footnotes in their assessments of white sisters' moral leadership. Stories about white sisterhoods that nobly ministered to African Americans free of concern for color during slavery—some, if not all, of which may be fictional—have regularly been offered to counter documentation of these sisters' discriminatory practices.[21] Many scholars also routinely cite select white sisterhoods' willingness to teach African American children during the Jim Crow era and the relatively small number of white sisters who marched for racial justice in the 1960s as evidence of their pioneering racial justice activism in the Church.[22] These contentions, however, are possible only because the history of US Black Catholic sisters remains largely untold and misrepresented. This is true of the first generations of Black sisters, who ministered amid the nation's and Church's slaveholding elite in the nineteenth century, as well as those who waged pivotal battles to break down segregation in the Church and wider society in the twentieth and twenty-first centuries. That most white US sisterhoods steadfastly refused to admit African-descended people—on equal terms or otherwise—for most of their histories remains one of the Church's best-kept secrets.[23] Moreover, as Black sisters' testimonies reveal, when white sisterhoods did admit African Americans into their novitiates and convents, this rarely translated into integration—let alone sincere inclusion—without intense Black struggle and suffering.[24]

Subversive Habits takes white Catholic racism and the brutal histories of Catholic colonialism, slavery, and segregation seriously. Using race and gender as essential categories of historical analysis, this book not only tells the stories of African American Catholic sisters and their diverse struggles against discrimination but also demonstrates how their history fundamentally reshapes and revises narratives of the US Church and its relationship to the African American community. It also turns critical attention to women's religious life in the Roman Catholic Church as one of the fiercest strongholds of white supremacy and one of the most consequential battlegrounds of the African American freedom struggle.

This book contends that the photograph of Sister Mary Antona Ebo marching with her Black counterparts to a segregated altar in a segregated profession ceremony in a segregated church in 1947 (figure Intro.2) offers a far more honest representation of the story of Catholic nuns in the Black freedom struggle than any of the now-iconic and widely accessible images of her or mostly white sisters marching for racial justice in the 1960s. The 1947 image captures the extraordinary efforts that white sisters—even those considered racially progressive—engaged in to enforce Black subjugation in their communities. It also illustrates that the earliest and most committed proponents of racial equality in women's religious life—those who were willing to suffer greatly in the face of unrelenting discrimination in order to lay bare and contest the evil of white supremacy—were Black Catholic sisters. Beyond the five pioneer Black Sisters of St. Mary, whose complaints about their racist mistreatment eventually forced SSM leaders to agree to fuller integration in 1950, the photograph documents the presence of two members of the Oblate Sisters of Providence (OSP), the modern world's first successful Black Roman Catholic sisterhood.[25]

Long before the legal and legislative victories achieved by the civil rights movement in the 1950s and 1960s, members of the nation's African American Catholic sisterhoods initiated and served as foot soldiers in some of the earliest campaigns aimed at dismantling racial segregation and exclusion within Catholic boundaries. Decades before the *Brown v. Board of Education* decision, for example, the leadership councils of the Black sisterhoods pried open the doors of Catholic higher education to secure the accreditation of the Black-administered Catholic educational system.[26] Since the early nineteenth century, the Black orders had also preserved the vocations of scores of devout Black Catholic women and girls denied admission into white sisterhoods in the United States, Canada, Latin America, and the Caribbean solely on the basis of race. Even Ebo had been preparing to enter

FIGURE INTRO.2. On June 9, 1947, Elizabeth Louise Ebo of Bloomington, Illinois; Hilda Rita Brickus of Brooklyn, New York; Pauline Catherine Townsend of Washington, DC; Mary Antonette Gale of Pine Bluff, Arkansas; and Bessie Lee Hardy of Philadelphia, Pennsylvania, professed their first vows as members of the Sisters of Saint Mary (now the Franciscan Sisters of Mary) in St. Louis, Missouri. Two members of the historically Black Oblate Sisters of Providence, whose order had served in St. Louis since 1881 and had broken some of the earliest racial barriers in the archdiocese can be seen seated on the right. Members of the Oblate Sisters of Providence regularly attended the investiture and profession ceremonies of pioneering Black sisters in white congregations in a show of solidarity and support. Courtesy of the American Catholic History Research Center and University Archives at Catholic University of America.

the historically Black OSP upon her graduation from nursing school before white SSM leaders finally lifted their ban on Black members in 1946.[27]

In narrating the history of racial segregation and exclusion in female religious life and the wider Church, this book recovers the story of Black Catholic sisters as vanguard antiracist educators, desegregation pioneers, and champions of Black women's leadership. Without knowledge of this largely suppressed history, one cannot begin to understand why Ebo and scores of Black nuns like her began appearing in civil rights marches and clamoring to participate in the Church's white-led racial justice initiatives both before and after Bloody Sunday.[28] Nor can one fully appreciate why many of these same Black sisters (who like Ebo had desegregated their white orders and/ or a host of other Catholic and secular institutions in the decades before Selma) finally came together in Pittsburgh to form the NBSC in 1968 and fought so hard to tell the stories of their lived experiences in public venues afterward.[29] Rather than being politically neutral or significantly late to the fight for racial justice, as many have argued, these Black sisters were already veterans of a long and tenuous freedom struggle within the Church. One need only shift the focus to the boundaries of Roman Catholicism, the nation's oldest, largest, and arguably most influential Christian denomination, to bear witness to this history. *Subversive Habits* finally offers the lens. In so doing, this book makes visible a long and sustained tradition of Black Catholic women's resistance to white supremacy. It also reveals an equally long and strident history of white Catholic resistance to racial equality, one that has gone unexamined—and in far too many cases has been explicitly denied.

Recasting the History of the African American Freedom Struggle

Subversive Habits broadens understandings of the long fight for African American freedom by turning attention to the social, educational, and political struggles waged by Black Roman Catholic sisters from their fiercely contested beginnings in the nineteenth-century slave South to the present day. Charting these battles upends one of the most enduring myths about African American Catholics, religious and lay, namely, that they were largely absent from or indifferent to the campaigns against institutionalized white supremacy. Despite copious evidence to the contrary, a seminal monograph on the early US Church inexplicably argued that "Catholicism rarely touched Black slaves" in the United States, "left no legacy of resistance" among enslaved Black people, and "built no solid foundation for future Black social and political activity."[30] Influential studies by historians John T. McGreevy and Father Cyprian Davis also contributed to the myth of Black Catholic political conservatism and complacency about white racism. Citing a white Jesuit priest who in 1961 "publicly wished for a Catholic version of Martin Luther King, Jr.," McGreevy wrote, "To the disappointment of liberals, few African American Catholics—clergy or laity—took leadership positions in the civil rights movement." He also characterized Black Catholics as "culturally conservative" during the 1950s and 1960s.[31] A decade before, Davis had concurred. While Davis pointed to the near exclusion of Black men from the priesthood from the period of slavery through the 1950s to explain why there were no Catholic Kings in the 1960s, he still wrote, "By and large Catholics, either black or white, were not in the forefront of the civil rights movement [of the 1950s and 1960s] or among the leadership of protest organizations."[32] However, Davis initially missed that many Black lay Catholics had initiated, spearheaded, and sustained formal and informal assaults on legal segregation from the earliest appearance of Jim Crow laws through to America's civil rights years. Davis and McGreevy also overlooked a more extensive history of Black Catholic activism against racism within Church boundaries spearheaded by Black women, religious and lay.[33]

In the past two decades, new scholarship has brought greater attention to the role of Catholicism in early American slave resistance and demonstrated how free Black Catholics, especially women and girls, used their faithfulness and membership in the Church to challenge anti-Blackness and carve out greater autonomy and mobility in their lives before the federal abolition of slavery.[34] Sustained attention to the brutal conditions of Catholic slavery and the abolitionism of individuals like Lydia Hamilton Smith, the longtime partner of radical Republican Thaddeus Stevens, has revealed how enslaved and free Black Catholic women and girls also fought to dismantle slavery.[35] Recent studies on the Catholic interracial and long civil rights movements have retrieved from the margins the stories of scores of Black lay Catholics who were local and national leaders in postemancipation freedom struggles. Their names include early South Carolina civil rights activists and suffragists, the famed Rollin sisters; early public transportation boycott leaders Aristide Mary and Homer Plessy; Chicago Catholic Worker founder Dr. Arthur Falls; A. P. Tureaud, Sr., an influential attorney for the National Association for the Advancement of Colored People (NAACP); Montgomery bus boycott plaintiff Mary Louise Smith; Freedom Summer martyr James Chaney; and Student Nonviolent Coordinating Committee leaders Lawrence Guyot and Diane Nash.[36] Attention has also been paid to the long fight to develop a substantial African American Catholic clergy and to the story of Black priests and Black Power.[37] Nevertheless, scholarly analyses of Black Catholic activism are still hindered by a desire to address the lack of a Catholic King. As one scholar of the Black Catholic movement in the 1960s and 1970s concluded in 2018, "Although there may not have been any Black Catholic equivalent of Martin Luther King, soon enough there were Black Catholic Malcolm Xs, Stokely Carmichaels, and Angela Davises."[38]

Because King—a minister born and shaped in the independent Black Baptist tradition—was not the only civil rights leader of significance, *Subversive Habits* moves beyond the futile search for his equivalent in the white-dominated Catholic Church. Instead, it builds on scholarship that has recovered the activism of African American women and girls who initiated, led, and sustained many local and national struggles for Black freedom and equal rights. Long before there were Black priests in the United States, there were Black sisters, who waged many of the first successful struggles against white supremacy and racial segregation in the Church, struggles that preceded and enabled the Black Catholic revolt of the late 1960s and early 1970s.[39] Indeed, this book reveals that before there were Catholic Angela Davises, there were plenty of Catholic Elizabeth Eckfords, Ruby Bridgeses, and Vivian Malones—Black Catholic women and girls who desegregated all-white Catholic parochial schools and academies, colleges, hospitals, and convents. In fact, many of the Black sisters who came of age politically in the 1960s and 1970s had desegregated their public and Catholic elementary and high schools and colleges as well as participated in the secular fight for civil rights before entering religious life.[40]

In recovering Black sisters' educational and political activism, *Subversive Habits* offers important new insights into the history of Black Catholic protest and the role of Black women's traditions of Catholicism in Black resistance to white supremacy. Since the late 1960s, scholars have generally identified three waves of Black Catholic activism: the rise and fall of the Colored Catholic Congresses, which layman Daniel Arthur Rudd led from 1889 to 1894; the rise and fall of the Federated Colored Catholics of the United States, which early NAACP leader and layman Dr. Thomas Wyatt Turner led from 1924 to 1933; and the Black Catholic revolt of the late 1960s, which led to the separate organization of the nation's Black priests, sisters, and laity and the establishment of the National Office for Black Catholics in 1970.[41] Scholarship on these movements reveals that African Americans have always desired to participate fully and equally in Church life, especially in the areas of worship, education, hospital care, and the clergy. But scholarly works have usually considered only the fight to develop an African American clergy to be synonymous with the Black Catholic fight for equality and justice in the Church.[42] Unlike their Protestant, Muslim, and non-Western counterparts, African American Catholics were long denied formal male religious leaders from their own communities.[43] Historians have argued that the racist exclusion of African American men from the Catholic priesthood and the US episcopacy into the twentieth century robbed Black Catholics of legitimate spokesmen and effective racial justice advocates within the Church.[44] This assertion, however, recognizes only men as agents of historical change and fails to acknowledge that Black sisters had important roles as Black Catholic spiritual leaders and as some of the earliest champions and educators of Black priests.

To expand understandings of Black Catholic resistance and illuminate how often it intersected with secular Black freedom campaigns, this book also turns critical attention to the leadership of Black sisters in the long struggle for Black Catholic education. The fight for literacy and quality education has long been a cornerstone of the African American struggle for freedom and justice. Yet the African American pursuit of Catholic education (and white resistance to it) remains largely neglected in histories of the civil rights movement and the broader struggle for Black liberation. While the Black Catholic population remained relatively low, hundreds of thousands of Black parents, Catholic and non-Catholic alike, regularly sought out Catholic schools as potential safe havens for their children to escape nonexistent, underfunded, and/or overcrowded public schools, from slavery through the Jim Crow era. During the desegregation era and even today, Catholic schools, especially those led by Black nuns and other Catholics committed to quality Black education, remained attractive to African Americans in large part because of their relative affordability and the hostile receptions that many Black youth received in white-led integrated schools, both public and private. Indeed, Black sisters' vanguard struggles for educational equality and dignity, combined with their pioneering commitments to teaching Black history and training "race leaders," demonstrate that they were formidable prophets of American Catholicism and democracy long before they began marching for racial justice in the 1960s and 1970s.

Subversive Habits also illuminates the emancipatory dimensions of Black female celibacy within religious life. Scholars of race and sex have long documented how white denial of Black female virtue was central to the social construction, maintenance, and defense of white supremacy in secular and religious realms.[45] Unrelenting and systematic attacks on the moral character of Black women and girls not only helped to justify centuries of unprosecuted racial and sexual violence visited on Black bodies and communities but also profoundly shaped the protest strategies that Black women and girls developed to survive.[46] However, the entries of Black women and girls into the consecrated ranks of religious life in the Roman Catholic Church have been widely overlooked as political and arguably feminist acts of bodily liberation and respectability.[47] While records offering insights into the inner thoughts of Black sisters from the nineteenth century are rare, the vehemence with which white Catholics opposed the very idea of Black sisters and characterized them as morally suspect is abundantly documented. Indeed, in a white-dominated and patriarchal society and Church that often opposed interracial marriage in law and custom, the very idea of a Black bride of a Christ imagined as white was nothing short of insurrectionary. In the early 1970s, NBSC members also wrote and spoke extensively about the radical dimensions of their vows of chastity. Many went so far as to link their celibacy to Black liberation and explicitly challenge the masculinist ethos of many Black Power advocates, who sought to allow Black women to contribute to the movement only through motherhood.[48] Black sisters' oral testimonies also underscore the liberatory and "radical," as one sister put it, dimensions of rejecting the traditional confines of motherhood and marriage through embracing the celibate religious state.[49] While those I asked why they had entered religious life always replied they had felt the call and desire to serve God, the women interviewed for this study also often noted the limited employment opportunities available to them before the civil rights movement. "I could only have been a teacher, a nurse, or a maid" was a common remark. Moreover, the current and former Black sisters interviewed often alluded (without prompting) to the "perils" they faced as Black women in the secular world. One former sister mentioned the frequent rape of Black domestic workers in white households.[50] This book, then, encourages historians of the Black freedom struggle to take seriously the spiritual, intellectual, and political activism of Black nuns as they navigated and challenged the racist and sexist contours of their church and wider society.

Rethinking the US Catholic Experience and the "Black Church"

Surveying the lives and struggles of African American nuns reveals that Black Catholics have never been footnotes in the history of the US Church or the wider nation. As such, *Subversive Habits* calls on scholars to expand their understandings of the US Catholic experience and turn more attention to the great diversity of the Black religious experience. Like in Latin America and the Caribbean, Catholicism was the first Black articulation of

Christianity in the land area that became the United States. In fact, much of early African American history (which includes the first recorded Christian marriage in what became the United States) and Black resistance to slavery and white supremacy took place within Catholic boundaries.[51] That hundreds of thousands of African American parents, Catholic and non-Catholic alike, seeking to overcome racial inequalities in the public school system, consistently turned to the US Catholic Church to educate their children over the centuries is also significant. Yet the story of Black religion and Black protest, like US Black religious history, is primarily narrated as a Protestant story, while US Catholic history is still overwhelmingly framed as a story of European immigrants, beginning in the antebellum urban North.[52] This book specifically builds on a new wave of scholarship seeking to foreground the African foundations of American Catholicism, center Black Catholic experiences, and move beyond the limited framing of the US Black Catholic community as "a minority within a minority."[53] It also takes a direct cue from a 2014 roundtable discussion published in the *Journal of Africana Religions*, which reminded scholars that "most of the people who have lived their lives under the sign of Catholicism [in the Americas, including the Caribbean] have been Native American and African descended, not European."[54]

Black women's religious life in the United States dates back only to the early nineteenth century. However, African American sisters were among the nation's pioneering nuns and led some of earliest US congregations of women, Black and white. Moreover, scores of the over 2,500 African American women and girls known to have entered religious life can trace their lineage to earliest days of the North American Church and the free and enslaved Black Catholics whose labor, suffering, and faithfulness built it.[55] Some Black sisters also have direct and even biological connections to the earliest European Catholic families in North America, including the famed Carrolls and Spaldings, who supplied the US Church with three of its earliest bishops and a pioneering white female congregational leader.[56]

The stories of Black sisters who converted to the faith also offer invaluable insights into the leading roles that African American women and girls often played in the making of US Catholicism. This is especially true of those who participated in the great migrations of Black southerners and Caribbean natives to the industrial North, Midwest, and West in the twentieth century. Many of these women's lives also intersect with the larger story of African American political and cultural protest in notable ways. Sister Francesca (Edeve) Thompson, the second African American Sister

of St. Francis of Oldenburg in Indiana, for example, was the child of pioneer African American stage and screen actors Edward and Evelyn (née
Preer) Thompson.[57] Sister Mary Reginalda (Barbara) Polk, an Alabama
native who entered the Sinsinawa Dominicans in Wisconsin in 1948, was
the daughter of famed Black photographer and Tuskegee Institute professor Prentice Herman Polk.[58] Boston native and early Black Sister of Notre
Dame de Namur William Virginia (Dolores) Harrall was a maternal cousin
of civil rights leader and National Council of Negro Women founder Mary
McLeod Bethune.[59]

Much of the scholarship on the growth of the African American Catholic population outside of the South in the twentieth century has centered
the efforts of the relatively small number of white priests and sisters who
expanded their ministries to the Black migrant and immigrant arrivals.
However, this study reminds scholars that Black sisterhoods, Black laywomen, and, later, individual Black sisters in white congregations were
also leading participants in this great missionary and evangelization endeavor. The general councils of Black sisterhoods regularly received and,
when able, answered requests from sympathetic white priests and often
desperate Black laywomen ministering in communities that had endured
decades of neglect and racist mistreatment in their respective dioceses. In
one remarkable example from the 1940s, the archdiocese of Detroit invited
the OSP to staff a storefront Catholic mission called Our Lady of Victory,
which had been established by a Black laywoman named Anna Bates in
1943. In the previous decades, Bates had walked five miles to and from
St. James Catholic Church, the only white parish in her community that
would not violently turn away the Black faithful. For more than ten years,
Bates had repeatedly petitioned the archdiocese to create a parish open to
Black Catholics in the northwest area of the city, to no avail, but eventually
persuaded the white Sisters, Servants of the Immaculate Heart of Mary to
offer instruction to the Black youth in her community. However, it took the
Detroit Massacre of 1943 and the much-celebrated arrival of the OSP from
Baltimore, Maryland, in 1948 before Bates's dreams of a safe and welcoming
Catholic Church and school for Black Detroiters would be fully realized.[60]

Also, the plethora of written and oral history sources consulted for this
study rarely credited the missionary labors of white sisters and priests with
Black conversions to Catholicism in the twentieth century. Instead, the vast
majority of Black converts in these sources noted that they followed the
leads of family members, Black neighborhood friends who were cradle
Catholics, or devout Black laywomen ministering in their communities.

When asked who modeled the life of prayer and service to which they had been called, almost all my interviewees cited the faithfulness, selflessness, and deep spirituality of family members, male and female, not white religious. Several Black nuns or their family members also championed pious Black laywomen who recognized and nurtured Black vocations to religious life.[61] For example, Washington, DC, native Angela White, who in 1956 desegregated the Sisters of Charity of Cincinnati in Ohio, fondly recalled how a devout Black laywoman and teacher at her public elementary school named Dr. Armeta Leach took her to daily Mass during the lunch hour and regularly wrote her letters of encouragement after White entered religious life.[62] In another poignant example from the historically Black Hill District of Pittsburgh, a Black laywoman and day care operator named Sarah Degree singlehandedly brought scores of Black people to the faith after World War II. Among them was Freda Kittel, who in 1958 became the first African American known to be admitted into a white sisterhood in Pittsburgh.[63] Shortly after Degree's death in the 1980s, Kittel's brother, Pulitzer Prize–winning playwright August Wilson, lambasted the diocese of Pittsburgh for failing to honor Degree's legacy of service and evangelization. "Every Catholic I knew that lived in the Hill District was a Catholic because of Miss Sarah," Wilson recalled. "If there was ever a saint, it was Miss Sarah. . . . If she was white, they'd have a Miss Sarah Degree Child Care Center or something." Such recollections underscore the vital roles that Black laywomen always played as evangelizers and spiritual and educational leaders in Black communities, roles too often overlooked, misrepresented, or altogether omitted from histories of US Catholicism.[64]

At its core, then, this book is a work of historical recovery and correction. So many forces have willfully conspired to silence the history of nation's Black sisters and their many struggles within and outside of the Catholic Church. Several documented examples show white sisters and others individually and collectively working to erase Black sisters' lives and labors from the historical record in the name of white supremacy.[65] The best-known cases involve white sisters, including members of leadership councils, blocking access to and even destroying archival materials documenting the Black heritage of their order's earliest members. Leaders of the Sisters, Servants of the Immaculate Heart of Mary, for example, colluded for nearly a century to suppress knowledge about the order's two African American foundresses, former OSP members who passed for white.[66] In 1928, one Immaculate Heart of Mary leader in Michigan wrote, "We are convinced that silence is the fairest, wisest, and most agreeable way of committing to oblivion this subject."[67] In the 1930s, the order's leaders even undermined an attempt launched by Father Leonard DiFalco, a Brooklyn priest, to have their chief foundress canonized, out of fear that her racial heritage would be rediscovered.[68]

White sisters and others have also grossly misrepresented the origins and (in some cases) the continued existence of formal and informal anti-Black admissions policies in white sisterhoods, usually in favor of narratives of white Catholic saviorism.[69] One illustration of this deliberate erasure involves the Sisters of the Blessed Sacrament (SBS), established by Saint Katharine Drexel, ironically the Catholic patron saint of racial justice. For much of the late nineteenth and twentieth centuries, the SBS—organized after the nation's first five self-identified African American sisterhoods—operated the nation's largest network of Catholic elementary and high schools designated for African Americans and Native Americans. The well-resourced order, which relied heavily on Drexel's trust left to her by her financier father, also established Xavier University of Louisiana, the nation's first historically Black and Catholic institution of higher education.[70] However, from the order's founding in 1891 to 1950, the SBS systematically excluded African American and Native Americans from its ranks, with the exception of one Native American woman admitted to a lesser rank in 1893.[71] For decades, white SBS members tracked their Native American pupils with vocations to other white orders, and they told their Black American pupils, whom they tracked to the Black sisterhoods, that they could not admit them to the SBS, at the request of the leaders of the Black orders and/or because of the racial segregation laws of the South.[72] During Drexel's canonization process, SBS members and their supporters publicly maintained that the community's exclusionary admission policies were not rooted in racism but rather in a sincere desire not to draw from the ranks of the Black sisterhoods.[73] However, the record is clear. There is no archival or other credible documentation that the Black superiors ever made such a request to Drexel. Instead, in 1893, the racially derogatory views of the SBS's founding white members and their unwillingness to live with Black women on equal terms were central factors in the order's vote to exclude Black and Native American candidates.[74] Moreover, when the order finally voted to accept Black members in 1949, pressure from white priests, not from the SBS's white members, forced their governing council to take the historic vote. Even then, the council initially voted to accept only two or three Black candidates at a time, seemingly to ensure that a Black majority did not develop.[75] Such realities underscore just how much white supremacy and the color of Christ's brides mattered to white sisters, even those professing a commitment to racial and educational justice.

Ultimately, *Subversive Habits* is an intentional exercise in African American women's historical truth telling. Most of my subjects and the struggles they waged are unknown outside of small Catholic circles. As such, I have opted to present this history in narrative form, using Black sisters' stories to frame my analysis of their lives and struggles for justice, equality, and democracy. Because so many people have never seen an African American nun, I have also included several photographs. Many of these images have been hidden away in Church archives or preserved in the private collections of the sisters and their families. Like the written and oral evidence, the visual record of Black sisters has been essential in documenting their lives and the history of racial segregation and exclusion in female religious life. In a few cases, photographs are the only surviving documentation of a Black sister's existence accessible to researchers, especially when a congregation has not maintained a formal archive or has blocked research access to the archive or a specific sister's file.

America's Real Sister Act

Despite Black sisters' nearly two-hundred-year history in the United States, Whoopi Goldberg's performance as Dolores Van Cartier/Sister Mary Clarence in the *Sister Act* film franchise remains the dominant interpretation of an African American Catholic sister and the desegregation of a white congregation in the nation. That the morally ambiguous fictional character of Mary Clarence is very loosely based on an actual African American nun and sainthood candidate who desegregated her order is perhaps the best testament to how Black sisters' history has been disfigured and erased in national memory.[76] In the pages ahead, I provide an essential counternarrative, what the historical record reveals to be the real sister act: the story of how generations of Black women and girls called to the sacred life of poverty, chastity, and obedience navigated and fought against racism, sexism, and exclusion to become and minister as consecrated women of God. In the face of often unrelenting discrimination, Black sisters overcame unimaginable obstacles and broke some of the nation's most difficult racial and gender barriers. At various points in their history, many also made gutwrenching compromises and accommodations to white racism that contemporary readers may find unacceptable. One must understand that Black sisters—like other Black Catholics who refuse to abandon the faith—never wanted to surrender *their* church to racists and others who could not fully affirm Black humanity and dignity. Like other African American activists fighting for justice, Black sisters who stayed in hostile congregations and endured pernicious discrimination in their church understood their sufferings as a necessary sacrifice in the fight to serve their communities and ultimately defeat the sin of white supremacy. African American sisters also took their sacred vows, especially obedience, seriously. However, as Sister Rose Martin (Kathryn) Glenn, the only African American woman to enter and remain in the Missionary Sisters, Servants of the Holy Spirit in Techny, Illinois, explained in 2011, "My vow was to God, not them. They were going to have to put me out" and seemingly disgrace God in the process.[77]

Because it is impossible to narrate this history without confronting the centrality of white racism in the American Catholic experience, white Catholics are also an integral part of this study. During and after slavery, white Catholics, religious and lay, were some of the bitterest and most violent opponents of racial equality and Black self-determination. Others served as some of the sincerest and most important allies that Black sisters and the larger Black Catholic community had in their fight for freedom, justice, and equity. Depending on the time, region, and circumstance, white Catholics were often an uneasy and complicated mixture of both.

Subversive Habits unfolds chronologically in seven chapters. More than two and a half centuries after the Roman Catholic Church introduced African slavery and ninety-seven years after the first European nuns arrived to minister in what became the United States, European and white American ecclesiastical authorities finally permitted African-descended women and girls called to religious life to profess vows as nuns. For these pioneering Black sisters, embracing the consecrated celibate state constituted a radical act of resistance to white supremacy and the sexual terrorism built into the nation's systems of chattel slavery and segregation. Chapter 1 chronicles their fiercely contested entries into the nation's pioneering Black sisterhoods and a small handful of white congregations during slavery and the early years of Jim Crow. This chapter not only foregrounds the white supremacist commitments of the nation's earliest European and white American bishops, priests, and sisters but also demonstrates how Black sisters and their supporters navigated this opposition to establish many of the nation's earliest Catholic schools, orphanages, and nursing homes open to Black people. In seeking to embrace the celibate religious state, devout Black Catholic women and girls dared white Catholics to live up to a core teaching of the Church: that all lives mattered and were equal in the eyes of God. They also seeded antiracist sentiments in the Church, formalized Black Catholic women's resistance to white domination, and challenged one of the most insidious tenets of white (Catholic) supremacy: the idea that Black people, and women and girls especially, were inherently evil, immoral, and sexually promiscuous.

Chapter 2 examines Black sisters' first explicit and successful challenges to racial segregation and exclusion. As in the secular domain, the struggle for Black education within Catholic boundaries was never politically neutral or divorced from the larger struggle for Black freedom and rights. In 1916, for example, the nation's seventh Black Catholic sisterhood formed, prompted by impending state legislation that sought to ban white teachers from instructing African American children, and vice versa, in Georgia. After World War I, laws across the country began mandating state accreditation of private schools. Like their white counterparts, the leadership councils of the Black sisterhoods were faced with the monumental task of obtaining higher education for their members to secure the certification of their schools and ensure that Black Catholic parents could uphold their canonical duties to provide a Christian education for their children. Yet most of the nation's Catholic colleges and universities explicitly barred US-born Black people, even Black religious, from admission, solely based on race. This chapter examines the hidden struggles waged by the African American teaching sisterhoods to desegregate Catholic colleges and universities to secure the accreditation of the Black-administered Catholic educational system and to preserve African American access to quality Catholic education in the decades before the *Brown* decision.

The struggle for Black Catholic education was deeply connected to the Black Catholic fight to enjoy all the rights and privileges of their church, including entering religious life. Catholic schools not only served as the primary vehicles of evangelization in the African American community but also constituted some of the most important spaces in which priests, sisters, and members of the laity identified and nurtured prospective Black candidates for religious life. Because white nuns made up the majority of sisters ministering in Black Catholic schools by the turn of the twentieth century and outnumbered white priests by significant margins in most locales, they exerted enormous influence on the growth of the national Black sister population and the culture of the larger Church. Many white sisters and priests teaching Black youth not only regularly enforced ideas of white superiority and Black inferiority in their interactions with their Black pupils and their parents but also actively discouraged Black vocations. However, after World War II, the formal and unwritten anti-Black admissions policies of white sisterhoods increasingly came under attack as changing racial attitudes and the explosive growth of the Black Catholic population outside of the South led to a marked increase in applications to white orders. Chapter 3 examines the often behind-the-scenes battles waged to desegregate the historically white and white ethnic Catholic sisterhoods. Drawing on previously sealed Church records as well as the oral and written testimonies of pioneering Black sisters in white orders, this chapter documents the measures white leadership councils and individual white sisters took to keep African Americans out of their congregations or prevent them from staying after admission. It also documents the extraordinary measures that Black candidates and a growing number of white Catholics committed to the principles of social equality took to break these barriers down.

As the nation entered the classical era of the civil rights movement (1954–68), not only did African American entries into white orders increase, but the secular Black freedom struggle greatly influenced many who entered. Many early Black sisters in white congregations understood their admissions and ministries to white Catholic communities as inherently connected to the broader freedom struggle. Unlike their secular counterparts, though, Black sisters who desegregated previously white congregations usually did so away from the protection of news cameras, their families, and the faith communities that had nurtured their vocations. They were usually also required to desegregate the faculties or staffs of their orders' schools and hospitals as well as the all-white neighborhoods, parishes, and sundown towns where their orders' convents and ministries were often located. Chapter 4 recovers the history of this hidden activism, charts Black sisters' overlooked participation in local and national marches for civil rights, and explores how some Black sisters brought some of the ideas, methods, strategies, and idealism of the movement into the Church before and after the reforms and activist-oriented mandates of the Second Vatican Council. It also documents the challenges that many African American sisters encountered as they tried to move into secular and Church-sponsored campaigns for the racial justice.

Chapter 5 examines the watershed formation of the NBSC in 1968 and the early story of Black nuns and Black Power. The inaugural NBSC meeting marked the first time that members of Black and white US sisterhoods gathered on a national stage to discuss racism in the Church and wider society. The NBSC's creation not only gave Black sisters an independent platform to initiate a national campaign of racial justice reform but also facilitated an outpouring of public testimonies from Black sisters documenting their experiences of racism and sexism in the Church. This chapter pays special attention to the NBSC's efforts to confront long-standing anti-Black racism in women's religious life and stop the increasing numbers of Black sisters departing religious life as a result. It also charts Black sisters' entries into secular campaigns aimed at dismantling institutional racism during America's Black Power years.

Chapter 6 chronicles the diverse ways Black sisters responded to the crises of Black Catholic education and vocational losses in the 1970s. As in secular society, white-directed desegregation in the Church often resulted in the closing of long-standing high-performing Black and Black-majority Catholic schools. Those led by the Black sisterhoods and located in inner-city and historically Black communities were especially vulnerable to closure despite ever-increasing Black demands for Catholic schools. By 1970, halting the mass closings of Black Catholic schools and the Black vocational losses that partially contributed to this crisis became the chief priority of Black sisters and the larger African American Catholic community. This chapter pays particular attention to Black sisters' involvement in the struggle for community-controlled schools, their efforts to radically transform Black Catholic educational curricula to reflect the changing times, and the efforts to keep Black sisters—most of whom were educators—in religious life.

Despite the NBSC's many achievements, the steady departures of Black sisters from their orders and the increasing successes of massive white resistance to equal rights legislation in the 1970s signaled an important new turning point. For the first time, the African American sister population, like the wider populations of priests and sisters, was clearly declining, with no immediate solutions to reverse the trend. Chapter 7 takes Black sisters through the crucible of the last quarter of the twentieth century and into the first decades of the twenty-first. It focuses on their continued efforts to preserve African American female religious life and Black Catholic education as well as their efforts to support the development of Black women's religious life in sub-Saharan Africa, outside the cultural domination of European and white American sisterhoods. This chapter also briefly examines the revolutionary ministry of Sister Thea Bowman, the first and only Black Franciscan Sister of Perpetual Adoration of La Crosse, Wisconsin, who in the 1980s emerged as one of the Church's most visible and beloved critics of enduring racism and sexism; the overlooked activism of Black sisters in the struggle for women's ordination; and the implications of the growing numbers of African sisters in the nation.

Charting African American sisters' freedom struggles reminds us that there has always been an articulation of US Catholicism that understood that the lives and souls of Black people mattered. For most of their history in the nation, Black sisters never made up more than 1 percent of the national population of Catholic sisters.[78] Yet they have been more than consequential figures in the story of American Catholicism and the fight against racism, sexism, and exclusion in the Church and wider society. Indeed, when one considers the kinds of barriers that African American sisters routinely broke over the years, many of the women whose stories fill the pages ahead deserve to be not only known but also championed as we champion the nation's most famous Black freedom fighters. Black sisters' epic journey in the United States is a remarkable story of Black resilience, faithfulness, and possibility. It also serves as another cautionary tale about ignoring and underestimating the prevalence of anti-Black racism in religious communities. It is my greatest hope that I have done justice to African American sisters' stories. Any mistakes are my own.

1. "Our Sole Wish Is to Do the Will of God"

THE EARLY STRUGGLES OF BLACK CATHOLIC SISTERS IN THE UNITED STATES

We had a very hard time for we had many enemies who wanted to degrade our dear little community as poor as we were. . . . We were persecuted by the Sisters of St. Joseph in this city. They tried all they could to make us take off our habits. That was after forty-five or fifty years that we had worked and suffered to have a religious habit. No one would think that we were anything if we were not dressed in the holy habit. —SISTER OF THE HOLY FAMILY MARY BERNARD DEGGS, *No Cross, No Crown*

Apologists for US Catholic slavery and segregation have long maintained that the Church embraced anti-Black racism to accommodate the status quo of secular society and protect itself as a persecuted religious minority.[1] As one historian put it, "No aspect of the life of . . . women religious . . . so emphasizes the fact that they were women of their times, influenced by the culture they lived in, as the issue of slavery."[2] However, a closer survey of the Church's foundational engagement with African enslavement in the Americas and an examination of the trials faced by the earliest generations of Black Catholic women and girls called to religious life in the United States tell a radically different story. While anti-Catholicism was certainly present in North America by the mid-seventeenth century, the Catholic Church not only introduced African slavery in the Americas but also spearheaded its violent growth in most of Europe's "New World" colonies, including what became the United States.[3] Spanish Catholics successfully inaugurated

African slavery in Florida in the sixteenth century, more than fifty years before the arrival of the first enslaved Africans in the English-controlled Virginia colony in 1619.[4] In the 1660s, the English and Irish Catholics who established the Maryland colony also oversaw the enactment of some of North America's earliest laws codifying race and slavery, including the 1663 statute that made slavery an inheritable and lifelong condition and the 1664 statutes that penalized interracial marriage and eliminated Christian baptism as an avenue for slave emancipation.[5] In fact, at various moments before the US Civil War, Catholics with Spanish, French, English, and Irish origins, including religious orders of men and women, constituted the largest slaveholders in Florida, Maryland, Louisiana, Missouri, and Kentucky.[6] Like most prominent white lay Catholics, the nation's inaugural European and white American bishops, priests, and sisters also promulgated white supremacy, championed racial segregation, and vehemently opposed the admission of African Americans into religious life, especially on equal terms with whites.[7]

Beyond the anti-Black admissions policies of white congregations, the greatest testament to the ferocity with which white Catholics rejected Black religious vocations is that historians cannot say with certainty who the nation's first Black Catholic nun was. The realities of racial passing and archival erasure suggest we may never know her name or the exact circumstances of her life. What is clear is that the first African-descended women and girls known to profess consecrated vows in the United States in 1824 were not the first to seek entry into religious life. In 1819, for example, a priest from New Orleans wrote the inaugural bishop of Louisiana and the two Floridas and offered "a few girls of color desiring religious life" to support the US branch of the Religious of the Sacred Heart of Jesus (RSCJ), established in the Missouri territory in 1818.[8] In response, Sister Rose Philippine Duchesne (now a Catholic saint) wrote her superior in France, proposing to admit the potential candidates from New Orleans to solve her order's inability to locate "suitable" servants at Missouri's first Catholic convent and school. Although the French-born Duchesne suggested that these "girls of color" wear the order's regular habit, she requested they be admitted at third-class status, below the "converse sisters," who performed manual labor, and "choir sisters," who taught in schools.[9] For his contribution, Bishop Louis-Guillaume-Valentin DuBourg, a French native of the Caribbean slave colony of Saint-Domingue (now Haiti) and former president of Georgetown College (now University) in Washington, DC, encouraged Duchesne to consider only candidates of mixed African and

Native American descent, who he declared might otherwise be reduced to "prostitution." The slaveholding DuBourg—who went on to found an academy that became St. Louis University in Missouri—suggested that any Black candidates be "admitted to a sort of subaltern profession, with a different habit than converse sisters." He also reiterated to Duchesne soon thereafter inaugural US bishop John Carroll's defense of anti-Black disdain and segregation "as a prejudice that had to be kept as the last safeguard of morals."[10] Duchesne's superior in France, Sister Sophie Barat, also now a saint, granted her request, "provided that it is not known that [the girls of color] are members of the society." "Do not make the foolish mistake of mixing the whites with the blacks," Barat wrote. "You will have no more pupils. The same for your novices; no one would join if you were to receive black novices. We will see later what we can do for them."[11] Although seemingly nothing came of these tacit approvals until 1948, when the order admitted its first Black candidate in New York, African American requests to enter the RSCJ, which came to own over 150 enslaved Black people, did not cease.[12] In 1831, for example, Duchesne was still writing about "the girls of color who want to leave the world," proposing then the creation of a separate auxiliary order of Black Sacred Heart Sisters to accommodate the requests, even as her order expanded its holdings in enslaved human chattel and resisted abolition.[13]

The case of the Ursuline Sisters of New Orleans, who arrived from France in 1727 and became the first order of Catholic nuns to minister in the land area that became the United States, is even more instructive. Historians Emily Clark and Virginia Meacham Gould have argued that the Ursulines' educational and evangelization efforts among free and enslaved African-descended women and girls led to the great expansion of Louisiana's Black Catholic population, facilitated the development of an Afro-female-dominated Church in New Orleans by the early nineteenth century, and planted the seeds for the second successful African American Catholic sisterhood.[14] However, the historically Afro-Creole Sisters of the Holy Family (SSF) in New Orleans formed in 1842 specifically because white sisterhoods ministering in Louisiana, including the slaveholding Ursulines, refused to admit African American candidates into their ranks.[15] Indeed, after the Louisiana Purchase in 1803, the Ursulines, then under the leadership of the French-born Thérèse de Sainte Xavier Farjon, famously wrote to US president and fellow enslaver Thomas Jefferson asserting their status as "moral" slaveholders to secure formal recognition of their rights, protections, and property—material and human—as new residents of the expanded nation. The Ursulines, who eventually owned over two hundred

African Americans and never advocated for slavery's abolition, argued they took up "the cause of the Orphan, of the helpless child of Want, of the many who may be snatched from the paths of vice & infamy . . . & be trained up in the habits of virtue and religion to be happy & useful."[16] Like Dubourg's attack on Black female morality sixteen years later, the Ursulines' slandering of the moral character of Louisiana's Afro-Creole and Black female populations—while ignoring the sexual brutality of the slave system, which they upheld and perpetuated—cannot be simply understood as an acclimation to a hostile anti-Catholic and anti-Black environment. By the nineteenth century, attacks on Black female virtue were part and parcel of a long-standing European Christian discourse about color, holiness, and power that gained new traction in the sixteenth century with the global spread of Christianity and the rise of the transatlantic slave trade, in which the Catholic Church played foundational and leading roles.

To be sure, records indicate that women of African descent established the world's first female Christian monasteries in northeastern Africa in either the first or fourth centuries, predating the development of consecrated life for women in Europe by almost a century.[17] The ancient African tradition of women's religious life not only survived into the modern era but eventually played a leading role in repulsing the first European (and Jesuit-led) attempt to colonize Abyssinia (present-day Ethiopia) and convert the African Christian nation over to the Roman rite of Catholicism.[18] Whereas Portuguese Catholics failed in eastern Africa in the seventeenth century, they thrived in western and central Africa, where they established the first Roman Catholic chapel in sub-Saharan Africa in the late fifteenth century and inaugurated the transatlantic slave trade in the early sixteenth century.[19] With a series of papal bulls, including Pope Nicholas V's *Dum Diversas* in 1452 and Pope Alexander VI's *Inter Caetera* in 1493, the Church not only sanctioned the perpetual enslavement of non-Christians and the Catholic trade in human beings but also authorized European Catholic invasions of Africa and eventually the Americas.[20] While European engagement with race making and racial othering dates back at least to the medieval period, under these new Catholic doctrines, Europeanness (and later whiteness) emerged as a protected and even "holy" status within and outside Catholic boundaries.[21] At the same time, non-Europeanness, especially Africanness (and later Blackness), increasingly became synonymous with evil, hypersexuality, and moral debasement. European and white American Catholic officials actively shaped this emerging discourse by colonizing and enslaving Indigenous and African people, creating formal laws based on Spanish and Portuguese notions of blood purity (which came to signify a person free of African ancestry), and systematically excluding Indigenous and African-descended people from religious life or relegating them to a subordinate status within European (and later white American) congregations and the wider Church.[22] In Brazil, which received the largest number of enslaved Africans transported to the Americas during the transatlantic trade and became home to the largest Black Catholic population in the "New World," the first Church-approved Roman Catholic sisterhood to freely admit African-descended women and girls was not established until 1928.[23] In Africa, the first sisterhood organized outside of Ethiopia was not established until 1858 in Senegal, and most European and white American Roman Catholic orders ministering on the continent formally barred Africans from equal membership up through the Second Vatican Council, held from 1962 to 1965.[24]

Thus, the successful formation of African American sisterhoods in the United States during the first half of the nineteenth century was a revolutionary development in the modern Roman Catholic Church. It was also a by-product of the Black Catholic–led slave revolution in the French colony of Saint-Domingue launched in the late eighteenth century, which cemented the foundation of abolitionism throughout the Americas.[25] During the rebellion, thousands of free and enslaved Saint-Domingue residents and others from neighboring islands fled to the United States, with many settling in port cities, including Baltimore, New Orleans, New York, Philadelphia, Richmond, Norfolk, Charleston, Mobile, and Savannah.[26] The humanitarian crisis that resulted from the influx of mostly French-speaking refugees, who were overwhelming Catholic, and the refusal of most white Church leaders to extend equitable resources to the Black faithful prompted Black Catholics to take the lead in providing essential services to these displaced communities. Scholars of the Catholic Church have long cited Pope Gregory XVI's 1839 condemnation of the slave trade for making some in the Church amenable to abolition and the more equitable treatment of Black Catholics.[27] However, the inauguration of modern Black women's religious life resulted specifically from the dramatic increase of the nation's Black Catholic population in the late eighteenth and early nineteenth centuries and the great expansion of US land territory in 1803 from the Louisiana Purchase—both of which resulted from the Haitian Revolution and preceded Gregory's *In Supremo Apostolatus* by more than three decades.[28]

Despite unrelenting white opposition, the admissions of the first generation of African-descended women and girls into US religious life marked a new beginning in the Black struggle for freedom, dignity, and bodily integrity in the religious institution most responsible for the rise of African slavery in the Americas. These pioneering African American sisters' spiritual successes struck at one of the central tenets of white supremacy—the racist belief that Black people were innately immoral and sexually promiscuous. Through their social service ministries to African American communities, especially in education, these Black brides of Christ not only institutionalized Black Catholic resistance to white supremacy in religious life but also forced the slaveholding Church to acknowledge Black humanity and commit resources (albeit minimal) to its Black faithful in unprecedented ways.

North America's First Black Sisters

Since the late nineteenth century, scholarly consensus has been that the first "Negro sisters" in the United States were members of a short-lived and all-Black auxiliary unit of the Sisters of Loretto at the Foot of the Cross (SL) located in the "Catholic Holy Land" of Kentucky.[29] Established in 1812 by Father Charles Nerinckx, a Belgian missionary priest, and Mary Rhodes, a member of a prominent and slaveholding Maryland Catholic family who migrated to Kentucky in the early nineteenth century following the Louisiana Purchase, the SL was one of the first two Catholic sisterhoods with a US foundation.[30] The SL also relied on the labor and sale of more than forty enslaved Black people to fund, build, and sustain their missions before the Civil War.[31] Nerinckx, who directed much of the construction of the Church's earliest buildings in Kentucky, desired to establish a ministry to the region's substantial Black Catholic population, most of whom had migrated from Maryland with their enslavers beginning in the late eighteenth century. Thus, Nerinckx, according to one early SL chronicler, soon "caused a few young negro children to be adopted in Loretto" for the purpose of developing a Black sisterhood to minister to the area's largely neglected Black population.[32] The original rule of the SL, written by Nerinckx, seemingly also made provisions for enslaved women and girls called to religious life to serve as oblates, whom the rule described as candidates "that offer themselves, or are offered to spend their life, or part of it, about the Society," distinct from the order's associates and penitents.[33]

In May 1824, twelve young women "offered themselves at Loretto for the little veil," three of them the community's "blacks, who received nearly all the votes!" To signify the Black sisters' subjugated status in the order, "their dress" and "offices and employment" were to be different. While the

Black candidates were to "keep the main rules of the society," they also had separate rules and were not permitted to take perpetual vows "before twelve years of profession."[34] One nineteenth-century source noted that two additional Black candidates entered the Loretto auxiliary soon thereafter.[35] However, a dispute with the community's confessor and future titular bishop of Bardstown, Kentucky, Father Guy Chabrat, forced Nerinckx out of Kentucky soon after the 1824 ceremony. Nerinckx died in Missouri that same year, and the French-born Chabrat quickly disbanded the Black Loretto congregation, deeming the time as one scholar put it "premature for colored nuns."[36] Soon thereafter, Chabrat suppressed the original Loretto rule; drafted another one without associates, oblates, and penitents; and burned nearly all of Nerinckx's writings and books.[37] This destruction, along with a later fire at the Loretto motherhouse and the SL leaders' decades-long suppression of public references to the order's slaveholding past, seemingly erased much of the archival and oral history evidence of the early African American dimensions of the Loretto congregation, including the suspected African heritage of Loretto foundress Mary Rhodes and several other early Loretto members.[38] Nonetheless, the verifiable details of the Loretto foundation reveal that all three of the nation's major cradles of Catholicism—Kentucky, Louisiana, and Maryland—produced significant numbers of Black vocations to religious life during the earliest days of the US Church. While the all-Black Loretto community proved short-lived, the next two African American sisterhoods withstood white opposition.

Like most of the nation's earliest white sisterhoods, the historically Black Oblate Sisters of Providence (OSP) in Baltimore and the historically Afro-Creole SSF in New Orleans began when a small group of devout laywomen who desired to consecrate their lives to God and address the need for Catholic education for children—especially girls—secured the support of a priest willing to direct the sisterhood. The African American congregations also responded to the refusal of European and white American sisterhoods to admit African-descended candidates. Despite the limited evidence documenting their early lives and experiences, it is clear that many founding members of the OSP and SSF communities evidenced a revolutionary commitment to Black education and clear vocations to religious life long before the Church's slaveholding leadership expressed a willingness to approve and supervise separate Black congregations.

The story of Catholic sisters in the fight against racial and sexual injustice in many ways begins with early Oblate Sister of Providence Mary Aloysius, born Anne Marie Becraft, although she was not the nation's first Black nun. Before she became the eleventh woman admitted into the OSP in 1831, Becraft achieved a saintlike status in her hometown community of Georgetown in Washington, DC.[39] In 1820, when she was only fifteen years old, Becraft—described in the first national report on education as the "most remarkable colored young woman of her time in the District, and perhaps, of any time"—established one of the earliest schools open to Black children in the nation's capital.[40] Over the next decade, Becraft transformed her school into the nation's first Catholic day and boarding academy for Black girls, winning crucial support from a Jesuit priest stationed at the racially segregated Holy Trinity Catholic Church and the French-transplanted community of Visitation Sisters, the second order of nuns to minister in the original thirteen states.[41] According to the chief surviving account of Becraft's life, the Visitation Sisters gave her instruction and briefly assisted her at her academy, which in 1827 became known as the Georgetown Seminary and was relocated across the street from the Visitation Convent and Academy, where over eighty enslaved men, women, and children labored against their wills, and around the corner from the Jesuit-led Georgetown College, where more than three hundred enslaved people did the same.[42] That Becraft not only dared to establish a Black Catholic school amid the nation's and the Church's slaveholding elite but also routinely marched her "troop of girls, dressed uniformly . . . in procession . . . to devotions on the sabbath at Holy Trinity Church" in the veritable hell of DC slavery, underscores the subversive and emancipatory nature of Catholicism in the hands of African American women and girls fighting white supremacy.

That surviving records document that Anne's father, William Becraft, was "the natural son of Charles Carroll of Carrollton," the only Catholic signer of the Declaration of Independence, and a free woman of color who worked in Carroll's household, also matters.[43] One of the early nation's largest enslavers, Carroll was a descendant of one of the first European families to settle in Maryland and an early benefactor of the US Church. He was also a cousin to the slaveholding Jesuit priest John Carroll, the nation's first Catholic bishop and the first president of Georgetown College (later University).[44] In addition to her reported "uncommon intelligence . . . extraordinary piety and . . . elevation of character," Anne Becraft being Charles Carroll's granddaughter may help to explain why some slaveholding priests and sisters supported her Black educational endeavors despite their insurrectionary dimensions. The suspected African American offspring of other white US founding fathers and their relatives, like the Costins and Dandridges of Mount Vernon, also operated schools for Black children in DC during the same period.[45] Still,

Becraft's African heritage barred her admission into the Visitation order, eventually forcing her to turn over the leadership of her school to a former student and leave Georgetown to enter religious life in Baltimore.[46]

Elizabeth Clarisse Lange (figure 1.1) and Marie Balas had also broken new ground in Black Catholic education before they met Father James Joubert, the Sulpician priest who helped them officially form the OSP in 1829. All three—Lange, Balas, and Joubert—had fled to the United States as a result of the slave rebellion in Saint-Domingue in the early nineteenth century.[47] Settling in Baltimore among the city's growing French-speaking refugee population, Joubert entered St. Mary's Seminary in 1805 and was ordained five years later. Shortly thereafter, he joined the Sulpician order, which established the nation's first Catholic seminary in 1791 and through Bishop DuBourg helped Elizabeth Seton, another future saint deeply entangled in the history of slaveholding, to establish the first Catholic school (for girls) in Baltimore in 1808 and the Sisters of Charity, the first Catholic sisterhood with a US foundation, in nearby Emmitsburg, Maryland, in 1809.[48]

The first order of priests in the original thirteen states, the Sulpicians ministered to Baltimore's Black Catholic populations during the late eighteenth and early nineteenth centuries. Specifically, the transplanted French order of slaveholding priests permitted free and enslaved Black Catholics to worship on a segregated basis in their St. Mary's Lower Chapel beginning in 1796. The Sulpicians also allowed one member to conduct religious instruction for the city's Black faithful.[49] In 1827, Joubert succeeded to these responsibilities and soon contemplated establishing a school for Black Catholic children to address the refusal of most of the city's white-administered schools to educate them.[50] While seeking support for this endeavor, Joubert in 1828 became aware of Lange and Balas, who had been conducting a free school for the children of Black Caribbean refugees out of Lange's home for "a number of years."[51] Although not officially sponsored by the Church, Lange and Balas's school likely facilitated additional Catholic evangelization among Baltimore's Black population and helped the two best friends to preserve their vocations to religious life.[52]

Like most devout women, Lange and Balas had also been active in Baltimore's Catholic confraternities for women since 1813, and during their first meeting with Joubert, they told him "that for more than ten years they [had] wished to consecrate themselves to God for this good work, waiting patiently that in His own infinite goodness He would show them a way of giving themselves to Him."[53] While it is unknown when and to which white-led sisterhoods Lange and Balas had sought admission and

FIGURE 1.1. Servant of God Mary (Elizabeth Clarisse) Lange (ca. 1784–1882), chief foundress of the Oblate Sisters of Providence, photographed a few years before her death. A French- and Spanish-speaking Saint-Dominguan of African descent, Lange fled to the United States with her mother following the progression of the slave rebellion in Saint-Domingue (now Haiti) in the early nineteenth century. Lange's fiercely contested journey to becoming the first African American mother superior underscores the transnational dimensions of early US Black Catholicism and illuminates the strident commitments that most of the nation's earliest Catholic bishops, priests, and sisters had to white supremacy and Black subordination. Courtesy of the Archives of the Oblate Sisters of Providence, Baltimore, Maryland.

experienced rejection, only the Carmelites (1790), the Visitation Sisters of Georgetown (1800), and Seton's Sisters of Charity (1809), all slaveholding orders, preceded the OSP in the diocese of Baltimore, the nation's first Catholic diocese.[54] Viewing it as "better to start a society of religious, who would be kept together by their vows and their piety," as a way to make Lange and Balas's school permanent and assist the friends in becoming consecrated women of God, Joubert helped Lange, Balas, and another Saint Dominguan woman, Rose Boegue, secure a separate house to relocate their school and begin their novitiate in June 1828.[55] Sometime later, nineteen-year-old Almaide Maxis Duchemin, the US-born daughter of a Saint Dominguan émigré nurse and a British major, whom Lange and Balas had raised and educated, also joined them.[56]

Despite finding a champion in Joubert, the four OSP charter members faced vigorous opposition from Baltimore's wider clerical and slaveholding community. White priests by and large declared the future sisters of color a "profanation of the habit."[57] Several threats were made against the women, and Joubert noted, "These good girls . . . admitted to me that after all they had heard said, only through obedience would they be determined to take the religious habit."[58] With the local archbishop's encouragement and approval of the community's constitution, Joubert and the four candidates cautiously proceeded. Pope Gregory XVI's formal approval of the OSP congregation in 1831, eight years before he condemned the slave trade, gave the diocesan order even more protection.[59] However, virulent white resistance to the OSP persisted, resulting in minimal financial support from the Church, erasure from the earliest Catholic publications documenting female religious life, and routine verbal and physical threats of violence, including white attacks on their second school and convent in Baltimore in 1857.[60] Not even the Oblates' valiant service to Baltimore's community, including Archbishop James Whitfield, during the great cholera epidemic of 1832 could overcome the anti-Black animus of the city's white Catholics, including the clergy.[61] Nonetheless, the OSP and their school, later St. Frances Academy, the first formal Black Catholic school in Baltimore, endured. Several St. Frances alumnae, including Arabella Jones, a woman with close ties to the family of President John Quincy Adams, went on to found other prominent schools, often Catholic, for Black youth in the nineteenth century.[62] Notably, in 1835, when the Sulpician superior requested the services of two OSP members to assume the management of the domestic and infirmary duties at their seminary, OSP superior Mother Mary (Elizabeth Clarisse) Lange also won further recognition of her sisters' consecrated status and critical protections for her members forced to undertake the perilous work among the slaveholding priests and priests-in-training. Specifically, Lange secured "separate accommodations and eating facilities . . . and the exclusion of visitors from the seminary kitchen" for her members. "We cannot give our consent, but under certain conditions," Lange courageously wrote. "Our sole wish is to do the will of God."[63]

Like their predecessors in Baltimore, Henriette Delille, Juliette Gaudin, and Josephine Charles, the three foundresses of the SSF in New Orleans, were free Catholic women of mixed African and European ancestry with expressed vocations to religious life but no opportunities to pursue them.[64] The early SSF members also had deep roots in the slaveholding American Church and sought to live free from the moral degradation and sexual exploitation routinely forced on African-descended women and girls.

Under Spanish and later French slavery, free women and girls of color living in the Louisiana territory had few legal rights and limited options outside marriage and the pervasive system of concubinage known as *plaçage*. Under that system, white European or Creole men entered formal long-term relationships with free and enslaved Indigenous, African, and mixed-race women and girls. Although segments of society, including the Church, publicly condemned these civil unions, they were commonplace in New Orleans and elsewhere by the late eighteenth century. At formal dances, often known as *quadroon balls*, young Catholic women and girls of color would be formally presented to prospective European or white Creole male suitors, who were also often Catholic. If a match were secured, a contract would be drawn up, usually between the girl's mother and the suitor, stipulating financial support, housing, and sexual relations.[65]

Extant Church and community records make clear that the SSF foundresses understood plaçage to be sexual slavery, restricting free women and girls of color—already limited or barred from entering marriage and religious life—from living lives of virtue and contributing to attacks on the moral character of Black women and girls. Most, if not all, of the women who entered the order before 1865 were products of plaçage and thus had firsthand knowledge of its exploitative nature. Sister Mary Bernard (Clementine) Deggs, the order's first historian, wrote, "All of the first sisters were of the very first families of the city, and only one Sister Suzanne Navarre, was a stranger from Boston. As for the rest, they were all natives of this state, but their fathers were all foreigners—some French, Spanish or German. They were descended from the first settlers of Louisiana."[66] Though cofoundress Juliette Gaudin was actually born in Cuba to a free woman of color and a French-born father, who fled the slave rebellion in Saint-Domingue, the other early SSF members save for Navarre were Crescent City natives and members of prominent Afro-Creole families with European fathers.[67] Surviving records even indicate that SSF chief foundress Henriette Delille (figure 1.2) was the great-great-granddaughter of Claude-Joseph Villars Dubreuil and an enslaved woman he owned named Nannette, also known as Mary Ann. Dubreuil, one of Louisiana's largest enslavers, was also the inaugural French royal engineer whose free and enslaved Black crews cleared much of the land area of New Orleans, built the city's first canals and levees, and erected its earliest structures, including the Old Ursuline Convent, which ironically Delille would never be permitted to enter as a candidate for religious life because of her African heritage and unwillingness to pass for white.[68] Evidence also suggests Delille entered into a plaçage arrangement with an older European man in her late teens or early twenties and bore one or two children who died in infancy.[69]

While some scholars have speculated that Delille's experience with plaçage likely prompted her call to religious life, the story of Josephine Charles, the third SSF cofoundress, makes clearest that the order was formed as a direct act of protest against slavery and sexual exploitation. Deggs, for example, documented that Charles, the daughter of an Afro-Creole mother and German father, fiercely resisted her older sister's attempts to groom her for potential suitors at a quadroon ball.[70] After the Civil War, Charles—by then the congregation's leader—mortgaged several properties inherited from her father in an effort to sanctify sites in New Orleans associated with racism and slavery, especially the abuse of Black women and girls.[71] One of the earliest properties that the order purchased under Charles's leadership, for example, was a former slave traders' pen on Chartres Street that the SSF used to establish their St. Mary's Academy for Girls in 1867. As Deggs explained, "Many sins had been committed at that place, not only sins, but the most horrible crimes. It must have been the will of God that our sisters should buy the place to expiate the crimes that had been committed there."[72] In 1881, Charles also purchased the French Quarter's Orleans Ballroom, which had hosted some the city's most (in)famous quadroon balls during slavery. According to Deggs, the Orleans Ballroom had been "a den of sin."[73] However, from 1881 to 1955, the site served as the new home of the SSF motherhouse and their St. Mary's Academy.[74]

Although the historical record does not note exactly when the three SSF foundresses first sought admission to religious life and experienced rejection, Delille, Gaudin, Charles, and a few other early SSF members

FIGURE 1.2. Venerable Henriette Delille (ca. 1812–62), chief foundress of the Sisters of the Holy Family sometime after 1852, the year she professed her first vows and her order's members began wearing black percale gowns to signify their consecrated status more formally. Born in New Orleans to a free Afro-Creole mother and a French-born father, Delille possessed a clear commitment to evangelizing and educating the city's free and enslaved Black population during the antebellum period. However, her order's ties to slaveholding and initial refusal to admit nonelite women circumscribed its impact in significant ways before the Civil War. Archives of the Congregation of the Sisters of the Holy Family, New Orleans.

were among the students and teaching assistants of Sister Sainte Marthe Fontière, a member of the French-based Religious Hospitallers of Saint Joseph.[75] In 1823, Fontière—at the invitation of Bishop DuBourg and with financial support from the city's free African American community—established the St. Claude School for free girls of color in New Orleans, effectively assuming the educational training of free African-descended girls from the slaveholding Ursulines, who abandoned the work sometime in the 1820s.[76] Many other early SSF members received instruction from the slaveholding RSCJ, which began teaching the catechism to the enslaved and providing rudimentary education to free persons of color (on a segregated basis) in Convent and Grand Coteau, Louisiana, as early as 1821.[77] During her tenure in New Orleans, Fontière also tried to establish her own community, or an American branch of a French order, that would minister exclusively to free and enslaved African Americans and seemingly accept young women of color as candidates for religious life.[78] However, the French nun was unsuccessful.[79]

After Fontière's departure from New Orleans in 1832, the administration of her school was briefly transferred back to the Ursulines before another Frenchwoman, Jeanne Marie Aliquot, took over in 1834. Although Aliquot, a biological sister of an Ursuline, arrived in New Orleans in 1832 with the intention of entering the Ursulines, fate intervened. According to SSF oral tradition, Aliquot fell into the Mississippi River while disembarking from her ship. After being rescued by a Black man, she vowed to minister for the remainder of her life to the city's African American community.[80] When Aliquot took over Fontière's school, she also began a lasting association with the Afro-Creole women who established the SSF.[81]

In 1836, Aliquot sold the St. Claude School back to the Ursulines, with the stipulation that the nuns continue the school's mission of educating African American girls. Aliquot then helped Delille and Gaudin organize an interracial and later Afro-Creole lay sisterhood, the Congregation of the Sisters of the Presentation of the Blessed Virgin Mary, to minister to the city's free and enslaved Black population.[82] By 1840, select members of this confraternity, including Delille, Gaudin, and Charles, had left their family homes to live together in a quasi-consecrated state under the directorship of Father Etienne Rousselon, the founding pastor of St. Augustine, a parish organized for the city's African American Catholics. In 1840, New Orleans bishop Antoine Blanc wrote to Rome to have the Sisters of the Presentation affiliated with the Sodality of the Blessed Virgin Mary.[83] Rome's approval in 1842 marked a turning point and became the order's official founding date.

The oral tradition of the SSF also records that in 1850 Delille and Gaudin underwent novitiate training with the RSCJ in Convent, Louisiana, in St. James Parish.[84] Two years later, Delille, Gaudin, and Charles professed their first vows.[85] However, severe obstacles remained. In addition to suffering persecution from those opposed to the presence of African-descended nuns in the city, the SSF faced strident resistance within the Church from those who, according to Deggs, told their spiritual director that he "would never be able to make anything out of us" and "never find any vocations among our class of people who loved their pleasure so much."[86]

Unlike the OSP in Baltimore and the nation's white congregations, ecclesiastical authorities in New Orleans forbade SSF members from wearing habits (clothing to signify their consecrated status) during the early decades of their existence. According to one SSF source, Antoine Blanc, who became the first archbishop of New Orleans when it was elevated to an archdiocese in 1850, prevented the sisters from wearing habits and making public vows to illustrate the Church's opposition to abolitionism, since some anti-Catholic nativists and proslavery ideologues promoted the myth that Catholic enslavers readily freed women who expressed a desire to enter religious life.[87] According to another community source, the order's first spiritual director advised the sisters to avoid wearing a traditional habit so as to appear without pretension and avoid threatening the status of white nuns, and other white women, in the city.[88] Such thinking would certainly have aligned with laws during the colonial and early national periods that sought to control, subjugate, and criminalize the city's free women of color. In 1786, city officials passed the infamous "tignon law" in response to Spanish King Charles III's demand to "establish public order and proper standards of morality" with respect to the "large class of mulattos and particularly mulatto women." The law not only banned African-descended women and girls from wearing fine clothing and jewelry and adorning their hair with jewels and feathers but also required free women of color to wear a kerchief to cover their hair. Historian Virginia Meacham Gould has argued that this law let the governor "symbolically reestablish" these women's ties to slavery and remind them of their subjugated place in New Orleans.[89] While Rousselon may have wanted to protect the early SSF members from public rebuke and potential violence, barring them from wearing a traditional habit upheld the same thinking that led Spanish colonial leaders to claim that Black female immorality—not European immorality and the institution of slavery—caused the growing number of sexual liaisons between European men and African-descended women.

In the 1870s or early 1880s, the SSF finally won the right to wear habits.[90] But before the Civil War, the congregation did not allow the denial of this recognition to circumscribe their ministries. Under Delille, the order established the nation's first Catholic ministry and nursing home for the elderly and infirm, especially the formerly enslaved.[91] They also established a school for free girls of color affiliated with St. Augustine Catholic Church, taught the catechism to the enslaved, and continued evangelizing in the African American community.[92]

While both the OSP and SSF educated free and enslaved Black (as well as a few white) children before the federal abolition of slavery in 1865, the SSF enforced separation between free and enslaved in their school like most white congregations engaged in this work during the period.[93] While white sisters' spiritual propagation of white supremacy and embrace of class stratification drove their segregationist policies, Sister Mary Bernard Deggs noted that the SSF's decision to instruct free and enslaved children separately was in response to complaints from free Afro-Creole parents who did not want their children educated on an equal basis with enslaved children or those "whose mothers had been slaves."[94]

Like most of their European and white American male and female counterparts and many Afro-Creole elites, at least two of the early Sisters of the Holy Family also owned enslaved people.[95] Because many of the earliest SSF members (whose names are lost to the historical record) left the order after Delille's death in 1862, the extent and nature of the order's slaveholding may be irrecoverable.[96] However, it seems clear that the Afro-Creole sisters did not themselves traffic in human flesh or use physical violence to control their enslaved property as most of their white male and female counterparts routinely did.[97] Nor did the SSF order support the Confederacy during the Civil War as white slaveholding Catholics did.[98] Records reveal only that Delille owned at least one human being while in religious life, and Gaudin owned at least two people during her lifetime. The two best friends seemingly inherited their enslaved human property from their families. While Delille made clear provisions in her last wills and testaments for the protection and emancipation of Betsy, the enslaved woman in her "possession," it is unclear whether Gaudin still owned the woman named Melania and Melania's son when she entered religious life.[99] In the SSF's first written history, Deggs also noted that the French-born Aliquot, who remained close to and sometimes resided with the Afro-Creole sisters, also brought "two or three slaves" to work for the community in its early years.[100]

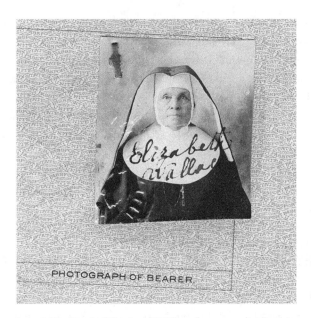

PHOTOGRAPH OF BEARER

FIGURE 1.3. Sister Mary Ursula (Elizabeth) Wallace (1848–1930). More than to Mother Josephine Charles, early community historian Sister Mary Bernard (Clementine) Deggs attributes the admission of the Sisters of the Holy Family's first formerly enslaved member, Cloé Preval, to Wallace, whom Deggs misidentifies as Sister Elizabeth Wales and repeatedly derides as a troublemaker. Wallace, who spoke English, Spanish, and French fluently, was a native of Holmes County, Mississippi, and according to one source the first principal of the order's St. Mary's Academy. After the Sisters of the Holy Family split bitterly over Preval's admission in 1869, Wallace, whom Deggs also describes as a "brilliant scholar," left and tried multiple times to start her own congregation before entering the Oblate Sisters of Providence in 1891. She taught in Cuba for over eighteen years and remained in the community until her death. Courtesy of the Archives of the Oblate Sisters of Providence, Baltimore, Maryland.

Like their European and white American counterparts, the ssf also initially employed a restrictive admissions policy based on color, class, and previous condition, accepting "only those of free and well-known families" and, according to Deggs, refusing "an Indian, red skinned."[101] The order ended its exclusionary policy in 1869 by admitting a formerly enslaved woman, Cloé Preval (later Sister Mary Joachim), which required the intervention of the order's second spiritual director, a new archbishop, for whom Preval worked as a cook, and the moral leadership of three members, including Sister Elizabeth Wallace (see figure 1.3), a Mississippi native who later departed the ssf for the osp, and the nonslaveholding ssf cofoundress Josephine Charles, who according to Deggs rejected social distinctions and "above all things . . . loved justice." Preval's admission en-gendered a bitter fourteen-year split in the congregation, underscoring the elitism and colorism of many of the order's early Afro-Creole members despite their unwavering commitments to evangelizing and educating the enslaved and formerly enslaved.[102]

By contrast, the foundresses of the OSP never enslaved people. While documented financial support received from Lange's father in Cuba sug-gests that she and the community might have indirectly benefited from the institution in their early years, the OSP never accepted enslaved people as a part of their members' dowries or relied on the labor of enslaved people in their daily lives or ministries. Nor did the early OSP members exhibit the anti-Black animus or classist attitudes of most of their white and Afro-Creole counterparts.[103] In fact, before the Civil War, the order admitted at least eight formerly enslaved women into their ranks. In 1855, the OSP even admitted a woman still legally held in bondage by Emily Harper, a local white laywoman who like Anne Marie Becraft was a granddaughter of Charles Carroll of Carrollton.[104] The decision to admit former bonds-women made the OSP the first US sisterhood to reject the racist and sex-ist belief that a woman born in slavery lacked the virtue required to enter religious life in the modern Roman Church.[105] The lives of the early OSP members, especially chief foundress and sainthood candidate Mother Mary (Elizabeth Clarisse) Lange, also provide essential counterpoints to those who attempt to defend or excuse their slaveholding and segregation-ist peers as simply people "of their times."

Despite the OSP's and the SSF's contrasting commitments to racial equality before the Civil War, the successful formation of the two sister-hoods was nothing short of remarkable. Although their designation as "colored" orders relegated them to the lowest status in the Roman Church and left them vulnerable to the whims of slaveholding and discriminatory archbishops, embracing the celibate religious state enabled Black Catho-lic women and girls to contest racist and sexist assaults on their humanity and morality, the ideological and legal cornerstones of white supremacy. That these two Black sisterhoods were founded in cities that contained two of the nation's largest slave ports and markets, where Black women's and girls' nude bodies were abused, displayed, commodified, and sold on a daily basis—often by members of their own church—is also significant.[106] The OSP's and SSF's ministries forced the nation's earliest Catholic officials to declare with their actions and words (however grudgingly) that the lives and souls of free and enslaved Black people mattered in fundamental ways.

The existence of these Church-approved African American congregations of sisters also helped ensure the survival of the Black Catholic community through slavery and created new possibilities for devout Black Catholic women and girls in the United States, Canada, and the Caribbean denied admission into European and white American sisterhoods owing to their color. Meanwhile, leaders of white sisterhoods made a few exceptions in the nineteenth century for African-descended women and girls who sought to suppress their Black identities, endeavors that met with mixed results.

Racial Passing in Early US Female Religious Life

Consensual interracial intimacy and the rampant sexual abuse of Black women and girls produced hundreds of thousands of African-descended people whose skin color and hair texture enabled them to move across society's manufactured racial boundaries and access the privileges and protections of whiteness during slavery's reign. As early as 1835, this racial ambiguity allowed certain US-born Black women and girls to enter predominantly or exclusively white orders with equal status. Although the nation's earliest white sisterhoods formally and informally barred Black candidates, several, including the Ursulines, the SL, and the School Sisters of Notre Dame in Baltimore, admitted non-Black Latina and Native American candidates early in their tenures.[107] While these non-Black sisters of color were often, but not always, admitted at the rank of lay or house sisters and relegated to domestic and agricultural labor, their admissions underscore that the earliest white sisterhoods were committed to what theologian Katie Grimes calls "anti-Blackness supremacy," a form of white supremacy rooted in New World slavery where Africans and their descendants became uniquely stigmatized and were subjugated to specific forms of individual and structural violence and discrimination.[108] An ability to pass for white or simply non-Black, then, sometimes led early white congregational leaders to make exceptions for select African American women. Such decisions not only required secrecy but also prompted a backlash if discovered.

For example, in 1835, the Dames de la Retraite, a French transplant community in Charleston, South Carolina, surreptitiously admitted a woman "known to be a mulatto," prompting protest within and outside the Church. However, the superioress, who had assisted the woman in securing "foreign papers stating she was white," insisted to Charleston's inaugural bishop, John England, that the woman was white. Despite England's demand that

FIGURE 1.4. Mother Theresa (Almaide) Maxis Duchemin (1810–92), charter member of the historically Black Oblate Sisters of Providence and chief foundress of the predominantly white Sisters, Servants of the Immaculate Heart of Mary, in exile wearing the habit of the Grey Nuns of Ottawa, Canada, in 1867. Courtesy of Sisters, Servants of the Immaculate Heart of Mary Archives, Monroe, Michigan.

the woman be removed to forestall white mob violence, evidence suggests that she remained.[109]

In 1843, the death of Father James Joubert, the unexpected withdrawal of white ministerial support, and an archdiocesan-led effort to suppress the OSP pushed cofoundress Sister Theresa (Almaide) Maxis Duchemin (figure 1.4) and another member, Sister Charlotte (Anne Constance) Schaaf, to pursue racial passing as a way to preserve their futures as nuns.[110] After a failed attempt to enter an order in Belgium in 1844, Duchemin, with the support of a Belgian Redemptorist priest ministering in Baltimore and Sulpician leader Father Louis Deluol, forged a plan to start a new order.[111] In 1845, Duchemin and Schaaf left the OSP to establish the first Catholic sisterhood and school for girls in Michigan. Another sister had made plans to join the Michigan sisterhood, but early OSP historian Sister M. Theresa Catherine (Sarah) Willigmann noted that Sister Stanislaus (Josephine) Amanda soon "received word from Sister Therese not to come as her color was too dark."[112] Initially named the Sisters of Providence, the Michigan community was quickly renamed the Sisters, Servants of the Immaculate

FIGURE 1.5. Mother Mary Rosina (Margaret) Wightman (1825–94). Despite a successor's attempt to erase her from the congregation's archive, a photo survived. Courtesy of Archives of the Sisters of Charity of New York, Bronx.

Heart of Mary (IHM).[113] Duchemin also dropped her mother's surname and began to call herself simply Mother Theresa Maxis.

Although IHM foundations in Michigan and later Pennsylvania flourished under Maxis's leadership, her attempt to suppress her African heritage was never successful. By 1859, repeated conflicts with bishops in Michigan and Pennsylvania, who regularly used racially derogatory language to describe Maxis's mixed-race heritage, forced the IHM foundress to seek refuge with the Grey Nuns of Ottawa, Canada.[114] Save for a thwarted attempt to enter the School Sisters of Notre Dame in Baltimore in 1868 as a white woman, Maxis remained in Canada until 1885 when the IHM in Westchester, Pennsylvania, finally allowed her to return.[115] After Maxis's death in 1892, white IHM leaders and others colluded to erase Maxis and Schaaf from the order's history as its foundresses, instead identifying and celebrating the order's third member as their foundress.[116]

The story of Sister Mary Rosina (Margaret) Wightman (figure 1.5), who entered the of Sisters of Charity of New York in 1848, followed a similar trajectory. She was born in Charleston, South Carolina, in 1825 to either a free or enslaved African-descended mother and an English planter father.[117] During her sixty-nine-year tenure in the order, Wightman led the community's St. Lawrence Academy in Manhattan and its military hospital during the last year of the Civil War. She also held several congregational offices, including "Treasurer, Assistant Mother, and Mistress of Novices."[118] In 1891, Wightman was elected as the order's superior, an office she held until her death in 1894.[119] However, upon the discovery of Wightman's African heritage after her death, one of her successors attempted to destroy "everything in the archives that pertained to her—except a prayer book and rosary."[120]

Fifteen-year-old Martha Healy may have been the last US-born African-descended person to enter a historically white sisterhood before the Civil War. Born into slavery in 1840 near Macon, Georgia, Martha was the eldest daughter of an Irish plantation owner and an enslaved woman who was seventeen years his junior.[121] Like her better-known brothers, James Augustine (the nation's first African-descended Catholic priest and bishop), Patrick Francis (the first African American Jesuit and Catholic college president), and Alexander Sherwood (a priest who became the first African American to earn a doctorate in canon law), Martha self-identified as Irish and never publicly embraced her mother's African heritage.[122] In 1853, she entered the order of her educators, the Congregation of Notre Dame in Montreal, Canada. However, in 1863, Martha departed religious life to marry and passed for Irish for the remainder of her life.[123]

Given the secrecy that racial passing required and the documented erasures of the African heritage of some pioneering Black members of white sisterhoods in the nineteenth and twentieth centuries, it is likely that other US-born African-descended women entered white orders in the United States and beyond before the federal abolition of slavery. For example, the oral traditions of the Daughters of Charity in Baltimore suggest as much.[124] The first congregational history of the SSF in New Orleans also reveals that three of the ten women who entered the order before 1862 departed the United States during the Civil War and attempted to enter orders in France.[125] While Deggs noted that none of these candidates' attempts proved successful, select African-descended women could gain admission into religious life in France as early as the seventeenth century and throughout its growing slave and colonial empire by the nineteenth century.[126] Though racial passing would continue in female religious life, it remained fraught with challenges and dangers, especially as the nation confronted the promises of Black freedom and terrors of white redemption after the Civil War.

African American Female Religious Life after Emancipation

The federal abolition of slavery in 1865 removed one of the greatest impediments blocking African American access to US religious life. However, widespread white Catholic resistance to Black emancipation and citizenship rights left the future of the African American Catholic community uncertain following the Civil War. While significant pockets of long-standing Black Catholics lived in northern port cities like New York, Philadelphia, and Boston, the vast majority of the nation's Black Catholics lived and labored in the South at the time of emancipation. Because most southern white Catholics supported the Confederacy and consequently opposed the Thirteenth, Fourteenth, and Fifteenth Amendments, southern parishes became especially volatile spaces for the Church's Black constituencies. In New Orleans, for example, interracial Catholic parishes of whites and free people of color had been the status quo during slavery.[127] However, most white Catholic New Orleanians not only supported the campaigns that sought to restore white rule in the former slave South but also took concrete measures to further subjugate African Americans within the Church. This often translated into Black Catholics being forced into segregated pews, to the back of Communion lines, and eventually out of white parishes and other Church institutions altogether.[128] When the New Orleans archbishop began mandating racial segregation in the city's parishes in the 1880s, the SSF were forced from their longtime parish, St. Mary's, and required to attend daily Mass at St. Louis Cathedral.[129] For grand ceremonies and masses at the Cathedral, which most sisters and priests attended, whites routinely insulted Black faithful and eventually prevented the parish's Black children under SSF direction from participating in the choir.[130] White sisterhoods also willfully disregarded the SSF's place as the first order with a motherhouse in the state and forced them to the back of the cathedral. Even though the African American order "went to the expense of putting up a small gate" at their pew "to prevent anyone from going in before" them, it proved "all in vain, for others would break the gates saying that they were the oldest in the church and had the right to pass in front" of the SSF.[131]

Other white sisters who arrived in New Orleans after the SSF's foundation also took advantage of the violent anti-Black climate to assert their dominance over the African American congregation. For example, sometime after the Civil War, the Little Sisters of the Poor, a French order that established its first ministry in New Orleans in 1868, confronted SSF leaders and demanded that they change the name of their home for the elderly and former slaves so that it would not be confused with the Little Sisters' home.[132] During Reconstruction, the Sisters of St. Joseph of Medaille (CSJ) from LePuy, France, even led a public campaign to have the Afro-Creole sisters remove their newly approved habits, arguing that they were too similar to the habit of the CSJ's lay (lowest-status) sisters. This was to ensure that African American sisters would be recognized as the most inferior nuns in the archdiocese.[133] In an especially egregious episode, New Orleans archbishop Napoléon-Joseph Perché, one of the Church's strongest advocates for southern secession and slavery's continuation, responded violently at the sight of a young novice sister sent by Mother Josephine Charles to model the SSF's long-desired habit and ask for its approval.[134] According to SSF oral and written history, Perché yelled, "What do you think you are?" and accused the young sister and her congregation of being "too proud" before sending her out of his office crying. Only after the intervention of the SSF's second spiritual director did Perché begrudgingly approve the SSF habit "with the addition of the Cord of St. Joseph in white wool" to appease the complaints of the Sisters of St. Joseph.[135]

The OSP, who survived the crisis of the 1840s, experienced another increase in white opposition to their presence after the Civil War. In 1863, the order accepted its first mission outside of Baltimore to staff Philadelphia's only Black Catholic school, which the Jesuits oversaw.[136] During the day, three OSP members taught Black youth at the Blessed Peter Claver School at a time when African Americans were still excluded from the city's public schools.[137] At night, the sisters ran a literacy school for adult Black women, many of whom were the mothers of the sisters' pupils and formerly enslaved. While the Jesuits and the city's Black Catholics gratefully received the Black sisters' presence, white city residents, including Catholics, fiercely resisted it. According to the OSP's oral tradition, white Philadelphians regularly subjected the Black sisters to verbal insults, pushed them off sidewalks, and threw garbage at them, among many other "severe trials."[138] By 1871, financial difficulties and unrelenting white racism forced the OSP to withdraw from Philadelphia.[139] It would take ninety-three years before the order returned to the so-called City of Brotherly Love to take up a ministry.[140]

Even when Catholic institutions remained open to Black people, white Catholics, religious and lay, mandated rituals of white domination and Black dehumanization that soured many long-standing Black Catholics. Misusing Black donations, preventing Black parents from attending their children's first Communions in white parishes on an equal basis, and subjecting the Black faithful to "petty persecutions" and intolerable humiliations as well as overt violence in parishes across the country led to a substantial exodus from the Church.[141] While it is unclear how many Black Catholics were living in the United States at the time of emancipation, historians have estimated that tens of thousands left the Church between 1865 and 1900.[142] One source suggested that as many as sixty-five thousand left in just one section of Louisiana.[143]

Black Catholic departures were also fueled by the white hierarchy's staunch refusal to commit resources to and invest in an educational and spiritual infrastructure for the Church's long-standing Black constituencies. While representatives of white Protestant denominations poured into the South after the Civil War to establish schools for the freed population and created opportunities for Black leadership in their respective ranks, the white-led Catholic Church focused its resources on the rapidly increasing European immigrant population and actively sought to abandon its long-standing communities of Black faithful. At the Second Plenary Council, held in Baltimore in 1866, for example, the vast majority of the southern prelates, led by the New Orleans delegation and the archbishop of St. Louis, fiercely opposed the adoption of a concrete plan of action and special ministry for the African American community, including a proposal to found "Negro sisterhoods" in their respective locales to lead the work. Like their secular segregationist counterparts, these men argued that matters regarding "the Negro" should be left to local (white) rule.[144] In undermining Black equality and racial justice, such a strategy ensured white domination in the Church, especially in areas where the Black faithful, mostly former slaves, constituted significant portions of the Catholic population.

Even when individual white bishops and priests sympathetic to the plight of African Americans recruited white American and European orders of men and women to minister within the African American community, the results often came at the expense of racial equality and Black Catholic self-determination. White priests and sisters who entered the Black apostolate, for example, rarely saw African Americans as their social, intellectual, and moral equals. Instead, the African American community was largely presented to and viewed by these white Catholics as a missionary field, despite its long-standing roots in the North American Church. Catholics had had a steady presence since the sixteenth century in what became the United States, but the nation was designated a mission territory and would remain under the direct control of the Vatican until 1908.[145] As such, many of the earliest European and white American religious who came to labor in the African American community during Reconstruction and the early decades of Jim Crow actively worked to undercut the long-standing leadership of Black sisters and laywomen. Most telling, most of these priests and sisters also vigorously opposed the admission of African Americans to religious life, especially on equal terms with whites.

The history of the St. Joseph's Society of the Sacred Heart, better known as the Josephite Fathers, in Baltimore, for example, is marred by its members' strident commitments to white supremacy and opposition to Black female leadership, beginning in the 1870s and 1880s. Recruited by Baltimore archbishop Martin Spalding, a former slaveholder from Kentucky's "Holy Land," after the Second Plenary Council failed, Josephite founder Reverend (later Cardinal) Herbert Vaughn dispatched four members of his order from England to Baltimore in 1871 to assume the pastoral care of the African American Catholic community there.[146] Not only would the earliest generations of Black men and boys who entered the Josephite community face well-documented opposition, but the Josephite ascendency also proved disastrous for ministries that Black Catholic women had established and maintained in Baltimore.[147] As historian Diane Batts Morrow has revealed, the inaugural Josephites resented being given spiritual directorship over the OSP upon their arrival and worked diligently to dismantle the Black sisterhood.[148] In addition to actively promoting the insidious myth that Black Catholics did not want priests of their own race to cover up their own opposition to training Black men, the earliest Josephites spread the lie that Black Catholics preferred white nuns over Black sisters as teachers.[149] In their correspondence, Josephite leaders regularly characterized OSP members in racially derogatory ways, calling the order "a huge failure," openly questioning the sisters' competence as teachers, and regularly professing a preference for working with white nuns over Black nuns.[150]

Because OSP members intentionally stopped keeping annals (daily records of the community's activities) after hostile interactions with the Josephites, the depth of the white priests' resentment and opposition to them is not attested in detail. However, by 1875, the Josephites had devised a plan to bring English nuns to Baltimore to take over the city's Black female-led Catholic ministries, including an orphanage established and administered by a devout Black laywoman, Mary Herbert.[151] The Josephites also planned to place the OSP order under the administration of the English sisters as "a kind of extern 3rd order of Colored Girls."[152]

In 1881, Josephite Father John Slattery, pastor of Baltimore's historically Black St. Francis Xavier Catholic Church, recruited four Franciscan Sisters from Mill Hill in London with the initial goal of taking over Herbert's

FIGURE 1.6. Sister Xavier (Frances) Johnson (ca. 1858–93), Franciscan Tertiary of Mill Hill. Courtesy of the Archives of the Sisters of St. Francis of Assisi, St. Francis, Wisconsin.

orphanage for Black youth without her knowledge or consent.[153] Despite Herbert's protests, the Franciscan Sisters, with Slattery's support, took charge of her orphanage, renaming it the St. Francis Home and incorporating it in 1882.[154] Although Herbert was removed from her institution, the white nuns hired two "very good colored women," Cecelia Buchanan and Frances Johnson, to assist them.[155] Johnson, a formerly enslaved woman who converted to Catholicism under Slattery's spiritual direction in 1877, also had a vocation to religious life.[156] In 1883, she traveled to London to enter the Franciscan order (figure 1.6). Although she had been told that she would be admitted on an equal footing, the Mill Hill superior ultimately decided to train Johnson as a Franciscan tertiary, equal in status to a lay sister, citing the precarious nature of US race relations.[157] She was also given a different habit than her white counterparts. In 1887, Johnson, then known as Sister Xavier, returned to Baltimore and labored at St. Elizabeth Home until her death in 1893, and the order did not admit another Black candidate until the 1960s.[158]

Slattery's opposition to the OSP and Black women's leadership in the Church more broadly did not cease. In 1890, according to the annals of the Sisters of the Blessed Sacrament, Slattery asked the order's foundress, Sister (later Saint) Katharine Drexel, then in the process of founding an order to minister exclusively in Native American and African American communities, to establish "a mixed white and Black, choir and lay community."[159]

Slattery, the son of Irish immigrants, was by then the first superior of the independent American branch of the Josephites. Though one of the first white priests to advocate the ordination of Black priests, Slattery steadfastly opposed Black sisters unless they were under the control of white nuns.

Unlike Slattery, Drexel did not deny the suitability of Black women and girls for religious life. However, like the Josephite superior, Drexel was a racial paternalist who viewed Black people as the objects of white missionary zeal and uplift, not equals. Indeed, when Drexel completed her novitiate with the Religious Sisters of Mercy in Pittsburgh in 1891, the heiress and recent Catholic convert took a fourth vow in which she pledged "to be the Mother and Servant of the Indian and Negro Races," seemingly oblivious of or indifferent to the deep Catholic roots of many African American and Native American communities.[160] Like the Mill Hill sisters, Drexel and the Sisters of the Blessed Sacrament would also quickly prove unwilling to admit and live with Black women and girls on equal terms, which effectively tabled Slattery's plan.[161]

Despite such strident white opposition to Black Catholic agency and self-determination, Black sisterhoods' membership rolls steadily rose nationally to more than 200 during the first decade of the twentieth century. Between 1865 and 1905, for example, the OSP grew from fewer than 30 to 103 members, with women and girls traveling from as far west as St. Louis, Missouri; as far north as Canada, specifically Ontario and Nova Scotia; and as far south as Louisiana, Texas, and Cuba to join the order.[162] The SSF grew from 8 members in 1865 to 101 in 1905, with several arriving from Louisiana, Missouri, Kentucky, Mississippi, Texas, and the Caribbean.[163] Much of the increase in the SSF order followed the termination of the order's exclusionary admission policies in 1869 after the New Orleans archbishop removed Juliette Gaudin, Henriette Delille's successor, from office and appointed Josephine Charles to lead the community. This facilitated the admission of Cloé Preval, whose journey from slavery under Catholic auspices to freedom in the cloister epitomized the revolutionary possibilities of religious life after the Civil War.[164]

Beyond the growth of the OSP and SSF, Black female religious life expanded in important ways after Reconstruction. In the last two decades of the nineteenth century, three new Catholic sisterhoods for African-descended women and girls were organized. In 1882, for example, the hardening of the color line and the unwillingness of two Afro-Creole women to align themselves with the African American community led to the formation of the nation's fifth congregation of African-descended sisters. In 1872, twin sisters Marie Emilie and Marie Gouley, Afro-Creole natives of New Orleans who could pass for white, entered the historically white St. Walburg Monastery in Covington, Kentucky, as candidates for the Order of Saint Benedict.[165] One year later, they received the order's habit and took religious names. Over the next eight years, the sisters professed simple vows and prepared to become choir sisters. However, in 1882 only Marie was permitted to make perpetual vows for reasons that remain unclear. After an attempt to transfer to the order's Trinity Convent in New Orleans failed, Marie Emilie set out to preserve her vocation by founding a new congregation.[166]

Few records have survived about the Sisters of Our Lady of Lourdes, as Marie Emilie's order was known, in New Orleans. However, Church directories indicate that the congregation grew to number nine, with most, if not all, being members of the Gouley family, including Marie, who departed the Benedictines in 1888. According to historian Roger Baudier, "Down the years, [the Sisters of Our Lady of Lourdes] always opposed strenuously any effort to induce them to join the Holy Family Congregation."[167] From 1900 to 1920, the sisterhood operated a small academy for white children in New Orleans that proved to be their major source of income. However, financial difficulties, combined with the order's small and aging membership and their unwillingness to expand their ministries to the Afro-Creole and wider African American communities, seemingly sealed the congregation's fate. The last surviving member died sometime in the twentieth century, curiously in the care of the SSF.[168]

Between 1887 and 1888, a bitter dispute within the SSF, seemingly over whether or not expand the congregation's ministry outside of Louisiana, spurred the formation of the nation's fifth Black sisterhood.[169] In 1887, St. Louis archbishop Peter Kenrick invited the SSF to work among the archdiocese's Black Catholic population, most of whom had formerly been enslaved and who had largely been abandoned by white Church leaders after emancipation. Although Mother Marie Magdalene Alpaugh declined the invitation, deeming her congregation "too small to undertake work in that distant city," Sister Teresa (Laurencia) Jacques, the local superior and principal of a SSF school in New Orleans, "decided to go to Saint Louis and take up the work."[170] According to SSF records, Jacques and two other members, Mary Clare (Julia) Stephens and Mary Ignatius (Anna) Jones, absconded from their convent and took the train north. After becoming aware of the sisters' actions, Alpaugh sent a telegram to Kenrick, describing the three as "fugitives." Kenrick instructed the three nuns to return to New Orleans, but they traveled instead to Convent, Louisiana, in St. James Parish, where Jacques's mother worked as a cook at Jefferson College, a seminary sponsored by the Marist Fathers.[171] Although Jones soon returned to New Orleans to live with her mother, Jacques and Stephens remained in Convent, teaching the catechism to the area's Black Catholics. Within a year, the two sisters received permission from the New Orleans archbishop to organize a new African American sisterhood under the supervision of the Marist priests.[172]

While very little documentation exists on the Sisters of the Third Order of Saint Francis, which operated from 1888 to 1913, the community was stationed at St. Michael's Catholic Church in Convent, where the sisters taught at its school (initially sleeping on the school's floors at night) and then in public schools.[173] Father Firmin Coppin, a Marist priest who served as the order's first spiritual director, provided no financial support to the "sisters of color." However, after confirming with the New Orleans archbishop that they "were not fugitives," he supported their desire to expand their ministries to the Black community in Convent.[174]

Between 1888 and 1898, the Black OSF in Convent admitted at least five women, all natives of Louisiana or Maryland. Among them was Eliza Barbara Williams, a cradle Catholic from Baton Rouge, Louisiana. Williams eventually took the religious name Sister Seraphine (or Seraphim) and became the order's assistant superior before the beginning of the twentieth century. Around the same time, the archbishop of New Orleans prevented the order from admitting any additional members, for unknown reasons. In 1901, all seven members of the order applied for admission into the OSP in Baltimore.[175] Ultimately, though, the sisters remained in Convent until 1913, when Jacques died. After that, the New Orleans archbishop suppressed the order, and two of the three surviving members entered the SSF. Williams, however, traveled to Baltimore to enter the OSP novitiate, where she took the name Mary Theodore.[176]

Ironically, the nation's sixth African American sisterhood (established in 1889) was also known as the Sisters of the Third Order of Saint Francis and led by a pious African-descended woman from Louisiana. The congregation's Afro-Creole and Native American foundress, Mother Mathilda (also Matilda, Mathilde) Beasley, was likely born into slavery in New Orleans in 1832 or 1834. "Owned" by James Taylor, she gained her freedom sometime before 1850 and then traveled to Savannah, Georgia, where she appeared on an 1860 register of the state's free Negroes. By day, Mathilda Taylor worked as a seamstress and a waitress in a restaurant owned by her future husband, Abraham Beasley. By night, Taylor (according to some sources) operated

FIGURE 1.7. This photograph is believed to feature Mother Mathilda Beasley (1832/1834–1903), the African- and Indigenous-descended foundress of Georgia's first order of African American nuns, the Sisters of the Third Order of Saint Francis. Another photo, likely of Beasley's stepdaughter-in-law, has long been mistaken for her. Courtesy of the Georgia Historical Society.

a secret and illegal school for Black children through the 1850s. In 1869, Taylor was baptized into the Catholic faith and soon thereafter married Beasley. Upon inheriting her husband's estate following his death in 1877, she bequeathed some or all of it to the local Catholic Church for ministries to African Americans. Soon thereafter, Beasley reportedly sailed for York, England, in 1885 to enter a novitiate of the Poor Clare Nuns. Two years later, she returned to Savannah and established the St. Francis Home for Colored Orphans. In 1889, Beasley formed an order of African American sisters and was soon called Mother Mathilda (figure 1.7). She transformed her orphanage into a school and renamed it the St. Francis Industrial and Boarding School for Girls.[177]

Despite its early successes and growth, Beasley's order began to falter financially in the early 1890s, whereupon she sought to forge a coalition with the Sisters of the Blessed Sacrament (SBS), headed by Katharine Drexel.[178] However, Beasley's attempt to save her order precipitated the formal exclusion of women of color from the SBS in 1893.[179]

Like many white sisters who began ministering in the African American community during slavery and the Jim Crow era, Drexel had to be encouraged to enter the Black apostolate by a white priest. Shortly before she established her order in 1891, Drexel's spiritual confessor persuaded her to expand her singular desire to minister to Native Americans and include African Americans.[180] Thus, when Savannah bishop Thomas Becker wrote Drexel in 1893 asking her to consider incorporating Beasley's fledgling sisterhood into her order, the superior gave it thought.[181] Soon thereafter, Beasley and a member of her order traveled to suburban Philadelphia to plead their case directly.[182] However, during Beasley's visit, the SBS formally voted against admitting African Americans and Native Americans into their ranks. An entry from the SBS annals from 1896 recounted the 1893 decision, citing "the strong racial feeling now existing in this country with respect to the Indian and Colored Races," "social prejudice" among potential white recruits, "the innate sensitiveness of both Indians and Colored," and the "existence of two large and flourishing communities for Colored Sisters."[183] Although the SBS annalist characterized Beasley as a "very saintly colored woman," the white order even refused to provide novitiate training for the Black order's sisters.[184]

Ironically, a few weeks before Beasley's visit, the SBS had admitted a "Seneca Indian," Georgiana Burton, as a house sister, meaning she was relegated to cooking and cleaning. However, the SBS's unwillingness to accept African American sisters prompted the order to place a moratorium on admitting Native American women. Moving forward, SBS leaders directed Native American applicants to other white orders, and Black applicants to Black sisterhoods.[185]

After being dealt what she described as the "fatal blow" by Drexel, Beasley returned to Savannah and attempted to forge a coalition with the Missionary Franciscans of the Immaculate Conception (MFIC), a white order who had operated a school for the children of ex-slaves in nearby Augusta, Georgia since the late 1870s.[186] Although the MFIC had admitted a Black former pupil, Frederica Law, into their novitiate in Rome, Italy, to train as a lay sister in the early 1880s, there is no evidence that the order ever admitted another Black candidate in Georgia.[187] Correspondence between Beasley and Josephite John Slattery in 1898 also reveals serious tensions between the Black OSF and the white MFIC, whom Beasley had invited to assist in her ministry.[188] While not mentioning specific problems, Beasley wrote, "I am going out in the cold world to be alone until I pass for I see [plainly] that I [can't] stay with them. . . . It is sad to give up the mission, but better give [it] up, then let them make me do it as I see they will."[189]

Although surviving records suggest that Beasley, who died in 1903, and the remaining Black OSF members lived and labored alongside three MFIC members for the first few years of the twentieth century, no existing evidence suggests the two orders ever officially merged.[190] For example, when Hannah Geary of Savannah and Ella Pollard of Annapolis, Maryland received their habits in 1901, the *Savannah Morning News* reported that they "received the habit of the Third Order Regular of St. Francis of Assisi," not the MFIC habit.[191] Moreover, when the Black-owned *Savannah Tribune* reported on the death of the last surviving member of Beasley's order in 1910, the article implied that "Sister Francis" had maintained her vows in some form of isolation from the MFIC or local Church officials. The tribute to "Sister Francis" characterized her as "the last colored nun in our city" and lamented that the OSP and SSF foundations in Baltimore and New Orleans were distant from Savannah.[192] The writer did not expect that the MFIC, which remained active in Savannah's African American apostolate for the next several decades, or any other white order in the diocese would recruit any additional Black members. Instead, the writer opined that if there were to be African American sisters in Savannah, the nation's "great communities of colored nuns" would have to supply them.[193] Such would also be true for much of the rest of the nation in the years to come.

The Enduring Problem of the Color Line

In 1900, Dr. W. E. B. Du Bois, the first African American to earn a PhD in history and a future founder of the National Association for the Advancement of Colored People (NAACP), included a group photo of the Sisters of the Holy Family in his award-winning "Exhibit of American Negroes" at the World's Fair in Paris (figure 1.8).[194] In transforming the order into an international symbol of Black progress from slavery to freedom, Du Bois foregrounded the subversive and emancipatory power of Black female virtue. The Atlanta University professor also unknowingly showcased to a global audience the revolutionary growth of the historically Afro-Creole sisterhood, then under its first non-Creole superior, Mother Mary Austin (Ellen) Jones.[195] Jones's appointment as the head of St. Mary's Academy in 1889 and her historic election as superior in 1891, at the age of thirty, signaled an important shift in the congregation and a test of whether the former slaveholding order could accept the leadership of a dark-skinned,

FIGURE 1.8. This 1898 group photo of the Sisters of the Holy Family, featured at the 1900 Paris World's Fair, reflects their color diversity, made possible by the admission of the order's first ex-slave member. No photos of Sister Mary Joachim (Cloé) Preval exist. However, Mother Mary Austin (Ellen) Jones, the order's first non-Creole and arguably most successful superior, is seated fourth from the left. To Jones's immediate left is Sister Anne Marie (Harriet) Fazende, one of the order's original six members and a descendant of the famed Spanish Catholic Pintado family, responsible for surveying much of Florida and Louisiana during the colonial era. Courtesy of Archives of the Congregation of the Sisters of the Holy Family, New Orleans.

English-speaking woman who was also the daughter of seemingly emancipated Black Catholics from Maryland.[196]

Under Jones's leadership from 1891 until her premature death in 1909, the SSF thrived in an unprecedented way. Membership rolls increased from 40 to 105, and the SSF's bank accounts swelled.[197] As dowries increased, Jones also launched an aggressive fundraising campaign in 1892 that brought the SSF into the national spotlight and even gained the attention of women's rights activist Susan B. Anthony.[198] The resulting financial stability let Jones expand SSF ministries and open fourteen Black Catholic schools in southern

Louisiana, Texas, and Arkansas.[199] With support from the Afro-Creole Catholic businessman Thomy Lafon and others, Jones also expanded SSF missions in New Orleans, establishing the School for Boys in 1891 and the Lafon Home for Boys in 1892 and expanding the order's Old Folks Home with a men's annex in 1896.[200] In 1898, she established the order's first mission outside of the United States, an educational ministry to the Garifuna, the largely African-descended and formerly enslaved Indigenous of Central America, in Belize. The SSF went to Belize in response to the refusal of the Jesuits and the Religious Sisters of Mercy to admit Garifuna youth into their schools there.[201] With resources that paled in comparison to those of her white Catholic and Black secular counterparts, what Jones accomplished was remarkable. A writer for New Orleans's Catholic newspaper, the *Morning Star*, even observed at her untimely death at forty-eight that "if one-half of the sums that have filled the coffers of Booker T. Washington had been placed in the hands of Mother Austin the fruits would be visible now in every section of the South."[202] Thus, Du Bois's inclusion of the SSF congregation as a shining achievement of Black excellence amid Jim Crow discrimination was more than fitting.

Eight months later, at the first Pan-African Conference in London, Du Bois for the first time declared "the problem of the twentieth century" to be "the problem of the color line."[203] Two years later, in 1903, Father Joseph Anciaux, a Belgian priest ministering in Virginia, sent an explosive missive to the Holy See in Rome documenting the rampant anti-Black discrimination and segregationist practices to which Black Catholics were subjected in the US Church. Anciaux drew specific attention to the exclusionary admissions policies of the white sisterhoods. "In every convent of religious women, a girl having a little Negro blood in her veins is immediately rejected," he wrote. "It does not matter at all that she is well-educated, pious, pure, and truly Catholic, so long as she seems Negro or there is the slightest suspicion of color."[204] Anciaux mistakenly considered all US convents to have white leaders. He was also seemingly unaware of the exceptions that a few white sisterhoods were willing to make for select racially ambiguous African-descended candidates. Nonetheless, Anciaux rightly underscored the leading roles that white sisters—who already outnumbered priests in some places by five or six to one—played in enforcing white supremacy within Church boundaries.[205] And as the US Church expanded its social welfare infrastructure in white and nonwhite communities, the influence of white sisters only widened.

Although white religious who ministered in Black communities were subjected to racist insults and routinely ostracized by other white Catholics, few held egalitarian views on race or embraced racial justice as a tenet of their ministries.[206] In fact, many white sisterhoods remained committed to racial segregation and exclusion even to their own detriment. When Irish immigrant Margaret Healy Murphy in 1893 established the Sisters of the Holy Ghost (later Spirit) and Mary Immaculate in San Antonio, Texas, to minister to African Americans and Mexican Americans, white resistance plagued her educational work. Murphy was also severely precluded from expanding the order's ministries owing to her inability to attract white American women to join her ranks. Like Drexel and the SBS in Philadelphia, Healy regularly recruited candidates from Ireland, who often held anti-Black attitudes, and her order remained opposed to admitting Black women to the congregation until after World War II.[207] The first US-born white woman to enter the Holy Ghost Sisters did not do so until 1919.[208] However, when Mary Louise Glenn—the first graduate of the order's historically Black Blessed St. Peter Claver School to enter religious life—sought to become a sister in 1896, she had to travel from San Antonio to Baltimore to enter the OSP.[209]

Racial ambiguity would continue to facilitate the admission of select African American women into white sisterhoods through the Jim Crow era. However, these exceptional entries generally depended on a white community's willingness to live with a racially indeterminate woman on equal terms and almost always required that this candidate cut ties with her visibly Black family members. In 1904, for example, the Sinsinawa Dominican Sisters, headquartered in Wisconsin, admitted as a candidate Rollena Thompson (later Sister Reynold), one of their former pupils from Kansas City, Missouri, who could pass for white. The order did not discover Thompson's racial secret until her mother, Fannie (whose African American heritage was visible), unexpectedly visited the motherhouse. While the congregation's leadership permitted Thompson to remain and pass for white, it did not accept its next African American candidates until after World War II.[210]

Though Thompson proved willing to hide her Black heritage in order to enter and remain in religious life, many racially ambiguous Black candidates steadfastly refused to do so.[211] Indeed, when twenty-two-year-old Rebecca Clifford, a native of Lynchburg, Virginia, had the opportunity to enter a white sisterhood in 1905, she refused because the unnamed order in Philadelphia agreed to admit her only if Clifford consented to not have her Black mother visit her at the convent.[212] As Clifford reportedly explained to one of her former SBS educators, who also barred her from admission on account of race that same year, "That I should not have my mother visit me I think positively wrong and not the Will of God. My mother is making a great sacrifice in giving up her only daughter to God. She is doing it most willingly. Should I impose an unnecessary sacrifice upon her?" Clifford also maintained, "My decision in this is that the white people have many to work for them, but the Colored People have very few. They are my own people and I think God wants me to give them the first place, and I don't think I would be blessed if I were to do otherwise."[213]

While it is unclear exactly how many racially indeterminate African-descended women and girls entered white orders during the Jim Crow era, most who became sisters seemingly opted not to do so. The group photographs of the African American sisterhoods are filled with women and girls who, like Clifford, could have passed for white but instead chose to serve the Black and Afro-Creole communities that had nurtured them. These young women's decisions ensured the survival and growth of the African American sisterhoods. Their stories also counterbalance the better-known examples of the Healy siblings, including younger sisters Amanda and Eliza, who also entered religious life, and the IHM foundresses, who all passed for white to maintain a clear social and political distance from the African American community.[214] In articulating a commitment to struggle for racial justice through Black Catholic education and an unwavering allegiance to the African American community, Clifford joined thousands of Black Catholic laywomen who during slavery and Jim Crow forged an emancipatory tradition of the faith free from the most violent aspects of white supremacy. These Black women undertook critical catechetical work in Black communities; organized and fundraised for Black Catholic missions, parishes, schools, and orphanages; nurtured Black vocations to religious life; and entered Black congregations, spearheading the fight to preserve and expand the faith among Black people. Twenty-one years later, Clifford, then serving as the elected leader of the OSP, would stand strong again when Catholic segregation and secular law threatened to dismantle the Black-administered Catholic educational system and endangered the survival of the African American teaching sisterhoods.

2. "Nothing Is Too Good for the Youth of Our Race"

THE FIGHT FOR BLACK-ADMINISTERED CATHOLIC
EDUCATION DURING JIM CROW

The Catholic Church in America stands for color separation and discrimination to a degree equaled by no other church in America. . . . The white parochial schools even in the North exclude colored children, the Catholic high schools will not admit them, the Catholic University at Washington invites them elsewhere, and scarcely a Catholic seminary in the country will train a Negro priest. —DR. W. E. B. DU BOIS to JOSEPHITE JOHN B. GLENN, March 24, 1925

In early August 1933, Mother Mary Consuella (Rebecca) Clifford, the superior of the Oblate Sisters of Providence (OSP), faced a crisis of epic proportions. In the previous month, she and Bishop Emmet M. Walsh, head of the diocese of Charleston, had communicated their mutual desire to secure accreditation for the nascent high school department of the city's Immaculate Conception (IC) School before the 1933–1934 academic term.[1] Because IC was one of only thirty-five Black Catholic high schools in the nation and the first of its kind in South Carolina, its ability to grant state-accredited diplomas was paramount to champions of Black Catholic education. That Black sisters led this state-of-the-art high school in the heart of the former Confederacy also heightened the political stakes.

During the first half of the twentieth century, access to high school education remained elusive for most African Americans, especially in the segregated South. All-white state governments not only refused to invest equitably in Black public education but opposed building enough Black high schools to be proportionate to the Black population.[2] South Carolina spent over four times more educating a white child than a Black child, and only about 12 percent of the state's African American youth aged fourteen to seventeen were enrolled in a secondary school in 1933. By comparison, approximately 60 percent of the state's white youth in that age group were pursuing a secondary education that year.[3] In Charleston, only the Avery Normal Institute (the state's first post-1865 secondary school for African Americans) and the publicly controlled Colored Industrial School were open to Black youth when the OSP arrived in 1917, and neither school had state accreditation.[4] For Black Catholic parents seeking to uphold their canonical duty to provide their children with a Catholic education, the absence of a Catholic high school for Black Charlestonians had been an especially bitter pill to swallow.[5]

Although Charleston's only Catholic secondary school, Bishop John England High School, led by the white Sisters of Charity of Our Lady of Mercy, had opened in 1915 and earned accreditation by 1930, the institution strictly excluded African Americans.[6] Thus, the 1930 opening of IC's high school department in a new $80,000 facility struck a hard blow against racial exclusion.[7] Yet Clifford and Walsh found themselves in an embarrassing predicament as IC's first students rose to twelfth grade in the 1933–1934 school year. Recently revised South Carolina Department of Education rules required IC to have four degreed teachers before it could award state-certified diplomas. However, only two members of the faculty—Sisters Mary Angela (Martha) Wade and Mary Edwina (Veronica) Holley—held bachelor's degrees in August 1933. Clifford and Walsh's ambitious campaign to provide South Carolina's African American citizens with their first accredited Catholic high school stood on the brink of failure.[8]

Episodes like the IC debacle played themselves out in dioceses and archdioceses across the United States after World War I, as state legislation began requiring the certification and advanced training of private school-teachers. Although the Catholic Church, which operated the nation's largest independent school system, had fiercely resisted earlier secular attempts to regulate its educational facilities, ecclesiastical authorities largely reversed their stance in the postwar years. Believing that state approval would elevate the standards of Catholic education and bolster the Church's expansion projects, Church leaders embraced the national campaign for accreditation. As a result, the higher education of sisters—on whose underpaid labor the Catholic educational system depended—became a top priority for Church school boards and the leadership councils of teaching sisterhoods.[9] However, white clerical demands that all Catholic teachers become state certified posed a seemingly insurmountable challenge for the Black teaching sisterhoods. Church mandates and canon law dictated that all Catholics be educated in Catholic schools. Yet most US Catholic colleges, universities, and normal institutes systematically excluded African Americans from admission on the basis of race.[10] As a consequence, the Black teaching sisterhoods had to secure the higher training of their members and the accreditation of their schools with minimal support from their church.

This chapter counters narratives that contend that Black Catholic sisters were politically conservative during the most brutal years of Jim Crow. The Black sisterhoods' struggles to expand their networks of schools for Black youth in the former slave South and later into the urban North, Midwest, and West—and the staunch resistance they faced—illuminate the deeply political dimensions of the fight for Black Catholic education, especially when administered by Black nuns. Like their lay and secular counterparts of the era, the leadership councils of the Black sisterhoods believed that the collective destiny and fate of the African American community in the quest to defeat Jim Crow segregation was contingent on a substantial expansion of Black educational opportunities. Beginning in the 1920s, their belief that segregation greatly hindered Black educational progress and that Black youth deserved every opportunity to develop their minds and souls under Catholic auspices brought the Black sisterhoods into alliance with a small cadre of progressive white priests and sisters and a national network of Black lay leaders and activists committed to dismantling the color line within and outside of the Church. Although formal segregation and exclusion would persist in the Church, including in Catholic higher education, through the 1960s, the ability of the Black leadership councils to pry open the doors of many Catholic colleges and universities in the three decades before the 1954 *Brown v. Board of Education* decision constitutes an important chapter in the history of the Black freedom struggle. The responses of white Catholics to Black demands for Catholic education and the attacks on Black Catholics by non-Catholic segregationists also offer better insights into the Church's lackluster and often adversarial commitments to the African American Catholic community during the nadir of American race relations.

Why Black-Administered Catholic Education?

In November 1889, Daniel Arthur Rudd, editor and chief proprietor of the *American Catholic Tribune*, the nation's first newspaper produced for and by Black Catholics, made it plain: the way for white Catholics to "bring the Negro" into the Church was to first pray and then support existing Black Catholic institutions, especially those led by Black nuns and laywomen. "Build up to respectable proportions the convents of the Oblate Sisters at Baltimore, St. Louis, and Leavenworth," Rudd wrote. "Rebuild the Convent of the Sisters of the Holy Family at New Orleans. Wherever there is a Negro school where secular teachers are employed let the teachers be of the race."[11] At a moment when white Church leaders, especially the Josephites, and others were conspiring to push Black sisters and Black laywomen out of their pioneering ministries and actively suppressing Black vocations to religious life, Rudd's championing of Black women's educational leadership—seen as essential to developing and nurturing future "race leaders"—was an important intervention. Not only did Rudd, a former slave of the Jesuits in Bardstown, Kentucky, who was fluent in both English and German, declare Black women key to the Black Catholic community's growth, but he also refuted the insidious white Catholic refrain that Black people did not want sisters of their own race to minister to them.

Earlier that year, Rudd had organized the first meeting of the Colored Catholic Congress to create a national network of Black Catholic leaders to chart their community's future, fight back against Jim Crow segregation, and defend what he believed to be the Church's great potential to attract more African Americans. Among the delegates to the first congress were Father Augustus Tolton, the nation's first self-identified Black priest, and James Alexander Spencer, a Black educational leader and state legislator from Charleston, South Carolina.[12] Over the next five years, men and women delegates to the Colored Catholic Congresses repeatedly called on Black Catholics and the Church to take the lead in opposing white supremacy and the descending shadow of Jim Crow segregation in the nation. "The Catholic Church alone can break the color line," Rudd declared in 1891. "Our people should help her to do it."[13] The meeting participants also called on the all-white hierarchy to eliminate racial barriers in the Church or at least commit equitable resources to its Black constituencies, especially in education. From their collective perspective, the survival and growth of the Black Catholic community hinged on preserving and expanding the Black

Catholic educational system, which required supporting Black sisters and laywomen in their ministries.[14]

During slavery and immediately following its federal abolition, Black nuns and laypeople—often in the face of staunch opposition and violence—established or staffed many of the first Catholic elementary and high schools freely open to African Americans across the South, including in Washington, DC; Baltimore, Maryland; St. Louis, Missouri; Charleston, South Carolina; the Kentucky towns of Bardstown and Louisville; and the Louisiana towns of New Orleans, Donaldsonville, Lafayette, and Mandeville.[15] In several instances, the erection of the Catholic schoolhouse preceded the building of the church. In Washington, DC, for example, the school that seeded the creation of the capital's first parish for African Americans, St. Martin de Porres (and later renamed St. Augustine), was established in 1858, sixteen years before the church's erection.[16] Similarly, in Lake Charles, Louisiana, the Sacred Heart Catholic School, called for, funded, and built by the city's leading Black Catholics in 1909, preceded the construction of the church—also funded and built by Black Catholics—and the arrival of the first pastor by a decade. In these schools, Black sisters or Black lay teachers, like Sacred Heart's legendary Naomi Eleanor Figaro, a former pupil of the Sisters of the Holy Family (SSF), usually ministered to long-standing Black Catholic populations, who increasingly found themselves either subjected to humiliating segregation in or barred from Catholic institutions that the labor, sale, and donations of Black Catholics had built.[17]

As early as 1868, the former slaveholding Sisters of Loretto began staffing newly established Black Catholic schools in Lebanon and New Haven, Kentucky. In the 1870s and 1880s, they were joined by a handful of other white congregations, including the formerly slaveholding Sisters of Charity of Nazareth in Kentucky and the Sisters of Charity of Leavenworth in Kansas (but originally from Kentucky and later Nashville, Tennessee), who also began supplying teachers for and establishing separate schools for Black youth across the South and in the Midwest.[18] Meanwhile, other congregations that taught Black youth in some fashion during slavery, in the decades immediately after slavery, or both—like the Ursulines and Carmelites in New Orleans and Sisters of Charity in Mobile, Alabama—abandoned the African American apostolate for the next several decades.[19] In 1835, Sisters of Charity of Our Lady of Mercy in Charleston briefly operated a school for Black youth, before white mob violence and threats compelled Bishop John England to order the closure of all schools open to Black people.[20] The Our Lady of Mercy Sisters reopened and administered the school in the 1840s before withdrawing from the Black apostolate for the next fifty-four years. In 1867, though, members of Charleston's Black Catholic community, including legislator James Spencer, founded a school attached to the city's first Black parish, St. Peter's, and Black laywomen ran it.[21] In 1902, the Our Lady of Mercy Sisters assumed teaching duties at St. Peter's school and soon opened IC elementary school to accommodate increasing demand.[22] However, the white nuns withdrew from the African American apostolate again in 1917, prompting Black Catholics and then Bishop William Russell, a native of Baltimore, to appeal for Black sisters to lead the diocese's Black schools. Within a decade, the OSP, who arrived in the fall of 1917, had nearly tripled enrollments at IC alone, and by 1930 opened Charleston's third Black high school since emancipation.[23]

In addition to helping raise literacy rates, conduct catechetical work, and expand Black educational opportunities, Black-led Catholic schools regularly produced female and male vocations to religious life. Notably, Black sisters, despite constituting less than 1 percent of the national sister population, educated and served as spiritual role models for more than half of the first two generations of Black priests, including the first Black Josephite, ordained in 1891, and three of the first four priests produced by the nation's first all-Black seminary, run by the Society of the Divine Word in Bay St. Louis, Mississippi, in 1934.[24] The fourth Black priest of the Society of the Divine Word, Father Vincent Smith, was born in Lebanon, Kentucky, in 1894. His mother, Mary Eliza Spalding Smith, had been enslaved by the extended family of early US bishops and slavers John Lancaster Spalding and Martin Spalding and Mother Catherine Spalding, the foundress of the Sisters of Charity of Nazareth. According to her obituary, Smith was "highly regarded" by the city's "white and colored residents," suggesting that she was also a spiritual leader. Vincent Smith, who later became the first Black Trappist monk, also had an aunt, Sister Mary Joachim (Rosalia) Spalding, his mother's sister, who became a member of the SSF and likely also played a role in nurturing his vocation.[25]

Although Black Catholics' desire for Black priests never wavered, white ecclesiastical opposition to the substantial development of an African American clergy remained firm, hampering evangelization efforts and leading most African Americans to conclude that Catholicism was "the white man's religion." After being denied opportunities to lead Black Catholic parishes in New Orleans, Chicago, and Washington, DC, despite having vocal Black Catholic support for the assignments, John Joseph Plantevigne, the third Black Josephite priest, raised the alarm at a conference for missionaries held in DC in 1909. "The blood of the Negro boils in resentment of a 'Jim Crow' system in the Catholic Church," he declared. "Negroes have followed their masters into the Catholic Church, but have fallen away in great numbers because they have not been given an active part in the organic life of the Church. . . . The Negro wants Catholic priests, non-Catholic people are accustomed to colored ministers and refuse to enter the Catholic Church under white priests."[26] Sixteen years later, in an editorial condemning rampant white Catholic segregation and racism in the North, W. E. B. Du Bois echoed Plantevigne's critiques: "Because Catholicism has so much that is splendid in its past, it is the greater shame that 'nigger' haters clothed in episcopal robes should do to Black Americans in exclusion [and] segregation . . . all that the Ku Klux Klan ever asked."[27] Despite steady Black Catholic demand for Black priests, the thirty-four Black priests ordained to the priesthood in the United States between 1909 and 1946 would be overwhelmingly prevented from leading African American parishes and completely barred from the episcopacy.[28]

Catholic educational opportunities for African Americans did, however, expand in important ways. Because the Black sisterhoods never had the membership numbers to satisfy the high demand for Catholic schools administered by Black sisters and because ecclesiastical leaders generally preferred sisters rather than laywomen to lead Catholic schools when available, efforts to recruit additional white congregations into the African American apostolate significantly increased. Heightened Vatican attention to the plight of Black Catholics in the United States also fueled select Church leaders' increased commitment to Black Catholic education. In response to Father Joseph Anciaux's damning 1903 letter to the Holy See outlining the racist mistreatment faced by African American Catholics, for example, US Church leaders established the Catholic Board for Mission Work among the Colored People in New York City (CBMWCP) in 1907 to support the African American apostolate.[29] Though often paternalistic in its approach to addressing Catholic anti-Black racism and restricted to fundraising, distribution of money, and publicity, the board, led by Father John E. Burke, the white pastor of New York City's historically Black St. Benedict the Moor Church, proved consequential in its support of the Black sisterhoods. The board paid the salaries of several Black sisters and later offered crucial support to the Black sisterhoods in their fight to gain access to Catholic higher education.[30] The CBMWCP also played a leading role in recruiting additional white sisterhoods into the African American apostolate, eventually paying the annual salaries of over two hundred white sisters ministering in southern Black communities, including the well-resourced Sisters of the Blessed Sacrament (SBS) under the leadership of Katharine Drexel.[31] However, as the Catholic Church began to commit more resources to establishing separate Black schools, white resistance to Black Catholic education also grew.

White Opposition to Black Catholic Education

The Catholic Church's financial support of its Black schools always paled in comparison to its support of its white institutions. Nonetheless, the Church came to play a significant role in African American education as Jim Crow matured. In 1916, the Church operated 112 schools for approximately 13,507 Black youth nationwide—the most schools of any predominantly white religious denomination.[32] By 1920, that number had grown to 144 schools for approximately 19,048 Black youth, the overwhelming majority of whom were southerners.[33] By 1941, there were approximately 44,939 Black youth in some 237 predominantly or all-Black Catholic schools, including 64 junior and senior high schools, with white sisters making up more than 750 of the 1,064 nuns teaching in them.[34] When contrasted with the Black Protestant and public educational systems, these numbers may seem negligible. However, Black Catholic education constituted a significant threat to America's racial status quo, especially in the South.

In many areas, Catholic schools led by Black and white nuns were the first, or among the first, educational institutions open to African Americans and eventually were among the earliest to be accredited. In Baltimore and St. Louis, for example, the OSP opened four of the earliest elementary and high schools open to Black people. In New Orleans, the SSF in 1867 established St. Mary's Academy for Colored Girls, which in 1882 became the first secondary school open to African Americans in all of Louisiana.[35] The all-white Sisters of Charity of Nazareth assumed the leadership of the Colored Industrial Institute, Arkansas's first formal school for Black youth, in 1889. They also led several of the earliest Black schools opened in Kentucky and the first accredited Black high school in Alabama, the Holy Family Institute.[36] In many cities and towns, Catholic schools for Black youth were also consistently ranked among the highest achieving, drawing interest from within and outside of the Black Catholic community.

Because Black Catholic schools provided African American parents with additional educational options for their children under Jim Crow, their physical structures and staffs became frequent targets of racial harassment and violence. In 1881, for example, racist whites in Baton Rouge, Louisiana, drove the SSF out of town after only one year of running a school at the interracial but segregated St. Joseph's Church. It would take fourteen years before the African American sisters returned to open another school, which thrived and eventually seeded the development of Baton Rouge's first African American parish, St. Francis Xavier.[37]

In 1894, local whites in Tampa, Florida, burned down the St. Peter Claver School, Florida's first Catholic school for Black youth, in the name of white supremacy. In a note left at the scene, the arsonists argued that they had no "ill feeling to the Catholic Church" but objected "to a negro school in the midst of the white & retired resident portion of the city." The criminals, who went unpunished, also warned that any attempt to rebuild there would be met with more violence directed at the Jesuits and two white Sisters of the Holy Names of Jesus and Mary who administered the school, as well as the town's other Catholic churches. While the school was rebuilt in a Black community, local white opposition to Black Catholic education remained strong.[38]

In white Catholic communities, violent opposition to Black-led Catholic schools also manifested. In 1921, OSP members stationed in St. Louis withstood a months-long terror campaign waged by their neighbors after the sisters relocated their St. Rita's Academy and Convent to the affluent and all-white riverfront community of Carondelet. Neighboring property owners, many of them Catholics, sought to evict the sisters and their twenty-four girl students and orphans—who had to be brought to the house in groups of two and three under the protection of two white male escorts—by any means necessary. After a failed attempt to have the sisters' renovation permit revoked, Carondelet residents appealed to Archbishop John J. Glennon to have St. Rita's relocated to a section of town where they would not be "objectionable." Although Glennon strictly enforced racial segregation throughout the archdiocese, he declined to intervene since the Black nuns had purchased the property via a white surrogate with their own money. Soon thereafter, the sisters' white neighbors resorted to extralegal violence. White youths regularly vandalized the sisters' property, throwing rocks and making obscene gestures. Then an armed white night watchman hired by the OSP members intercepted a white man (believed to be a neighbor) breaking into the convent through a window. After the incident, a police detail was assigned to the property to protect the sisters and

FIGURE 2.1. This photograph of the sisters, students, and orphans of the St. Rita Boarding and Day Academy in St. Louis, Missouri, was taken in 1922, one year after the racist assault on the institution. Three of the sisters and several of the girls pictured lived through the violent episode. Courtesy of the Archives of the Oblate Sisters of Providence, Baltimore, Maryland.

their students around the clock. Although white opposition endured, the Black sisters and their academy, which soon became St. Louis's first Black Catholic high school, remained (figure 2.1).[39]

Because Black Catholic schools were almost always interracial spaces (with white teachers and Black pupils, or Black sisters and white priests), these institutions posed a unique threat to the racial and religious order of the largely Protestant South, eventually drawing the attention of some of the region's most powerful racists. In 1922, for example, Billie Mayfield Jr., an ex-colonel in the Texas National Guard and the Ku Klux Klan's candidate for Texas lieutenant governor, called for violence against the "colored convent."[40] In his newspaper, *Colonel Mayfield's Weekly*, he noted that the white priest attached to the Sacred Heart School in Ames, Texas, led by the SSF, "preaches to mixed audiences at Aims [*sic*]" and "gives communion to whites and blacks at the same altar." He also believed that the SSF were instructing white children. "I tell you people, the effort to Catholicise the colored man is fraught with the gravest danger," Mayfield wrote. "We don't want any negro Catholics in this country who will be subservient to a foreign ruler who believes in social equality."[41]

Although the "white children" at the Sacred Heart School were actually mixed-race children from the New York Foundling Asylum, Mayfield's rage at the perceived social transgression was telling.[42] Had the three SSF members been "mammies" to white children or lay maids to the white priest, no white resistance would have manifested. However, because they were nuns, educational leaders, and spiritual role models free from state supervision, these Black women threatened the foundations of segregation.[43]

A few days later, unknown persons placed a note on the rectory door of Father Alexis LaPlante, the white Josephite who headed the Sacred Heart mission in Ames. Signed "K.K.K.," the letter threatened to dynamite the mission's school and church and demanded that LaPlante immediately leave town. If he refused, the letter threatened, the writers would tar and feather him publicly.[44] In response, a contingent of armed Black Catholic men from Liberty County stood guard at the Church and convent attached to the school for several weeks.[45] While no physical acts of violence occurred toward LaPlante or the SSF, opposition to Black Catholic education remained strong, especially on the state level and from Protestant proponents of white supremacy or anti-Catholicism.[46]

Mayfield's attack on the Sacred Heart School and convent explicitly linked Catholic evangelization, education, and Black equality. The Klan leader also articulated growing white Protestant fears over expanding Black Catholic education in the South. "No color line in the Catholic Church and 18,000,000 colored Catholics in the south," he proclaimed. "What would we be into?"[47] Although the Catholic Church upheld racial segregation in most of its institutions, its social teachings, which affirmed the life and dignity of every person, threatened to undermine white domination over Black southerners. Because Black Catholic schools also served as the primary vehicles for evangelization in African American communities, attacks on these institutions became part and parcel of local, regional, and national campaigns aimed at demonizing and circumscribing the growing Catholic population.

After World War I, anti-Catholic sentiment significantly increased across the United States, spurred by the resurrection of the Ku Klux Klan, nativist immigration laws designed to severely restrict Catholic immigration from southern and eastern Europe in the 1920s, and acts of overt violence against

Catholics, white and nonwhite alike.[48] The violence and laws targeting Catholics in the South were also deeply influenced by the centuries-long campaign of white resistance to African American education and literacy.[49]

Thus, southern legislatures began passing bills to authorize state inspection of convents, parochial schools, and other private institutions; to prohibit the carrying or drinking of alcohol, including sacramental wine, at churches; to authorize the taxation of church property; to authorize compulsory public school attendance for children; and to indirectly criminalize Black Catholic education.[50] In Florida, for example, state representatives introduced anti-Catholic bills in the 1913, 1915, and 1917 legislative sessions, one of which forbade white teachers from teaching Black students, and Black teachers from teaching white students. House Bill 415, signed into law in 1913, provided that violators could be fined up to $500 and imprisoned for six months. Because the bill was not explicitly anti-Catholic in its text and was instead widely viewed as a "negro" issue, it failed to elicit any protest in prominent Catholic news outlets. However, its enactment seriously affected the state's Black Catholic schools, which were then exclusively staffed by white sisters.[51] This threat was realized when three white Sisters of Saint Joseph were arrested and briefly detained in 1916 for operating their Black Catholic school in Saint Augustine, the formal birthplace of Black and Catholic history in the United States.[52] That same year, a similar law pending in the Georgia state legislature precipitated the establishment of the nation's seventh African American sisterhood.

The Formation of the Handmaids of Mary

When Georgia state legislator J. B. Way introduced a bill seeking to "prohibit white teachers from teaching in colored schools and colored teachers from teaching in white schools" in 1915, he inadvertently spurred the resurrection of Black female religious life in Savannah. If passed, the measure would have effectively barred African American students from Georgia's Catholic school system, then staffed solely by white sisters.[53] While the crisis could have easily been averted if any of the white sisterhoods teaching in the diocese's four Black parochial schools had had Black members or sought to welcome vocations among Savannah's Black Catholic population, none did so. However, Father Ignatius Lissner, a member of the Society of African Missions stationed in Augusta, Georgia, concluded that "the future of the mission to the Negro lies in the colored sisters, brothers, and priests."[54]

FIGURE 2.2. The inaugural Handmaids of the Most Pure Heart of Mary in 1917. The Handmaids, who affiliated with the Third Order of Saint Francis in 1930, were the first Roman Catholic sisterhood organized in explicit protest against a Jim Crow segregation law in the United States. Courtesy of the Franciscan Handmaids of the Most Pure Heart of Mary, New York.

Seeking to circumvent the impending law, Lissner first asked the Black sisterhoods whether they could establish a ministry in Savannah. When neither order had sisters to spare, he sought a pious Black laywoman to lead a new Black teaching sisterhood. He traveled across the South, including to Washington, DC, where a white Marist priest stationed at the Catholic University of America informed him about Eliza Barbara Williams, then living in the city. A former assistant superior of the suppressed all-Black Franciscan order in Convent, Louisiana, and a former OSP novice, Williams was working as a domestic, answering the phone and door, for the Sisters of Notre Dame de Namur at their Trinity College (now Trinity Washington University) when Lissner visited her. Williams immediately agreed to lead the new community and offered Lissner her life savings.[55] By October 1916, she had moved to Savannah and begun identifying potential candidates in Georgia, South Carolina, and Ohio. Within a year, the Handmaids of the Most Pure Heart of Mary numbered ten and staffed the St. Anthony School in West Savannah (figure 2.2).[56] By early 1923, the Handmaids had also admitted women from Kentucky, Massachusetts, New York, Louisiana, Pennsylvania, and the Caribbean, including Mary Christine Gallavaga (later Sister Mary of the Presentation), an African-descended woman raised by the Carmelite nuns in Cuba.[57]

However, the Handmaids' tenure in Savannah proved short-lived. While local Black Catholics provided them with provisions, local whites, especially sisters, regularly expressed disgust at the reemergence of an order of Black nuns in their midst. Lamenting that no white sisters welcomed or visited the Handmaids, Lissner wrote, "As real Southerners they could not believe that a colored woman could make a real Religious Sister. I was blamed for the mistake. 'It is a shame' they said. 'Father Lissner will soon find out his mistake. He may give them the veil but what will prevent them from stealing chickens and telling lies?'"[58] Local white sisters exhibited willful amnesia about the legacy of Mother Mathilda Beasley and her Black order, who had helped to inaugurate and sustain Catholic ministries to Savannah's African Americans.

The racial antipathies of white Catholics, as well as rampant anti-Catholic sentiment in the state, ultimately doomed the Handmaids in Savannah. Following a series of bitter disputes with Savannah's bishop, Benjamin Keiley, over Lissner's proposal for an integrated seminary in the diocese, Lissner departed Savannah in 1920 for Tenafly, New Jersey, to establish his short-lived seminary there. His absence left the Handmaids without a clerical ally, making them increasingly vulnerable to growing anti-Black and anti-Catholic hostilities.[59]

Little information survives about the Handmaids' forced exile from Georgia, which began in 1921. However, Bishop Keiley, a former Confederate soldier from Virginia who held racially derogatory views about African Americans and persons of Jewish heritage, dismissed the Black sisters from their teaching positions soon after Lissner's departure and replaced them with white sisters.[60]

To support themselves, the Handmaids operated a laundry business at night and begged along the Savannah waterfront on weekends. However, escalating white hostility prompted them to join the growing Black exodus from the state. In 1921, Williams took a small band of Handmaids to Tenafly, New Jersey, to serve as domestics for the priests of the Society of African Missions and seek out a northern mission.[61] During this time, Lissner sought a congregation to assist the Handmaids with their novitiate training. After "a few years" of asking Mother Katharine Drexel for help, she finally consented to take one Handmaid, Sister Mary Dorothy (Cecilia) Hall, a native of Georgetown, Kentucky, who could pass for white, into the SBS novitiate in Pennsylvania.[62]

Back in Savannah, white hostilities remained high. In a letter to Father Lissner dated July 27, 1923, for example, Williams, who had returned to check on the remaining members of her congregation, lamented the white opposition to Lissner's plan to assign Joseph John, the first Black alumnus of Saint Anthony's Mission House to West Savannah. She reported that local whites stopped her in the street to express their disgust. "Now we meet the Colored Sister," they caustically remarked. "Next we will be meeting the colored priest." Williams also documented the opposition of the white Franciscan sisters who staffed the city's Black Catholic schools. The Missionary Franciscans of the Immaculate Conception specifically complained that it was enough that Savannah already had Black sisters and it did not need a Black priest.[63]

Ultimately, Savannah's new bishop, Michael J. Keyes, fearful of white opposition, rejected John's assignment, later stating that he wanted mission work among African Americans in his diocese left to willing white priests and presumably only white sisters.[64] For Williams, the bishop's opposition to Joseph must have been infuriating. In 1913, racism in the Josephite order combined with white Church leaders' refusal to assign Black priests to Black parishes drove her cousin, Father John Joseph Plantevigne, insane and led to his early death at age forty-two.[65] A decade before John's death, his brother, Albert LeForest Plantevigne, who left the Catholic Church to become a Congregationalist minister, had been lynched by whites for opening a Black school in Point Coupee, Louisiana.[66] Keyes's opposition to Black-administered education and Black priests in Savannah, then, was terrible déjà vu for the Black foundress. Voicing her frustration to Lissner, Williams wrote, "The Japanese . . . Italians . . . Chinese . . . Africans have priests. Why can't the American Negroes?"[67] For Williams and other African American Catholics, the fate of Black Catholics remained uncertain if white religious with minimal commitments to racial justice continued to be in charge of the African American apostolate. But there was nothing she could do.

By the close of 1923, Williams relocated the remainder of the Handmaids to New York City to minister to Harlem's expanding southern Black migrant and immigrant communities. There the sisters took over a property left to the Church to become the city's first Black Catholic nursery, later named St. Benedict the Moor. Soon thereafter, they began teaching at the all-Black St. Benedict the Moor School in lower Manhattan and opened a food pantry and soup kitchen on Staten Island. In 1930, the Handmaids affiliated themselves with the Third Order of Saint Francis, becoming the Franciscan Handmaids of the Most Pure Heart of Mary (FHM) and established St. Mary's, their first primary school for Harlem's African American and Caribbean immigrant youth, in their convent. In 1941, the sisters assumed the administration of Harlem's newly established St. Aloysius Catholic School and cemented the foundation of Black-administered Catholic education in the archdiocese of New York City.[68] Though the FHM found stability and security in New York, the racial hostilities that drove them from Savannah would remain constant in the Church and society at large.[69]

White Catholic Racism in the African American Apostolate

In 1925, the Supreme Court's decision in *Pierce v. Society of Sisters of the Holy Names of Jesus and Mary* guaranteed the right of Catholic (and other private) schools to operate in the United States.[70] While the laws designed to criminalize Black Catholic education were nullified, others demanding teacher certification for private schoolteachers continued to challenge Black sisters. So did enduring white racism.

As noted earlier, white priests and sisters who led ministries in the African American community before the 1960s—like their Black counterparts—regularly faced harassment by white supremacists and others opposed to Black Catholic education. Within the Church, white religious who led schools for Black youth also faced ostracism from other white Catholics, who routinely called them "nigger sisters" or "nigger lovers" and subjected them and their charges to harassment and occasional violence.[71]

Nevertheless, white sisters and priests working in the Black apostolate were almost always able to retain the privileges of whiteness, which guaranteed them automatic social protections unavailable to Black sisters. In most cases, white sisters could avoid eliciting significant physical violence. When the three white Sisters of Saint Joseph were arrested and jailed in Florida in 1916, for example, two were immediately bonded out of jail.[72] Moreover, when the school's principal refused the bond offer, the judge allowed her to be held at the convent in the custody of a priest rather than in the county jail. Some historians have suggested that St. Augustine's bishop, Michael Joseph Curley, orchestrated the sisters' arrest to test the limits of the 1913 law. When the court finally ruled that it did not apply to private institutions, white sisters teaching in the Black apostolate in Florida were protected from further legal molestation.[73]

Black sisters, however, received minimal support from white ecclesiastical authorities when faced with white supremacist violence. At best, white clerics remained reserved in their defense of Black sisters and their schools. At worst, they upheld the social order without apology or concern. In fact, in a 1939 interoffice memo regarding the Klan's activities toward Catholics

FIGURE 2.3. During the Jim Crow era, African-descended women and girls from across the United States, Canada, Central America, and the Caribbean denied admission to European and white American sisterhoods often traveled hundreds and even thousands of miles away from their hometowns to enter the African American sisterhoods. Five of the daughters of Charles and Emma Burks of the historically Black St. Augustine Catholic Church in Louisville, Kentucky, entered the Oblate Sisters of Providence in Baltimore, Maryland, in the 1930s and 1940s owing to the anti-Black admissions policies of the white orders ministering in their home archdiocese. Four Burks sisters remained in the order until their deaths. Courtesy of Sylvia Miles.

within the National Catholic Welfare Conference, Director Frank Hall noted to his supervisor, Monsignor (later Bishop) Matthew Brady, that he had been informed that "the Klan now plans to concentrate on the matter of Negroes and Jews and not to worry to any great degree about Catholics."[74] Such statements document a profound indifference toward Black life and suffering, including for Black Catholics, among white Catholics working in the highest positions in the Church.

White religious who led Black ministries were also not free of the anti-Black racism that circumscribed Black lives and institutions. During Jim Crow, most white religious who ministered in African American communities firmly opposed the desegregation of religious life and usually, but not always, directed their pupils with expressed vocations to the Black congregations (figure 2.3). Also, the written and oral records of religious and lay

Black Catholics raised in that era are inundated with examples of the racial humiliations and abuses that white religious regularly enforced and perpetrated in both predominantly white and Black institutions.

In some instances, the abuse suffered by Black Catholics was sexual or had sexual undertones. For example, in 1897, upon her graduation from Holy Cross Catholic Elementary School in Lynchburg, Virginia, the family of future OSP superior Mother Mary Consuella Clifford removed her from the Church for two years after Thomas Donovan, a white Josephite priest and the order's future superior, "victimized" one of the Black laywomen who led the school. It is not clear what Donovan did to "Miss Lillie Reed," but it was traumatic enough that the Black community turned against him and that Clifford, who was eventually sent away to a Catholic boarding academy, narrated the episode to her community members decades later.[75] Saundra Ann Willingham, who grew up Black and Catholic in Cincinnati in the 1940s and later entered religious life, vividly recalled a white priest who would give each child a nickel if they let him touch them sexually.[76] While the sexual abuse of Black youth and adults in white-led parishes and schools remains grossly understudied, the available archival and oral history record documents that these were not isolated incidents and that they date back to slavery.[77]

Other kinds of abuses suffered by Black Catholics reflected the daily rituals of white domination and Black subordination in Jim Crow life. In white parishes that formally barred Black faithful, the arrival of Black Catholics seeking to worship could and often did meet with violence. In a May 12, 1891, letter to Katharine Drexel, for example, Father Augustus Tolton noted that two days earlier he had administered death rites to a Black laywoman who "had been nine years away from her duties because she was hurled out of a white church and even cursed at by the Irish members." "She sent for me and thanked God that she had me to send for," Tolton wrote.[78] African American migrants and Caribbean immigrants to New York City in the 1930s recalled one white priest in central Harlem who "stood on the steps [of his parish] with a bullwhip, chasing the niggers away."[79] Similarly, when former School Sister of Notre Dame Louis Mary (Carolyn) Quadarella's Italian father took her to Nativity of the Blessed Virgin Mary in the diocese of Brooklyn to be baptized in 1945, the priest hatefully refused and instead directed her father to the borough's designated Black parish, St. Peter Claver.[80] In the years before archdiocesan-mandated desegregation in 1948, records even reveal that a white monsignor who led Immaculate Conception Catholic Church in northwest Washington, DC, regularly called the police to remove Black worshippers who dared enter the sanctuary.[81]

In white parishes that permitted Black worshippers, white priests deliberately passed over Black Catholics, including youth, at the Communion rail; used separate vessels for the Eucharist and Communion wine for Black and white parishioners; and relegated the Black faithful to separate pews (sometimes behind screens) and to the back of Communion lines. Even in parishes where Black laywomen and sisters cleaned and cooked for white priests, these same men sometimes put on gloves before offering Black Catholics the Eucharist, jokingly referred to Black sisters as "necessary evils," and rarely, if ever, offered homilies explicitly condemning racial injustice.[82]

In their interactions with Black youths and their parents in Black Catholic schools, white priests and sisters also regularly enforced the Jim Crow order. White religious casually and maliciously used the *n*-word, used unjust corporal punishment, denigrated African American culture, and often openly referred to their African American charges as "heathens" and "savages" in need of white missionary zeal.[83] Although scholar Matthew J. Cressler has argued that white religious who used such racially derogatory terms to describe their Black pupils "carried no ill intent," the exclusionary practices of white religious orders, the archival and oral history record documenting the anti-Black animus of white religious, and the emotional, psychological, and physical scars carried by Catholics of color who suffered raced-based mistreatment in white-led Catholic missions, parishes, and schools indicate otherwise.[84] Civil rights leader and cradle Catholic Diane Nash, for example, was haunted by a disturbing encounter with a white SBS member while enrolled at the grade school attached to Chicago's St. Anselm Catholic Church in the late 1940s. The white nun told Nash, "You know we love God because we deal with the least of God's people." Unsure how to respond, Nash remained silent.[85] Nash also recalled days when the white sisters required their girl pupils to wear their hair in Shirley Temple curls, completely disregarding the complexities of Black hair and often privileging light-skinned students like Nash with hair textures that could easily be transformed into long ringlets.[86]

Basketball Hall of Fame coach and cradle Catholic John Thompson Jr. also experienced racially antagonistic mistreatment from the white religious in Washington, DC, and southern Maryland, where his family's roots in the US Church began. In addition to being relegated to the back of Communion lines and into separate pews at white parishes during the 1940s, 1950s, and 1960s, Thompson suffered verbal and emotional abuse from a white priest who told him that he "might grow up to be a murderer one day."[87] The School Sisters of Notre Dame (SSND) who staffed Our Lady of Perpetual Help were hardly any better. When the white nuns failed to diagnose Thompson's illiteracy and his need for eyeglasses, they instructed his mother that he should be sent to a school for "the retarded." However, Thompson's devout Catholic mother instead enrolled him in a public school, where he thrived under the tutelage and nurturing of a Black woman teacher. Although Thompson's superior athletic abilities won him admission into DC's historically white Archbishop Carroll High School, the mistreatment he endured from white religious left its marks.[88]

Most Black parents and guardians knew well that many white Catholics ministering in the African American community did not endorse racial equality, and they tried to shield their children from the most pernicious aspects of that racism. Indeed, when fifteen-year-old Rosa Marshall, a future OSP superior, informed her father that she desired to become a member of the Sisters of Charity of the Blessed Virgin Mary (BVM), her high school educators in Memphis, Tennessee, in 1942, he firmly responded no, without providing an explanation. Initially distraught, Marshall came to understand her father's protectiveness two years later when her BVM high school counselor informed her that she could not enter the community because she was Black. When the crestfallen Marshall later told her father of the exchange, he simply responded, "I was wondering when you were going to get it."[89]

In some cases, though, Black parents and guardians forcefully pushed back against the racism of the white religious educating their children. For example, Sister Josita (Mary Frances) Colbert vividly recalled an instance when a male relative confronted the white Franciscan Sisters of Glen Riddle who staffed Baltimore's St. Peter Claver Catholic School after their callous mistreatment of her in the second grade. Because Colbert had forgotten to bring a signed form to class, her white sister instructors forced her to travel back home in the rain without an umbrella to retrieve it. When she returned home soaking wet and sick, Colbert's relative immediately traveled to the school, lambasted the nuns for their behavior, and instructed them to "never do that again."[90]

When Gwynette Proctor, another future nun, and her siblings desegregated Baltimore's Blessed Sacrament Elementary School in 1958, her cradle Catholic parents regularly traveled to the school to confront the white SSND for their failures to protect their children. During the Proctors' first year at Blessed Sacrament, their white classmates' parents regularly threw trash at them and spat on them as they walked to the school's entrance. However, the white sisters never rebuked the offending parents or offered comfort to their Black pupils. In another jarring episode, after Proctor broke her ankle at school, the white nuns opted not to call her parents immediately or take her to a Black hospital as they did not want to journey into the Proctors' middle-class Black neighborhood, perceiving it to be dangerous. Instead, the white nuns put Proctor in a taxicab alone and sent her home, calling her mother only after they did so. An older Black woman in her neighborhood subsequently took Proctor to the hospital, and Proctor's parents returned to the school the following day for another bout with the SSND.[91]

Because the Black sisterhoods never had enough members to staff all the nation's Black Catholic schools or take over the ministries white sisters bungled, many African American parents had to negotiate the racism of the white sisters and priests as best as they could. This meant not only confronting white religious when necessary over the mistreatment of their children but also regularly supplementing their children's education with Black history and art lessons when their instructors attempted force white supremacist and self-abnegating attitudes onto their Black pupils. Indeed, when Phillis Sheppard, a former Sister of Providence, was reprimanded by her first-grade teacher for drawing the baby Jesus brown, as she had seen in her home, she proudly remembered how her mother "marched" to her school the next day to confront the offending white nun and principal and educate them on the matter.[92]

In egregious cases of white incompetence and abuse, though, sustained protests from Black Catholic parents sometimes forced white pastors to acquiesce to Black Catholic demands for Black nuns. In 1914, for example, Black Catholic complaints over the mistreatment of Black youth educated by the Holy Ghost Sisters resulted in an all-out revolt against the mostly Irish nuns at their Holy Redeemer School in San Antonio, Texas. African Americans objected to "the disciplinarian nature of the all-white staff," who they argued "treated them as inferiors" and gave preferential treatment to white and Mexican American faithful in a church designated for African Americans. Unyielding calls for Black nuns at Holy Redeemer eventually persuaded a local white Josephite priest to recruit the SSF to come to San Antonio, where they took over the administration of the school and parish in 1914.[93]

To be certain, anti-Black animus among select Afro-Creole SSF members persisted into the twentieth century, regularly manifesting in disparaging remarks by these sisters about "American Negroes" and favoritism toward Creoles and/or light-skinned African Americans in their schools and convents. However, African American Catholics still preferred some prejudiced Afro-Creole sisters committed to serving their communities over racist white ones.[94] Indeed, the ministries of Black nuns, especially in the South, extended well beyond the classroom. Black sisters not only lived in the Black communities they served but also regularly visited the homes of their pupils, the sick, and the imprisoned. Black sisters regularly led weekly catechism classes for Catholic students enrolled in public schools and summer vacation Bible schools, and they were visible members of the communities they served. When the OSP took up a ministry at St. Peter Claver Catholic Church in St. Paul, Minnesota, in 1944, the sisters and members of the Black parish even worked together to launch a bowling alley in the church's basement to raise funds to open the school and build a convent in 1951.[95]

Many Black youths educated by Black and white nuns also recognized the differences in their respective educators' commitments. Earline Greenfield, a cradle Catholic from St. Louis, Missouri, recalled the shock she experienced after graduating from the all-Black Holy Angel School in Kinloch, Missouri, and entering the marginally integrated Mercy High School in University City, Missouri, in 1957. At Holy Angel School, Greenfield felt loved and protected by the SSND, especially "Sisters Gladys and Helen Marie," two of the order's earliest Black members, and the OSP members who assumed the administration of the Black Catholic school in 1955.[96] At Mercy High School, however, Gourley's experience with the Religious Sisters of Mercy, who fiercely resisted the integration of their own ranks in St. Louis, was markedly different.[97] Although Greenfield, an honors student, reported that she got along well with her white classmates, she noted that some of the white Mercy nuns were overtly hostile and discriminatory to the school's small contingent of Black students. Greenfield specifically recalled that Black girl students were required to wear longer skirts than their white counterparts and that a few nuns oversurveilled and regulated Black students' behaviors resulting in a steady decline in the school's Black population during her time there. "Sister Rosaria thought she was the head of the Ku Klux Klan by the way she acted," Greenfield remembered. Moreover, when Greenfield's classmates elected her as the school's first Black May Day queen during her senior year, several white sisters and many of her classmates' parents openly disapproved, especially since she would receive a crown and potentially have a white male escort. Though Greenfield's win was upheld, she never forgot the controversy that emerged because of it.[98]

Sister Mary Judith Therese (Mercilite) Barial, who was taught by the predominantly Irish Sisters of the Holy Ghost in her hometown of Pascagoula,

Mississippi, and the African American SSF as a boarding student at their St. Mary's Academy for (Colored) Girls during Jim Crow, also recognized the differences between her educators' commitments to the Black communities they served. While Barial, a brown-skinned Afro-Creole, maintained that she received a quality education under both orders, she noted that her white elementary school sister instructors maintained a clear social distance from their Black pupils and their families outside of school. "We knew them only at school but not in our neighborhoods," Barial reflected. When the absence of a Catholic high school open to Black girls in Pascagoula forced Barial's parents to send her away to New Orleans to St. Mary's Academy, she immediately discerned the difference. "I felt at home [with the Holy Family Sisters]," she stated. Unlike with her former white sister-educators, Barial knew that her SSF educators wanted and expected her to succeed academically and professionally, color notwithstanding. Thus, when she decided to enter religious life in 1958, she applied only to the order of her African American educators.[99]

Even when Black sisters were available, though, white prelates and priests sometimes ignored Black Catholic demands for Black teachers because they preferred that white sisters lead the schools under their jurisdiction.[100] Such opposition drove the Handmaids from Georgia. Sometime in the 1930s, Charleston's bishop, Emmet Walsh, even confided to the OSP's white chaplain, Josephite Father John Gillard, that he preferred white sisters because Black sisters were "more expensive."[101] Black orders rarely received equitable financial support from the all-white hierarchy or the Church-led annual appeals and could not rely on substantial monies from incoming dowries or donations, unlike many of their white counterparts. Consequently, securing the labor of Black sisters could be costly. Black sisterhoods sometimes had to purchase or rent homes for their members at higher rates owing to exploitative real estate practices or rent private cars or hire drivers to transport them to new missions to avoid the ever-present dangers of Jim Crow travel.

While white racism sometimes made Black sisters "more expensive," the fact remains that many white religious openly opposed and resented Black sisters' educational and spiritual leadership. Like white sisters and priests ministering in the Black community, Black teaching sisters regularly endured racist taunts, including being routinely labeled as "the little nigger sisters" by their adversaries both within and outside of the Church.[102] And just as their fellow white religious often ostracized them, white priests and sisters active in the African American apostolate often maintained a clear social distance from their Black counterparts, often excluding Black sisters from local meetings and social gatherings, pushing them to the back of Communion lines, and regularly subjecting them to condescending behavior.[103] Many of these white priests and sisters considered themselves experts on educating and handling the Negro and deeply resented when Black parents and youth expressed a preference for and followed the instructions of Black sisters over white religious.[104]

The oral histories of members of Black orders also document their experiences of racism from white sisters at the annual meetings of the National Catholic Educational Association. By the 1940s, Black teaching sisters regularly attended these professional gatherings on a segregated basis. Sister Mary Alice (Innocence) Chineworth, an OSP member, recalled that most white sisters who attended refused to speak to Black sister-participants and rarely acknowledged their presence. Chineworth also noted that Black sisters were never consulted or invited to be formal speakers at the National Catholic Educational Association conventions during Jim Crow, and topics related to Black Catholic education or the teaching of Black history were rarely on the agenda before the civil rights movement.[105] However, the widespread popularity of Blackface minstrelsy and other forms of racist miseducation in white Catholic parishes and schools staffed by white religious, especially the Irish, through America's civil rights years is well documented.[106] So, too, are instances in which white sisters enforced segregation, deliberately thwarted academically talented Black students, and actively encouraged the anti-Black animus, bullying, and violence of their white pupils and others under their spiritual guidance.[107]

The refusal of white religious ministering in Black schools to teach Black history and art was another distinct manifestation of their commitment to white supremacy. As early as 1915, schools led by the OSP taught Black history in the formal celebrations of Negro Emancipation Day.[108] Following the establishment of Negro History Week (later Black History Month) in 1926, all three Black sisterhoods formally inaugurated the teaching of Black history and culture in their schools. By 1946, OSP leaders required each grade level to create their own Negro History Week programs, a survey of which reveals elaborate celebrations of African, African American, and Black Catholic history (figure 2.4).[109] These weeklong events usually featured the singing of the Negro national anthem, "Lift Every Voice and Sing," and African American spirituals.[110] At the elementary level, students routinely performed skits in which they recited poems by Black intellectuals and freedom fighters and documented the history of Black Catholics

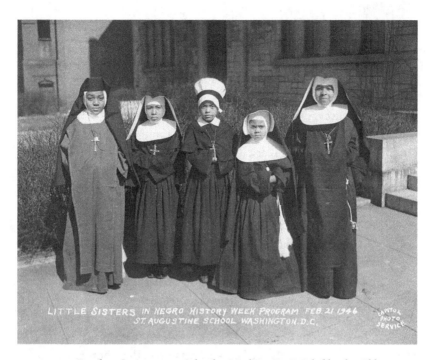

FIGURE 2.4. Pupils at St. Augustine School in Washington, DC, led by the Oblate Sisters of Providence from 1908 to 1998, celebrate Negro History Week in 1946. From left to right, the students don the habit of the Franciscan Sisters of Mill Hill, the second habit of the Oblate Sisters of Providence, which was modified and approved in 1906, the original habit of the Oblate Sisters of Providence, the habit of the Sisters of the Holy Family, and the habit of the Franciscan Handmaids of the Most Pure Heart of Mary. The four teaching sisterhoods worked exclusively in the African American apostolate during the most turbulent years of Jim Crow segregation. Courtesy of the Archives of the Oblate Sisters of Providence, Baltimore, Maryland.

in the United States. At the high school level, students often wrote essays on these same topics as well as on the contributions of Africans, especially Catholics, to world civilization.[111] In 1949, the Oblates and their students at St. Alphonsus School in Wilson, North Carolina, even won national praise from poet Langston Hughes, who celebrated Negro History Week at the school that February.[112]

Because books provided by diocesan school boards rarely included materials on Black history and culture that were accurate or free from demeaning depictions of African-descended people and white supremacist revisions of American history, Black teaching sisters developed their own curricula, reading lists, and assignments on the topic to supplement their lessons.[113] At gatherings of interracial councils and interracial groups of sisters working in Black communities, Black sisters also regularly encouraged white sisters leading Black Catholic schools to incorporate "Negro history" into their curricula and emphasized the importance of "Negro educators."[114] However, few white orders—including the SBS—taught Black history before the civil rights gains of the 1950s and 1960s. In fact, in several instances, the teaching of Black history in schools led by historically white sisterhoods was inaugurated by Black laywomen who taught alongside the white nuns, by pioneering Black nuns in those orders, or by members of Black sisterhoods who integrated the faculties of white-led schools.[115]

However, the most conspicuous evidence of white Catholic opposition to Black sisters' educational leadership was the persistence of anti-Black admissions policies at the nation's Catholic colleges and universities, even as state boards required teachers to attain higher education to secure their schools' accreditation. Given the new standards, Black-administered schools without accreditation would fall behind their white counterparts, providing greater ammunition to white Church leaders already opposed to Black-run Catholic schools and Black leadership in the Church.

Through the Jim Crow era, the largely Irish SBS supplied the most teaching sisters to the African American apostolate. Mother Katharine Drexel also used her sizable trust to subsidize a great expansion of African American Catholic infrastructure and at times support Black civil rights causes. In addition to offering critical funding to support the building or restoration of many Black Catholic churches and schools—which had often been established by Black Catholics—the SBS operated the largest network of Black Catholic elementary and high schools, overwhelmingly located in the South. In response to Afro-Creole and Black protests against the anti-Black admissions policies of white Catholic colleges and universities, the SBS also founded Xavier College (now Xavier University of Louisiana), the first Catholic institution of higher education for African Americans, in 1925.[116] By 1928, Xavier would be among the few accredited Catholic colleges open to Black sisters seeking to preserve the Black-administered school system. However, even Drexel and her SBS congregation had to be persuaded to support the Black sisterhoods in their protracted struggle for teacher certification and school accreditation after World War I.[117]

The Early Struggle to Desegregate Catholic
Higher Education

As a private institution, the Catholic Church was never legally obligated to enforce state segregation laws within its boundaries. However, as these pages have demonstrated, racial segregation and exclusion were also Catholic traditions. Most of the nation's Catholic colleges and universities—all led by white priests and sisters—upheld the racial status quo during Jim Crow and placed Black congregations in an extremely precarious position in the era of teacher reform and private school accreditation. While the nation's growing network of private and state-supported Black colleges and universities would accept Black sisters, Black Catholic leadership councils were reluctant to send their members to non-Catholic institutions in violation of Church law. Minutes from a 1927 meeting of the OSP general council, for example, reveal that during a visit to their motherhouse that year, US apostolic delegate Pietro Fumasoni Biondi stressed that the sisters "should not be allowed to attend non-Catholic colleges."[118] Required by Church leaders to secure the accreditation of their schools but banned from Catholic higher education on the basis of race, Black sisters mobilized to forge secret agreements with willing white ecclesiastical leaders, priests, brothers, and sisters. However, it was not easy.

For example, in 1920, when the bishops who served on the executive board of the CBMWCP appealed to all US white sisterhoods to help the Black sisters circumvent racial segregation and earn their teaching certificates, only one order, the Sisters of Charity of Seton Hill (SCSH), responded affirmatively. Only after several years, more pressure from the board, and pleas from the Black sisterhoods did a few more white orders—including the Benedictine Sisters in Atchison, Kansas; the SBS in suburban Philadelphia; and the SSND in Baltimore—decide to help.[119] Most of the nation's more than five hundred white sisterhoods refused. Even the Sisters, Servants of the Immaculate Heart of Mary, which had been founded by two OSP members and operated three colleges for women in 1920, declined to help Black teaching orders pursue higher education until after World War II.[120]

Once admitted, Black sisters still faced barriers. For example, oral testimonies and the archival record indicate that Black sisters encountered resistance to their presence on campus and inside classrooms. According to OSP records, members also endured racial slurs and slights from their white peers and instructors. Sometimes Black sisters addressed such abuses head-on. For example, when a white male professor at the Catholic

University commented on "something [that] reminded him of a Negro's kinky head," an OSP member confronted him after class and "told him that she belonged to the Negro race and that she did not like the comparison."[121] These occurrences soon forced the OSP leadership council to devise rules and suggestions for sisters entering college to prevent such confrontations. In one striking example, OSP members were instructed to "pay no attention to any remarks relative to the Negro race—whether made by white Sisters, the Professor, or secular students." If such remarks occurred, sisters were advised not to repeat them to any OSP member as it might cause "a violation of charity."[122] Oblates who attended Villanova learned to laugh away the insults of white sisters who "decided that the Oblates are Mexican Sisters" since they could not "conceive that colored people can be lady like."[123] Others embraced a code of silence and deference that would come back to haunt them years later. Nonetheless, the very fact that Black sisters were able to enter several Catholic colleges and universities and earn as many normal certificates and bachelor's and master's degrees as they did during this period testifies to their courage, determination, and faith. Two key educational victories also offer a glimpse into the hardships that Black sisters faced and the possibilities of interracial cooperation in the early fight to desegregate Catholic higher education.

The Secret Desegregation of Loyola University of the South

In 1921, the SSF leadership council launched the first major assault on anti-Black exclusion in higher education in the Deep South. One year earlier, Louisiana had begun requiring the certification of private schoolteachers, threatening the future of the state's only African American sisterhood and their growing network of Catholic schools. With their sisters barred by their race from admission to the state's only Catholic university and college with education departments, the Jesuit-led Loyola University of the South and St. Mary's Dominican College, administered by the Dominican Sisters of St. Mary, SSF leaders decided to establish an accredited normal institute at their motherhouse.[124] Before this, like for many of their white counterparts, SSF higher education had been piecemeal at best. The SSF sisters with the most teaching experience led the normal school's summer classes. The SSF leaders also hired white private university instructors. However, the latter practice caused a severe financial strain on the order's budget, and

SSF records reveal that the individuals hired were ineffective.[125] As a result, Mother Mary of the Sacred Heart (Victoria) Jourdan, the SSF superior, sought the assistance of the archbishop of New Orleans, John Shaw, who also served as the president of the CBMWCP, and subsequently expressed her concerns to its membership.[126]

In the spring of 1921, a pamphlet the board prepared and distributed made the special appeal. Titled "The Colored Sisters: A Plea for Fair Play and Equal Opportunity," it indicted the Church for "heartlessly" excluding Black sisters from Catholic higher education, including summer classes. Calling for at least six annual scholarships (two for each Black order) to be established at accredited US Catholic colleges and universities, the pamphlet cited the leading example of the SCSH, who in 1920 had been the first and only white order to respond to the board's appeal to staff a normal school for Black sisters. It concluded, "We Catholics owe this to these wonderful women not only for what they have done and suffered, but to equip them properly for their tremendous future work for the Church and for Negro Womanhood. We of the white race have done much to degrade Negro Womanhood, as is incontestably proven by the presence of 5,000,000 mulattoes in our midst. We ought to make some reparation."[127] In acknowledging the rampant sexual abuse of Black women and girls by white men and boys during and after slavery, and in framing their appeal in the language of reparations, these white bishops opened an avenue for the Church to confront its role in the nation's sins of anti-Black racism, slavery, and segregation and to support some of the earliest Catholics to organize against these systems.

Still, only Mother Mary Joseph Harvey, the SCSH leader in Greensburg, Pennsylvania, answered the bishops' appeal for help in 1921.[128] Working secretly in conjunction with the SCSH, Archbishop Shaw, and Father Francis X. Twellmeyer, the Jesuit superintendent of the archdiocesan school system and director of the summer school and extension program at Loyola, the CBMWCP financed the entire operation, providing teaching supplies, paying the white sisters' travel fees and salaries, and arranging for them to reside with the white Religious of the Sacred Heart of Jesus during the summer. Under this arrangement, Loyola granted the academic credits the SSF earned, and the sisters subsequently applied to the state for teaching certificates.[129]

On June 22, 1921, six SCSH members started six weeks of work as the inaugural staff of the Holy Family Normal School (see figure 2.5).[130] Upon the session's conclusion, one of the sisters published an article in *Our*

FIGURE 2.5. Sisters of Charity of Seton Hill instructing Sisters of the Holy Family at the clandestine Holy Family Normal School in New Orleans during the Jim Crow era. Courtesy of the Archives of the Sisters of Charity of Seton Hill, Greensburg, Pennsylvania.

Colored Missions, the CBMWCP's monthly newsletter, in which she confessed a conversion of her understanding of Black people. "I have heard so often that . . . ['the Negro'] . . . is lazy, that he will not work. These colored sisters work. They could not have worked harder." When asked whether her order would return to the South, she added, "Please God we shall form the habit of going back to the South . . . Summer after Summer, as long as we are needed."[131] And for the next thirty-six years, SCSH members returned annually to New Orleans to operate a summer normal school for the SSF.[132]

Yet as soon as the African American sisters started earning teaching certificates with credits from Loyola, the state's segregationist leadership became suspicious. In 1929, the Louisiana State Board of Education opened an investigation into the legality of the arrangement, and it remained vigilant.[133] When Father Harold Gaudin, a Jesuit priest and segregationist, became president of Loyola in 1937, he terminated the university's sixteen-year association with the SSF.[134] Despite pleas from the SSF superior, letters from SCSH and CBMWCP leaders explaining his predecessor's arrangement, and copies of the SSF's transcripts with the Loyola University seal, Gaudin denied that Loyola had ever been a part of the arrangement. He also ordered all records of the endeavor contained in the university's files closed.[135]

After Loyola ended its support, Xavier, then fully accredited, affiliated itself with the normal institute and ensured its survival. Xavier's SBS leaders also offered full-tuition scholarships to any SSF member desiring a bachelor's or master's degree.[136] However, the SSF members who had not yet received their teaching certificates were forced to begin their coursework anew, having lost their Loyola credits. Loyola's white registrar's refusal to certify their matriculation also meant that some sisters were denied a renewal of their state teaching certificates.[137]

Although the first desegregation of Loyola University proved short-lived, it enabled the SSF to begin securing accreditation for their schools throughout Louisiana and in Florida and Texas. A predecessor to the famed Freedom School project launched by the Student Nonviolent Coordinating Committee in 1964, the Holy Family Normal School was a radical experiment in interracial Catholicism, education, and democracy. By 1940, the educational partnership between the SCSH and SSF also resulted in the establishment of a scholarship program that enabled the Black sisters to matriculate at the SCSH's Seton Hill College in Pennsylvania. In 1944, Sister Mary Esperance (Emma) Collins received her Bachelor of Arts degree in biology, becoming Seton Hill's first Black graduate (figure 2.6)[138] Over the next thirty years, sixteen other SSF members earned their bachelor's degrees from the institution.[139] Through the Jim Crow era, the educational institutions the SSF staffed were consistently among the highest-achieving schools for African Americans in Louisiana.[140] In fact, of forty-eight Black Catholic high schools open across the nation in 1941, the SSF operated six in Louisiana and Texas, with only one not yet accredited.[141]

The OSP and the Reintegration of the Catholic University of America

In 1917, "after many unsuccessful attempts to obtain help from various religious congregations," Mother Frances (Marie) Fieldien inaugurated the higher education of the teaching members of the OSP with the secret support of the all-white Xaverian Brothers in Baltimore.[142] That year, Fieldien, a native of Ottawa, Canada, successfully appealed to Brother Isidore Kuppel, the Xaverian congregation's US provincial, who agreed to assist the

FIGURE 2.6. Sister Mary Esperance (Emma) Collins, Sister of the Holy Family, in her yearbook photo from Seton Hill College (now University). Courtesy of the Archives of the Sisters of Charity of Seton Hill, Greensburg, Pennsylvania.

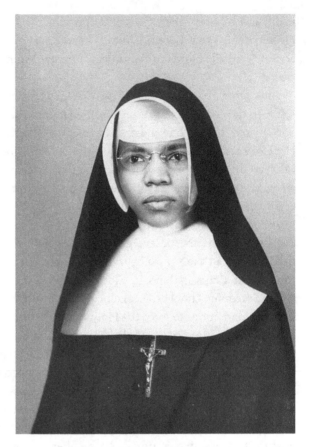

Black superior with the creation of a summer school at the OSP's mother-house.[143] Initially led by Brother Simeon Jolivet and the Oblates who already had degrees, the OSP summer school provided sisters who entered the order without teaching diplomas the critical training necessary to begin classroom instruction.[144] However, with the expansion of state laws requiring teachers at private schools to have normal certificates and bachelor's degrees in order for those schools to be accredited, Fieldien and her successor, Mother Mary Consuella Clifford, increased their appeals to the white sisterhoods and male religious orders that operated colleges in order to meet the new standards and secure their schools' accreditation. With the support of a small cadre of willing white provincials and school administrators, they secretly became the earliest Black students at Mount St. Scholastica College (now Benedictine College) in Atchison, Kansas, in 1923; Villanova College (now University) in Villanova, Pennsylvania, in

1924; St. Louis University in St. Louis, Missouri, in 1927; and the College of Notre Dame of Maryland—the nation's first Catholic college for women to award a four-year bachelor's degree—in Baltimore in 1929.[145] Unlike the SSF in their arrangement with Loyola, OSP members physically desegregated these institutions, though most often only their extension and summer classes.

By the early 1930s, OSP leaders set their sights on reintegrating the Catholic University of America (CUA) in Washington, DC. Founded by US bishops as an institution of higher learning for men, the CUA had accepted Black applicants from its foundation in 1889.[146] However, beginning in 1914 and in response to increasing anti-Black antagonisms in the nation's capital, including President Woodrow Wilson's authorization of segregation within the federal government, university leaders placed a moratorium on admitting American-born Black students. When the ban persisted after the conclusion of World War I, Black lay Catholics organized on the local and, soon, national level to address it and the broader practice of racial segregation and exclusion in the Church. The series of white-on-Black massacres that swept the country, including Washington, DC, during the summer and fall of 1919 only intensified Black Catholic concerns about the clear emergence of a color line at the CUA. [147]

On November 3, 1919, Howard University professor Dr. Thomas Wyatt Turner, writing as chairman of a Washington, DC–based group calling themselves the Committee for the Advancement of Colored Catholics, sent a twenty-page typed missive to Giovanni Vincenzo Cardinal Bonzano, the Vatican's Apostolic Delegate to the United States. After outlining the Jim Crow conditions African American Catholics experienced, he pointed to the Church's continued neglect of the Catholic education of African American children. Especially disconcerting to Turner was the abrupt change in the admissions policy at the Church's national university, especially the refusal of the Catholic Sisters' College at the CUA to admit Black nuns to its summer session.[148] "Catholic authorities have gone far ahead of non-Catholics and far ahead of city, civic practices in oppressing and discriminating against their fellow Catholics," Turner wrote to Bonzano in 1919.[149]

For the OSP, the Catholic Sisters' College at the CUA was their desired choice for higher education. Opened in 1911, the college was organized to provide teacher training primarily to sisters. However, it was also open to female public and private schoolteachers. By 1919, the college had instructed over 200 white laywomen and 1,800 sisters representing 151 congregations from across the United States and Canada. Because of the CUA's position as the national Catholic university and its proximity to their motherhouse in Baltimore and their ministries in Washington, DC, the Sisters' College was ideal. However, efforts to persuade university officials to lift the ban on Black people would take more than a decade and the rise and fall of another powerful Black lay organization, the Federated Colored Catholics of the United States (FCC).[150]

Organized in 1924, the FCC, led by Turner, was an outgrowth of the Committee against the Extension of Race Prejudice in the Church, and part of its mission was "to advance the cause of Catholic education throughout the Negro population."[151] As a Black lay-led organization, the FCC promoted racial pride and Black self-determination and called for an immediate end to racial segregation in the Church, especially in education. The organization found the systematic exclusion of African American Catholic teaching sisters from most Catholic colleges and universities especially egregious. As a result, its Black leaders, many of whom were also founding members of the National Association for the Advancement of Colored People (NAACP), were often at odds with its white clerical members, who both resented Turner's leadership and feared reprisals from whites if segregation ended.[152]

Before 1930, the FCC's relationship with the Black sisterhoods was informal. Turner was an active member of Washington, DC's historically Black St. Augustine parish, whose school had been staffed by the OSP since 1908. While the OSP certainly had known about the FCC since its founding, members did not formally participate until 1929 when eight Oblates attended the convention's High Mass at Baltimore's St. Peter Claver Church. In 1930, at the sixth convention in Detroit, the FCC made a special appeal for equal opportunities for Black Catholic boys and girls "called to the priesthood or to the religious life" and for them "to receive such educational facilities as are necessary for the same."[153] One year later, fourteen OSP members (ten stationed in St. Louis and four from Baltimore) and two SSF members from New Orleans participated in the FCC convention as delegates, with OSP Mary Laurentia (Catherine) Short (figure 2.7) delivering an appeal for support for her congregation's fight against segregation in Catholic higher education. Noting that it was a "source of pride" for her order to contribute to the advancement of Black literacy and higher education, Short argued that "nothing is too good for the youth of our race" and called the Black Catholic community to stand behind her order "by founding scholarships, establishing burses, and making generous contributions towards providing

FIGURE 2.7. Washington, DC, native Sister Mary Laurentia (Catherine) Short matriculated at Saint Louis University in 1927. She earned her AB in education in 1935, quietly becoming the Jesuit institution's first Black graduate. Courtesy of the Archives of the Oblate Sisters of Providence, Baltimore, Maryland.

university training."[154] Such, Short declared, was critical if the OSP were to be successful in helping Black youth reach "the highest potentialities of the race" and become leaders in their communities.[155]

At the 1931 meeting, FCC delegates also openly condemned lynching and US imperialism; passed resolutions "demanding equality of opportunity in worship, education, and economics"; and "expressed their resentment at being called a 'problem' by whites," presumably including priests and sisters.[156] Such proclamations drew praise within the African American protest community and aligned the FCC with the most militant Black civil rights organizations of the era.

The FCC's increasing radicalization, however, drew widespread criticism from white Church leaders. Following the 1931 meeting, white priests ministering in the African American community mobilized to derail the organization, offended by its blistering critiques of white Catholic racism.[157] Led by Jesuit Fathers John LaFarge and William Markoe, the priests devised a plan to oust Turner from his own organization, reorganize the FCC under a different name (which erased its African American roots and leadership), and transform it into a moderate entity that advocated "interracialism" and a gradualist approach to desegregation, successfully doing so at the 1932 and 1933 meetings.[158] Josephite Father John Gillard, the paternalistic white OSP chaplain who fiercely supported the sisters' efforts to obtain Catholic higher education, also worked behind the scenes to discredit Turner and undermine attempts by former members to reorganize the FCC under its original name, mission, and leader.[159]

Despite the subversion of Turner's leadership, the FCC's efforts at forcing the CUA to lift its ban on African Americans between 1931 and 1933 paid off. In 1932, Baltimore archbishop Michael Joseph Curley, the FCC's spiritual adviser, began exerting pressure on CUA administrators to again admit African American students to the school's summer sessions. In a June 6, 1932, letter to Bishop James Hugh Ryan, the CUA's rector and president, Curley specifically advocated the admission of the OSP. "I am afraid we are going very far now yielding to prejudice when we exclude the Colored Sisters from the school," he wrote. "It is a matter that I really think should get some consideration."[160] While Curley did not say what precipitated his actions, the FCC's growing militancy and Black sisters' steady demand for Catholic higher education were undoubtedly influential.

In fact, two months after Curley wrote to Ryan, the FCC penned a letter to Pope Pius XI pleading for an end to racially discriminatory practices in the Church, specifically citing the CUA case. Noting that Black Catholics supported the university through annual collections, the FCC pointed out that the CUA regularly accepted non-Catholic white students, while several elite white colleges and universities admitted African Americans.[161] However, Curley remained cautious.[162]

The timidity with which even progressive white Church authorities approached racial injustice, however, threatened the integrity of the Black-administered Catholic educational system. It was also the root cause of the 1933 crisis at Charleston's IC High School. In fact, when Bishop Walsh attempted to blame Mother Clifford (figure 2.8) for failing to provide "a properly qualified staff" for IC's high school department, the fifty-year-old Black superior took the forty-one-year-old white bishop to task.[163] Clifford maintained Church-mandated deference when she wrote to Walsh in August 1933, even as she eloquently outlined the race-specific challenges that her order faced in the struggle for school accreditation. "We are taking every opportunity to make our Sisters as well equipped for the class room

FIGURE 2.8. Mother Mary Consuella (Rebecca) Clifford. Courtesy of the Archives of the Oblate Sisters of Providence, Baltimore, Maryland.

as any white Sisters," she wrote. "It might truly be said that if Catholic institutions of higher learning had opened their doors to our Sisters sooner and with greater welcome, neither Your Excellency nor I would be in the present embarrassing situation as regards the Immaculate Conception High School."[164] In this rare rebuke, Clifford found Walsh's indignation unjust when he, along with the rest of the hierarchy, remained silent and complicit in the Church's institutional racism.

To stave off the crisis at IC, Clifford suggested that the bishop secure two degreed teachers from Xavier College for the upcoming school year to ensure state approval of the high school diplomas to be awarded in the spring. The superior then guaranteed Walsh that she would have two additional degreed Sisters to send to Charleston the following year.[165] However, the long-term fate of the high school department rested on the shoulders of Mary of Good Counsel (Helena) Baptiste and Mary Consolata (Lydia) Gibson, whom OSP leaders had selected to integrate the Catholic Sisters'

College during the 1933–34 academic term. For the CUA's 1933 summer term, OSP leaders had brokered a secret agreement with Archbishop Curley, their chaplain, and select university officials to permit Gibson and two additional OSP members to attend.

However, the agreement brokered for Baptiste and Gibson for the 1933–1934 term, according to OSP records, held higher stakes. If Baptiste and Gibson earned superior grades, CUA officials agreed to reopen all its classrooms to all African Americans permanently.[166] And like most Black women desegregation pioneers before and after them, the two Black nuns did not falter. On June 13, 1934, Baptiste and Gibson earned their bachelor's degrees from the CUA, becoming the institution's first Black graduates in more than a decade and its first Black women graduates.[167] While their academic excellence ensured the formal termination of the school's ban on African American students, informal barriers and challenges remained for future Black students.[168] Nevertheless, three months later, Gibson and Baptiste joined the IC high school staff, ensuring its permanent state accreditation one year later. Although the Avery Normal Institute is widely considered the first accredited secondary school for African Americans in Charleston, records indicate that IC granted its first state-certified high school diplomas in 1934, one year before Avery, and was formally recognized as a state-accredited school in 1935, the same year as Avery.[169]

Over the next five years, the OSP quietly desegregated the academic-year sessions at Rosary College (now Dominican University) in River Forest, Illinois, in 1937 and Maryville College (now University) in St. Louis, Missouri, by 1938. In 1940, OSP members also took special summer courses at Webster College (now University) in suburban St. Louis.[170] Like their secret admission at St. Louis University in 1927, the entry of these OSP members at Webster, led by the Sisters of Loretto, did not result in the immediate termination of the institution's formal ban on Black students. Instead, it simply permitted Black sisters to obtain the academic credits they needed to secure state approval of their institutions and expand their educational ministries. By 1941, the OSP operated four of the nation's forty-eight Black Catholic high schools, and two of those institutions (IC in Charleston, South Carolina, and St. Frances Academy in Baltimore, Maryland) had state approval.[171] In the case of the OSP's St. Rita's Academy in St. Louis, which earned its accreditation from the all-white University of Missouri in 1945, it was the first of only two Black Catholic high schools to operate in the archdiocese of St. Louis during the Jim Crow era.[172]

AFRICAN AMERICAN SISTERS' FIGHT to obtain school accreditation had far-reaching consequences for the Black community and the Church as a whole. By 1941, the Black teaching sisterhoods operated an elite network of parochial schools and boarding academies for the African American community. In fact, during Jim Crow, the OSP, SSF, and FHM (in 1931 FHM members became some of the earliest Black students at Manhattan College) administered many of the highest-ranked schools for African Americans in Louisiana, Texas, Maryland, Missouri, South Carolina, and New York City.[173] In 1941, only three of the fifteen nonaccredited Black Catholic high schools in the nation were led by Black nuns. By contrast, the white SBS and the Franciscan Sisters of Baltimore, formerly of Mill Hill, operated five of these nonaccredited institutions, while the two Black Catholic high schools operated by white male orders both lacked state approval.[174]

Because white congregations' discriminatory practices and exclusionary admissions policies continued to limit their effectiveness in crucial ways, schools led by Black sisters remained desirable to many African Americans, especially as the Black Catholic community began to migrate out of the South. In response to complaints from Black Catholic migrants unsatisfied with the work of white orders, white pastors and bishops continued to flood Black orders with requests to start schools in their respective locales. In one poignant example from 1932, Jesuit Father Arnold J. Garvy, a professor at Loyola University in Chicago, appealed to the OSP to come there and assist the SBS in the Black apostolate, noting that while the white sisters "did very excellent work," they "did not at all satisfy the colored people for representatives of their own race." In addition to acknowledging the Church's neglect of Chicago's growing Black community, Garvy documented that an increasing number of Black female vocations were being lost owing to the discriminatory admissions policies of local white sisterhoods. Garvy mentioned specifically "a remarkable young colored girl" who had "for seven years . . . been wishing to become a Sister" and had established a "catechetical center" to meet the spiritual, educational, and social needs of the city's growing Black Catholic population. That same year, the woman and two other Black Catholic women in Chicago (recent migrants from Louisiana) took their case to the annual FCC meeting in New York City. There they presented letters from "a group of ten or more" desiring "the establishment of a convent" in Chicago because of the "great and fertile field" there and their fears of being "hampered by the restrictions inevitable in the South" if they joined the OSP or SSF.[175] Ultimately, two members of the group did join the SSF in New Orleans with plans to help the order establish a convent in Chicago, while the leader of the catechetical center joined the FHM in New York City.[176] Chicago's first Black nuns, OSP members, did not arrive until 1941. They came in response to the efforts of a group of Black laywomen who in 1938 mobilized, fundraised, and successfully appealed to Chicago archbishop Samuel Stritch to establish a Black parish (Holy Name of Mary) in the South Side's largely neglected Morgan Park neighborhood.[177] While the OSP would face virulent opposition to their leadership from the parish's first white pastor, who openly derided their intellect, regularly insulted the parish's African American families, and often terrorized the school's Black pupils, the Black sisters endured and eventually thrived in their ministry.[178]

Over the next two decades, Chicago's Black Catholic community would become the largest Black Catholic population outside of the South.[179] The midwestern city would also experience some of the most turbulent battles over public and private desegregation, with white Catholics, religious and lay, often leading massive resistance efforts.[180] While scholars generally attribute the explosive growth of Chicago's Black Catholic population during the Great Migration to the relatively small number of white sisters and priests who extended their ministries to the city's new arrivals, the circumstances that brought the OSP to the city and prompted interventions by Black laywomen in ministering to the needs of the city's Black Catholic migrant population before them underscore just how tenuous the situation was in the 1930s and 1940s. These accounts, along with the plethora of accounts of the mistreatment endured by Black youths and adults in white-administered Catholic institutions, also suggest that white Catholic racism and paternalism actually circumscribed the population increase in Black Catholics outside the South and hindered Black retention in the Church as the twentieth century progressed.

Indeed, two years before her order's arrival in Chicago, Sister Mary of Good Counsel Baptiste cogently outlined why Black sisters' leadership and expertise would always be needed in the African American educational apostolate in her master's thesis, completed at Villanova College. Like many in her congregation who had been denied admission to the orders of their white educators based on color, Baptiste, a former SBS pupil, knew well the limitations of white nuns teaching in Black communities and the deficiencies caused by their racial antagonisms, even if unconscious. In addition to highlighting the leading roles that Black nuns played in nurturing and preserving Black vocations to religious life, Baptiste documented the mistreatment that Black children in Black Catholic schools received from white nuns, who sometimes expected "less of colored children" and failed to develop what Black sociologist Kelly Miller described as the "best powers and possibilities of Negro youth."[181]

Baptiste even went so far as to describe the OSP as "conservative radicals," individuals who found the strategic balance between the radicalism of Black intellectuals and freedom fighters like W. E. B. Du Bois and Carter G. Woodson and the conservatism of Booker T. Washington. Baptiste, who then led her order's St. Francis Academy in Baltimore, also argued that Black sisters—like their secular counterparts in Black public and private schools—were consciously part of the African American freedom struggle. "Many . . . [Oblate Sisters] come from the South where they have lived under great injustice and restraint," she wrote. "They know the temper of the South which accepts as axiomatic white supremacy and they would be foolhardy to advocate any theory or system which would bring overt acts of violence upon their heads or the heads of their pupils. At the same time, they are not unaware of the injustices of this bi-racial set-up. . . . They are courageous enough to renounce wrong as wrong with no cringing on questions of morality."[182] Though Baptiste contended that successful teachers of Black youth had to equip their charges with "a wider perspective than that of the race," she maintained that a quality Black education always had to instill racial pride, which came "only after the child has learned that Africans have contributed to civilization along important, if unrecognized lines."[183] Baptiste's Black nationalist and activist vision of Catholic education would be realized and enhanced in OSP schools across the country in the decades that followed.

While segregation and exclusion persisted in the Church, the successful accreditation of schools led by Black sisters and the expansion of these institutions outside of the South undermined the practices of white supremacy within Catholic boundaries in significant ways. Black sisters' desegregation victories in Catholic higher education and their commitment to producing race leaders trained to chip away at racial exclusion also left the Church's segregation practices and policies on more unstable ground as Americans returned from World War II.

After 1945, assaults on segregation would intensify both within and beyond Catholic boundaries. As the Church expanded its "missionary" efforts in the African American community and assumed a leading role in the fight against communism, its segregationist practices increasingly became moral and political liabilities. The Second Great Migration of African Americans out of the South also had a monumental impact on the Church. While the

OSP and SSF joined the migration, an even greater number of white sisters entered the African American apostolate as white lay Catholics abandoned their inner-city parishes and schools to escape integration.[184] Tens of thousands of southern Black migrant children and first- and second-generation Caribbean immigrant children entered these institutions, propelling not only African American conversion rates but also an explosion of Black vocations to religious life. Although most white orders would continue to reject African American applicants, a small number of white priests and sisters joined Black Catholics in fighting to dismantle anti-Black policies and preserve the vocations of young Black women and girls desiring to enter religious life.

3. "Is the Order Catholic Enough?"

THE STRUGGLE TO DESEGREGATE WHITE
SISTERHOODS AFTER WORLD WAR II

I myself know of a congregation in a largely non-Catholic region of this country which has had requests to start schools in 19 different cities, but simply has not enough womanpower. The superior has had novenas made in honor of Blessed Martin de Porres for plentiful vocations—but if Blessed Martin de Porres sent her two dozen Negro applicants, it is quite doubtful whether they would be accepted. Many other institutes which complain about the scarcity of vocations have drawn a color-line on would-be applicants—yet continue to pray for more vocations to arrive at their door. —FATHER RAYMOND BERNARD, SJ, *America*

In February 1946, Mother M. Genevieve Crane, leader of the Religious Sisters of Mercy (RSM) in Chicago, received distressing news: a white priest was "sending in an application for two colored girls to enter the novitiate" of her community. Faced with what she described as "the problem of accepting colored girls as postulants," Crane wrote to her superiors in Washington, DC, asking for guidance and prayers.[1] Like all Catholic sisterhoods in the 1940s, the RSM, who operated one of the largest US networks of Catholic schools and hospitals, were always in desperate need of more members to support their ministries.[2] However, like most white female congregational leaders, Crane and the members of the Mercy General Council had no desire to admit Black women and girls into their ranks. This had been the case since the first RSM members arrived in the United

States from Ireland in 1843, and it remained true even as the congregation expanded its educational ministries significantly to the African American community during the Great Migrations of Black southerners and Caribbean immigrants to the urban North, Midwest, and West. As Mother M. Bernardine Purcell, head of the US Mercy Union, explained in an emergency missive sent to Vatican official Pietro Cardinal Fumasoni Biondi four months later, "The problem is forced upon us because of the number of colored students we now teach in our schools." In addition to admitting that "the Sisters in general would not welcome colored subjects" into the order's "present novitiates," Purcell outlined the challenges of creating a separate novitiate and eventual "all-Negro province," which the council had proposed, as they and other European and white American orders had previously done in Africa, Latin America, and the Caribbean to evade desegregation by African-descended candidates.[3] However, the global defeat of Nazism and changing Church teaching on racism left Purcell uneasy implementing policy without input from the Roman Curia, the Church's highest governing branch. "From your vantage point," Purcell wrote Fumasoni Biondi, "you have an all-overview of the colored question as well as an intimate knowledge of the teaching and attitude of the Church toward the problem."[4]

The anti-Black admissions policies and practices that systematically barred women and girls of African descent from entering white and white ethnic US sisterhoods had permitted only eleven documented exceptions between 1900 and 1944, with all but one involving candidates who could pass for white or were racially ambiguous.[5] No white order had terminated its exclusionary practices as a result of these admissions, and no records indicate that these orders even considered taking such steps. In fact, most white councils either unknowingly admitted these Black women or accepted them because the candidates were willing to deny their African heritage. Even then, white congregations never guaranteed Black candidates' acceptance or long-term security. For example, in 1930, the RSM in St. Louis, Missouri, dismissed Mildred Dolbear, a postulant from Mobile, Alabama (figure 3.1), after someone from the "former Mobile motherhouse" alerted the Mercy council in DC to Dolbear's Afro-Creole heritage, including a grandmother of "pure negro blood and black in color." Mother M. Carmelita Hartman, the first elected head of the US Mercy Union, told her subordinate in St. Louis in December 1929, "I hope she is not already in the novitiate because I could not allow her to remain."[6] In the one documented case before 1944 in which a white order accepted a visibly

FIGURE 3.1. After her dismissal from the Religious Sisters of Mercy in 1930, Mildred Dolbear entered Monte Maria Monastery of the Visitation in Richmond, Virginia, where she successfully passed for white, professed vows as Sister Peronne Marie, and died in 1963. Courtesy of Marie Feeney.

Black woman, the Poor Clare Sisters of Bordentown, New Jersey, admitted Harriet Dayson, a "West Indian" native of New York City, in 1936 only "with the intention that eventually she would establish her own house." When the separate house never materialized, the order dismissed Dayson, a 1935 graduate of Hunter College, in 1941.[7]

However, the global campaign to defeat Nazism and fascism ushered in a monumental change in Catholic doctrine on race and racism. In 1943, the Vatican's formal endorsement of the doctrine of the Mystical Body of Christ rejected the legitimacy of racial and national distinctions and emphasized equality among the followers of Christ, signaling to some that Jim Crow segregation could no longer stand in the US Church. The propagation of *Encyclical Mystici Corporis Christi* and surging Black demands for civil and human rights during World War II also empowered a new generation of African American Catholics to push forward in their complaints against segregation and exclusion within Church boundaries.[8] Less than three months after the encyclical's release in June 1943, two young African American laywomen sought to enter Saint Louis University and Webster College, inaugurating an all-out assault on the anti-Black admissions policies of white Catholic institutions in the St. Louis archdiocese.[9] One year later, two other African American laywomen applied to enter the novitiate of the all-white Dominican Monastery in Catonsville, Maryland, and the debacle that followed ultimately secured the first major victory in the long struggle to desegregate US female religious life.[10]

Before World War II, formal complaints about white congregations' anti-Black admissions policies had emanated almost exclusively from Black Catholics. However, after the Dominicans in Catonsville rejected the two Black applicants in 1944, two professed sisters and a postulant left the order with a plan to establish the nation's first racially inclusive monastery. After numerous rejections from white bishops across the country, the three white Dominicans finally received permission to launch their radical experiment in Alabama, in the small rural town of Marbury, thirty miles north of Montgomery. "The purpose of this new foundation is the acceptance of Negro postulants who wish to lead the life of cloistered religious," Prioress Mary Dominic of the Rosary, OP, explained in the Josephite monthly the Colored Harvest soon after the monastery's opening in the fall of 1944. "Here every opportunity will be given to colored girls who feel called to the contemplative life to try their vocation and God willing, become one day Dominican Nuns of the Perpetual Adoration and Rosary."[11] In 1922, the organization of an all-Black contemplative branch of the Good Shepherd Sisters in Baltimore—the nation's eighth African American sisterhood—created the first opportunities for visibly Black women and girls to pursue such vocations in the United States.[12] The Dominican monastery in Marbury and the order's immediate admission of several young Black women, including Lalia Jones of Chicago and Geraldine Mouton of Lafayette, Louisiana, finally provided a second option.[13] News of the interracial monastery's founding also prompted a small number of white leadership councils, including that of the contemplative and former slaveholding Baltimore Carmelites, to begin rethinking the morality and utility of their policies.[14] However, more pressure would be required before most white Catholic sisterhoods would even consider opening their ranks to African

Americans. This was especially true of the nation's historically white apostolic sisterhoods.

Unlike contemplative orders, whose members have minimal contact with the outside world and whose primary vocation is prayer, apostolic orders engage in public works like teaching, nursing, and social work. Such realities meant that desegregating apostolic communities held higher political stakes and placed heavier responsibilities on the Black women and girls who sought to enter. Pioneering Black sisters often had to integrate not only their new order but also its institutions of higher education; other convents, schools, and/or hospitals; the parishes in which their congregations ministered; and the often racially hostile communities and sundown towns in which most white Catholic institutions were located. Moreover, unlike their secular counterparts who desegregated public institutions before and after *Brown v. Board of Education* in 1954, the Black women and girls who desegregated white congregations generally did so in severe isolation, away from the protection of news cameras and the Black people and institutions that had nurtured their vocations.

This chapter turns critical attention to this largely overlooked dimension of the post–World War II African American freedom struggle. Nearly two decades before Black civil rights activists launched their highly publicized "kneel-in" protests at southern white Protestant churches to test their tolerance for integrated worship and desegregate the nation's "most segregated hour," scores of young Black women and girls began battling for racial equality and justice in some of the nation's oldest strongholds of white supremacy and racial segregation: white-run Catholic convents and their affiliated institutions.[15] Between 1945 and the opening years of the Second Vatican Council, Black sisters waged private, public, and spiritual battles as they sought one of the Black freedom movement's most ambitious goals— radically transforming the hearts of white Christian segregationists from vessels of anti-Black hatred to facilitators of interracial agape love. In tracing the lived experiences of the first two generations of this forgotten group of Black freedom fighters, this chapter makes visible the tremendous courage and activism of these Black women and girls and the small cadre of white priests and sisters who helped them. It also documents the extraordinary lengths many white leadership councils and individual sisters—some of the nation's fiercest segregationists—went to evade meaningful integration, openly defying Church reform and changing racial attitudes.

Two years after the interracial Dominican monastery opened in Alabama, the Sisters of St. Mary (SSM), a nursing order founded by German immigrants and headquartered in St. Louis, made Catholic headlines when it announced it had admitted its first African American candidates.[16] In July 1946, Elizabeth Louise Ebo of Bloomington, Illinois; Hilda Rita Brickus of Brooklyn, New York; and Pauline Catherine Townsend of Washington, DC, became the SSM's first Black candidates. Five months later, African Americans Mary Antonette Gale of Pine Bluff, Arkansas, and Bessie Lee Hardy of Norfolk, Virginia, also entered the order, setting in motion one of the Church's most important experiments in racial integration after World War II. Rather than being a reactionary decision to changing attitudes in the Church, the SSM's desegregation had deep roots. It resulted from these young women's determined efforts to enter religious life and minister as nurses—something that visibly Black Catholic women could not do before 1946—and unyielding Black and interracial Catholic protest against segregation in St. Louis, especially between World Wars I and II.

In 1933, for example, SSM leaders made history when they reorganized their previously all-white St. Mary's Infirmary into the nation's first Catholic hospital and nursing school for African Americans. Before this, Catholic hospitals in St. Louis, as in most areas of the country, refused to treat Black patients.[17] Even the dental clinic at Saint Louis University's School of Medicine refused to serve the Oblate Sisters of Providence (OSP), though the university had secretly opened its doors to the Black order in 1927.[18] St. Louis's Catholic hospitals, usually administered by white sisterhoods, also refused to train or hire African American physicians, while Catholic nursing schools, also often administered by white orders, barred Black students.[19] Precipitated by decades of Black Catholic protests against their exclusion from the Catholic health-care system and the SSM's decision to build a new, all-white St. Mary's Hospital in the suburbs in the late 1920s, the 1933 establishment of the all-Black St. Mary's Infirmary and Training School, affiliated with Saint Louis University's School of Medicine, marked an important victory.[20] Although the opening of the Black St. Mary's did not overtly challenge segregation in the Jim Crow diocese, it did reflect the growing influence of Catholic interracialism and organized Black Catholic protest in St. Louis. It also signaled to many in the local struggle that the SSM might serve as a significant future ally.

During World War II, the ssm's indirect and direct support of campaigns to integrate the nursing ranks of the US military and Webster College in St. Louis, respectively, raised the order's public profile in the fight for racial justice even higher. Although the ssm was not affiliated with the National Association of Colored Graduate Nurses, the Black organization that initiated the protest campaign that resulted in the integration of the Army and Navy Nursing Corps in 1945, the St. Louis order took full advantage of the federal subsidies that created the US Cadet Nurse Corps in 1943 to combat nursing shortages at home and abroad.[21] Because the National Association of Colored Graduate Nurses worked to secure a nondiscrimination clause in the Bolton Act that created the Cadet Nurse Corps, 3,000 of the nearly 180,000 students trained as cadet nurses were African American. And among the over eighty young women who entered the cadet program at St. Mary's Infirmary was Elizabeth Louise Ebo, who expressed her desire to enter religious life.[22]

Also in 1943, ssm leaders publicly supported Mary Aloyse Foster's attempt to desegregate Webster College, garnering substantial attention in the national Black community. With other members of the Sisters' Conference on Negro Welfare, a small interracial St. Louis organization of nuns (figure 3.2), the ssm worked behind the scenes to secure Foster's admission to the all-white Catholic women's college.[23] Although the Sisters of Loretto (sl), who administered Webster College, initially agreed to admit Foster that fall, segregationist archbishop John Joseph Glennon secretly encouraged the nuns to reverse their decision, which they quickly did.[24] In response, Foster's supporters took their protest to the front page of the Pittsburgh Courier, one of the nation's most influential Black-owned newspapers. Unaware of Glennon's duplicity, the Courier's editors published a scathing open letter to the sl superior denouncing her leadership council's unanimous decision to rescind Foster's admission. Written by white Catholic interracial crusader Ted Le Berthon, the missive cited support for Foster from several white St. Louis priests and sisters who championed the young woman's devout faith, impeccable academic record, and strong work ethic. Among Foster's "enthusiastic" supporters quoted in the article was Mother M. Celeste, ssm, the superintendent of the Black St. Mary's Infirmary, where Foster had worked for a year and a half after graduating from high school.[25]

Despite the national publicity surrounding the Foster case, the sl did not reverse their decision. But the media attention and pressure from an appeal from Mattie Williams and her daughter, Ethel, members of the city's Black St. Malachy parish, to address the admissions bar at Saint Louis

FIGURE 3.2. Members of the historically Black Oblate Sisters of Providence were founding members of the Sisters' Conference on Negro Welfare in 1943. This 1946 photograph features some of the conference's members. Pictured from left to right: six Oblate Sisters of Providence (numbers 1 and 5 in second row, 2 and 6 in third row, and 1 and 3 in fourth row); two Sisters of the Blessed Sacrament (numbers 1 and 2 in bottom row); two Maryknoll Sisters (number 3 in bottom row and number 1 in third row); three School Sisters of Notre Dame (numbers 4 and 5 in bottom row and number 1 in top row); four Sisters of the Precious Blood (numbers 2 and 4 in second row, number 4 in fourth row, and number 2 in top row); six Sisters of Saint Joseph of Carondelet (number 3 in second row, numbers 3, 4, and 5 in third row, number 2 in fourth row, and number 5 in top row); and two Daughters of Charity (numbers 3 and 4 in top row). Courtesy of the American Catholic History Research Center and University Archives at Catholic University of America.

University (SLU) in the fall of 1943 prompted a small cadre of white Jesuits at the university to push their leadership to reconsider the ban on African American students there.[26] In the summer of 1944, SLU's admission of five Black students, though not Ethel, finally broke the color bar in higher education in the Jim Crow South. In the fall of 1946, Webster College became the second institution of higher education in the former slave South to knowingly admit an African American, Janet Irene Thomas, a non-Catholic.[27] While most of St. Louis's white Catholics and most of the priests and sisters teaching at SLU and Webster vigorously opposed integration, the installation of Joseph Ritter in the episcopacy following then-cardinal Glennon's death in 1946 ensured that segregation in the archdiocese would finally be addressed on the ecclesial level.[28]

But although the SSM proved invaluable allies to St. Louis's Black Catholic community in their fight against racial barriers in education and health care, its leaders' commitment to racial equality literally stopped at the doors of their motherhouse. It is unknown whether any Black women or girls sought admission to the SSM before its Black hospital and nursing school opened in 1933. However, community records indicate that Popes Pius XI and Pius XII verbally encouraged SSM superiors "to found a Negress nursing community" as early as 1930.[29] Archdiocesan records also reveal that sister-instructors at St. Mary's began rebuffing student inquiries and requests to join the nursing order from the first day of class in 1933. The SSM leaders initially denied these requests by simply citing "the difficulty and racial question." But the congregation's involvement in the Sisters' Conference on Negro Welfare, the US Cadet Nurse Corps, and the Foster case gave aspiring candidates and a handful of supportive white priests the necessary moral ammunition to push the order to act.[30]

In 1943, Hilda Rita Brickus, a cradle Catholic from Brooklyn, New York, wrote to Father Alphonse Schwitalla, dean of the School of Medicine and Nursing School at SLU, informing him of her desire to enter nursing school and pursue a vocation to religious life. Although Schwitalla denied Brickus's request to enter SLU, he put her in contact with SSM superior Mother Mary Concordia Puppendahl, who invited her to finish her education at the city's Black St. Joseph High School with the expectation that she would enter St. Mary's soon thereafter. It is not clear if Schwitalla or the SSM explicitly told Brickus that she could enter the SSM in 1943, but she traveled to St. Louis that year under the impression that she would be permitted to do so. She also lived with the SSM on a segregated basis at St. Mary's Infirmary while completing her high school education, which she did in

1945. However, the SSM forced Brickus to wait another year before accepting her.[31] This was because SSM leaders had no intention of accepting Brickus on an equal basis—or the eight other Black candidates who had expressed interest in joining their community between 1943 and 1945. In a letter to Pope Pius XII in 1944, Puppendahl revealed that they had delayed establishing a Black nursing order for financial reasons and because of their unwillingness to have Black and white women living together on equal terms. There was "no building near St. Mary's Infirmary in which to house the Postulants and Novices," Puppendahl claimed, indicating that the Black candidates would not live with the white candidates admitted into the order the same year.[32]

Although Puppendahl led the Black candidates to believe they would be accepted into the SSM on an equal basis, SSM leaders worked behind the scenes to establish a separate, all-Black community that would not be affiliated with their congregation.[33] The SSM envisioned that "with careful nurturing in 25 to 30 years" this separate order would become autonomous and "qualified to assume complete control of the [Colored] Infirmary and convent."[34] The SSM's leaders also hoped that these Black sisters would eventually staff future Black-only Catholic hospitals across the nation, insinuating that the order eventually planned to withdraw from the African American apostolate.

Stiff opposition from the candidates, Archbishop Ritter, and several white priests ultimately forced SSM leaders to abandon that plan. However, they moved forward in establishing a separate, all-Black SSM branch, with Puppendahl arguing that the separation of white and Black sisters was paramount and nonnegotiable.[35] In addition to building a separate novitiate for their Black candidates and barring them from entering the SSM motherhouse out of concern they would "be affected by the contrast," the SSM general council planned to extend the customary three-year period of temporary vows for the Black postulants in order to "guard against what has been considered a common negro tendency to instability and irresponsibleness."[36] In her first communication seeking volunteers for their "new" Black hospital in 1933, Puppendahl had expressed a similar derogatory view of African Americans. "Our zeal for souls should make us rejoice even though the work is repugnant," she wrote. "He can't help that his face is black. We might also have belonged to that unfortunate race."[37] That such hateful attitudes persisted after SSM sisters had worked for thirteen years alongside Black physicians and nurses and treated African American patients at St. Mary's Infirmary reveals how deeply entrenched the congregation's anti-Black animus was. It also clearly documents the often-hidden forces of racism with which early Black candidates in white orders had to contend.

Because most observers remained unaware of white SSM leaders' segregationist commitments, the order's publicized admission of five visibly Black candidates in 1946 gave unprecedented hope to people nationwide who opposed segregation in female religious life. News of the breakthrough also encouraged other white orders to dismantle their own color bars. Three months after the SSM admitted its first three Black candidates, for example, the Missionary Sisters Servants of the Holy Ghost (later Holy Spirit), a white sisterhood working in the African American apostolate and headquartered in Techny, Illinois, issued a direct call for "colored" vocations in the *St. Augustine's Messenger*, a Catholic periodical published by the Society of the Divine Word and devoted to the Black ministries.[38] The magazine's editors also listed six additional white communities that had expressed willingness to accept "colored girls and young ladies as members."[39] Of those orders, three were contemplative. Two had ministries in the African American apostolate, and only one, the Marbury Dominican nuns, was located in the Deep South.[40]

The historic *St. Augustine's Messenger* list became the first draft of an unofficial guide to Catholic sisterhoods that Black women and girls and their spiritual advisers came to rely on when beginning the application process. Like *The Negro Motorist Green Book*, an annual guidebook that helped African Americans avoid the dangers and humiliations of racial segregation and white violence while traveling, this list (and those to come) offered institutional hope to Black women and girls seeking to enter white orders to whose missions and charisms they felt called.[41] It also further emboldened a small cadre of white priests and sisters committed to integration to begin publicly exposing the color bar in religious life and exerting pressure on other white sisterhoods to open their ranks.

Among this progressive cadre of white priests was Father Raymond S. Bernard, a Jesuit who began conducting formal investigations of white sisterhoods' admissions policies. In 1949, Bernard published an article titled "Jim Crow Vocations" that included an expanded list of US-based orders willing to accept "qualified Negro applicants."[42] Among these twenty-two congregations, only a few actually had Black members: the Missionary Sisters of the Immaculate Conception in Paterson, New Jersey, who accepted Olivia Williams of Austin, Texas, in 1947; the Religious of the Sacred Heart of Jesus (RSCJ) in the Bronx, who admitted twenty-four-year-old Mamie Louise Jenkins, also of the Bronx, in 1948; and the Ursuline Sisters in New Rochelle, New York, who admitted twenty-year-old Jennie Ellen Seabrook of the Bronx and Charleston, South Carolina, in 1949. While Williams was admitted right out of high school, Jenkins and Seabrook had desegregated their orders' colleges before entering religious life.[43]

Although the white orders willing to accept Black women and girls in 1949 represented only a tiny fraction of the nation's 650-plus Catholic sisterhoods, Bernard's list documented a clear change in congregations' public postures regarding racial segregation. It also gave the young and idealistic Jesuit hope. For Bernard, the Church's segregationist practices weakened its moral standing in the fight against communism and limited its evangelization efforts among Black people.[44] As such, terminating the color line in religious life was essential to preserving the integrity of the Church. "Distortions, misinterpretations, and prejudiced policy of some communities need to be balanced and offset by the disclosure of the unsuspected opportunity for Negro vocations," Bernard explained in 1949. "This listing given here will prove that restrictive admission is not official to the Church and will present true facts on a growing trend. It is bound to lead to the collection of more data and a long-range improvement, preserving the good reputation of those religious who draw no color line."[45] Over the decade, though, Bernard would learn that few white religious drew "no color line" and that anti-Black animus and segregationist practices in the nation's white and white ethnic convents would not be easily uprooted.

Confronting the Limits of White Mercy in the Black Apostolate

Before World War II, most Black female vocations to religious life were drawn from the South, where most Black Catholics resided and consequently where most white sisters and priests with ministries to African Americans labored. When confronted with admission requests from African Americans during this time, white religious, male and female, regularly cited secular segregation law and custom, which banned interracial equality and cohabitation (outside of domestic service), and generally tracked Black candidates to the Black sisterhoods. As mentioned, the Sisters of the Blessed Sacrament also falsely claimed that the leaders of Black sisterhoods requested that they not admit Black candidates so the candidates would go to Black sisterhoods instead.[46] Such evasive strategies allowed white sisters and priests to help preserve Black vocations while concealing and upholding formal anti-Black admissions policies.

However, as millions of Black southerners and Caribbean immigrants entered the urban industrial North, Midwest, and West after World War II, white priests and sisters who expanded their ministries to African Americans in those areas could not readily rely on the tactics of their southern counterparts. This was especially true if they expected to win souls and secure conversions among the new Black arrivals in their cities. While thousands of Black Catholic faithful participated in the Great Migration in the mid-twentieth century, most Black Americans who entered the northern, midwestern, and western strongholds of white Catholic America were not Catholic. Nonetheless, postwar white Catholic suburbanization and educational demands from Black parents not only fueled African American enrollments in Catholic schools but also precipitated high rates of Black conversion to the faith during this period.[47] Between 1950 and 1960 alone, US Black Catholics increased from 398,111 to 615,964, with dioceses in Los Angeles, Chicago, Philadelphia, and New York City doubling or nearly doubling their Black numbers.[48] As a result, white orders that expanded or adopted ministries to Black Americans in these areas experienced a marked increase in applications from Black women and girls, often their former pupils. Although secular law upheld the constitutionality of segregation outside the South, Church doctrines emphasizing the moral righteousness of social equality and the genuine desire of some white priests and sisters to maintain and spread the faith into Black migrant communities left the anti-Black admissions policies of white sisterhoods (as well as diocesan seminaries and orders of men) on shaky ground. So, too, did the Church's rampant anticommunism and the increasing belief among white Catholic interracialists that the Church's segregationist practices would push potential African American converts to join the Communist Party.[49]

Because applications to religious life required a letter of recommendation from a candidate's spiritual confessor, and African American parishes were long denied the leadership of Black priests, white priests ministering in Black migrant communities emerged as essential allies in the fight to integrate female religious life. However, many white priests belonged to segregated white communities, and some opposed admitting Black women and men into religious life. Those who may have opposed segregation on principle were still likely to direct Black candidates to Black sisterhoods out of legitimate fear that if Black women and girls applied to the white orders, they would either endure a racist rejection or suffer racial mistreatment if admitted. In 1949, a white Josephite priest ministering in Beaumont, Texas, expressed the latter sentiment to future Oblate Sister of

Providence Magdala Marie Gilbert when she decided to seek admission into the Maryknoll Sisters and asked him for a letter of recommendation. "Indeed not," the Josephite stated. "All that community is going to do is make you a domestic. I will send you to the Oblates in Baltimore."[50] Such attitudes and realities among white religious would continue to fill the ranks of the Black orders with candidates from across the country through the era of Vatican II.

Some white priests, however, began to challenge white female leadership councils to reconsider their discriminatory policies. In addition to providing enthusiastic letters of recommendation for Black candidates, these priests often wrote to white orders to ask about their admissions policies related to Black candidates. This enabled the priests to construct their own lists of congregations willing to accept African Americans while sparing those under their spiritual direction the pain of a racist rejection. It also permitted these men to appeal directly to white superiors and leadership councils in the name of catholicity.

In early December 1946, for example, Father John F. O'Brien, a white assistant pastor at Harlem's Church of the Resurrection, sent a brief missive to the provincials of all the white orders ministering in the New York City metropolitan area. While O'Brien simply asked each congregation for its admission requirements, he concluded with a searing moral question. "Is the order Catholic enough to accept colored vocations?" he asked. "I am in a colored parish and am immediately concerned with this information."[51] While his letter did not produce immediate changes, he put congregational leaders and others across the country on notice about an impending campaign to address the morality of their discriminatory policies.

Mother Mary Assumpta Knobbe, the RSM provincial in Tarrytown, New York, for example, directed O'Brien's query to the head of the Mercy Union, Mother M. Carmelita Hartman, then already confronting application requests from African American girls in Chicago. "It would be a help to know whether the postulants entering the Providence novitiate from Belize or candidates to any other of our novitiates are mulattoes or dark skinned," Knobbe wrote. "Any suggestion that you can make which will aid me to answer Father's letter prudently will be appreciated."[52] Hartman's response did not mention that the RSM had recently voted to permit the Omaha province to admit a Belizean candidate of African descent who could pass for white.[53] She also made no reference to the order's plans to establish an all-Black RSM province headquartered in Chicago. "I see nothing for you to do but tell Father O'Brien that we do not accept colored applicants," Hartman wrote. "Some of the postulants that have been admitted to the novitiates in Providence and Scranton are dark-skinned but they are not mulattoes. These candidates are Portuguese and therefore white."[54]

Hartman's position is instructive in two central ways. First, like many white orders at the time, the RSM had proven itself willing to admit African-descended applicants who could pass for white, especially those born outside of the United States. As early as 1938, for example, the RSM General Council discussed admitting African-descended candidates from their missions in Belize. This was nine years after Hartman called for removing Mildred Dolbear from the St. Louis novitiate for passing for white. While Afro-Belizean admission was "kept in abeyance " until 1944, the general council in 1945 approved the admissions request of "a young lady from [Belize]" with "colored blood on her maternal grandmother's side" whose "colored heritage [wa]s not perceptible."[55] She was admitted despite her "illegitimate" birth "with the proviso that she never be sent to Belize for duty," seemingly because the order did not want to encourage additional Afro-Belizean vocations then.[56] The general council's willingness to make an exception for this Belizean candidate confirms historian Irma Watkins-Owens's contention that white Americans held Black immigrants, especially those whose accents and cultural traditions aligned with European customs, in higher regard than native-born African Americans.[57]

Second, Hartman's strident opposition to admitting US-born Black women and girls in 1946 is also significant because the RSM was then perceived as progressive on race. While most Mercy hospitals across the country still refused to treat Black patients, the RSM, which operated one of the nation's largest and most distinguished networks of academies, universities, and hospitals, was among the earliest white congregations to expand its educational ministries to African American youth outside of the South after World War II.[58] In 1946, the RSM in Chicago, who constituted the order's largest US province by 1941, also made headlines when their St. Francis Xavier College graduated its first African American student and admitted three additional Black students.[59] Yet that same year, applications from two African American girls seeking to join the order initiated a panic, revealing just how much color, ethnic heritage, and segregation mattered at the highest levels of leadership.

The RSM's leaders in Chicago and DC not only characterized Black applicants as "problems" before they ever stepped foot inside the convent but also evaded desegregation by voting to establish a separate and unequal all-Black juniorate in Chicago for US-born candidates. The leaders were willing to establish the juniorate (for high school girls) only because they believed the order would be able to assimilate younger girls into the congregation's white and European culture more easily.[60] Although Vatican leader Pietro Cardinal Fumasoni Biondi endorsed the plan for the juniorate and eventual all-Negro province that year, the proposal was tabled after Chicago's Cardinal Samuel Stritch expressed concern about a potential backlash, describing his archdiocese as a place where "the problem of segregation" was "bitterly contested."[61]

Previously sealed records of white leadership councils between 1946 and 1954 offer invaluable insights into how far many white female superiors were willing to go to keep their communities "white" before the dawn of the modern civil rights movement put added pressure on the Catholic Church to address its practices of segregation and exclusion. Although the white congregations, like the RSM, had firm policies banning US-born Black candidates, most of these practices were informal. As such, local and national records, including general council minutes and correspondence between superiors, depict how the sisters individually and collectively devised ways to evade desegregation and even suppress Black vocations.

Some, like the Chicago RSM provincial M. Genevieve Crane, regularly complained about sister shortages while unapologetically rejecting Black candidates. In 1949, Crane even argued that the extension of the order's educational ministries to "several colored schools" had cut off their sources "for prospective white postulants."[62] In 1950, Crane's successor, Mother Domitilla Griffin, upheld the bar even as an internal survey revealed that 546 Chicago RSM members favored accepting Black candidates, with 269 opposed. In response, Griffin wrote, "I feel that many of the Sisters are not aware of the problems involved in this step," such as the "assignment for duty of colored girls teaching white pupils" and "the attitude of Pastors and parents if such should be the case." She also wondered how a policy of "assigning colored subjects to only colored schools" would be "accepted by the colored and by those in sympathy with them."[63] At no point did Griffin cite Catholic social teaching or plans to challenge the anti-Black attitudes of the 269 sisters who opposed integration. In fact, in November 1950, the Mercy council in Chicago concluded that "a separate Province" for colored candidates who met "certain requirements" was the only feasible answer.[64] Notably, that same fall Mercy leaders in Chicago expressed an openness to admitting a Chinese American candidate who had inquired about admission, underscoring the council's specific anti-Black animus.[65]

Despite increasing ecclesiastical demands for their labor, Mercy leaders from Portland, Oregon, to New York City continued to rebuff inquiries from African American women and girls through 1954.[66] The RSM General Council even instructed members in Chicago to deliberately suppress attempts to nurture Black vocations among their students. For example, in 1951, Sister Jean Marie Boyd, the white principal of Chicago's St. Malachy High School, identified a promising vocation in one of her students and asked whether she should help students nurture their vocations for the RSM community or direct them to the three white sisterhoods in Chicago then known to be admitting Black candidates.[67] In response, the RSM General Council strictly prohibited Boyd from both nurturing vocations and directing them to any other white orders, noting that the latter "would, in effect, be equivalent to stating that we have a policy of not accepting them."[68]

In another duplicitous move, RSM leaders in 1952 informed Father Raymond Bernard, who had inquired about their policy toward Black candidates, that the order had had a favorable policy toward the admission of "qualified Negro girls" since the previous year.[69] This was technically true because the RSM in Burlingame, California, had admitted a Black candidate in 1951, initially unbeknownst to and without the permission of the general council.[70] However, that same year, Mercy Union head Mother Bernardine Purcell supported the decision of the RSM superior in suburban St. Louis to reject a "colored" applicant. This came after the order's name appeared on the *St. Augustine's Messenger*'s list of novitiates willing to admit Black candidates. In a panicked letter to her DC superiors, Mother M. Hildegarde Schuman, RSM, wrote, "It is putting us in an embarrassing position to know how to reply. We do not think that a novitiate so Southern in sympathies and prejudices as ours, is at this time, ready to meet this issue."[71] Purcell advised the St. Louis superior to allow God's will to direct her decision and said, "I think you could truthfully advise the applicant in question to enter [another order] closer to home."[72]

In early 1953, while still working hard to keep African Americans out of their US ranks, the RSM General Council considered an appeal from the independent Sisters of Mercy in Jamaica—a branch "made up chiefly of colored, black, and Chinese Jamaicans" who sought admission into the US Mercy Union.[73] Despite Purcell's expressed belief that "this acceptance will present many problems" and her expectation that "future candidates would also be drawn from these sources," the council voted to admit the Jamaican Mercy Sisters to the Union that same year, underscoring white Mercy leaders' preference for Black candidates born outside of the United States.[74]

Such blatant contradictions in the order's policies toward US Black candidates and African-descended candidates elsewhere forced the RSM leaders to develop a more concrete policy in 1953. One month after the vote to accept the Jamaican Mercy Sisters, Purcell instructed the mother provincials and sister mistresses under her authority how to respond to inquiries from "interested members of the clergy" and others regarding the admission of US-born Black candidates. She maintained that the congregation could not "as an Institute establish a policy for the acceptance or rejection of such applicants" because "such a policy would . . . be contrary to the wishes of Holy Mother Church." However, the superior described "the admission of Negro and other dark-skinned girls" as "a local problem." She told her subordinates that an African American accepted into the order "should be of superior type, preferably above average in character and education, with a good social and religious background," which she argued "would compare very favorably with the other Sisters." This policy enabled the RSM to publicly champion their "sisters of Negro blood" in their missions outside the United States, while still upholding their informal bar on US-born Black candidates, making exceptions only for extraordinary African American applicants.[75]

Over the next decade, the RSM continued to expand their educational ministries to African Americans, while remaining deeply committed to anti-Black exclusion in their ranks. Two years after the *Brown* decision, the RSM in Philadelphia admitted the order's first US Black candidate who would remain. In the mid-1940s, two of Cora Marie Billings's maternal aunts, who later became Oblate Sisters of Providence, had suffered racist rejections from the Mercy congregation in Philadelphia.[76] Thus, when Billings, the great-granddaughter of an enslaved man who labored for the Jesuits at Georgetown University, was admitted (figure 3.3), she aimed to persevere in religious life no matter what. She would become one of fewer than six African American RSM members to do so. In the Chicago province, where the RSM taught thousands of African American students and where the Black Catholic community experienced its greatest growth during the twentieth century, records indicate that the order never accepted a single Black candidate.[77] These realities not only underscore the conspicuous limits of the Mercy charism when it came to African American applicants but also expose white sisters' inability to see past race and color even when admitting Black candidates could have expanded their ministries, ensured the growth of their congregations, and produced potentially hundreds of additional vocations to religious life.[78]

FIGURE 3.3. Cora Marie Billings, seen here at her 1956 reception ceremony, is also believed to be the first self-identified African American admitted into a white sisterhood in the Philadelphia archdiocese. Billings, who took the religious name of Marie Immaculée, is the maternal granddaughter of John Aloysius Lee Sr., the second African American graduate of Philadelphia's historic Roman Catholic High School, and the great-granddaughter of William Henry Lee, an enslaved man who labored for the Jesuit priests at Georgetown College (now University) in Washington, DC. Courtesy of Sister Cora Marie Billings, Religious Sister of Mercy.

The Impact of the *Brown* Decision

Although the US Catholic bishops waited four years to publicly endorse the 1954 *Brown* decision and even ignored a deathbed order from Pope Pius XII on October 8, 1958, while doing so, select white bishops, priests, and sisters committed to desegregation used the landmark decision ruling segregation in public schools unconstitutional to push white orders to open their ranks to Black women and girls.[79] In some cases, individual sisters extended invitations to their Black pupils with clear vocations to religious life. Others continued to write letters of inquiry on behalf of Black candidates and visit white superiors to personally advocate for young Black women in their parishes and dioceses. However, most white congregations remained firmly opposed to the desegregation of their ranks by African Americans.

In the 1950s, Father Raymond Bernard became deeply aware of the extent of the anti-Black animus present in white congregations when he conducted three questionnaire surveys among the nation's female congregations to ascertain their policies regarding the "admission of qualified Negro girls" and published the results.[80] Although the number of white communities open to accepting African American candidates steadily increased, Bernard's surveys, conducted in 1951, 1954, and 1957, revealed that it never constituted even half of US orders. In 1951, for example, only 156 of the 553 US novitiates surveyed had policies allowing admission of "qualified Negro girls"; 51 responded unfavorably, 66 were doubtful, and the remaining 280 communities failed to respond. In 1954, out of the same 553 novitiates, 193 had favorable admissions policies, 19 responded unfavorably, 5 were doubtful, 127 were "unsettled officially," 23 stated "no policy given," and 186 communities failed to respond.[81] Although 290 orders reported to Bernard in 1957 that they had favorable admissions policies toward Black candidates, he found in 1958 that roughly 55 percent of the 355 African Americans who inquired about admission to the favorable respondents of his 1957 survey had not carried through with their applications or remained with their orders.[82] For Bernard, the results, especially the vocational losses, not only documented the persistence of anti-Black admissions policies and practices but also revealed that expressed willingness to consider Black candidates did not always translate into sincere, permanent, or even actual desegregation. Indeed, when faced with increasing pressure to admit Black women and girls, many white orders continued to direct Black candidates to the Black orders. Many white leadership councils and vocational directors also developed new strategies to evade integration at every stage of the application process.

For example, many white congregations began requiring prospective candidates to submit photographs.[83] This became more common after 1954 as many Black applicants stopped identifying their racial background in their written inquiries. In the years before Catholic desegregation, spotting a letter from an aspiring Black candidate unknown to a white order had been fairly easy because historically Black Catholic schools and parishes often had the names of African and other Black saints, like St. Augustine, St. Monica, and Blessed (later Saint) Martin de Porres. Catholic directories also identified "colored" parishes with a special designation. Even when the name of an applicant's all-Black school or parish did not readily reveal her heritage, the order of priests and sisters attached to the institution usually did. However, the Great Migration and white flight dramatically altered the inner-city landscapes of the Catholic North, Midwest, and West. Some historically white Catholic schools gained notable populations of Black students or transformed into predominantly Black or all-Black institutions, save for the sisters and priests.[84] As such, screening applications for race became increasingly difficult. Indeed, when the vocational director of the SL in Kentucky received an inquiry from Marjorie Ann Rideau, a graduate of their Holy Name Elementary in Los Angeles, in 1955, the white nun wrote the order's local superior in California. Because Holy Name had undergone a demographic shift, Rideau's French Creole surname likely raised a red flag. As such, the Kentucky director asked the Los Angeles superior bluntly, "Do you know this girl? Can you tell us if she is a Negro?"[85]

In orders willing to seriously consider African American applicants, other obstacles remained. Although leadership councils usually voted on every candidate, some communities let their entire congregations vote when Black women and girls were under consideration, a remarkable exception in the otherwise authoritarian rule of pre–Vatican II orders. Such happened with the first Black women admitted into the Sisters of Notre Dame de Namur (SNDdeN) in California, Ohio, and Massachusetts.[86] And when Linda Taylor (later Sister Marie de Porres) applied to become a Sister of the Holy Names of Jesus and Mary in California, the leadership council asked the young women admitted with Taylor if they were okay with her Black heritage before the group ever set foot in the convent.[87] This was not done for white candidates.

Another strategy employed by white superiors to limit or block African American admissions was requiring Black applicants to take numerous medical tests to prove their physical and psychological "fitness" for religious life. In spring 1955, a white Sister of St. Joseph of Carondelet (CSJ) who taught at the moderately integrated Rosati Kain High School in St. Louis, Missouri, invited eighteen-year-old Barbara Moore (later Sister Ann Benedict) to apply for admission into her congregation. Though the invitation proved pivotal, Moore recalled that she had to take multiple medical tests at different hospitals before CSJ leaders approved her application that fall. Later, Moore, the CSJ's first African American member, discovered that her white counterparts were only required to have their blood pressure taken, suggesting that Moore's racial heritage was the true concern of the community's leaders.[88]

Color and ethnic heritage also continued to matter to white leadership councils and priests recommending Black candidates to white congregations.[89] In addition to sometimes championing only light-skinned applicants, whom paternalistic whites expected not to exhibit racial militancy and whose complexion would not readily reveal the order's desegregation, priests recommending Black candidates of Caribbean or Louisiana Creole heritage often made special note of this in their supporting letters.[90] In his statement for Loretta Hassell, who in 1956 became the first Black person admitted into the Sisters of Charity in New York in the twentieth century, Father Joseph Donachie, who used every resource at his disposal to secure Hassell's admission, attributed Hassell's "wonderful Catholic background" to the fact that her "parents are from the West Indies."[91] Similarly, in his recommendation letter for Marjorie Rideau's application to the SL, Father Michael J. Condon emphasized that Rideau's parents were Creoles and "of good stock."[92]

Reflecting the class and ethnic divisions present in many white orders, white Catholic obsession with color and ethnicity combined with anti-Black racism ensured that some light-skinned Black applicants continued to pursue racial passing to gain admission to or remain in white congregations.[93] The School Sisters of St. Francis even mandated that two of their earliest Black candidates—Elizabeth Holley of Colorado Springs, who entered the order in 1941, and Sandra Smithson, a Nashville, Tennessee, native who entered in 1953—pass for white and deny their Black heritage to their peers and pupils.[94]

Employing racial quotas was another way white orders limited the desegregation of their ranks.[95] Beyond the Sisters of the Blessed Sacrament, who initially restricted their admissions of Black women and girls to "two or three" per year during the 1950s and 1960s, a superior of the SNDdeN in Ohio explicitly told Helen Weind (later Sister Teresita) that she could not enter in 1960 because the order had already taken two Black candidates that year and thus had reached their quota.[96] In the case of the Oblate Sisters of Providence (OSP), between 1962 and 1963, its leadership council received a series of letters from one of their former students at Chicago's all-Black Holy Name of Mary School who had desegregated the Mantellate Sisters Servants of Mary in the 1950s and was requesting an immediate transfer to the congregation of her elementary school educators. According to Sister de Sales, the historically Italian order had decided not to admit "any more colored."[97]

It is unclear how many Black vocations to religious life were lost to this racist quota system. [98] But some Black women refused to be denied. Women, like Phillis Rae Johnson of Detroit and Yvonne Irvin of New York, followed in the footsteps of several of their nineteenth-century foremothers and left the United States to enter congregations accepting of their

FIGURE 3.4. Phillis Rae Johnson of Detroit, Michigan, professed her vows as Sister Marie Lutgarde at the Notre-Dame de l'Assomption Abbey in Rogersville, New Brunswick, in 1952. She remained in the French Canadian Trappistine order until her death in 1994. Johnson is one of at least nine African American women known to have departed the United States to enter religious life after confronting the anti-Black admissions policies of the nation's white sisterhoods. Courtesy of Lois Wheeler.

vocations.[99] Johnson sought to enter a female monastery upon her 1948 graduation from Wayne State College.[100] Although the Magdalens in Grand Rapids, Michigan, accepted their first Black member, Mae Frances Mallory, in 1948 and the Carmelites in New Hampshire accepted their first Black member, Shirley Snead (the 1949 valedictorian of the OSP's St. Frances Academy in Baltimore), in 1950, all of Johnson's admissions inquiries to northern monasteries from 1949 to 1950 were rebuffed.[101] Undeterred, she took French classes and applied to a French-speaking community of cloistered Trappistines in Canada, which she entered in 1951 and took the religious name Marie Lutgarde (figure 3.4).[102] After being rejected by every white sisterhood in New York City in 1957, Yvonne Irvin wrote to the Congregation of Divine Providence in Melbourne, Kentucky, to ascertain their admissions requirements, only to be rejected again when the order requested her photo. In response, Irvin studied French, becoming fluent, and applied for admission into the Congregation of Divine Providence's original branch in Saint-Jean-de-Bassel, France. In 1962, Irvin entered the French novitiate. One year later, she professed her first vows as Sister Antoine de Jesus.[103]

The obstacles faced by Black Catholic women and girls who sought entrance to the communities of white nuns to whose charisms they felt called underscore the inability of most US white female congregational leaders to exercise moral authority on desegregation. In 1959, shortly before he departed religious life, Jesuit Raymond Bernard lambasted leadership councils who continued to uphold the color line in an article in *America*. "Vocations come from the Holy Spirit, not from human administrators," he wrote. "Thus they are not to be thwarted by shortsighted humans who may raise the foolish fears of racist prejudice as an obstacle to the working of Divine Wisdom."[104] Yet the anti-Black admissions policies and practices of white congregations continued through America's civil rights years, resulting in the loss of hundreds, if not thousands, of Black female vocations and difficult journeys through religious life for those Black candidates admitted.

Massive Resistance behind Convent Walls

For many early Black candidates in white congregations, gaining admission was only the first hurdle; many faced daily obstacles that threatened to stop their progress to the profession of full vows. Some barriers were cultural. Indeed, white congregations that often reveled in racist caricatures of Black people, actively frowned on actual Black cultural traditions, including Black spirituals and gospel music, and promoted strict adherence to European food, linguistic, and holiday customs.[105] White congregational leaders also routinely failed to consider practical differences between Black and white women, such as differing hair care. For example, the Dominican Sisters of Peace in Columbus, Ohio, lost their first Black candidate, a young woman from Washington, DC, in 1946 after only a month, in part because the superiors disapproved of the candidate's need "take care of her hair" every three days.[106] Along a similar line, when Angela White and Ethel Baker of Washington, DC, entered the Sisters of Charity in Cincinnati in 1956, White immediately noticed the absence of Black hair-care products and Black-specific toiletries in the order's storage rooms. Although white hair-care products and other daily beauty and hygiene products specific to white women were regularly available, White and Baker had to use their limited funds to purchase such items on their own.[107] Such fundamental lapses of cultural understanding detail how ill-prepared white orders, even those open to integration, were for Black members. While some white superiors simply failed to consider such differences because of their limited or nonexistent experience with Black people, others explicitly demanded that their Black members assimilate to whiteness as well as to the rigid structure of the order.

Indeed, many rank-and-file members of white sisterhoods routinely engaged in behavior that pressured some Black candidates to degrade their racial heritage and assimilate to the local culture of their orders. In her early years at St. Rose Convent in La Crosse, Wisconsin, Sister Thea (Bertha Elizabeth) Bowman, who entered the Franciscan Sisters of Perpetual Adoration as an aspirant at age fifteen in 1953, routinely deflected questions and teasing about her hair texture and southern mannerisms. She also stopped breaking into song when she felt happy because her superiors disapproved. In one particularly disturbing encounter, one of the older members of the community told Bowman, "Black people go to nigger heaven together with the dogs and other animals." Because Bowman knew her parents, who had feared such mistreatment, would remove her if they learned of the abuse, she remained silent about her pain and endured what one white sister later admitted was the order's attempt to mold their first (and only) Black sister into "a southern Wisconsin white woman."[108]

While Bowman eventually learned how make her "Blackness" more palatable to her white counterparts, Sister Daniel Marie (Jannie) Myles confessed to internalizing the ubiquitous racism of her white counterparts when she entered the School Sisters of St. Francis in 1949. Myles was unaware of Elizabeth Holley's pioneering presence in the order since Holley had been instructed to pass for white and was by then away from the motherhouse. Thus, Myles went through the formation process desperately alone. "I tried to act and talk and live white, because it was the only way I'd be accepted at all in the convent," Myles remembered. "And I forgot my own culture, my own Black parents down South, and tried my best to be what the white nuns wanted me to. . . . The other sisters always laughed at me for the way I talked and walked. And I tried not to resent their laughter. In fact, I tried to laugh right along with them."[109] During her postulant days, Myles was also bullied to the point that she stopped speaking in class, which her classmates and others attributed to "Negro sullenness." The nun who taught Myles's freshman English class even told her, "There's only so far that you can go in this classroom, and that's up to a grade C. So it doesn't really matter if you don't talk." Despite such opposition, Myles continued to seek common ground and sisterhood with her white counterparts. "During Recreation time, I'd walk up to sisters and they'd turn away. . . . I used to pray to God to change me—change me and not them—so I'd be acceptable to them, and they wouldn't turn away when they saw me coming. Some of the sisters, when I tried a little group, would tell me, 'No, get out of here.' This was after I did everything I knew how to try to become white. . . . I was ashamed of being Black then and nobody really let me be as white as I tried."[110] Not until the entries of additional self-identified Black candidates in the late 1950s would Myles find friendship and sincere sisterhood in her order.

Like Myles, many early Black sisters faced obstacles designed to antagonize them and drive them out of religious life. For example, when Dolores Harrall, the first African American graduate of Boston's Bishop (now Cardinal) Cushing High School, became the first US-born Black person to enter the SNDdeN in New England in 1955, several of her white counterparts made it a point to show her during community meals that they would not touch or use the same cups, plates, and utensils she did. Others regularly burned Harrall's bedsheets and mattresses rather than use them after she did. During community swimming activities, Harrall also routinely suffered the indignity of watching her white counterparts depart the pool immediately after she entered.[111]

Not every Black woman and girl who entered a white order experienced such hateful resistance to their presence. Sister Francesca (Edeve) Thompson, who was racially ambiguous in her religious habit, reported that she faced no significant racial animosities when she became the second African American woman admitted into the Sisters of St. Francis of Oldenburg in Indiana in 1950.[112] Sister Rosella Marie (Janie) Holloman, the first and only African American member of the Sisters of Charity of St. Augustine in Cleveland, Ohio, to remain, also characterized her experiences with racism in religious life as benign. Holloman credited her superior and the relatively small size of her order with her exceptional experience. Unbeknownst to Holloman when she entered the order in 1950, her superior held a meeting of the sisters and instructed them that Holloman was not to be molested in any way based on her color. Earlier that same year, Floyd Begin, a white auxiliary bishop in the diocese of Cleveland and champion of racial equality, had visited the leadership council of every sisterhood ministering in the city and urged them to end their bans on the admission of African Americans. In the case of the Sisters of Charity of St. Augustine, established in the diocese in 1851, Bishop Begin gave the leadership an hour to decide during his visit. In response, the order's leaders took a hurried congregational vote, largely in favor of desegregation. While Holloman noted that a few members of her order rarely if ever spoke to her, they never acted on any overtly racist impulses.[113]

However, many early Black sisters in white orders faced routine physical bullying, deliberate ostracism, their white counterparts' refusal to use the same bathroom facilities as they did, and racist verbal taunts.[114] At her first profession ceremony, for example, five of the sisters with whom Sherrill Adams entered the Baltimore province of the School Sisters of Notre Dame (SSND) loudly yelled "nigger" in unison and snickered as she walked down the back path of the motherhouse to join her family. Adams, a cradle Catholic with deep roots in Louisiana, was also routinely forced to wait extended periods of time to be assigned to one of the order's schools to teach because most of her white counterparts steadfastly refused to live and dine with her on nonsegregated terms. Adams's admission to the SSND congregation had been subject to a general chapter vote in 1962, and such pernicious votes continued after she professed her vows. Indeed, Adams recalled that on more than one occasion white members of her order took votes on whether or not to accept her into their convents, teach with her, or simply host her for a meal.[115]

Some US Black sisters, like many Latina sisters, were also denied the opportunity to pursue higher education by their superiors.[116] Instead, they were relegated to in-convent domestic labor like cooking, "hidden in laundries," or forced to serve as telephone operators.[117] Such strident hostilities resulted in early departures by several pioneering Black sisters, many of whose records are closed to researchers. For those who remained, their early years in the convent were often devoid of socializing and friendship. While time and spiritual perfection sometimes won these sisters sincere friends and allies in their orders, many others persevered in their vocations in desperate isolation. Many also learned how to counter verbal taunts and attacks with smiles and deferential behaviors. "When I cried in my room at night, I made sure nobody knew it," remembered Sister M. Martin de Porres (Patricia) Grey, the first African American admitted into the RSM in Pittsburgh. "When I was with the sisters, or anybody for that matter, I kept smiling through my hurt."[118] Early in her tenure in the Pittsburgh Mercy community, Grey, who faced hate-driven harassment from several peers and her novice directress, also stopped talking, prompting one concerned Mercy leader to put Grey in art classes to help her express herself in a different way.[119]

Many white superiors and leadership councils anticipated the back-lash from members committed to white supremacy and segregation. Yet few did much to protect their early Black candidates. In 1956, when Angela White (who took the religious name Sister Mary Angela de Porres) entered her Cincinnati congregation, the bullying by the order's racist members knew no bounds. When the older white nuns harassed her with names like "pickaninny" and cracked jokes about not being able to see the order's Black candidates when the lights were turned out, White recalled, "I did not get angry. . . . I would just smile." She also prayed God would not allow her to become like the women who terrorized her. However, when the order's novice director repeatedly threatened White with expulsion after she began regularly experiencing sickness and fainting spells during community prayer, the eighteen-year-old began to crack. Unsure to whom to turn, White initially kept quiet about the emotional and psychological abuse. However, after another near-fainting spell caused her to leave community prayers again, White walked to an exit door of the motherhouse and stood there. After several hours, the superior of the community asked White to explain herself, at which point the teenager burst into tears and detailed what was happening to her.[120]

Although the local superior verbally reprimanded the offending novice director, she did not remove White from the director's supervision or remove the director from her post.[121] In fact, white sisters caught publicly bullying their Black counterparts were rarely punished for their actions, and no records indicate that white sisters who antagonized Black members or expressed racist sentiments were ever dismissed from their orders for those actions. Anti-Blackness, in other words, was not considered immoral or disqualifying for religious life.

White resistance to Black sisters also mounted outside convent walls as an increasing number of Black sisters professed vows and began working in their orders' hospitals and schools. Confused or repulsed by the sight of a Black woman in a religious habit, white adults and children often taunted and verbally assaulted Black sisters.[122] In hospitals and public health settings, white patients sometimes refused to be treated by Black sister nurses.[123] While stationed at a white hospital in Gadsden, Alabama, Sister Mary Ann (Mae Harriet) Henegan, an early Black Trinitarian nun, also vividly recalled a white male doctor who refused to address her as "Sister" while affording the title to her white counterparts.[124]

In school settings, some white parents openly questioned the credentials of Black sister-teachers and balked at their children developing positive relationships with their Black instructors.[125] Other white parents refused to permit Black sisters to instruct their children. In 1962, for example, outraged white mothers withdrew their children and picketed a Catholic grammar school in Chicago following the assignment of a Black sister to teach there.[126] Holding placards decrying the "black nun," the mothers sustained their public protest for several days.[127] Similarly, when SNDdeN John Bosco (Violet Marie) Dennis was assigned to teach math and science in Columbus, Ohio, in 1967, a cross was burned in front of the convent.[128]

Such vitriolic opposition to the presence of Black sisters in white Catholic institutions underscored the need for true moral leadership to ensure the retention and safety of Black sisters, and a few white sisters and priests rose to the challenge. After the cross burning, for example, the SNDdeN superior in Columbus threatened to expel any students who participated in the threatened boycott of Sister Dennis.[129] After Sister Cora Marie Billings was assigned to teach at the all-white St. Michael the Archangel School in Levittown, Pennsylvania, in 1961, shortly after the nationally publicized attacks on the community's first Black residents, the white pastor of St. Michael also acted to provide the necessary protection.[130] Years after her tenure at St. Michael, Billings learned from a member of her order whose father had participated in the Levittown violence that St. Michael's pastor had held a special meeting for the men of the community to inform them of Billings's impending arrival and instructed them to leave her alone.[131]

However, some congregations responded to real (and anticipated) opposition from white parents and students by forcing Black sisters to withdraw. Such was the case for Brenda Marie Williams, who entered the Sisters of the Holy Family of Nazareth (CSFN) in Chicago in 1957. Between 1898 and 1916, the historically Polish order had admitted at least three US-born mixed-race women—the adopted daughters of the community's first US provincial. But they did not admit another Black candidate until 1955, when Barbara Jean LaRochester of Brooklyn, New York, entered the community in Philadelphia.[132] Upon her own entrance as an aspirant in Chicago, Williams "learned to read and speak Polish" in preparation to teach in her order's schools. After completing three years of instruction at Loyola University Chicago and earning her teaching certificate, Williams also briefly taught in one of her order's Chicago schools. However, when the time came to profess her perpetual vows, the CSFN council refused to permit Williams to do so, stating only that "they felt her vocation was not for their Polish order."[133]

In a 1965 letter, the CSFN provincial superior, Mother M. Getulia, described Williams as "a polite and sociable person—easy to get along with others; thoughtful of others and helpful." She also characterized Williams as a "good student" with a "God endowed ... vocal voice" and "an avid reader." Nevertheless, the superior maintained that Williams did not have a vocation for their order, citing only Williams's "free excess to reading ... sometimes to the neglect of other duties."[134] During the early years of desegregation, white congregational leaders routinely cited potential opposition from white parents and students to the presence of Black sisters in white Catholic schools and parishes to justify their exclusionary policies. However, Mother M. Getulia's letter confirmed that sometimes the fiercest opposition to Black sisters' presence in white congregations emanated from within the convent walls. On July 16, 1963, CSFN leaders forced Williams to withdraw.

Williams's vocation to religious life would, however, be saved when she returned to Chicago's South Side and began volunteering at Holy Name of Mary School and Church, staffed by the OSP. Although Williams waited two years before sharing her story with the local superior, Mother Mary Angela Wade reacted swiftly. Impressed by Williams's work ethic and distraught over the mistreatment the young woman had suffered, Wade soon wrote to her own superior in hopes that the OSP leadership council would intervene, as it had done for several early Black sisters in hostile white orders in the previous decade. In 1965, Williams left Chicago and entered the OSP novitiate in Baltimore.[135]

As is the case with most Black women and girls who came up against the color bar in white sisterhoods and were pushed out for one reason or another, the specifics of Williams's story remain hidden from the public. However, white congregations' exclusionary practices came under a national spotlight after the Civil Rights Act passed in 1964. As an increasing number of Catholics, Black and white, entered the public fight for civil rights, other white Catholics led massive resistance campaigns to desegregation, marking a conspicuous dividing point in Catholic America.

In November 1964, ABC hosted a nationally televised panel discussion titled "Racism and the American Catholic" that aimed to shed light on the widening gulf between "the attitude of many [white] Catholics toward Negroes" and "the principles expressed by the American bishops" in recent pastoral statements condemning racism as a moral sin.[136] Joining three priests—two Black and one white—for the discussion, Sister Maria Mercedes (Aurelia) Oliver, the vocational director for the all-Black Franciscan Handmaids of the Most Pure Heart of Mary, focused her remarks on the enduring problem of the color line in female religious life. Like her fellow

Black panelists—Father Rollins Lambert, who in 1949 became the first African American ordained in the Chicago archdiocese, and Father Elbert Harris, who in 1960 became just the sixth ordained Black Josephite priest—Oliver blamed the Church's problem of racial division on white Catholic America and its long-standing failure to adhere to the Church's most basic social teachings when dealing with Black people. In addition to noting that the Church had lost "many Negro vocations to the sisterhoods because of the prejudicial policies of many religious orders," Oliver spoke at length about the disbelief and hostile reactions that she still regularly encountered from white Catholics, including priests, when she identified herself as a Catholic nun. When the panel's white moderator, Josephite Father Philip Berrigan, asked if the Church had "lost the Negro," Oliver answered no. "It has not lost the Negro provided that it recognizes its mistake and corrects it now."[137] Five months later, the struggle for Black voting rights in Selma, Alabama, provided the Church with a monumental chance to demonstrate its commitment to racial justice. It also brought a significant cadre of Black sisters into the streets in solidarity with the secular fight for civil rights and in protest against racism in the Church.

4. "I Was Fired Up to Go to Selma"

BLACK SISTERS, THE SECOND VATICAN COUNCIL,

AND THE FIGHT FOR CIVIL RIGHTS

[I am the] Ku Klux Klan's dream girl. I am a Negro, a Catholic, and a nun.
—SISTER MARY FRANCESCA THOMPSON, OSF

When Sister Mary Antona Ebo descended the steps of a chartered plane from St. Louis, Missouri, in Selma, Alabama, on Wednesday, March 10, 1965, Edmundite Father Maurice Ouellet, pastor of the city's only African American Catholic Church, momentarily stood still. Three days earlier, an all-white force of mounted state troopers, city police, and deputized citizens had teargassed and savagely beaten some six hundred peaceful Black voting rights marchers during an attempt to cross Selma's Edmund Pettus Bridge. The carnage of Bloody Sunday, as it was later called, had rocked the moral conscience of the nation and prompted the Reverend Dr. Martin Luther King Jr. to call the nation's religious leaders to Selma to stand in solidarity with the brutalized marchers.[1] Although Father Ouellet, who had secretly been active in the local Black freedom campaign, knew several priests and sisters were to be among the supporters to descend on the city that Wednesday, he never imagined that Ebo, whom he did not know, would be among them. "She was as black as black could be," Ouellet later reflected. "And, I said to myself oh my God this is going to make a difference."[2]

The evening before, Ebo had been shocked into silence when her superior asked if she wanted to join a local delegation of religious leaders heading to Selma. In the previous nineteen years, Ebo, who had desegregated the order in 1946, had gained a "bad" reputation for her outspokenness on racial injustice. After learning about the Bloody Sunday violence from the Black women employees at St. Mary's (Colored) Infirmary where she worked, the forty-one-year-old nun had even remarked, "I would go to Selma if I wasn't wearing this habit."[3] Yet Ebo had hesitated before accepting her superior's invitation. In addition to fearing the dangers she would face as a Black woman—nun or otherwise—especially if the interracial group was arrested, Ebo had learned from a news report of the recent (and ultimately fatal) beating of the Reverend James Reeb, a white Unitarian minister, by white segregationists in Selma. "I didn't want to be a martyr," Ebo later reflected. "But it was either put up or shut up."[4] Indeed, when a reporter en route to Selma encountered Ebo on the following morning and asked her if she feared being injured, she responded, "I'm willing to die," revealing the depths of her commitment to the civil rights struggle.[5] When given an even larger platform to speak in Selma, Ebo seized the moment again.

Though the sight of a Black nun caused shock among the protesters gathered at Brown African Methodist Episcopal (AME) Chapel Church, and though the members of Selma's white segregationist establishment believed Ebo was a random Black woman pretending to be a nun to inspire the marchers, all recognized the significance of her presence that day and the symbolic power that a Black Catholic nun could bring to the secular freedom movement. So did Ebo. Thus, when civil rights leaders singled her out among the six nuns from St. Louis to address the crowd at Brown AME and later to make a statement to the press, Ebo did not shrink from the moment. Nor did she waste the opportunity to explain who she was and why she had come to Selma.[6]

"I am here because I am a Negro, a nun, a Catholic, and because I want to bear witness," Ebo declared.[7] "I feel it is a privilege to be here today . . . yesterday being a Negro I voted, and I would like to come here to say that I feel that every citizen, every Negro citizen, as well as the whites, has a right to vote and should be given this right."[8] She also confirmed to reporters that she was "a Negro" and "very proud of it."[9] With her brief but poignant statements, Ebo entered the public record on civil rights in a powerful way. Her presence among the first sisters to join the Selma protest also signaled a change in the public postures and attitudes of the nation's Black Catholic nuns toward the secular fight for racial justice.

Before the liberalizing reforms of the Second Vatican Council, the rigid tenets of religious life and structural racism in the Catholic Church had precluded most sisters committed to racial justice from formally joining or publicly supporting secular Black political organizations. To be sure, the Black sisterhoods had quietly desegregated several Catholic colleges and universities, pioneered the teaching of Black history in the Church, and supported inherently political endeavors for racial justice in Church-affiliated organizations during the most brutal years of Jim Crow. After World War II, young Black Catholic women and girls were often active in Catholic interracial groups as well as secular organizations like the National Association for the Advancement of Colored People (NAACP). Inspired by the burgeoning civil rights movement and their own lived experiences of racism, they had also desegregated many white sisterhoods and scores of previously all-white Catholic institutions. Yet the white clerical gutting of the Federated Colored Catholics of the United States in 1933 and white resistance to their presence in religious life had forced most Black sisters to retreat from expressing their racial and political consciousness in white Catholic spaces. As one early African American Sister of the Blessed Sacrament later explained, "Entering an order meant ceasing to be Black and looking upon what you grew up with as uncouth. You could do the Irish Jig, but anything African was taboo."[10] However, Black sisters as educators and desegregation foot soldiers never discontinued their commitments to racial justice.

This chapter explores the diverse ways in which Black sisters responded to secular fights for civil rights and Black liberation, especially after the Second Vatican Council. Black sisters were only a minority of the nuns who joined civil rights organizations and demonstrations during the mid-1960s. However, their relative invisibility and public silence on racial injustice in the secular arena did not signify political complacency. Rather, a close examination of Black sisters during America's early civil rights years reveals that many continued their long-standing freedom struggles against racial discrimination and exclusion within Catholic boundaries. When able, Black sisters also joined marches for civil rights, spoke out against racism in the Church, and increasingly challenged the anti-Black attitudes and practices of white religious in their respective locales. Their efforts resulted in towering achievements and in some cases forced their congregational leaders and peers to adopt more progressive stances on racial justice in the years before and after the pivotal Selma protests.

The Hidden Civil Rights Struggles of the
Black Sisterhoods before Selma

Although a small number of Catholic archdioceses and institutions of higher education had initiated racial desegregation before the pivotal *Brown v. Board of Education* decision of 1954, the white-dominated Church had remained a bastion of white supremacy before 1965. At best, the Church's all-white and male hierarchy maintained an ambivalent posture toward African American demands for civil and equal rights. At worst, they were among the fiercest opponents of racial equality and justice. The US Catholic bishops, for example, were the last among the leaders of the nation's twenty-five major religious denominations to endorse *Brown* when they finally did so in late 1958.[11] Even then, their historic pastoral letter, "Discrimination and Christian Conscience," offered no proposals for action but rather commended a "method of quiet conciliation."[12] The bishops' lukewarm support of the civil rights movement not only exposed the limitations of their moral competency when it came to Black people but also informally endorsed the actions of white Catholics who, in places like southern Louisiana and later across the North and Midwest, emerged as some of the most virulent and violent opponents of desegregation in the 1950s and 1960s.[13] Thus, when Black civil rights leaders expressed shock at the substantial participation of Catholic sisters and priests in the Selma protests, few took offense. From the perspective of Father Maurice Ouellet, in fact, the *white* Church was abysmally late.[14]

However, Black lay Catholics played leading roles in the long African American struggle for civil rights from Reconstruction through the 1960s and spearhead the efforts that secured Church-mandated desegregation in places like St. Louis and Washington in the years before *Brown*.[15] Struggles led by Black sisters against racial segregation and discrimination within Church boundaries also resulted in some of the nation's earliest desegregation victories, especially in the South. Indeed, when the Reverend Dr. Martin Luther King Jr. in his 1963 "Letter from a Birmingham Jail" saluted Catholic leaders in Alabama for opening Spring Hill College to Black students in the late 1940s, he was unaware that Black sisters' needs and demands for higher education, not inherent moral fortitude, had forced the Jesuits to initiate desegregation at the institution.[16] Even then, Jesuits in the Deep South and in other parts of the country still resisted the desegregation of their own ranks by self-identified African American men.[17]

After World War II, as the congregations of the Oblate Sisters of Providence (OSP) and the Sisters of the Holy Family (SSF) followed migrating

African Americans out of the South, their members continued desegregating Catholic colleges and universities near their new ministries. For example, in 1949, eight Holy Family Sisters stationed in Tulsa, Oklahoma, desegregated Benedictine Heights College in Guthrie, Oklahoma.[18] A decade before, the SSF arrived in Tulsa to staff the elementary school attached to St. Monica Catholic Church, the city's first parish for Black Catholics, established in 1925 in response to the devastating Tulsa Race Massacre.[19] Holy Family Sisters also entered several northern Catholic colleges in the 1950s and 1960s, including Mount St. Joseph College (now University) in Cincinnati, Ohio; Cardinal Stritch College (now University) in Milwaukee, Wisconsin; the College of Saint Teresa in Winona, Minnesota (now closed); and Marylhurst College (now University) in Lake Oswego, Oregon.[20] Beginning in the 1940s, Oblate Sisters stationed in Chicago, Minneapolis, and Detroit became some of the earliest Black students at DePaul University, Cardinal Stritch College (now University) and Mount Mary College (now University) in Milwaukee, the College of Saint Teresa, the College of St. Catherine (now St. Catherine University) in Minneapolis, and the University of Detroit Mercy.[21]

Both the OSP and SSF also continued to desegregate institutions in the South. In 1951, for example, two SSF members—Mary Letitia (Florence) Senegal and Mary Catherine (Cecilia) Waiters—were awarded scholarships to the Loyola University Extension Program with Senegal becoming the first Black student to officially obtain academic credit from the institution.[22] One year later, Norman Francis, a former SSF pupil, entered Loyola University's Law School. In 1955, he became the institution's first African American graduate.[23] Recalling his primary and secondary education half a century later, Francis noted that a Holy Family Sister had encouraged him to pursue higher education and helped him secure a scholarship.[24] In 1950, OSP members Mary Immaculate (Naomi) Smith and Mary Anselm (Catherine) Bentley became the first Black women to enter Loyola University of Maryland and the first Black students in the institution's graduate school, earning their master's degrees in 1953.[25]

The Franciscan Handmaids of the Most Pure Heart of Mary (FHM) also continued in their commitment to racial justice through their educational and social service ministries in New York City and by 1950 back in the Jim Crow South (figure 4.1). That year, Mother Mary Agnes Eugenia Cormier, the order's fourth superior general, sent four members to staff Christ the King Mission School in High Point, North Carolina, invited by the Franciscan Friars of the Atonement.[26] In 1951, the FHM joined the Society of African

FIGURE 4.1. This group photo of the Franciscan Handmaids of Mary was taken in 1950 in front of their motherhouse in New York City shortly before the departure of its first members to take up an educational ministry in the South in more than two decades. Courtesy of the Franciscan Handmaids of the Most Pure Heart of Mary, New York.

Missions, their order's male founders, at St. Cyprian Mission School in Georgetown, South Carolina, and in 1953, the order accepted the invitation of the Josephite Fathers to administer St. Thomas the Apostle School in Wilmington, North Carolina.[27] In resurrecting the order's southern educational ministries, the FHM joined the OSP and SSF in providing Black communities with what they desperately desired: quality Catholic education administered by Black nuns.

Even after the *Brown* decision, Black leadership councils remained deeply wary of white-administered desegregation, and they continued expanding the Black-administered Catholic educational system. Notably, the OSP opened St. Gabriel's Mission School in the all-Black town of Mound Bayou, Mississippi, in September 1954. Established in 1887 by two men formerly enslaved by the brother of Confederate president Jefferson Davis, Mound Bayou was a revolutionary venture in Black political leadership, self-determination, and self-reliance. Mound Bayou was also the only Mississippi municipality free of segregation (save for the train station depot), and all its eligible Black citizens voted.[28] Thus, when Father John Bowman, an African American priest from the Society of the Divine Word, arrived to establish a Catholic mission in 1949, he wanted only Black nuns to assist him.[29] No records indicate that the Oblates at St. Gabriel joined any of the pivotal civil rights demonstrations that erupted in nearby towns in the 1950s and 1960s. However, their school served as a haven for scores of Black parents in the area who sought Black-administered Catholic education for their children. The OSP also voted in every election and readily assisted in local efforts to train Black voters how to pass tests that required them to read and interpret obscure passages of the Mississippi Constitution until 1965, when the Voting Rights Act made such examinations illegal.[30]

As white-administered desegregation began to threaten their schools and the wider Black Catholic educational system in the late 1950s, the Black orders also fought to ensure their members' expertise was not overlooked by white Catholics staffing schools. In 1956, for example, OSP leaders were forced to halt plans to take over a white-administered Black Catholic school in Kansas City, Kansas, where there had been some "racial difficulty," after local church leaders decided that the *Brown* decision discouraged segregation. However, that same year, OSP leaders in a historic move assigned two members to desegregate the faculty of all-white Holy Rosary School in Minneapolis, Minnesota.[31] In 1957, the OSP also agreed to staff Our Lady Help of Christians, an all-white Catholic elementary school in Saginaw, Michigan.[32] Unlike most of their white counterparts, the OSP had never barred any person from their ministries based on color or race. In fact, the OSP and the SSF had taught white children in their schools in the nineteenth century, before Jim Crow changed white attitudes and secular law and custom prohibited Black sisters from doing so. However, the burgeoning exodus of sisters from religious life and their subsequent withdrawal from white Catholic school faculties left many dioceses and archdioceses desperate for sister replacements, regardless of color. Hiring nuns was much cheaper than hiring lay teachers, and that fact likely guided many of these decisions. Nevertheless, the OSP jumped at the opportunity to help break down racial barriers on the parish level. The same was also true for the FHM, who in 1958 integrated the faculty of St. Cecilia School in East Harlem and worked alongside the all-white Religious Sisters of Mercy.[33] As in their Black schools, Black sisters taught their white students Black history, art, and culture.[34]

Because most white sisters in Black, white, or integrated schools still did not teach Black history in the 1950s, Black sisters' offering of Black and Black Catholic history curricula put them in the vanguard of racial justice through Catholic education during America's civil rights years. At the annual meeting of the National Catholic Educational Association in New Orleans in 1950, an unnamed "Negro nun" even indicted white Catholic educators for contributing to the problems of racism by reinforcing anti-Black attitudes in their schools. "It is fine to say that the teaching of love of God and love of neighbor applies to all men," she declared. "But the real question is: how far do you go with that teaching? Do you teach that your neighbors are not only the members of your family or the people next door, but the people of other races? I know that you have to be specific, because we have experience in our schools in teaching our children not to hate the white children."[35] She openly questioned whether white Catholic educators, religious and lay, instilled the same explicitly antiracist values in their white and non-white students.

As many white Catholics mobilized to contest desegregation across the country, Black sisters continued to exercise superior moral leadership and uphold Catholic social teaching in their engagements with white people. During the 1950s, several graduates of schools operated by the Black sisterhoods desegregated white orders with the support and encouragement of their former educators.[36] In 1959, the OSP set another milestone when they admitted their first white member. Like the other Black sisterhoods, the OSP never barred white women and girls from joining, but no white woman or girl had ever applied. However, in 1958, Edith Humphrey, a forty-year-old Stanford-educated librarian and translator in San Francisco, wrote to OSP Mother General William (Alice) Hundley requesting information about the order's admission requirements. Called to religious life at the age of thirty-three when working with the Sisters of Mercy, Humphrey had previously contacted and applied to white orders but had been rejected owing to her advanced age and history of anxiety.[37] However, the OSP general council unanimously voted to admit Humphrey and give her "the usual trial" in their novitiate. The OSP minutes do not reveal why the council admitted Humphrey despite her advanced age, nor is there any evidence to suggest that OSP leaders attempted to dissuade Humphrey from entering the order based on race.[38]

Although the OSP would continue to admit white women—at least two entered in the 1950s and 1960s—applications from non-Black women and girls proved rare.[39] However, the white orders' enduring anti-Black admissions policies ensured that Black sisterhoods had a steady stream of applicants through the 1960s. So, too, did the unwillingness of white congregations to truly accept, nurture, and protect the Black candidates who desegregated their ranks. Through the 1960s, the OSP continued to receive transfer requests from pioneering Black sisters in white congregations in Illinois, New York, and New Jersey, including the Order of Saint Francis and the Sisters of the Precious Blood.[40] In 1963, the order also welcomed back two members, Sisters Mary Christella (Doris) White and Assisi (Frances) Jackson, who had left to desegregate white contemplative orders, the Franciscan Nuns of the Blessed Sacrament and an order of Poor Clare nuns, respectively. In both cases, the sisters were declared "undesirable" and voted out after a few years.[41]

While the reasons their monasteries dismissed White and Jackson remain unclear, many white convents remained fierce strongholds of racial segregation and exclusion during America's civil rights years. The two Oblates seemingly accepted their dismissals without protest. However, many Black sisters in Black and white orders increasingly found it difficult to remain silent about racism in the Church, and religious life specifically, as the secular freedom struggle progressed. Occasionally, this resistance emanated from Black leadership councils and older Black sisters. However, younger Black sisters who entered religious life following the *Brown* decision and were increasingly radicalized by the changing times emerged as the most vocal critics of Catholic racism and discrimination during this period.

The Forgotten Till Generation

As discussed in chapter 3, many Black women and girls who desegregated white sisterhoods after World War II became the first African Americans admitted to many of their congregation's schools, hospitals, and institutions of higher education and the first Black people to live in the hostile sundown towns and neighborhoods where many white Catholic institutions were located. While most Black sisters in white congregations did not frame their admission requests in the language of desegregation, the resistance that many faced at every stage of the process underscored the political nature of their entries into religious life at every turn. So, too, did their experiences of rejection, bullying, and cultural misunderstanding. Because many of the pioneering Black sisters in white congregations were southerners or first- or second-generation migrants to the North and had personal experience with the laws and customs of *de jure* segregation, they sometimes spoke on such issues with authority, even garnering empathetic ears among their white instructors and peers. For example, one white Benedictine sister in St. Joseph, Minnesota, attributed her awakening to the plight of African Americans to her college classmate Joyce Williams, who in 1949 became the first Black woman in the order. She recalled, "I had never heard of such things as lynchings. Joyce filled me in on how the Blacks were treated in Mississippi. And that kind of understanding filtered through to other students."[42] Because Minnesota was not free from the virulent white racism that resulted in the lynchings of people of color, Williams, who was repeatedly denied admission to the congregation owing to her color from 1944 to 1948, remained cautious but seemingly continued such conversations in the convent when finally admitted in 1949.[43]

By 1955, though, many Black applicants to white congregations were empowered not only by the expanding southern Black civil rights movement but also by the increasing efforts of Catholic interracial councils and youth groups against racial segregation in the Church. This was why Angela White, the great-granddaughter of enslaved Black Catholics from Upper Marlboro, Maryland, repeatedly rebuffed suggestions that she enter a Black sisterhood in 1955. As a student at the historically Black Paul Laurence Dunbar High School, White became active in local youth groups seeking to eviscerate the color line and set out to "change the world." As she recalled decades later, "I thought—when I wanted to become a religious— if I was doing this and I was a significant part of this organization trying to bring about racial togetherness, then why should I go into an all-Black community."[44] Thus, when a white Sister of the Holy Names of Jesus and Mary stationed at northwestern DC's St. Gabriel Catholic Church, which White's family had desegregated in 1953, caustically told her "not to bother about applying because they were not accepting Negroes," White did not retreat.[45] In fact, she endured rejections from all the white teaching orders ministering in DC that year before her local pastor secured her entry into the Sisters of Charity of Cincinnati that fall.[46]

When able, many pioneering Black sisters in white congregations also took advantage of opportunities to educate their white counterparts about the civil rights movement and wider Black freedom struggle. For example, when Sister Thea Bowman desegregated her order's Viterbo College in 1958, she became active in student groups and began championing Black history and cultural traditions in her classes.[47] In an article the college's literary magazine published in 1959, Bowman detailed African American life under Jim Crow in her hometown of Canton, Mississippi, and outlined the civil rights movement's aims. "I lived through the days when [Mississippi] Senator

[Theodore G.] Bilbo paraded up and down Main Street—his resolve to keep 'niggers' away from the polls," Bowman wrote. "I was not old enough to vote, but I am old enough to remember the Bilbo cartoons that plagued our papers and my elders' conversations of deceit, trickery, and violence used against Negroes at Mississippi polls. . . . [Negroes] are not clamoring for integration but they want equal rights—jobs, educational facilities, equitable public services."[48] Like many African Americans raised under Jim Crow, Bowman had witnessed firsthand the daily humiliations and sufferings of Black people in the name of white supremacy. As an adolescent, she had also been traumatized after witnessing the police murder an African American youth outside her bedroom window after he refused to say "Yes, sir" and "No, sir" to them.[49] Such violent experiences shaped Bowman's racial and political consciousness long before she entered Saint Rose Convent and helped her withstand their attempts to transform her into "a southern white Wisconsin woman."[50]

Bowman entered religious life before the 1955 lynching of Emmett Till. However, many other Black Catholic women and girls, like their secular counterparts, were inspired to join the fight for equal rights within and outside Church boundaries after Till's confessed murderers were acquitted. For thirteen-year-old Patricia Grey, Till's killing was "unfathomable" and life-changing. "I remember seeing that unforgettable, grotesque photograph of 14-year old . . . Till in his open casket in *Jet* magazine . . . and I recalled how incensed I was as a young teenager, wanting to do something and not knowing how to even talk about it," Grey declared decades later. "That picture left an indelible imprint in my memory."[51]

Although Grey would not be among those who organized the Student Nonviolent Coordinating Committee and pushed the civil rights movement forward in 1960, she did join another brave group of Black youth fighting institutionalized white supremacy, namely, the young people inspired to desegregate the nation's all-white convents and seminaries in the mid-1950s and 1960s.[52] After being barred admission to the Sisters of St. Joseph of Baden, Pennsylvania, on the basis of race in 1960, Grey, then nineteen years old, became the first African American admitted into the independent Pittsburgh community of the Religious Sisters of Mercy in 1961; there, she regularly endured verbal and physical bullying from her peers and novice directress.[53] However, she fought back with spiritual perfection and academic excellence. In one notable episode, though, after a series of racist encounters with an especially "nasty" woman in her band of entrants, who "admitted she hated all Black people," Grey and the woman engaged in a "real brawl." After some time and apologies, a tear-filled conversation between the two uncovered the white candidate's racist upbringing and facilitated what Grey later called a sincere transformation of her heart.[54]

Young members of the Black sisterhoods also increasingly proved willing to challenge the anti-Black racism and utter disrespect directed at them by white priests and sisters. In 1956, for example, twenty-five-year-old Holy Family Sister Marie Assumpta (Doris) Goudeaux caused a stir after she publicly lambasted a white sister-classmate at Louisiana State University for racist behavior toward the members of her order. Although most white sisters in New Orleans had historically avoided social interactions with the SSF in the name of white supremacy, Goudeaux was shocked that they continued to do so after the SSF initiated a program aimed at breaking down racial barriers between Black and white sisters. In 1955, the SSF moved from their longtime headquarters in the city's French Quarter to their new motherhouse on the city's east side.[55] Among its modern conveniences, the new SSF motherhouse featured an indoor swimming pool, a first among the local congregations. The SSF graciously invited local white sisters to share the luxury, which many did.

As Black and white sisters swam and socialized together that summer, a first for New Orleans, many SSF members—Goudeaux among them— thought they were forging real friendships with their white counterparts. However, when Goudeaux matriculated in the graduate school at Louisiana State University the following fall, she noticed that the white sisters with whom she had swum avoided her on campus. When she greeted them, they always turned and walked away. After a few weeks, despite the objections of other SSF members, Goudeaux finally cornered one of the white nuns and confronted her. To Goudeaux's dismay, the white sister admitted that her community members were explicitly forbidden to acknowledge or associate with Black sisters outside of the SSF convent. Stunned, Goudeaux responded that if Black sisters were unworthy to be spoken to in public, then white sisters should not feign friendship with them behind closed doors or take advantage of their pool. She also instructed the white nun to share her message with the other white nuns on campus. Although these white sisters continued their swim visits at the SSF motherhouse, Goudeaux refused to engage with them any further, to the chagrin of her congregation.[56]

Such newfound expressions of militancy among the SSF were not exclusive to the younger members, though. Members who served on the domestic and cooking staffs at the New Orleans archbishop's residence and the local archdiocesan seminary also began speaking out against long-standing mistreatment by white priests and seminarians—a significant

contrast to the SSF's seemingly apolitical behavior during the desegregation crises that struck New Orleans when the courts ordered the public
schools integrated in 1960 and Archbishop Joseph Rummel ordered an end
to segregation in the archdiocesan school system two years later.

Although most white Catholics in New Orleans, religious and lay, mobilized to resist public and Catholic school desegregation, a small handful of local white priests and religious ministering in the African American
community, mostly the Sisters of the Blessed Sacrament and the Josephite
Fathers, publicly supported integration.[57] The Sisters of the Blessed Sacrament, who administered several local Black Catholic schools and by
then had begun admitting Black women into their ranks, also publicly denounced the efforts of segregationist women's groups dominated by white
Catholics, like the infamous "Cheerleaders," who led some of the loudest
and most violent protests against desegregation in the city and surrounding areas.[58] Former SSF pupil Norman Francis, then serving as the dean of
men at Xavier College (led by the Sisters of the Blessed Sacrament), also
secretly and successfully fought to provide housing for the Freedom Riders
who arrived in New Orleans beaten and terrorized by white supremacists
in 1961.[59] During these tumultuous episodes, though, SSF leaders offered
no public condemnations of white violence.

While it is possible that the Afro-Creole-dominated order hesitated
because select Afro-Creole Catholics had also participated in the backlash
against the civil rights movement and Catholic school desegregation, fear of
white retaliation likely drove their public silence. An assaulted or murdered
African American nun would have garnered little sympathy in New Orleans,
where white Catholic segregationists proved themselves willing to bomb
white schools and convents that supported desegregation. Many SSF leaders
also viewed their educational ministries to African American communities,
their involvement in archdiocesan interracial justice programs, and their
hidden desegregation efforts at Loyola University (which included enroll-
ing two members as the institution's first full-time undergraduate students
in 1959) as the best testament to their commitment to the larger struggle.[60]

Thus, the only published SSF response to the 1962 desegregation crisis
appeared in an Associated Press photograph from April 24 (figure 4.2). In
it, the two Holy Family nuns who worked as domestics in the archbishop's
residence keep their eyes to the ground as they sidestep a placard-carrying
white laywoman protesting Rummel's decision to excommunicate the three
leading white Catholic segregationists eight days before.[61] The two sisters'
actions not only epitomized their community's public posture toward the

FIGURE 4.2. During Jim Crow and the early years of the civil rights movement, Black sisters rarely challenged segregation and open acts of racism in public. This was especially true when the perpetrators of racial violence and massive resistance to desegregation efforts were white Catholics. In this 1962 photograph, taken in New Orleans shortly after Archbishop Joseph Rummel excommunicated three prominent white Catholic segregationists, two Sisters of the Holy Family who served on Rummel's domestic staff avoid a protester outside the archbishop's residence. White Catholic laywomen—often armed with crucifixes, tiny coffins, and grotesque and sexualized insults—were among the most virulent foot soldiers of the anti-desegregation campaigns that swept New Orleans and nearby areas in the 1960s. Courtesy of the Associated Press.

crisis but also gave political fodder to segregationists, who accurately noted that local Church leaders upheld discrimination in religious life and relegated Black Catholics to subordinate roles.[62] However, taking the image at face value obscures the daring acts of resistance that the women and their predecessors who had been assigned to the archbishop's residence had recently undertaken.

Since 1869, with brief interruptions, SSF members had served on the domestic and cooking staffs at the New Orleans archbishop's residence. Soon after Notre Dame Seminary opened in 1923, the order assumed domestic duties there as well. Because of the African American sisterhood's precarious position in the segregated archdiocese, the sisters' complaints against mistreatment in those spaces were generally suppressed within the order. However, in 1959, sisters serving at the seminary revolted against the white priests and seminarians, and mediation proved necessary. The men accused the SSF, save for the local superior, of "discourtesy, uncooperation, & rebellion." One sister, "Miriam Teresa," was also accused of attacking a priest "severely and unjustly." On the other side, the SSF, backed by their superiors, complained of being "overworked," accused the white priests "of being very inconsiderate," and strongly insinuated that the priests treated them like enslaved persons. "Remember, we are ladies," Sister Miriam Theresa (Rose Marie) Bartholomy reportedly stated. Because the SSF refused to back down, the priests characterized the "whole tone of the sisters' comments at the meeting" as "discourteous and rebellious." In the end, however, the priests approved most of the SSF demands. The seminarians were subsequently barred from entering the kitchen while the sisters were working. The archdiocese also agreed to hire a full-time dishwasher, purchase extra tray carts, and require the seminarians to clean up after themselves better in the dining hall.[63] One year later, SSF superior Mother Marie Anselm (Marvel) Duffel sent a letter to all the pastors assigned to the schools, parishes, and missions staffed by her order and informed them that the SSF would no longer "wash and iron the Altar linens or clean the body of the church or even . . . supervise this work." Foregrounding the sisters' need to prepare for their classes and take care of their own "washing and ironing," Duffel asked for each pastor's "full understanding and willing cooperation."[64] Such behind-the-scenes victories were monumental even as Black leadership councils continued to mandate public silence from their members regarding the secular fight for civil rights. Following the opening of the Second Vatican Council, select sisters in Black and white congregations grew even more daring in their challenges to racial discrimination.

The Impact of the Second Vatican Council

Between October 1962 and December 1965, over 2,700 of the world's Catholic bishops gathered in Vatican City to bring the Church into the modern era. Called by Pope John XXIII shortly after his election in 1959, the Second Vatican Council, or Vatican II, also sought to increase the Church's relevance to worldwide struggles for justice and peace. Inspired by monumental societal shifts and upheavals resulting from Asian and African decolonization and American social movements demanding justice for the poor and marginalized, the council produced decrees calling for modernization in the Church and mandating major reforms in the liturgy and religious life.[65] In addition to loosening many of the regulations that had severely restricted sisters' movements and activities, Vatican II encouraged a celebration of the Church's ethnic diversity, including terminating the centuries-long tradition of saying Mass in Latin rather than in each community's native tongue. The council also exhorted all Catholics, as the "People of God," to engage fully with the world and "promote human justice," declaring social justice activism as a primary way of fulfilling the Church's mission.[66] Although many Catholics fiercely resisted many of the reforms and mandates, others readily and enthusiastically embraced the challenge. Vatican II finally gave activist-oriented sisters and priests the space to contemplate openly their place in the modern Black freedom movement. It also forced the all-white US Church hierarchy to take a clear position on racial justice as resistance to civil rights gains within Catholic boundaries grew stronger.

Before Vatican II, Catholics involved in civil rights organizations and secular campaigns for racial justice were primarily Black members of the laity. After 1962, significant numbers of white lay Catholics, most of whom were associated with the Catholic interracial movement, particularly the recently organized National Catholic Conference for Interracial Justice, began appearing in civil rights demonstrations across the country. Following Pope John XXIII's public condemnation of racial discrimination in his pastoral letter "Pacem in Terris" in April 1963, a small number of priests and sisters also began appearing in local and national civil rights marches.[67] Dialogues on racism in Catholic institutions also increased, and sometimes Black members of white and Black sisterhoods were invited to contribute. Sister Mary Francesca Thompson, the second Black Sister of St. Francis of Oldenburg, for example, became a popular speaker on racism in the Church in the early 1960s, decrying the evil produced by racial prejudice and sarcastically characterizing herself as the "dream girl" of the anti-Black and anti-Catholic Ku Klux Klan.[68] In 1958, Thompson had joined with early Black priest Clarence Rivers in popularizing and teaching the Congolese Mass, Missa Luba, in the archdiocese of Cincinnati before Vatican II reforms encouraged such cross-cultural embraces.[69] The FHM vocational director Maria Mercedes Oliver also made several Catholic headlines in 1964 decrying racism in the Church and detailing her own experience of being denied admission into the white congregations in New York City.[70]

Many scholars have cited the participation of seven white School Sisters of St. Francis in an organized picket against the anti-Black admissions policies of the Illinois Club for Catholic Women on the campus of Loyola University in Chicago in July 1963 as a seminal event in sisters' engagement with the civil rights movement. [71] However, many Black sisters were active in civil rights organizations and participated in marches and desegregation protests before entering into religious life. Some, like Sister of Charity of Nazareth Ann Barbara (Patricia) Haley, even brought the movement's tactics into their respective congregations. A few months before she desegregated the former slaveholding order in the fall of 1963, for example, eighteen-year-old Haley was arrested and jailed for leading her Black Catholic high school's delegation in the highly publicized youth marches for civil rights in Birmingham, Alabama. Within weeks of entering the convent in Kentucky's "Holy Land," Haley led a one-woman campaign to have her congregation desegregate its dining halls and the water fountains for its lay workers. Haley reportedly told her superiors, "I will not work in a segregated dining room, obedience or no obedience." The leaders of the Sisters of Charity of Nazareth soon ordered the removal of signs mandating segregation in their slave-built motherhouse, while Haley kept protesting other intolerable dimensions of racism in the order.[72]

Earlier that year in February, Oblate Sisters of Providence stationed at Detroit's Our Lady of Victory Catholic School made headlines when they protested a dictionary and history book used in the archdiocese's parochial schools "for their attitudes toward the Negro." Regarding the history text, Mother Mary Patricia (Elise) Ford argued that while "there is nothing in it that belittles Negroes . . . it is guilty of omission of those who made contributions," naming inventor Benjamin Banneker, scientist George Washington Carver, and education leader Booker T. Washington as examples of those missing. Because their superiors in Baltimore actively discouraged public acts of protest, the Detroit members' stand is notable.[73]

So, too, were the efforts of the Oblates stationed at the recently merged Saints Paul and Augustine Catholic Church in Washington, DC, at the time of the March on Washington for Jobs and Freedom. In addition to providing food and accommodations to out-of-town participants, at least two members defied Archbishop Patrick O'Boyle and their superiors in Baltimore and joined their students and parishioners in the national demonstration on August 28, 1963. Because O'Boyle, who delivered the march's opening benediction, had banned sisters from participating, the Oblates did not record their participation in their annals or inform their superiors.[74] Back in Baltimore, the OSP members at the motherhouse watched the march on television. If any saw their comrades, they did not record that in the annals either.[75]

Vatican II and civil rights victories also inspired Black sisters in white congregations to continue their individual struggles against racism in the Church. Besides continuing to desegregate white congregations, Black sisters began to break monumental leadership barriers. In 1963, Sister Ann Michael Boyd, a native of Washington, DC, and an early Black member of the Franciscan Sisters of Rice Lake in Wisconsin, became the first self-identified African American to be elected the superior of a white order.[76] That same year, Dr. Frances Douglass (figure 4.3), the first African American Daughter of the Heart of Mary, became the first woman of color to chair a department at Marquette University.[77] Douglass had also made history in Chicago in 1956, when she became the first African American to head a department at DePaul University, where she was one of only nineteen women faculty members.[78]

By 1964, Black sisters in white congregations also began appearing in local civil rights demonstrations. Even before the historic passage of the Civil Rights Act of 1964, which criminalized racial segregation and discrimination in the public sector, several white sisters and at least one Black sister joined local marches for equality, opportunity, and decent housing in Gary, Indiana, and St. Louis, Missouri.[79] However, the marches from Selma to Montgomery, Alabama, four months later marked the first time a notable portion of the US Church officially staked their claim in the Black civil rights movement.

Black Sisters and the Selma Protests

During the Selma campaign, hundreds of Catholic sisters from across the country unexpectedly joined the protest and generated a substantial amount of media attention, as well as backlash within the white Catholic community. The image of Catholic sisters dressed in the full habits of their orders marching in Selma and other cities under the banner of civil rights and human justice was especially powerful. It also alerted civil rights leaders and sisters themselves to the unique contributions that nuns as "symbols

FIGURE 4.3. Although historian Dr. John Hope Franklin is widely cited as the first African American to chair an academic department at a historically white institution of higher education, Sister/Dr. Frances Douglass began her tenure as the head of the psychology department at DePaul University in September 1956, the same month and year Franklin assumed the helm of Brooklyn College's history department. Because members of her order did not wear habits or take religious names, Dr. Douglass's status as a nun was not known to most of her colleagues at DePaul and later at Marquette University, where she became the first woman of color to chair a department in 1963. Courtesy of the Department of Special Collections and University Archives, Raynor Memorial Libraries, Marquette University, Milwaukee, Wisconsin.

of God" could make to the racial justice fight.[80] Although most sisters who participated in the Selma protest were white—as were over 95 percent of US sisters in 1965—a significant number of Black sisters also stepped forward to support Black voting rights. In so doing, this pivotal cadre of Black sisters firmly broke the taboo that had precluded most of their predecessors from publicly engaging in civil rights activism. It also gave greater incentives to Black sisters to bring their long-standing commitments to racial justice into the secular arena.

FIGURE 4.4. Sister Ann Benedict (Barbara) Moore (sixth from the left) with other Selma march participants from Kansas City, Missouri, in March 1965. The first African American member of her order, Moore went on to earn a master's degree in nursing and a doctorate in higher education administration. Courtesy of the Archives of the Archdiocese of Kansas City-St. Joseph, Kansas City, Missouri.

Three days after Sister Mary Antona Ebo's highly publicized stand in Selma, Sister Ann Benedict (Barbara) Moore, the first African American admitted into the Sisters of St. Joseph of Carondelet, joined a Selma delegation composed of sisters and priests from Kansas City, Missouri (figure 4.4).[81] Like Ebo, Moore was outspoken on racial injustice. She had also quietly kept abreast of the civil rights movement as she underwent spiritual training and entered college. Thus, Moore welcomed the opportunity to join the Kansas City delegation. Reflecting on her experiences in Selma years later, Moore vividly recounted the trip from the airport to the march, noting the white citizens with shotguns who had come out on their porches and lined the streets to intimidate the protesters.[82] She also recalled marching in the streets surrounded by the police: "The state troopers were there in full riot gear. . . . It was a metanoia for me because after that I felt that I had made a decision that if I was going to die, it was okay."[83]

Although Ebo and Moore were the only two Black sisters to march in Selma in 1965, several more participated in sympathy marches in cities across the North and Midwest. One of the most dramatic took place in New York City on March 14 when approximately fifteen thousand people, including over five hundred sisters, priests, and brothers, marched through the predominantly African American Harlem community. March organizers demanded Black voting rights and federal intervention to stop the violent state-sanctioned repression of Black voter registration campaigns in Selma.[84] Among the approximately three hundred Sisters of Charity of New York, the largest delegation of religious who marched that day, were two of the congregation's first professed Black members in the twentieth century (figure 4.5). Several members of the all-Black FHM also joined the demonstration.[85]

Reflecting on the Handmaids' participation decades later, Mary Bertha Alexander, formerly Sister Mary Concepta, FHM, noted that their participation had been spontaneous. In 1961, the FHM had integrated the faculty of New York City's Cathedral High School for Girls, where they taught alongside the Sisters of Charity of New York, many of whom were their former educators.[86] However, the Sisters of Charity who helped organize the Harlem march had not informed the FHM ahead of time. As the march crossed West 123rd Street, though, a Charity nun rushed to the FHM motherhouse to let them know. In response, several, including Alexander, left the convent to join the demonstrations.[87]

Another large Selma sympathy march was held in Pittsburgh. On Tuesday, March 16, three thousand Black and white residents, including several priests and sisters, marched from the predominantly African American Hill District to the new federal building downtown to protest the ongoing repression of Selma activists. Among the marchers was twenty-two-year-old Sister M. Martin de Porres Grey, Pittsburgh's first Black Religious Sister of Mercy.[88] Although Grey had requested permission to travel to Selma with her community's delegation, marching there the same day, her congregational leaders had refused, citing Grey's junior status. Mercy leader Mother Thomas Aquinas Carroll also stated that she did not want her community's only Black member becoming "too militant."[89] However, Carroll did allow Grey to lead the sixty-five-member student delegation from the order's Mount Mercy College in the local demonstration.

While no OSP and SSF members marched in Selma, archival sources and oral histories reveal that members of the two Black sisterhoods kept abreast of the struggle and supported it as they could. Sister Mary Consolata Gibson, for example, participated in a meeting of Baltimore-area sisters

FIGURE 4.5. Early Black Sisters of Charity of New York Rose Frederick (*left*) and Margaret Dean (*right*) marched at the front of their order's delegation in Harlem in March 1965. Courtesy of Getty Images.

in support of the Selma protest.[90] Thirty-one years earlier, Gibson had reintegrated the Catholic University of America. Convent annals and oral history also reveal that OSP and SSF members stationed throughout the country followed the marches, said prayers for peace in Selma, and were granted special permission to watch televised footage of the protests.[91]

Several Oblate Sisters of Providence stationed at Holy Name Catholic School and Convent in Chicago were also moved to greater action. Sister M. Virginie (Ruth Willa Mae) Fish, for example, requested permission to travel to Selma, but her superior, Mother Mary Angela Wade, refused. Decades later, Fish stated, "I was fired up to go to Selma. I wanted to go. So, I asked Mother Angela for permission and she said [in a low and deep tone]: 'Noooo!'"[92] Although Wade permitted Fish and the other OSP members to participate in the weekly activities of the Urban Apostolate of Sisters (UAS), a Chicago-based organization committed to racial justice, before the Selma protest, she refused to let her members participate in demonstrations.[93] Mother Wade, who had been one of the earliest African American students at Villanova College in 1925, considered the Black sisters' work at their school critical, and she was concerned about the unique dangers that Black sisters faced.[94] However, by 1965, Fish and the other younger sisters were not easily dissuaded.

Less than a month later, five Chicago Oblate Sisters, including Fish, attended a talk by Selma activist Father Maurice Ouellet, sponsored by the UAS. Speaking on the potential roles that Catholic sisters could play in the shifting Black freedom struggle, Ouellet urged the sisters present to become apostles for racial justice in the North. "Selma was the opening shot of the war," he proclaimed. "If SCLC [the Southern Christian Leadership Conference] comes to Chicago, they will need the Sisters."[95] Aware of the opposition mounting to Catholic sisters' growing participation in civil rights activities, Ouellet nonetheless encouraged UAS members to continue and even risk disobedience. He also warned his mostly white audience against assuming a paternalistic posture toward the African American community in the evolving Black revolution. "The Church has been slow," Ouellet reminded. "The Sisters and Priests in Selma have a fine reputation—not the Church as a whole." Of particular concern to Ouellet was the Church's ongoing failure to confront racial exclusion and discrimination within its own boundaries, especially within religious life. "The negro priests in [my] community have spoken to [me] about it and Father imagines that any negro Sister has had feelings of discrimination in some of the religious communities," he stated. "We are not always aware of our prejudices."[96] While light-handed with his rebuke of racism within religious life, Ouellet's early acknowledgment of the limitations of white priests and sisters seeking to become active in the secular fight for racial justice was significant. So, too, was his documentation of African American challenges to racism in his own order and his call for white UAS members to avoid taking a patronizing posture toward African Americans. "Work with the Negro, not for him," Ouellet warned.[97]

At the conclusion of Ouellet's talk, the five Oblates present requested a private conference with the priest, during which they spoke at length about their growing desire to enter the public fight for racial justice and the obstacles they faced in doing so. A few days later, the following entry appeared in the Holy Name annals: "After school . . . Sisters Michael, Josine, Donna Marie, Vincetta, and Virginie (driver) went to a[n] Urban Apostolate League to hear Father Maurice Luellet [*sic*], s.s.e. [Society of Saint Edmund] of Selma, Alabama speak of the Negro Apostolate and conditions in Selma. We felt as if we had met Christ Himself in the flesh. Father is tremendous in his Christian convictions."[98]

During the Selma protests, Ouellet realized the unique power that Black sisters could bring to the secular freedom struggle. Two weeks after Ebo marched in Selma, the white priest wrote her to convey as much.[99] Thus, two weeks after the uas meeting in Chicago, Ouellet bypassed the local osp superior and wrote directly to Mother Mary William Hundley in Baltimore to plead the case of the five Oblates whom he had encountered directly. "Never have I met sisters more enthused over the work that is being done in this country in the field of race relations," Ouellet remarked. "I could not help but think to myself what a tremendous impact these sisters could have in any community in which they might be working." Ouellet also encouraged Hundley to permit the young sisters to become more active. "I know that you will feel for their safety and this is certainly to be taken into consideration," he wrote. "However, I think that the time has come when oftentimes we must place personal safety aside and do what must be done in the name of the Church. As I spoke to the sisters I felt that they wanted to do so much."[100] From Ouellet's perspective, the participation of the osp and members of the other Black orders would be a significant asset to the struggle.

However, the position of Black superiors on their members' involvement in protest activities in early 1965 was clear. Though Black leadership councils unequivocally supported the aims of the civil rights movement and though select members of the osp would (without permission) march for open housing in Baltimore in November 1965 and participate in desegregation sit-ins in Orangeburg, South Carolina soon thereafter, the Catholic schools the Black orders operated faced an uncertain future with school desegregation, and to the Black councils that took precedence over any other racial justice matter.[101] As their communities underwent conciliar-mandated renewal after 1965, and as hundreds of white sisters became the face and force of racial justice in the Church, though, Black superiors would rethink their positions.

Historian Amy L. Koehlinger has argued that "the Selma protest proved to be a singularly powerful catalyst to arouse sisters to pursue apostolic works among African Americans."[102] Before that, most white sisters had routinely shunned that work, considering it beneath them, and as a rule ostracized sisters, white and Black, who labored in African American communities. However, after Selma and Vatican II's call to social justice activism, a significant portion of white sisters changed their public postures. Those who participated in the Selma protests found the experience transformative. As School Sister of Notre Dame Margaret Traxler remarked, "After Selma, you can't stay home again."[103] For others, Selma helped expand what it meant to be a Catholic sister. Long prohibited from direct engagement in civic and political affairs, sisters could now become advocates and activists, and many viewed the Black freedom struggle as a useful training ground for what many were then calling "new nuns."[104] As a result, hundreds of Catholic sisters entered the public fight for racial justice—some during free time from their traditional apostolic labors and others on a more permanent basis.

Many religious orders also received invitations from various racial justice organizations to contribute to local struggles. In the spring of 1965, for example, Kate Jordan, founder of the Pax Christi Institute (a secular institute of religious women) in Greenwood, Mississippi, invited the Benedictine Sisters in St. Joseph, Minnesota, to assist in Pax Christi's racial justice efforts. The order had been anxious to become involved in such an endeavor, and that summer they sent five sisters to assist in the educational and community work of Greenwood's Saint Francis Center, which Pax Christi administered. Inspired by the Freedom Summer of 1964, the Benedictines named their endeavor Operation Mississippi. The five Benedictines (two of whom were African Americans and native Mississippians) joined eleven Pax Christi members, fifteen seminarians, a layman, and six other nuns, who were all white, in conducting a host of summer literacy and arts classes aimed at raising the quality of African American life in Greenwood. The group also made home visits, prepared medications for the dispensary, and established drama clubs for the local children before returning to their regular teaching positions in the fall.[105]

In other instances, individual sisters created their own programs to uplift neglected African Americans or joined Black freedom organizations in their respective locales. Sister Mary Julian (Norma Fae) Griffin, the first Black Vincentian Sister of Charity in Pittsburgh, for example, did both while on her first teaching assignment at St. Jude High School in Montgomery, Alabama, in the mid-1960s. After school, Griffin conducted basic literacy classes for adults in the rural communities outside Montgomery and joined the local Black voter registration campaign. In 1964, she also became active in the Montgomery chapter of the Alabama Council on Human Relations, an organization at the center of the local civil rights movement. Griffin's subsequent involvement in direct-action initiatives and demonstrations against segregation in Montgomery quickly drew the attention and fury of local white Catholic leaders.[106]

Most sisters who gained substantial releases from their communities entered the freedom struggle through initiatives across the country sponsored by the Department of Educational Services (DES) of the National Catholic Conference for Interracial Justice (NCCIJ), headquartered in Chicago. Founded in 1964, the DES was organized "to increase awareness of racial justice issues among Catholics by improving the visibility and influence of the NCCIJ" in the Catholic community.[107] Following the Selma protest, the DES came under the leadership of Sister Margaret Traxler, who became in most Catholic circles the most visible sister associated with the fight for racial justice. Through a host of programs funded by antipoverty grants from the federal government or private philanthropic organizations, the DES funneled hundreds of Catholic sisters into the civil rights movement. Some programs were aimed at dispelling racist attitudes among white sisters, such as the DES's Traveling Workshops in Intergroup Relations. In these five-day workshops, led by a group of five sisters who traveled the country in a rented station wagon, sisters "explored the sources of human conflict—especially racial conflict—and strategies for resolution."[108] Other programs placed sisters into direct-action programs aimed at promoting racial justice "either by challenging white supremacy among [white] Catholics or by responding to specific needs in African American communities."[109] Some of these initiatives included sister-led summer academic enrichment camps for low-income Black children in Chicago and a program that placed northern sisters on the faculties of southern historically Black colleges and universities, in order to allow their regular Black faculty members to complete their doctorates.[110] Because participation in these efforts often required either temporary or permanent release from traditional apostolates, many of the sisters active in the early years came from larger communities that could afford to release members. Because of the systematic exclusion of Black women and girls from white congregations and the marginal population of the nation's Black orders, sisters released to participate and lead these Church-sponsored initiatives were overwhelmingly white, with minimal experience and knowledge of Black people or their history, limiting their impact from the beginning.

Although Black sisterhoods remained reluctant to allow their members to enter the Black freedom movement formally, many leadership councils did begin to loosen the restrictions that generally forbade their members' involvement as their communities underwent conciliar-mandated spiritual renewal. On October 28, 1965, the Second Vatican Council issued *Perfectae Caritatis*, in which Pope Paul VI addressed religious orders of men and women and called for radical reform. In addition to mandating that congregations undertake a substantial self-study of their communities, including their original charisms, *Perfectae Caritatis* encouraged orders to reimagine all facets of their life, including religious garb, living arrangements, religious observance, and enclosure, in order to become effective agents of change in the modern world.[111] Keeping their strict adherence to Church law, the three Black sisterhoods all began renewal in some fashion soon thereafter, ahead of their formal chapter meetings.[112]

Because the Black orders had pioneered Catholic service to the African American community and traditionally served the excluded, most Black superiors came to view entry into the secular fight for racial justice as an extension of their foundresses' legacies and their educational activism. Speaking at her order's 125th-anniversary celebration in New Orleans in 1967, for example, SSF leader Mother Marie Anselm Duffel reflected on the "new dimensions" required of the order in the wake of Vatican II and the changing dynamics of the Black freedom struggle. Announcing the order's new rallying cry of "SERVICE FIRST! SERVICE NOW! SERVICE ALWAYS!"—a play on the segregationist rallying cry of Alabama governor George Wallace—Duffel paid homage to the SSF foundresses and outlined a new course for the order. "Wherever opportunity opens a door—whether it be the integration of an erstwhile all-white faculty on any academic level, or whispering an act of love in the ear of a dying man or woman in our Home for the Aged," she proclaimed, "we deem it not only an obligation but also a blessing to be present."[113]

While Black leadership councils remained cautious about releasing sisters from their traditional educational duties, Black superiors increasingly permitted members to participate in Church-sponsored demonstrations and initiatives. This was particularly true when such efforts allowed Black sisters to demonstrate their educational preparedness and expertise—for instance, integrating faculties and serving on diocesan and archdiocesan educational boards—or to break new racial ground for their orders. In 1964 and 1967, the OSP received and accepted two additional missions to teach in all-white Catholic elementary schools in Lavonia and Three Rivers, Michigan, respectively, continuing their efforts to break down racial barriers in white Catholic spaces.[114]

In 1967, the OSP also released two members from their teaching duties in predominantly Black schools to help integrate historically white faculties in Florida and Minnesota. Sister M. Virginie Fish was released at Holy Names in Chicago to integrate the Benedictine faculty of St. Joseph Public School in Dade City, Florida, while Sister Concepta Marie (Clara) Moran integrated the Dominican faculty of Incarnation Catholic School in Minneapolis, Minnesota.[115] The order also released Sister Mary Monica (Elaine) Dean in 1967 to teach English at the historically Black Howard University in Washington, DC, her alma mater.[116]

Black sisterhoods took advantage of changes at administrative levels as well. In September 1965, SSF leaders accepted an invitation from New Orleans archbishop John Patrick Cody to have a member serve as one of the archdiocesan school supervisors.[117] It marked the first time that a Holy Family Sister had served in an administrative capacity on the Catholic school board. Two years later, the SSF reached out to their longtime educational allies, the Sisters of Charity of Seton Hill (SCSH) in Greensburg, Pennsylvania, to initiate a teacher exchange program to "bring about racial integration at the religious faculty level in the Catholic elementary schools" of the New Orleans archdiocese and the Pittsburgh diocese.[118] Although the SCSH had admitted two African American women, one each in 1957 and 1961, both departed the order in 1963.[119] The experiment in faculty integration between the SCSH and SSF involved four pilot schools in each archdiocese, in which the exchange teachers would live with the receiving community and serve as regular faculty members under the respective administration. Before the formal program began in the fall of 1967, the SSF had first offered the services of Sister Aquinata (Helen Marie) Cuillier to the SCSH's all-white Elizabeth Seton High School in Brookline, Pennsylvania. Unsurprisingly, when interviewed by the local Catholic newspaper about her historic assignment one year later, Cuillier refused to comment on the civil rights movement when asked. But she noted that she had incorporated "Negro history" into her high school lessons and spoke on the topic throughout Pittsburgh.[120]

By 1967, OSP and SSF members had integrated all-white Catholic school faculties in Florida, Oklahoma, and Pennsylvania; participated in sister-exchange programs with white orders in Pennsylvania; and worked in inner-city apostolate programs in Detroit, New Orleans, Chicago, and

Baltimore.[121] During the summer of 1967, the SSF also released a member to lead and coordinate a traveling race-relations workshop sponsored by the DES. She was the first member of a Black order to join the prominent sister-led racial justice organization.[122]

Even as they more formally entered the public fight for racial justice, Black sisters continued to blaze trails in Catholic higher education. For example, in 1965, Holy Family Sister Mary Reginald (Augusta) Carter made headlines when she received her doctorate in Spanish from Saint Louis University. Although Carter was celebrated for becoming the first African American nun to earn a PhD, the distinction secretly belonged to Daughter of the Heart of Mary Frances Douglass. Nonetheless, Carter soon thereafter integrated the faculty of the College of Great Falls in Montana.[123] Three years later, Holy Family Sister Mary Sylvester (Lovenia) Deconge became the third known African American sister to earn a PhD and the fifteenth Black woman to earn a PhD in mathematics in the United States, when she received her degree from Saint Louis University. Deconge subsequently became the first Black woman to join the faculty of Loyola University in New Orleans, where she taught from 1968 to 1971.[124] Although many Black sisters in Black communities held master's degrees (most of which they earned in religious life), time constraints and lack of community resources had prevented Black sisters from joining their white counterparts in the highest ranks of education. While at least two Oblates held doctoral degrees when they entered the order, the first Oblate to earn a PhD was Sister Mary Alice Chineworth, who in 1972 earned a PhD in psychology from the Catholic University of America.[125]

In 1966, the OSP made history in higher education again when they opened Mount Providence Junior College in Catonsville, Maryland (figure 4.6). An outgrowth of their accredited normal school, the Oblate Institute, Mount Providence also offered secular female students two-year associate's degrees in the liberal arts. During the college's dedication ceremony, then-senator Robert F. Kennedy heralded Mount Providence for its dynamic and innovative approach to education. Open to all women regardless of race, Mount Providence was the first US Catholic institution of higher education founded by a Black congregation.[126] After seven decades of sister-led Catholic higher education for women in the United States, Black sisters had finally joined their white counterparts as college founders and administrators.

Black sisters in white congregations also continued to blaze trails. For example, in 1966, Sister Mary Reginalda Polk, a Sinsinawa Dominican and a native of Tuskegee, Alabama, became the first Black principal of a

FIGURE 4.6. The dedication of Mount Providence Junior College, the first Roman Catholic institution of higher education established by a Black congregation, drew a host of city, state, and Church officials on September 12, 1966. Pictured from left to right are Sister Mary of Good Counsel (Helena) Baptiste, Sister Mary Consolata (Lydia) Gibson, Mother William (Alice) Hundley, Baltimore's Cardinal Lawrence Shehan, and US senators Robert F. Kennedy, Joseph Tydings, and Daniel Brewster. Courtesy of the Archives of the Oblate Sisters of Providence, Baltimore, Maryland.

Milwaukee Catholic school, at Saint Gall Church in Wisconsin.[127] In 1967, Sister Mary Antona Ebo was chosen to lead St. Clare Hospital in Baraboo, Wisconsin, making her the first Black sister to head a hospital in the United States.[128] As Black sisters in white communities pursued degrees paid for by their communities, many also became involved in campus movements, exposure that proved pivotal in raising their political consciousness. These opportunities especially encouraged Black sisters who had suppressed their racial identity to reclaim their heritage proudly, and it further encouraged some to become involved in the larger fight for racial justice and be more vocal about racial discrimination within their own congregations.[129] Indeed, in 1967, Black nuns were also counted among those famously marching for open housing in Milwaukee, Wisconsin, in the face of jeering, and often white Catholic, counterdemonstrators.[130]

However, as increasing numbers of Black sisters offered their services and expertise through Church-affiliated organizations and initiatives, many encountered opposition rooted in the legacy of white supremacy. For example, when Selma march veteran Sister Mary Antona Ebo applied for a staff position at the NCCIJ in Chicago in 1967, she encountered resistance within her order and during her interview with the organization's white priest and sister members. When appointed as the first Black director of the records department at her order's previously all-white St. Mary's Hospital in suburban St. Louis in 1966, Ebo had immediately integrated the unit's clerical staff. While serving on the Human Life Committee of the St. Louis chapter of the NAACP that same year, Ebo had also been involved in local civil rights campaigns, including the fight to integrate St. Mary's all-white staff of physicians.[131] Yet Ebo recalled that some white NCCIJ staff members openly questioned her qualifications for the position. While Ebo superiors' refusal to release her from her duties ultimately prevented her from joining the NCCIJ, Ebo remained deeply skeptical about the sincerity of the organization's white leaders, especially when they remained silent about racism within their own ranks.[132]

Black sisters in white orders who participated in racial justice initiatives or joined Black freedom organizations also experienced racially based challenges. For instance, Benedictine Sister Joyce Williams, one of the two Operation Mississippi sisters who were Black, later revealed that her participation had not been "a satisfying experience" and noted that she had "felt encumbered by the decisions of her [white] companions."[133] In Montgomery, Alabama, Vincentian Sister of Charity Mary Julian Griffin endured formal and informal threats from white archdiocesan officials and religious because of her civil rights activism and literacy campaign. When Griffin refused to halt her activities, she was dismissed from her teaching assignment.[134]

Such impediments to Black sisters' activism underscored the difficulties in breaking down structural barriers without Black Church leadership. Even whites active in the racial justice apostolate routinely failed to address individual and structural racism in the Church in meaningful ways. Although some sister-sponsored initiatives were aimed at dispelling racial and derogatory myths and stereotypes about Black people held by white Catholics, most programs placed white sisters with little experience working among African Americans or little knowledge of African American history into racial justice initiatives. Many white sister-leaders in the racial justice apostolate and in Black schools expressed disdain for calls for Black power and self-determination, which further demonstrated the inherent limitations of these white-led initiatives. Indeed, white sisters' newfound interest came off as hypocritical, insincere, and dangerous.

For Sister M. Melanie (Saundra Ann) Willingham, one of the first two African Americans admitted into the Sisters of Notre Dame de Namur in Ohio in 1960, the intractability of white racism in the Church, especially among sisters, proved more than she could handle by 1968. Early in religious life, Willingham had laughed away her peers' regular slights and anecdotes designed to make her "look like Stepin' Fetchit," the racist 1930s caricature.[135] Even when her novice directress "cautioned" her against having "inordinate race consciousness," Willingham resisted, secretly devouring the novitiate library's limited collection of African American literature. However, when in 1965 Willingham matriculated at the University of Dayton, she realized that it had not been enough.[136] "Young people with less experience than I were much more knowledgeable in the history, sociology, and psychology of our people," she later wrote. "They were able to argue and challenge while I could only sit back in ignorance. I was humiliated by my state of mind, it was white."[137] Wanting to become active in the freedom struggle, Willingham joined the local Catholic interracial council, only to find herself and her concerns misunderstood or dismissed by whites in the organization. "The more actively I involved myself in the . . . Council, the more threatened my fragile psychic equilibrium became," she wrote.[138] Despite the trial, Willingham initially committed to remaining in religious life. However, unyielding white racism in her order and a gut-wrenching experience while working for the DES in Cleveland led to Willingham's defection from religious life in 1968.[139] As she explained in an article for *Ebony* magazine that same year, "The march on Washington had fired me up, the bombing of [four] girls in Birmingham had enraged me, the assassination of Malcolm X had embittered me. None of these events seemed to capture more than the casual attention of my community," she wrote. "I eventually had to ask myself how I could justify such total identification with this institution which was not only white, but so racist and authoritarian that it cannot accept the factual reality that its schools were segregated; so racist that it cannot comprehend the message the d[ea]rth of black 'vocations' is testifying; so racist that it does not even know the meaning of the word paternalism and is far indeed from seeing itself implicated therein."[140] And Willingham would not be alone in her disillusionment.

The year 1968 would prove pivotal for most African Americans. While the urban rebellions of 1967 pushed the nation further toward racial crisis, the release of the Kerner Commission Report in February 1968 affirmed long-standing Black American critiques and placed the blame for the unrest firmly on white America. "Our nation is moving toward two societies, one Black, one white—separate and unequal," the report declared.[141] Although many white sisters active in the racial justice apostolate resisted calls for Black self-determination, a few working in the African American community began to voice their concerns about the dangers of white sisters' irrational opposition to "Black power" and their ongoing failure to acknowledge Catholic culpability in the nation's racial problems. In a February 13, 1968, letter to the executive committee of the Conference of Major Superiors of Women, Sister Mary Schultz, a Home Visitor of Mary, of Detroit wrote, "In our metropolitan area there is a serious white backlash— one of the most fanatical leaders being a Catholic. . . . Frankly, Mother, I find so many Sisters have no idea of the reality of racism in our midst—of the psychological damage we are doing. . . . How many of our Sisters know what is meant by Black Power?—the legitimate goals. . . . Catholics have a special obligation since they still constitute a major white institution in the cities."[142] Schultz, the foundress of a white congregation that had worked in Detroit's African American community since 1949 and begun admitting Black candidates soon thereafter, did not believe that white sisters should abandon the inner city, but she argued that they could not be effective "prophets in this struggle" if they remained uninformed about the true plight of African Americans.[143] However, the soul-chilling assassination of the Reverend Dr. Martin Luther King Jr. would prompt many Black Catholics to openly question whether even sincere white Catholics ministering to Black communities had the moral capacity to bring about the necessary changes. While Vatican II reforms had revealed that Black sisters had a rightful place on the front lines of the public struggle for racial justice, King's assassination set the stage for the emergence of a new kind of Black religious sister—one who proved willing to risk it all, including arrest and defection from religious life, to expose the depths of white supremacy in female religious life and rid white Catholic America of racism once and for all.

5. "Liberation Is Our First Priority"

BLACK NUNS AND BLACK POWER

To be celibate, black and committed gives promise and danger to life. —SISTER M.
MARTIN DE PORRES GREY, RSM, quoted in "Black Nun Pleads for 'God Convicted
Women,'" *Pittsburgh Courier*, December 5, 1970

On April 5, 1968, Sister Joyce Ruth Williams (figure 5.1) decided that she
had had enough of white Catholic racism. The forty-two-year-old Benedictine nun was also done suppressing her African American identity for the
false promises of universalism in her church.[1] Like many Black women who
desegregated white sisterhoods after World War II, Williams's journey in
religious life had been fiercely contested and peppered with gut-wrenching
experiences of racism. Between 1944 and 1948, Williams's admissions requests to the Order of St. Benedict in St. Joseph, Minnesota, had been rejected on the basis of race. In 1948, Mother Rosamond Pratschner had even
declared that the sisters did not know what the Mississippi native would eat
and maintained that there was "no work in the community" that Williams,
a recent graduate of the order's College of St. Benedict, could do if admitted into the order.[2]

When the 1948 election of a new prioress, Williams's college dean, finally
opened the order's doors to her in 1949, Williams, like many of her Black
peers in white congregations, decided to persevere even if it meant submitting
to some level of racial assimilation. She firmly believed that the Church's

FIGURE 5.1. Joyce Ruth Williams converted to Catholicism in 1944, just two years after migrating to Chicago from Summit, Mississippi. A regular volunteer at the city's Friendship House, she became inspired by the Catholic witness of founder Catherine de Hueck Doherty and the writings of Trappist monk Thomas Merton, shortly before feeling the call to religious life. Courtesy of the Order of St. Benedict at St. Joseph, Minnesota.

social teachings would eventually prevail over the sin of racism. The then-twenty-five-year-old math and science teacher also believed that serving as an example of Black excellence and spiritual perfection would help transform the hearts of those who disregarded Black dignity and humanity.[3]

However, the response of her students and congregation to the assassination of the Reverend Dr. Martin Luther King Jr. forever changed her. The day after King's murder, Williams announced the tragedy in her Religion in the Modern World course at Cathedral High School in St. Cloud, Minnesota, hoping to start a meaningful discussion. Yet Williams's all-white class reacted with silent indifference. Then, after a long and uncomfortable pause, a male student stood and declared, "Well that's one down, how many more to go?!"[4]

Until that moment, Williams had believed her presence was helping to break down racial barriers among the white people with whom she lived and taught. However, her students' callous reaction to King's assassination painfully exposed the futility and naivete of her campaign. Soon thereafter, Williams marched to the office of her superior and asked to be "freed" from her teaching duties so she could take up a ministry in a Black community. She also demanded to be seen for all she was.[5]

"I feel as a black woman, and a black nun in particular, that my place is with the black community," Williams stated. "If I am going to make a difference, I have to do it as a black person."[6] Although Williams's superiors assured her that her presence was "doing things for the students" and begged her to remain, she refused.[7] After seventeen years of ministry to white Catholics who could not care less about Black people, Williams was determined to chart a new path in religious life and stake her claim in the Black revolution. A few months later, Williams got the chance when Black sisters across the country formed a new political organization that denounced white racism as an "individual and institutional" sin and demanded monumental change—sending shock waves through their church. As the members of the National Black Sisters' Conference (NBSC) explained in their position paper one year later, "Our failure to speak out against this evil exposes us to the risk of miscarrying and betraying that sacred trust which God our Father has seen fit to place in our hands. . . . We black sisters cannot and will not tolerate any longer this total destruction of a great people."[8]

The formation and growth of the NBSC in the late 1960s and early 1970s reveal how a cadre of Black Catholic nuns committed to Black liberation seized the opportunity created by the rebellions that swept the nation following King's assassination. Determined to save their church's moral credibility and to become "relevant" in the Black revolution, NBSC members developed a new collective voice, style, and platform for Black Catholic sisters to demand racial justice in their church and society at large. Drawing on their foremothers' history and publicly testifying about their lived experiences of racism and sexism, these "new Black nuns" unapologetically embraced Black Power as a Christian demand and forged a Black woman–centered theology that positioned Black sisters in the vanguard of the changing freedom struggle—and rocked the Church in the process.

The Awakening of Black Nun Power

Vatican II's liberalizing reforms and social justice mandates enabled Black Catholics, especially religious men and women, to fight white supremacy within and outside Catholic boundaries in important new ways in the mid-1960s. However, King's assassination in 1968 proved a turning point for many African Americans—and the final straw for many Black Catholics. Although they and their forebears had exercised heroic patience in their individual and collective battles against anti-Black racism in their church, Black Catholics knew how culpable white Catholics were in fomenting and legitimizing the racial hatred that killed King.

As Father Clarence Williams, a founder of the Black Catholic Clergy Caucus and early NBSC supporter, later explained, until King's assassination, "We were in seminaries and convents where people accepted us as experiments. . . . You were trying to be a credit to your race; you were trying be as white as possible in your diction, in your conduct."[9] Some Black priests and sisters had even welcomed the cloister and priest collar as ways to run away from their identities and responsibilities—a strategy often employed to counter or mitigate the anti-Black bullying regularly experienced in white-administered Catholic institutions.

Writing in *America* in 1968, Sister Teresita Weind confessed to embracing assimilation and denigrating her African American heritage to lessen the sting of the racism she faced growing up Black and Catholic in Columbus, Ohio. "My peers, classmates, school teachers and co-workers made me feel like the under-dog," she wrote. "We were the first Negro family to move into a white community, and before I completed my secondary education all the white people had moved away."[10] Weind also revealed how her coping mechanism of self-hatred impacted her early journey in religious life. "Away from home, I lived behind a façade," she narrated. "So when I entered the convent, naturally I came with these habits. In the community of white sisters, I subconsciously dissociated myself from all black ties. I made a special effort never to speak about home, 'soul' food, customs, or anything 'black.' Even though I loved the black spirituals, I chose to keep my appreciation hidden. . . . For me to be 'in,' I thought I had to act 'white.' So before long I began to feel superior and consequently grew ashamed of my past."[11] However, King's assassination and the rebellions that followed proved pivotal for Weind, whose experiences in the cloister had left her unaware of who he was before his death.[12] In many other convents, seminaries, and parishes with African American Catholics, who kept abreast of and participated in the fight before April 4, 1968, King's death unleashed a righteous discontent.

In the case of the Oblate Sisters of Providence (OSP), members and the Black communities in which they served were distraught over King's murder. Although their annals rarely recorded civil rights events or sisters' emotions, an April 4, 1968, entry revealed anguish at the Holy Name of Mary convent in Chicago. "Dr. Martin Luther King shot and killed in Memphis Tenn," the OSP annalist wrote. "Horrible!—News every 15 minutes; Lost; Martin Luther King is dead!" The annals also documented the enduring shock of the assassination and the beginning of the Chicago rebellions. "Mention of & prayers for Martin Luther King at Mass," she continued. "Parents upset in afternoon; Many came for their children. Others were dismissed at 2:30; High School pupils in disorder Morgan Park & Fenger; Much disorder in Loop—West side—Fires—looting; King praised by all—Too Late; R.I.P." Four days later, five white Dominican Sisters from Chicago's St. Barnabas parish attended a memorial mass for Dr. King at Holy Name of Mary. Although the OSP welcomed the gesture of racial solidarity, the annalist's declaration "Too Late" signaled frustration with their white Catholic counterparts. That would only increase when Chicago's Irish Catholic mayor, Richard J. Daley, long suspected of having participated in the violence and looting of Black homes during the Chicago Race Massacre of 1919, instructed the city's mostly Catholic police forces to "shoot to kill" arsonists and "looters."[13]

Because nearly all Black convents were in segregated Black communities, members of the Black sisterhoods were often firsthand witnesses to the pain and fear that King's assassination caused African Americans at every socioeconomic level. Many were also moved to action as Black despair gave way to anger and rebellion. For example, Oblate Sisters of Providence Mary Marcellina (Shirley) Brooks and Alphonsa (Barbara) Spears, stationed in Washington, DC, left the protection of St. Augustine's Convent to provide medical aid to those wounded in the riots and police violence that swept the city. They also administered a food distribution center out of the historically Black parish.[14] On April 7, 1968, two Oblate Sisters of Providence, Mary Loyola (Frances Aileen) Holley and Mary Francine (Muriel) Johnson, stationed at St. Joseph Convent and School in Mobile, Alabama, took part in a memorial march for Dr. King.[15] Two days later, eight Sisters of the Holy Family, including Marie Assumpta Goudeaux, Judith Therese Barial, and Miriam Theresa Bartholomy, traveled to Atlanta to attend his funeral service and march in the subsequent procession.[16]

Before King's death, the mainstream white Catholic press had regularly amplified the opinions of white Catholics on racial justice, but Black Catholic voices were in especially high demand in the wake of the Black rebellions. Several young Black sisters spoke about their lived experiences of racism in the Church and indicted the moral bankruptcy of white Catholic America in the racial crisis. In a May 1968 op-ed in the *Catholic Review*, the nation's oldest Catholic newspaper, for example, Oblate Sister of Providence Mary Deborah (Julia) Johnson denounced the "deplorable sickness" of racism and rejected the "disgusting" fallacy that the so-called Negro problem caused King's assassination and subsequent violence. She also directed her frustrations squarely at her church. "Why is it that some bishops cry 'Don't get the Church involved,' when members of their diocese try to support marches and freedom campaigns," Johnson asked. "How 'involved' was the Church when racism within the structure of the 'universal' Catholic Church appalled many a Protestant, and many a Negro Catholic, who for years had to sit in the back of the temple of his welcoming unprejudiced God, or could only attend a 'colored' parish?" All too familiar with the Church's hypocrisy, Johnson was still willing to give the Church one last chance but not without an ominous warning. "While many can be lauded for their efforts toward equality for all men, much of the Church has been asleep to these racial concerns too long—and between minor stirrings it turns over again into a secure soundness. I fear that before long if it does not permanently arouse itself peacefully, the 'signs of the times,' of which it so frequently speaks, will incite a most startling and perhaps most unwelcome awakening."[17]

In the nation's interracial convents, the awakening to which Johnson alluded was already underway. While some Black sisters still felt stifled, others defected from religious life in explicit protest of white racism and ignorance. Sister Mary Florence (Rosaria) Floyd, the only Black member of the Daughters of St. Paul (FSP) in 1968, was in Boston with her community watching news reports on the rebellions in the city's predominantly African American Roxbury neighborhood when her superior remarked, "See how mean these people are." Floyd had endured other racist aggressions, but her superior's remark was beyond the pale. Decades later, Floyd wrote, "With her third grade education from Italy she thought that the colored people had killed Dr. King. My quiet reaction was that it was my people that she was calling mean."[18] Soon thereafter, Floyd, the daughter of NAACP leaders in Lake Charles, Louisiana, left the order to attend college and join the fight for racial justice.[19]

Many Black sisters lived among white religious who were unconcerned with Black suffering and death at the hands of white supremacists. School Sister of Notre Dame Nathan Marie (Sherrill) Adams was riding back to the convent with several housemates when the radio announced King's murder. The driver nonchalantly turned the radio off, and the others spoke about a different matter as if nothing had happened. Her counterparts' callous indifference was a hard slap in the face, as was another white School Sister of Notre Dame's declaration that the police should "just shoot the rioters" the following day. Because the School Sisters of Notre Dame taught Black children and had done so for decades, Adams was especially disgusted by these reactions, but the twenty-two-year-old nun did not feel called to leave her order yet. Instead, she went into the riot-torn areas of DC with a white priest to bring blankets and food to those affected by the uprisings.[20]

For Sister Sylvia Thibodeaux, stationed in Tulsa, Oklahoma, the site of a horrific white-on-Black massacre in 1921, white indifference would have been a blessing.[21] In 1967, the Sisters of the Holy Family (SSF) had selected Thibodeaux to desegregate the faculty of Tulsa's predominantly white Bishop Kelley High School. There, the white Sisters of Divine Providence and the white parents' organization had refused to accept her as a professional and an equal.[22] The parents' of Thibodeaux's students frequently labeled her a "socialist" and objected to her teaching history that exposed their children to "radical" ideas, such as those they contained in Upton Sinclair's *The Jungle*. Inside the convent, the Sisters of Divine Providence refused to use the same "facilities" Thibodeaux did, assigned her and a Latina sister to the "last rooms," and refused to sit by Thibodeaux at the dinner table.[23] Like many Black Catholics, Thibodeaux persevered in the face of such unholy discrimination. However, when whites in Tulsa, including most of her students' parents, openly celebrated King's assassination, Thibodeaux decided she had to leave her ministry. But Thibodeaux also knew her congregation's leaders would not approve a transfer solely based on racial discrimination.[24] One of the charisms of her African American order was to suffer gladly under the burden of white racism. Instead, Thibodeaux invited her superior, Mother Marie Anselm Duffel, for a visit, during which she witnessed how many of Thibodeaux's white nun housemates had abandoned their habits and openly dated the male religious at the school. Duffel soon approved Thibodeaux's withdrawal, even as a white nun complained that her loss meant the school could no longer qualify for federal funding as an integrated institution.[25]

King's death not only exposed the ugliest faces of white Catholicism but also set in motion a revolt that few white Catholics could have anticipated. Among those inspired to action was Sister M. Martin de Porres Grey, Pittsburgh's first Black Religious Sister of Mercy (RSM). As was true for many of her counterparts, Grey's journey into religious life had entailed overt racism and paternalism. But enduring the trauma of King's murder among women with whom she had "never felt at home" was especially distressing.[26] When Grey came upon white sisters discussing the crisis, they almost always turned quiet and cold. Everything came to a head as Grey and a group of sisters watched television footage of the rebellions. An older white nun marched into the room, approached Grey with a balled fist, and threatened her, yelling, "If anything happens to my family—" She stopped midsentence and stormed away. For Grey, then a seven-year member of the community, the attack was almost unbearable. However, when RSM leader Mother Thomas Aquinas (Elizabeth) Carroll learned of the incident, she offered unexpected support.[27]

Although she had championed Grey and spoken out on racial justice as president of the community's Mount Mercy College, Carroll, as a member of her order's leadership council, had previously hesitated over permitting Grey to become as active in the freedom struggle as she desired.[28] After King's assassination, though, Carroll completely reversed her stance. "What do you want to do for your people?" Carroll asked Grey. The fifty-five-year-old white superior also promised to support Grey in whatever she decided to do.[29] Ready to act but unsure how, Grey found direction a few days later when a Black priest from the Society of the Divine Word who was visiting Pittsburgh invited her to join an upcoming meeting of Black priests in Detroit, Michigan.[30]

The Black Catholic Clergy Caucus

Like their female counterparts across the nation, many Black priests took King's assassination as a clarion call to action. However, in 1968, only 177 of the over 58,000 US priests were Black, and fewer than 5 served in Black parishes.[31] While Black priests were not formally barred, as Black women were, from accessing power in the patriarchal Church, long-standing policies excluded Black men from most seminaries, lead pastorships in Black parishes, and the episcopacy with few exceptions. King's assassination and the calls for justice that followed created an opportunity to demand change. As such, Black priests followed the lead of their counterparts in the predominantly white Methodist and Episcopal denominations, who had revolted against racism in their churches earlier that year and begun demanding greater power and decision-making authority.[32] In fact, shortly before King's assassination, Father Herman Porter, a Black diocesan priest in Rockford, Illinois, and vice president of the Catholic Conference on the Interracial Apostolate, had called on the African American clergy to meet. King's murder and Mayor Daley's "shoot to kill" orders only underscored the urgency of Porter's call.[33]

News of the Black priests' meeting made its way to Pittsburgh through Father John Labauve, a Black Society of the Divine Word priest who in the early 1960s had worked there "doing street preaching" and returned in 1968 for a brief visit.[34] While touring St. James Parish in suburban Sewickley,

the home church of Sister M. Martin de Porres Grey, the white nuns introduced Labauve to an African American cook, who encouraged him to visit
Grey. Soon thereafter, Labauve made his way to Mount Mercy Convent and
engaged Grey in a conversation about religious life and the national crisis.
Deeply impressed with her intellect, spirituality, and passion for racial justice,
Labauve impulsively informed the young sister about the upcoming Black
priests' caucus. After Grey asked if she could attend, Labauve met with her
superior, who gave Grey special permission to travel with Labauve to participate.[35] However, the unexpected arrivals of Grey; Father Dan Mallette,
a white Chicago priest active in the Black freedom struggle; and Brother
Joseph Davis, an African American member of the Society of Mary, at the
exclusive meeting caused a stir. While Davis was a male religious, he was
not a priest and thus was initially excluded from the gathering.[36]

Because the Detroit meeting marked their first national gathering, the
approximately sixty Black priests in attendance fiercely resisted the presence of outsiders. While the group soon agreed to let Davis observe un-
officially, they steadfastly opposed Grey and Mallette. According to one
observer, Mallette left the caucus meeting with a smile and remarked, "I
expected this."[37] Grey, however, refused to budge, resulting in an ugly confrontation between the twenty-five-year-old nun and a hostile (and overtly
misogynistic) contingent of Black priests led by Fathers Lawrence Lucas,
George Clements, Rollins Lambert, William Norvel, and caucus organizer
Herman Porter.[38] Grey explained why she should be permitted to remain
and eventually won the support of a few priests, who convinced the group
to let her to stay as an unofficial observer. Grey's and Davis's presence and
interjections were not formally recorded, nor were they allowed to vote
on the group's draft statement to the nation's bishops, which declared the
Church to be "primarily a white racist institution" and called for greater
decision-making power for Black priests in the Church and Black communities.[39] Nevertheless, Grey's presence at the first meeting of the Black
Catholic Clergy Caucus proved pivotal, especially as the men recounted
their often gut-wrenching experiences of discrimination and abuse in their
respective communities or seminaries and the Church at large.

Listening to the priests' testimonies was a consciousness-raising experience for Grey.[40] However, she challenged them to consider Black sisters'
leadership and think more broadly about Black self-determination in the
Church. Grey reasoned that most African American sisters had experienced similar abuses, and she feared that without the support of Black
sisters, who she rightly guessed outnumbered Black priests significantly,

the priests' caucus might fail to wrest power from the Church's hierarchy. Thus, Grey broke protocol and spoke out against the priests' circumscribed vision of Black liberation. A few years later, Grey recalled:

> I got up and suggested they open the caucus to sisters and allow us to participate in it fully. I pointed out that there are too few black priests and too few black Catholics in the teaching body of the hierarchy. For this reason the black priests ought to combine forces with us and that maybe if this happens, our power will begin to be heard in the hierarchy. Well, it caused quite a stir, because they had a black male and a black female hang-up. I challenged them very openly on the matter, and I accused them of prejudice against their own women and of allowing themselves to be so dominated by their prejudices that they were acting irresponsibly toward the black people.[41]

Of particular concern to Grey was how fearful many of the priests were of the Church hierarchy and the potential loss of "their security," as well as what it might mean that many stated that they desired to become bishops and monsignors. She specifically worried that some of the men present would make compromises that adversely affected Black Catholics.[42]

Despite Grey's arguments, most priests present voted against including sisters in the caucus. In an act Grey saw as cowardice, the priests forced her to leave the room so she would not know who voted against her. However, a few priests, including Labauve, James Patterson Lyke, Charles Burns, and Joseph Abel Francis, a former SSF pupil and brother of soon-to-be Xavier College president Norman Francis, took Grey's criticisms seriously and suggested that she organize the nation's Black sisters in a similar fashion, which she already aimed to do.[43]

Organizing the NBSC

Back in Pittsburgh, Grey received permission to begin organizing a week-long gathering of the nation's Black Catholic sisters. Grey's fears that as a junior sister she lacked the authority to organize such a meeting were partially assuaged when she received written endorsements for the conference from Mother Mary Omer Downing, a Sister of Charity of Cincinnati and the president of the Conference of Major Superiors of Women, the largest organization of US women religious, and Pittsburgh bishop John J. Wright, who also served as chairman of the National Bishops Social Action Commission on Human Relations.[44] Mother Thomas Aquinas Carroll, the leader of the RSM offered the facilities of Mount Mercy College. Within days, Grey also received the assistance of another pioneering Pittsburgh Black nun, Vincentian Sister of Charity Mary Julian Griffin, who was on summer break from her teaching position in Montgomery, Alabama.[45]

In her inaugural letter to the nation's female superiors, sent in early May 1968, Grey stressed the gathering's necessity. She wrote, "The Negro priests strongly advised me to do something to bring all the Negro sisters in the United States together in order to evaluate the role of Negro sisters within the Church and their respective communities, to deepen their understanding of themselves and their people, and to determine more effective ways to contribute to the solution of America's racial problem."[46] Grey emphasized that Black sisters had to "support each other and understand [Black] people's position if [they were] ever to remain loyal members of [their] congregations."[47] Grey believed that a conference, being "educational" in nature, would be a better fit than a caucus.[48]

In a follow-up letter to sisters who committed to attending, Grey wrote, "I feel that we Negro religious women must use every ounce of our strength to help our people, our sisters, the parochial school, and the priests in parish work to actualize brotherhood."[49] She expressed hope that their actions and influence could help salvage the Church's reputation in the freedom struggle and the African American community. She also recognized that Black sisters alone should control the conference, without white oversight. "Many Mothers General, whether they have Negro sisters or not, have expressed in letters that they feel this should be a permanent conference," Grey wrote. "Of course, all of this and more will be up to the decision of us all."[50]

While a significant number responded positively and sent donations, most mothers general opposed the very idea of Black sisters meeting on their own terms. Beyond the clear threat that it posed to white authority in general, the NBSC threatened white supremacy in female religious life. To the 633 letters that Grey mailed, only 200 major superiors responded. And many of the responses were outright hostile. Several white superiors accused Grey of attempting to polarize the Catholic community along racial lines and refused to send any delegates.[51] Unsurprisingly, of those who replied, one-third had no Black sisters to send.[52]

Even when superiors expressed favorable opinions, they often revealed the profound racial tensions in their communities, and several noted that they had lost their only Negro sister soon after King's assassination. For example, Mother M. Mary Florence of the Sisters of Divine Providence in Kingston, Massachusetts, wrote, "I would have been happy and proud to send our one and only Negro Sister to the Conference (Aug. 18–24) but S. Mary Rose left the Community last week. Sister seemed happy but she told me she really was not and she wanted a family of her own. I asked Sister to send some other girls to us for we feel there is a gap here which we do not want."[53] In a similar vein, Sister Mary Daniel, provincial of the Sisters of Notre Dame de Namur in Ilchester, Maryland, applauded Grey's endeavor and said it would "result in much good for the cause of the racial justice." However, she wrote, "We do not have any members who qualify as Black Sisters and this I regret exceedingly. We did have one Sister but she left our community about a month ago."[54]

Learning that several pioneering Black sisters had departed from religious life within weeks of King's assassination demonstrated to Grey the profound crisis of anti-Black racism in white convents. So, too, did the responses from superiors who inadvertently revealed that white congregations continued to use formal and informal barriers to block or limit African American admissions into their ranks. For example, Sister M. Catalina of the Sisters of Saint Joseph in Milton, Massachusetts, wrote, "We do not have any Negro Sisters in our Community, Sister. This does not mean that we would not accept them, however. We did have two Negro applicants, but neither of them passed the physical examination."[55] Other communities such as the Sisters of Charity in Emmitsburg, Maryland—the first Catholic sisterhood with a US foundation—and the Sisters of the Holy Child Jesus in Rye, New York, noted that although they did not have Negro sisters in their US provinces, they did have scores in their African provinces and separate African congregations.[56]

Some African American sisters in white congregations also expressed uneasiness about attending a meeting only for Black sisters or initially failed to understand why a Black sisters' conference was even necessary. Sister Martin de Porres (Irma Jean) Coleman, the first African American accepted into the Sisters of Notre Dame de Namur, for example, had persevered in religious life in part by selectively dissociating herself from her Blackness. She had an Italian grandfather and did not readily identify herself as "a Negro" to her students, who generally perceived her to be a non-Black Latina or Filipina. Thus, when her superiors informed her about the meeting, Coleman agreed to attend primarily out of curiosity and because the gathering provided her an opportunity to see the East Coast—somewhere she had never visited. While mentioning her travel plans to her former teacher, Sister Amelia Rodriguez, Coleman even stated, "I've never seen a Negro sister." Stunned, Rodriguez stood Coleman in front of a mirror and asked, "Don't you look in the mirror?" The moment began Coleman's powerful awakening to what she had compromised in religious life. It also forced Rodriguez, who had in 1951 threatened to leave the order if Coleman was not admitted into the California province, to consider her own culpability in the community's suppression of Coleman's racial identity.[57]

Resistance from white superiors, a persistent cloister mentality, and enforced self-hatred among select Black sisters limited the reach of the NBSC even before its first meeting. However, mounting resistance from the historically Black sisterhoods, whose members accounted for over three-fourths of the total national population of Black sisters, proved most troubling to Grey.[58] Although several members of Black orders had responded publicly and passionately to King's assassination and its violent aftermath, most Black leadership councils remained opposed to their members' full engagement with the Black revolution. This was especially true of the SSF in New Orleans and the Franciscan Handmaids of Mary (FHM) in Harlem, whose Afro-Creole superiors remained skeptical of the Black Power movement.

Members of the FHM who participated in the Selma sympathy march of 1965, for example, recalled that their superiors had initially been open to the progressivism of the younger members. Mary Bertha Alexander, who entered the order in 1947, recalled that no one tried to stop those who joined the march through Harlem. Alexander and Barbara Ann Johnson, who entered the FHM in 1952, also recalled that the order was attracting some of the most talented young Black women in New York City and beyond in the 1960s.[59] However, after King's assassination, Mother Miriam Cecilia (Agnes) Cormier, the first African American school principal in the archdiocese of New York, became more conservative, voting against every progressive reform offered by the younger but fully professed members of the order.[60] On June 25, 1968, Sister Mary Immanuel (Patricia) Lucas reflected in her diary on the marked change in the posture of FHM leaders:

> It's hard to believe this is really happening to us. Every meaningful change that would attract young black women or even whites, now that they are running in herds to the inner city, is being either deleted or tabled. It almost seems like someone learned a new word and is trying to use it in every sentence. Delete this. . . . I move that we delete. . . .
>
> At lunch break when most of us were crying or just simply disgusted. Sister Elaine suggested we pray and sing "We shall Overcome." We did not overcome anything. The afternoon session was another disaster. Perhaps tomorrow will be better.[61]

While Cormier remained deeply suspicious of the NBSC meeting, the fifty-five-year-old superior agreed to send two delegates, one of whom she personally selected.[62]

Before responding to Grey's initial letter, SSF leader Mother Marie Anselm Duffel held a meeting at the congregation's motherhouse in New Orleans to discuss the matter. There, simmering tensions—between old and young, light-skinned and dark-skinned, and Creole and non-Creole—came to a head. A few sisters who supported the fight against racism remained hesitant to support the NBSC because of the derision some Black sisters in white congregations had directed at the Black orders. Although Duffel eventually agreed to send a delegate to the inaugural NBSC, she selected an older Afro-Creole sister who had vocally expressed her opposition to Black Power.[63] Complaints from several younger members who wanted to attend the meeting and pressure from local Black and white priests eventually prompted Duffel to select Sister Sylvia Thibodeaux, still stationed in Tulsa, as a second delegate.[64]

Many white sisters active in the Church's new racial justice apostolate also objected to the national organization of Black sisters. In the months leading up to the conference, Sister M. Martin de Porres Grey became a visible presence in Black liberation efforts, serving on the executive council of Pittsburgh's Black United Front, coordinating a summer Upward Bound college-preparatory program for underprivileged youth, and organizing a race relations workshop for Mount Mercy students.[65] In July 1968, Grey attended a national conference in Chicago organized and sponsored by the Department of Educational Services. By then, that organization, led by white sisters, had channeled hundreds of sisters, mostly white, into the Black freedom struggle.[66] However, the intractability of white supremacy in the Church, especially among religious, had limited the Department of Educational Services' efforts significantly. Beyond keeping Black sisters out of leadership positions, its leaders routinely employed white sisters who belonged to segregated orders and held derogatory views of Black people.[67]

Thus, when Grey voiced her concerns about ongoing racism and discrimination in the Church and the limitations it placed on Black sisters seeking to become active in the freedom struggle, many of the conference's white sister-participants responded with indignation. Some outright denied the allegations, but Grey pushed back. Concerned that many of the white sisters present spoke about the Black experience from a position of moral superiority and frequently disregarded Black humanity, Grey argued that Black people could and did speak for themselves. She also maintained that Black sisters had invaluable expertise to offer white sisters active in the racial justice apostolate. Yet many whites, especially sisters, refused to listen and accept them as equals.[68]

During the conference, Grey had an especially tense encounter with Department of Educational Services leader Sister Mary Peter (Margaret) Traxler.[69] Afterward, Traxler gave a damaging appraisal of Grey's presentation to a journalist for the *National Register* who reported that "the black militant nun [Grey] questions white Sisters teaching black children."[70] The article also falsely stated that Grey "resents white nurses nursing black patients" and told the white sisters in the audience to "get out" of the "black ghetto."[71] Though Traxler wrote the editor of the *National Register* expressing concern at what she characterized as the article's incomplete presentation of Grey's comments and its potential to result in "unintended harshness," the DES leader did not retract her negative response to Grey's criticisms or state plainly that Grey's comments were inaccurately reported, which Grey in her own letter to the editor maintained they were.[72] As a result, a substantial national controversy ensued as the young Mercy sister was still soliciting support for her conference. A few white superiors who were initially favorable to the NBSC threatened to rescind their support after reading the article. Among them were the leaders of the Sisters of the Blessed Sacrament (SBS), which had the largest population of Black sisters outside the Black orders. Grey also faced a substantial backlash within her own community.[73] The episode revealed the great barriers she was up against and the critical importance of a fair media platform.

Interestingly, efforts to discredit Grey and the NBSC in the press helped to spread the word about the meeting. Forced to do damage control by the clash with Traxler, who never personally apologized to her, Grey traveled across the country to meet with superiors and individual Black sisters to explain the purpose of the gathering. Several Black SBS members in Chicago also persuaded their white superiors to restore their support to the NBSC. In fact, white SBS superiors after meeting with Grey eventually agreed to send all their Black members.[74] Grey's travels and effective communication also ensured that news of the NBSC reached many Black sisters across the country. One noted to Grey, "Our black students on campus have let me know that they do not feel we are doing much for the cause. May we make all aware that we will be heard from in the future and that dreams for a whole America are held sacred by the black religious of America. May God prosper what you have so bravely begun."[75] A Black nun from Nairobi, Kenya, who was studying in the United States also wrote Grey, "My order

FIGURE 5.2. Photo of the National Black Sisters' Conference foundresses at Mount Mercy College (now Carlow University) in 1968. Courtesy of the National Black Sisters' Conference.

is a pure African order, and since I will be going back to teach, I am sure the experience with the Afro-American sisters and a share in their thoughts and problems will be very helpful to me in my future work."[76] Such enthusiastic responses helped buoy Grey, whom select white superiors continued to charge with polarizing the national sister community. Opposition from white sister-activists, like Traxler, who too often remained silent about racism within Church boundaries and in religious life especially, also underlined the necessity of organizing the nation's Black sisters at such a critical transition in the Black freedom struggle.

The First NBSC

On Sunday, August 17, 1968, more than 155 Black Catholic sisters representing seventy-nine congregations, forty-five US cities, the US Virgin Islands, the Bahamas, and the newly independent East African nations of Uganda and Kenya arrived at Mount Mercy College in downtown Pittsburgh for the first NBSC (figure 5.2).[77] They represented a diverse spectrum. Sister Mary Paul (Susan) Lee, OSP, and her niece, Sister Cora Marie Billings, RSM, were cradle Catholics, the granddaughter and great-granddaughter respectively of an enslaved man who labored for the Jesuit Fathers at Georgetown University. Other delegates were converts. Many were native southerners, others first- or second-generation migrants from the South or first- or second-generation immigrants from the Caribbean. Most were teachers, but some were college professors, hospital heads, and nurses. While most delegates were in their late teens and early twenties, the oldest, Sister Mary Consolata Gibson, OSP, who had reintegrated Catholic University of America in 1933 and earned a master's degree in theology at St. Mary's

College in Indiana in 1966, was sixty-one. Gibson was also the dean of her order's Mount Providence Junior College.[78]

Among the dozens of activists, educators, professionals, and religious leaders who gave presentations were Father Lawrence Lucas, vice president of the Black Catholic Clergy Caucus; Black psychologist Dr. Alvin Poussaint; Pittsburgh RSM leader Mother Thomas Aquinas Carroll; Selma march veteran Sister Mary Antona Ebo; Oblate Sister of Providence Mary Deborah Johnson; and Dr. Nathan Wright Jr., the urban affairs director for the archdiocese of Newark, New Jersey.[79] In a rather tense moment, Wright, who gave the conference's introductory remarks, asked the white audience members not scheduled to speak or serve as event transcribers, including local reporters, activists, and observers, to exit. All NBSC press announcements and invitations had clearly stated that most sessions would be closed to white observers, but some whites, including two Sisters of Loretto, ignored these directives.[80] While some Black sisters initially protested the exclusion of white observers and reporters, the group soon reached consensus that Black sisters must decide their next course of action without white interference and surveillance. Moreover, many participants agreed that certain aspects of their program needed to remain "family business" to ensure candid discussions.[81] White observers were still welcome, though, to attend Thursday's education panels and Sunday Mass, which featured Black gospel music, bongo drums, and other African-inspired cultural forms.[82]

Save for the conciliar-mandated chapter meetings and anniversary celebrations of the two oldest Black sisterhoods, a larger number of Black sisters had never before gathered in the United States. And for Black sisters in historically white orders, the mere presence of so many Black sisters was exhilarating. One sister stated, "I never knew there were so many Black Sisters in this country."[83] Some had even believed that they were the only Black sister in the country.[84] Eight Black sister-delegates from the Chicago area learned of each other's existence only through their participation in the first NBSC.[85] One of the two African delegates, who was the superior of her order in Kenya, noted that she "had only come into contact with one Black sister and one Black priest in her travels across the U.S." before attending the NBSC.[86] Another delegate even confessed, "For the first time in the eighteen years of my professed life, I am meeting four of the six other Negro members of my community."[87] Such reactions underscored the profound isolation in which many Black sisters in white congregation lived and reinforced the importance of Black sisters having a space of their own to think, share, and organize at such a critical moment in the nation's history.[88]

For most delegates from the three African American orders, the first NBSC was also profound. The OSP in Baltimore sent the largest delegation (twenty-nine sisters).[89] The predominantly white SBS sent the second-largest contingent (twenty-seven sisters), while the two remaining Black sisterhoods sent two delegates each.[90] Although Sister Sylvia Thibodeaux had permission to attend, difficulties in Tulsa had precluded her attendance, prompting the SSF superior to send another member of the order.[91] While the OSP superior sent delegates who had expressed interest or been active in the public fight for racial justice, the SSF and FHM superiors deliberately sent delegates perceived to be politically conservative.

Sister Loretta Theresa (Agnes) Richards, FHM, recalled that her superior selected her because she was "older" and not known to rock the boat. Although Richards was a descendant of Garveyites and had always felt called to serve as a member of a Black order, she reflected, "I wasn't particularly outspoken about political matters at that point in my life."[92] In an order that did not watch television or read newspapers regularly, it had also been difficult for her to stay informed about the Black freedom struggle. However, Richards intentionally selected Sister Jacinta Marie (Barbara) Johnson, a younger and more outspoken FHM member, to accompany her to the Pittsburgh meeting.[93]

Black sisters' long-standing marginalization in the Church left many delegates feeling ill equipped to talk about broad social issues at the first meeting. While many shared their personal journeys, testifying to their experiences of discrimination in religious life and the Church at large, "Black is beautiful" was still a revolutionary concept for many, particularly older sisters and those in white communities. Although the Black sisterhoods regularly taught and championed "Negro history," art, and culture, identifying as Black was jarring for many. Others in white orders testified about a culture of self-hatred that their orders explicitly and implicitly enforced.[94]

Sister of Charity Louis Marie (Beryl) Bryan, a native of Saint Thomas in the US Virgin Islands and a doctoral candidate at Columbia University at the time, for example, recalled with embarrassment two years later, "Those of you who attended the 1968 meeting in Pittsburgh might remember that even during the first few days there I had difficulty saying or thinking 'black' instead of 'Negro' or 'colored.' I shall never forget my own Freudian slip, booming out over the microphone trying to explain where I was coming from, and saying instead, 'I am a white sister from a white community.'"[95] A few delegates also directed attention to long-standing colorism in the SSF and the known practice of select light-skinned Afro-Creole sisters discriminating against Black Anglo sisters and their students.[96] Yet the delegates' public testimonies encouraged Black sisters to confront these issues head-on.

As the weeklong conference concluded, the delegates decided to form an institution from which to launch a national program of social justice and awareness led by Black sisters. They voted overwhelmingly to make the NBSC a permanent organization with an annual conference, established four regional divisions, and elected nine sisters to an executive board, three seats of which were reserved for representatives from the Black congregations.[97] The delegates also unanimously elected Grey to serve as the first president. In a press release, the NBSC announced, "Black Sisters Declare: 'BLACK IS BEAUTIFUL.'"[98] Shortly thereafter, Grey urged religious congregations to become relevant or risk further alienating or even losing their Black members. She also said, "It was unbelievable the many talents that were represented in this group. . . . I thought to myself how few religious communities are taking advantage of this great resource of black sisters. I also thought of how easy it can be for a black sister in a white community to lose her identity."[99] With little organizing experience and only four months of planning, Grey had convened representatives from Black and white orders under the banner of Black Power, bringing a mostly hidden cadre of Black churchwomen into the broader Black revolution. Reflecting on Grey's achievement decades later, Father Charles Burns, an early NBSC supporter, not only chided the founding priests of the Black Catholic Clergy Caucus for their chauvinism and "reprimand" of Grey at the Detroit meeting but also confessed that the NBSC was more meaningful. "She not only organized the Black sisters conference, but it was far better organized than the Black priests' caucus," Burns declared. "There was far more love there. There was far more intensity of purpose . . . so much beautiful work [done there]."[100] The leaders of the NBSC—a national organization that embraced the talents and expertise of Black Catholic sisters—aimed to initiate a major racial reformation in the Church. They also sought to become visible in secular Black society in new and important ways, triggering a new dimension in Black women's political activism.

Becoming "a Part of the Answer"

The delegates who attended the first NBSC were among the most educated Black women in the country. Many had broken some of the nation's oldest and most rigid racial barriers, often before the *Brown v. Board of Education* decision. As school principals, teachers, college professors, hospital heads, and nurses, many had also exercised leadership among Black and white Catholics. Unlike many Black priests, these women possessed an enviable skill set and could pinpoint areas for reform in the Church and beyond. Moreover, as Black nuns, they could draw significant media attention. However, many founding NBSC members wanted a strategic plan of action and better alignment with the Black revolution.

Coming out of the first conference, NBSC leaders sought to use the organization to salvage the Church's quickly deteriorating reputation in the African American community. However, Black sisters' conversations with non-Catholics and lay Catholics had revealed some uneasy truths. During a lively, but tense, conference session, Johnny Clark, a panelist and a Black undergraduate student at the University of Pittsburgh, had questioned Black sisters' relevance to the liberation struggle. Referencing two painful encounters that he had with Black nuns who refused to acknowledge him in a public setting, Clark argued that all nuns used their habit to distance themselves from non-Catholics, especially young Black men. Clark also referenced the miseducation that Black children received from white teachers in Catholic schools, "the hell" Black children caught if they mentioned Black history in those spaces, and the silence from Black Catholic leaders, especially religious, in confronting white Catholic racism.[101] Although some there challenged Clark to consider the Black sisterhoods' pioneering commitments to Black Catholic education that emphasized racial pride in their pupils, others admitted that by entering religious life in the predominantly white and racist Catholic Church, many African American religious had turned their backs on the Black community in soul-crushing ways.[102] Many had alienated themselves from Black culture and become acclimated to white supremacy. Some delegates from white orders confessed that they had deliberately sought to appear white to their peers and even felt good when whites noted that they did not see their color.[103] A few Black sisters in white orders even admitted that they had previously looked down on sisters in Black orders and Black Catholic institutions and refused to acknowledge Black congregational members when they encountered them in public spaces, often out of fear of white reprisals in their own orders.[104] Some delegates from the Black orders confessed to ambivalent feelings about Black sisters in white orders, sometimes rooted in having been rejected by such orders and sometimes resulting from painful encounters with Black members of white congregations who refused to acknowledge them in public.[105]

Many delegates also pointed to the Church's historically hostile posture toward African Americans, which had severely jeopardized its credibility in the wider Black community. Sister Joyce Williams, for example, testified to the cool reception that she had received from Black teachers in Chicago when she became active in an inner-city education apostolate led by white sisters during the summer of 1968. She noted that the sight of her habit discredited her with the secular Black teachers with whom she worked. Their experiences with racist and paternalistic white sisters had trained them to look at Williams as a Catholic sister first, not completely trustworthy and not authentically Black. Understanding that mistrust, Williams distinguished herself from the offensive white sisters with whom she worked, and that helped her succeed. Eventually, Williams also abandoned her veil in an act of solidarity with the people with whom she worked.[106]

The NBSC leaders understood that Black sisters—despite their individual efforts and the great work of the Black sisterhoods—had been invisible to most Black people. Consequently, these Black sister-activists realized that they needed to better demonstrate their commitment to Black liberation. They also had to rehabilitate the image of the Catholic sister and of the Church, since most African Americans viewed both as white and racist. Thus, NBSC members focused on promoting the image of the "new Black sister" by sharing their conference experiences and personal testimonies far and wide. Because of Grey's clash with Traxler and the media's failure to solicit a direct quote from Grey, which fueled the controversy, NBSC leaders also became media savvy, recognizing the critical importance of controlling the narrative about themselves and their forthcoming activism.

Upon returning to their congregations, NBSC delegates delivered written reports and oral presentations detailing the aims, objectives, and necessity of their new organization. Most also shared their conference experiences and thoughts on the Black revolution in personal conversations during recreation time or over meals. Some even began challenging their white peers who held racially derogatory views yet considered themselves allies and experts on "ministering to the Negro." For example, Sister M. Veronica Wanya, one of two African delegates to the first NBSC, openly challenged the hypocrisy of many of the white sisters in her community who ministered in Africa. She wrote Grey:

> I am now a bit more militant than I was before I attended the conference and I am proud of it. Some of the white sisters I live with were very happy that I came but others are very sorry that I was ever exposed to such things. . . . I make it worse when they [ask] me if I think missionaries should be going to Africa and I tell them if they

were going to preach Christ's love to the Africans, they should have stayed at home to teach their brothers how to love my Black brothers here and when all that is done they can go to Africa—charity starts at home. . . . I do not understand some of the American Christians. There is a parish here where the Pastor would rather throw a desk outside of the classroom than give it to a black child. Now what is that? There are days when I feel like abandoning my religious life but [it] is by the people like you that I want to join hands with because I believe that even though some are evil and ignorant many are good and fight for the right.[107]

Some NBSC delegates delivered formal presentations to their congregations. For example, Selma march participant Sister Ann Benedict (Barbara) Moore lectured to more than a hundred guests during Avila College's homecoming celebration on October 6, 1968. For Moore, then a nursing instructor at Avila, the Pittsburgh meeting had been "a wonderful week of study, prayer and charity." "We found a greater awareness of what it means to be black—to be 'black and beautiful,'" she stated. Moore emphasized the Christian aspects of Black Power to her white audience and cited the Church's failure to embrace the fight for racial justice as the major source of ongoing racial problems within Catholic boundaries.[108] While the responses that the NBSC foundresses received were often mixed, the political moment had created new opportunities to speak and act out against white supremacy.

The NBSC delegates also targeted and shared their stories in mainstream, Catholic, and Black-owned newspapers across the country. Because press access to the conference sessions had been limited, their articles often offered details that only meeting participants knew. Charged with promoting the image of the "new Black sister," delegates used their unprecedented access to the media to present their thoughts on racial justice, white racism, and the Church. Many also pushed back at the charge of separatism and embraced the calls for Black self-determination. "I really believe in [the] black front," Oblate Sister of Providence Mary Monica (Elaine) Dean told reporters from Washington, DC's *Afro-American*. "I really found [the conference] a sincere searching for the truth—awakening young people to see that we must do some re-writing of history books to give us a feeling of pride in this country. . . . Before black and white can unite, it is necessary to have this new black liberation front."[109]

Feeling renewed in their calls to religious life and empowered by telling their stories, many delegates began requesting permission to participate in the liberation struggle. This sometimes translated into becoming active in local Black Catholic lay caucuses; organizing Black studies clubs and weekend institutes, which included the teaching of Swahili, for the youth at their schools and in the neighborhoods in which they labored; requesting assignment transfers to serve in Black communities; holding antiracism workshops and seminars in their convents, parishes, and schools; and/or selling dashikis and other Black-inspired goods to raise funds for the NBSC and the wider Black Catholic movement. Some delegates also began attending meetings of prominent Black freedom organizations, such as the Southern Christian Leadership Conference, the Congress of Racial Equality, and the Black Panther Party, as well as a host of local Black freedom and community organizations. In Montgomery, Alabama, for example, Sister of the Blessed Sacrament Tarcisius (Beatrice) Jeffries joined Vincentian Sister of Charity Mary Julian Griffin, in the Montgomery Improvement Association and its Project Blackout, an economic boycott of white-owned businesses in the city's downtown district.[110] In Baltimore, Oblate Sister of Providence Mary Judith (Brenda) Williams became active in a host of Black protest and cultural organizations, included the SOUL School, founded by former Baltimore Congress of Racial Equality chair Benjamin "Olugbala" McMillan, where she taught courses in Black history and emphasized Black pride.[111] In May 1969, Sister Elfreda Chatman, the first Black Sister of the Humility of Mary, was arrested with twenty-two others after participating in a welfare rights sit-in at the Mahoning County office in Youngstown, Ohio.[112]

Black sisters in Detroit, under the leadership of Religious Sister of Mercy Mary Kimberley (Mildred) Clark, emerged as one of the most active NBSC regional committees. In September 1968, Clark invited all eighteen Black sisters working in the Detroit area; one Black priest, Father Donald Clark; and the archdiocese's only Black seminarian, Homer McClarty, to a meeting to unify themselves locally and chart an action plan.[113]

Soon thereafter, Black sisters in communion with hundreds of Detroit Black lay Catholics and clergy gained substantial local and national attention through their participation in local Black protest organizations, including the Black Panther Party. After witnessing members of the police's soon-to-be-infamous STRESS (Stop the Robberies and Enjoy the Safe Streets) unit murder two unarmed Black male teenagers outside a community center where she was working, Sister Marie Thomas (Elizabeth) Harris, the first professed Black Home Visitor of Mary, emerged as a powerful advocate against police violence in the Motor City. She called the first community meeting and press conference to denounce STRESS and led the campaign to remove the teens' killers from the Detroit police force.[114]

As a result of their activism, NBSC members emerged as preferred Catholic speakers on racial justice in many spaces. In early 1969, Sister Anita Robinson, a Benedictine Sister in Minnesota, reflected to NBSC president M. Martin de Porres Grey on this newfound popularity. "The six of us from here who attended the Conference have been invited and given panels at all the major Religious motherhouses in the state," she wrote. "We have spoken to Benedictines, Franciscans, Notre dames, and I even went to a group of Carmelites in their monastery (even though behind a grill). . . . We mostly speak on Black Power, White Racism, Miseducation, the Church and the Black Man, Black Religious in a White Community."[115] Finally recognized for their expertise in the racial justice apostolate, Black sisters used their opportunities to address Church issues, especially racism in religious life and spiritual formation programs. Speaking at the first NBSC, Saundra Ann Willingham, a former Sister of Notre Dame de Namur in Cincinnati, attributed her recent departure from religious life to such realities. "White religious women make it well-nigh impossible for Black religious women to exist as integral human beings in white orders," Willingham proclaimed. "They do this on a number of counts and on several levels but they make it impossible mainly by refusing to let the Black woman be black."[116] Speaking at a regional meeting of the Sister Formation Conference in 1969, Sister of the Blessed Sacrament Mary Cabrini (Anna) Cox implored white sisters to confront their own racism. Having suffered multiple admissions rejections from white orders in her native Iowa in the early 1950s, Cox stated, "Whites who attempt to teach . . . black [people] . . . how to love God and [their] fellowmen, yet refuse themselves to accept black candidates, to truly accept them, shout by their actions if not by their words, the pharisaical attitude denounced by Christ, 'Don't do as I do, do as I say.'"[117] In addition to calling public attention to the long-standing anti-Black racism and paternalism of many white sisters ministering in African American communities, especially educators, many NBSC members openly questioned the motives of white sisters involved in racial justice campaigns, suggesting that some, such as Traxler, were using the Black freedom struggle to gain credibility and fame in order to launch a national campaign for (white) women's rights and ordination.[118] Consequently, the NBSC initially refused to align with white sister organizations such as the National Coalition of American Nuns and Sisters Uniting, which they argued were exploiting Black suffering and false unity for personal and political gain. Although several NBSC members felt called to preaching, they also initially opposed joining white sisters who had begun advocating for women's ordination.[119] Little in their experience suggested that white female priests would be different from their male counterparts, who had mostly failed at making the Church a living witness for all people.

From the NBSC's standpoint, white sisters had tremendous work to do to become sincere allies to and effective leaders in Black communities. Speaking at a "Soul Weekend" at St. Michael's Community Center in Hartford, Connecticut, in early April 1969, for example, Grey told a room of over 150 white sisters that they "won't convert anybody until they convert themselves and their constituents." She noted that "liberal" whites were often "patronizing, paternalistic, and condescending" and wanted "freedom without risks." She argued that racism was a white problem and was often perpetuated by "good people who do not or cannot understand what the problem is." "They may perform individual acts of kindness or charity toward the black man," she stated. "But neither kindness nor charity is justice."[120]

Although she did not say so in Hartford, Grey had also discovered that some white sisters were entering the Black freedom struggle to pursue sexual encounters with Black men. At the 1968 Pittsburgh meeting, some NBSC delegates had suggested as much in private conversations. Some had also mentioned white sisters in their communities who secretly dated white priests and/or temporarily left their orders to have children.[121] Thus, most Black sisters were not shocked when *Review for Religious* published an explosive article documenting at least seventy-eight cases of ex-religious sisters—many with advanced degrees—expecting children out of wedlock with fathers who were "members of underprivileged minority groups," noting that "not one was a victim of rape."[122] The NBSC's members openly challenged the hypocrisy of white sisters—who had long used racist and sexist stereotypes about Black sexuality to keep Black people from religious life—attempting to teach Black people morals and civic values.[123] They took this stand in the face of a backlash against Black Power and expanding African American Catholic demands for justice in their church.

Fighting for Survival

More than anything, NBSC leaders believed the future of the Black Catholic community depended on their ability to become effective leaders in the Black revolution, remain in religious life, and increase their numbers. But their first meeting did not bring even 20 percent of the nation's approximately one thousand Black sisters together. Unsurprisingly, some white superiors continued to try and keep their Black members out of the organization's reach, refusing to inform their Black members about the organization or denying them permission to attend the conferences and regional meetings.

In the face of growing white opposition and Black Catholic hesitancy, several NBSC members worked to recruit additional Black sisters into their ranks. Sister Jayne Marie Simon, a Poor Clare nun in Omaha, Nebraska and one of only two Black contemplatives to attend the 1968 meeting, encouraged her peers to support the NBSC's "heroic efforts."[124] In the August 1969 issue of *Contemplative Review*, she wrote, "We contemplatives must emerge to stimulate a revolution in depth that hopefully will result in racial solidarity."[125]

Because over 75 percent of Black sisters belonged to Black congregations, while the nascent NBSC was primarily made up of Black sisters in white congregations, delegates from Black communities worked to rally their home congregations' support. The twenty-nine OSP members who attended the Pittsburgh meeting soon after delivered a position paper to their superiors emphasizing the Christian dimensions of Black Power and the critical necessity of the NBSC.[126] Three days later, the delegates held a Black Power forum for members at the order's Mount Providence Junior College. The platform called for their community to become "relevant" and endorse Black Power in five components: Black consciousness and racial pride and socioeconomic, political, cultural, and educational power. They proposed that every OSP school become a "cultural and resource center" for their communities and incorporate Black history and culture into all subjects, rather than teaching it separately as they had done for decades.[127]

Franciscan Handmaids of Mary Loretta Theresa Richards and Jacinta Marie Johnson tried to engage their conservative leaders in Harlem with the Black revolution, especially since many of their former pupils, including New York Black Panther Party members Joan Victoria Bird and Michael "Cetewayo" Tabor, both of whom were Catholic, were leading local efforts.[128] However, according to Johnson, Mother Miriam Cecilia Cormier overwhelmingly feared change. "The absence of strong generational leadership" ultimately led several FHM members to depart, sealing the congregation's fate.[129] Sister Mary Immanuel (Patricia) Lucas, sister of Black Catholic Clergy Caucus leader Father Lawrence Lucas, wrote in November 1968: "Ten years in the motherhouse and I can't stand it any longer. The community is stagnant, refusing to move ahead." She also documented the beginning of the exodus from her order, a fashion show in which "former novices model[ed] the clothes they were going to wear when they leave in a few weeks."[130] Among those to depart in late 1968 was thirty-three-year-old Johnson.[131]

In New Orleans, outside intervention and internal dissent persuaded SSF superior Mother Marie Anselm Duffel to let more members join the NBSC. At the Pittsburgh meeting, SSF delegate Mary Letitia Senegal had turned down her election to the NBSC executive board. Back in her congregation, she criticized the meeting, its young leadership, and the Black Power movement.[132] In response, Grey traveled to New Orleans to appeal directly to Duffel, who finally agreed to permit more SSF members to attend the next NBSC.[133] Sister Sylvia Thibodeaux soon after wrote Grey, noting that she was working to make her community aware of the "grave need" for the NBSC. "Know that there are many among us, who are loyal supporters, and are completely interested," she noted.[134] Thibodeaux offered to lead a substantial SSF delegation to the next conference, which she did. Soon thereafter, Duffel also permitted the NBSC to host a board meeting at the SSF motherhouse.[135]

From August 6 to 16, 1969, over two hundred Black sisters gathered at the University of Dayton in Ohio for the second NBSC, on the theme of Black Survival: Past, Present, Future. It immersed delegates in Black history, culture, theology, and spirituality and provided educational materials for their curricula and ministries. Speakers included noted Black civil rights activists Reverend C. T. Vivian, director of affiliates in the Southern Christian Leadership Conference, and Bernice Reagon, a member of the Student Nonviolent Coordinating Committee Freedom Singers and then an instructor at Spelman College, as well as noted Black theologians and historians Dr. Vincent Harding and John Henrik Clarke.[136] Like at the Pittsburgh meeting, white sisters and priests were restricted from most sessions, save for the "Soul" Mass and educational panels.[137]

At Dayton, NBSC delegates formalized the organization's structure and drafted their constitution. Twenty-one delegates, including sixty-two-year-old Oblate Sister of Providence Mary Consolata Gibson, wrote a position paper, "The Survival of Soul."[138] It pledged "to work unceasingly for the liberation of black people," denounced white racism, and articulated a "course of action to the end that all may be free, and in that freedom to become one in God."[139] It also maintained that despite centuries of oppression, Black people were still in proud possession of "that indefinable yet identifiable 'soul,'" which NBSC members would assert through political and social programs.[140] In fully embracing Black Power, NBSC leaders gave moral legitimacy to a political philosophy that most whites, including Catholics, impugned. In an interview given to the Black press earlier that year, Oblate Sister of Providence Mary Paraclete (Doris) Young, a member of the committee, argued that her order's long-standing educational ministry to Black girls was an expression of Black Power. Noting that Black Power included "self-respect, self-identity, and self-determination," Young simply concluded, "We've just found a name for what we've been doing all these years."[141]

The NBSC leaders also focused on the exodus of young Black sisters from religious life. At the second conference, the NBSC board found that over fifty of its members had departed religious life, and scores more planned to leave soon.[142] A few had left on relatively good terms and for reasons unrelated to the freedom struggle. However, most had either defected in protest or been forced out because of their involvement in Black liberation. In a widely publicized case, Oblate Sister of Providence Mary Judith (Brenda) Williams was dismissed in January 1969 after she spoke publicly on the utility of "spiritual" violence in the Black revolution, which OSP leaders had forbidden her to do.[143] Williams was devastated, especially as the OSP had rescued her vocation after a Polish order in Chicago had dismissed her on the basis of race six years earlier. Williams's dismissal, which was protested by NBSC leaders and a few white supporters, weakened a budding relationship between the NBSC and the order, which had been an early supporter.[144]

Black sisters in white orders also faced an onslaught of resistance to their rising racial awareness and political activism.[145] Among them was School Sister of Notre Dame Nathan Marie Adams, who, like many others, requested permission to work in a Black school and "get involved in [Black] community social and political activities" following the first NBSC. Her superiors, however, responded, "That is not the work of Notre Dame." When Adams cited the order's long-standing ministry to underserved communities, her superiors refused to budge, punishing her by delaying her perpetual vows for several years.[146] By extending Black sisters' formation periods, some white superiors seemingly hoped to drive young activists out of religious life and thwart the NBSC. Even Grey was prevented from taking her final vows in 1968, with one council member maintaining she "was not yet ready."[147] Grey, however, only had to wait one additional year.[148]

Some white Catholics also used on-the-job harassment to intimidate Black sister-activists, and some NBSC members lost their jobs because of their activism. For example, in May 1969, a white priest fired Sister Mary Julian Griffin from St. Jude High School in Montgomery, Alabama, after she refused to stop participating in freedom movement activities.[149] Already fully professed, Griffin returned to Pittsburgh to await reassignment to the racial justice ministry. However, many NBSC members were in temporary vows and consequently more vulnerable to dismissal, prompting NBSC leaders to develop a formal strategy to preserve and expand religious life for Black women.

In early 1970, the organization sent a questionnaire to US sisterhoods to gain a better statistical profile of Black women religious and track those leaving religious life. Many congregations refused to participate, but some returned questionnaires confirming NBSC leaders' fears about why Black sisters were departing. In one telling example, the Sisters of Providence in Issaquah, Washington, revealed they had lost their only two Black novices in the previous two years. The order's provincial superior wrote, "One postulant . . . said her being black had no bearing on her decision" and characterized the other as "defensive and race conscious. She did not receive permission to receive the holy habit."[150] Such statements confirmed the specific dangers Black sisters faced when they expressed racial pride and spoke out against injustice, while, as demonstrated in chapter 3, white sisters could be openly racist in their words and actions and never suffer any significant consequences. With the prospect of an even larger exodus before the 1970 meeting, NBSC leaders worked to develop programs and initiatives to ensure the growth of the Black sister population. They also began to articulate what can be called a Black Catholic women's liberation theology, which envisioned God as Black and understood female celibacy as a righteous act of Black liberation, as they continued to assert leadership in the fight against injustice in the Church.

"Celibacy Frees Us to Free Thousands"

The NBSC's members were deeply influenced by and contributed in important ways to what scholar James Cone termed Black theology in the late 1960s and 1970s.[151] Their conferences not only operated as spiritual and educational safe havens for Black religious struggling to negotiate white racism, but also served as early training grounds for Black Catholics seeking new forms of worship and preaching after Vatican II. Though many African American Catholic families listened to gospel music at home, and though some schools run by Black sisters taught Black history and art, including the "Negro spirituals," Black cultural and spiritual traditions were rarely incorporated into the Mass before the late 1960s.[152]

Answering the call of Vatican II that the faithful embrace the Church's multicultural dimensions, Grey brought African American Christian musicians and dancers to Dayton to help Black sisters and priests institutionalize African and African American spiritual traditions into the Mass.[153] Because Black priests were systematically denied the opportunity to lead Black parishes, the NBSC meetings were also the first spaces in which several Black priests offered Mass to an all-Black audience. Freed from white parishes' traditional restraints, these priests preached homilies that "went on for hours."[154] They applied Catholic social teaching to the everyday realities of Black lives, using themes of Black liberation, Black Power, and Black suffering. Black sister worshippers at NBSC Soul Masses often responded emotionally in the call-and-response tradition of African and African American spirituality.[155]

The Black sisters' conferences also served as some of first Catholic "classrooms" in which Black liberation theology was taught, discussed, and debated. Of Dayton's thirteen formal talks and presentations, six centered on Black spirituality and Black theology.[156] And the Black attendees were eager and critical learners and practitioners, which impacted the speakers. In his address on the need for a Black theology, Dr. Vincent Harding, a close advisor to the Reverend Dr. Martin Luther King, Jr., remarked he was moved to see Black sisters and priests "coming out of a white world . . . trying to move back into the dances of our homeland." "And I trust that you know even though they are called the 'Popcorn' and the 'Bugaloo' and everything else now, that they are the dances of our homeland," Harding proclaimed. "They are the dances that we danced a long long time ago before somebody told us that it was evil and sinful to dance the dances of our religion."[157]

Other presenters challenged the sexism inherent in the emerging Black theology, which centered Black men and largely erased Black women. Student Nonviolent Coordinating Committee activist Bernice Reagon, for example, used sex-inclusive language and discussed Black women as vital leaders and transmitters of Black cultural traditions. In his address on Black spirituality and revolution, Reverend C. T. Vivian noted that the audience of "nuns and sisters, all black and beautiful," reminded him of the critical role sisters played in Selma. Vivian also shared an anecdotal story about a white segregationist from Mississippi who had a near-death experience and briefly experienced heaven. Asked what God was like, he replied, "She's black."[158]

Black theology offered a new language and analysis through which Black sisters could demand racial justice in the Church and position themselves as natural leaders. In "The Survival of Soul," NBSC members declared:

We black religious women see ourselves as gifted with the choicest of God's blessings. The gift of our womanhood, that channel through which the Son of God Himself chose to come into the human race, endows us with those qualities and prerogatives which are designed for the deliverance of humanity.... And the gift of our religious vocation makes accessible to us that union with Christ which guides us to the task, strengthens our determination, and sustains our efforts to free ourselves and our black brethren from the intolerable burden forced upon us as the victims of white racism.[159]

In this document, Black sisters showed themselves to be early theorists and practitioners of Black womanist theology—which centered the experiences and perspectives of Black women—in the United States. By committing themselves to Black liberation and asserting themselves as capable leaders in the changing freedom struggle, NBSC members joined other Black women of the era who fiercely rejected the sexist notion that only Black men should lead.

After Dayton, the influence of Black theology became readily apparent in Black sisters' presentations and talks. Speaking to her nearly all-white congregation in late 1969, Humility of Mary Sister Elfreda Chatman, for example, argued that a just church could "be intelligible only in terms of a Black person's insistence that knowledge of one's own identity—one's self, nation, culture, religion, God—is indispensable to a creative life for the individual and for all people." Anticipating allegations of Black separatism, Chatman explained, "It is not the principle of integration—that is, total acceptance without discrimination—which we question, but our destiny as a people." She also declared that Black Catholics wanted to "be shown positive images of blackness in our Church" as they sought "to free" themselves "from the deep feelings of self-rejection, cultural alienation, and social estrangement which have pervaded and corrupted" their "personalities."[160] While Chatman declared that Black sisters sought a church that gave them the freedom "to worship a Black Messiah, a God Who created us black and loved the beauty of His Creation," some, like Sister Joyce Williams, frequently retold C. T. Vivian's story in which God appeared to discriminatory whites as a Black woman. Williams also often drew on biblical understandings of restitution when calling for white atonement for racism: "If you steal from me my good name, you have to give it back."[161] The NBSC leaders' embrace of Black theology and Black pride was part of the evolving freedom struggle, in which "Black Power" and "soul power" enabled Black people to counter years of anti-Black miseducation and its impact on Black people's thinking and worship styles.[162]

Thus, by the third NBSC meeting, held at the University of Notre Dame in August 1970, the tone, conversations, and appearances of most African American sisters, priests, and seminarians had changed. Many of the over two hundred attendees donned secular attire, dashikis, or other African-inspired dress. The NBSC president, Sister M. Martin de Porres Grey, underwent one of the most dramatic transformations, not only abandoning the modified RSM habit she had worn at previous conferences but also sporting a short Afro, big hoop earrings, and stylish clothes inspired by America's rising soul culture. The Notre Dame meeting also featured a maturation of the Soul Mass and panels in which Black sisters fully embraced the Black revolution.[163] As NBSC vice president Sister Marcellina Brooks put it in her address, "No longer can it be said that religious do not know what's happening. Many black religious are what's happening."[164]

Organized under the theme Celibate Black Commitment, the Notre Dame conference sought to understand the roots of the Black vocational crisis and assess the Black Catholic future in the Black freedom struggle. Delegates also renewed their vows of celibacy, noting their utility in such times of great social change and upheaval.[165] In her address, Sister of the Holy Family Theresa Perry linked celibacy to Black freedom, saying, "To be celibate means that we have dedicated ourselves totally and completely to building the new . . . to ushering in the future. . . . The challenge is to free yourself enough so you can free other people."[166] Similarly, Grey argued, "To be a celibate woman, to be a black woman, to be a committed woman—knowing that you have all three of these strains of power simultaneously swimming in your body of woman pronounces promise and danger for yourself, your fellow sisters, your friends—men, women and children."[167] In declaring celibacy a radical act of Black liberation, NBSC members powerfully challenged the masculinist ethos of certain segments of the Black protest community that regarded Black women as able to contribute only through motherhood. In demonstrating themselves to be formidable leaders in the Catholic fight for racial justice, they also challenged the misogyny and sexism of many of their male counterparts who had initially believed Black sisters needed to stand behind Black priests in their quest for Black power in the Church.

Indeed, by 1970, the NBSC arguably stood in the vanguard of the Black Catholic movement. Headquartered at Mount Mercy College with a full-time staff of six sisters, a secretary, and a printing press, the organization claimed membership of over 350 sisters and ex-sister affiliates. It had a powerful media platform and the unconditional support of Pittsburgh leader Mother Thomas Aquinas Carroll, who the following year was elected president of the Leadership Conference of Women Religious (formerly the Conference of the Major Superiors of Women). In many respects, the NBSC had also overtaken the Department of Educational Services as the nation's most prominent sister-led racial justice organization. In 1970, the NBSC served as the model for both Las Hermanas, a racial justice organization of Chicana and Latina nuns, and the National Black Catholic Seminarians Association, and it helped each organization's leaders develop their mission statements and organizational structures. The Black seminarians, who like Black sisters were excluded from the Black Catholic Clergy Caucus, organized their association at the NBSC's Notre Dame conference.[168]

But just as the NBSC was finding direction and expanding its reach, support for transformative racial change in the Church began to drop. Driven largely by shock and guilt after King's assassination, a notable number of white ecclesiastical authorities and Church leaders had been willing to listen to Black demands for racial justice within Catholic boundaries. Several archdioceses, dioceses, religious congregations, and Catholic organizations had also provided substantial financial support to the Black Catholic movement in its early years. However, white allies in the Church increasingly became endangered species. Progressive white priests and sisters who had supported the Black Catholic movement also departed religious life in droves—often in protest against rising racial and political conservatism in the Church. Some Black Catholics remained skeptical of the utility of Black Power and opposed the outspokenness of some Black priest and sister leaders. The NBSC leaders, however, pledged to move forward despite the risks. As Sister M. Martin de Porres Grey explained in her 1970 presidential address, "The NBSC is a radical movement. A radical movement does not incorporate every person in its course."[169] The opposition to the NBSC would remain steady. However, the growing crisis of Black Catholic education, specifically the mass closings of Catholic schools in Black and inner-city communities, soon united even the most conservative Black Catholics in the fight to preserve their communities' prized possessions and chief evangelization vehicles.

6. "No Schools, No Churches!"

THE FIGHT TO SAVE BLACK CATHOLIC
EDUCATION IN THE 1970S

Education and religion are the first two subversive forces that an oppressed people can use to liberate themselves. Religion is the guts of all human life; it can be used to silence a people or deliver a nation. —NATIONAL BLACK SISTERS' CONFERENCE, "NBSC Practicability Study," 1972

On Monday, April 5, 1971, representatives from Baltimore's Black Catholic Lay Caucus traveled to the motherhouse of the Oblate Sisters of Providence (OSP) for an urgent meeting with Mother Mary of Good Counsel Baptiste. Distraught over the threatened closing of scores of Black Catholic schools across the nation, the caucus's members aimed to develop a long-term solution with the sixty-four-year-old superior. They also sought to warn Baptiste of a duplicitous local campaign then underway. "Some priests have initiated long range plans to close black schools staffed by the Order," the delegates charged. "In order to shift attention from their plans and motives they will attack and deliberately antagonize the Sisters in hope that the Order will withdraw. They will then place the blame for the school closings on the sisters." The caucus warned that the assault would only "escalate and intensify" and stressed the need for "strong black leadership" and unity among Black Catholics. They also called for rejection of the survival tactics many Black Catholics had long employed to remain in their church. "The traditional Negro Catholic responses that 'white is right' must be replaced with an objective and analytical assessment of the role we, as blacks, have played in the perpetuation of the oppression of our people," the delegates asserted. Although the representatives acknowledged the unique pressures that Black sisters faced from both "black and white Catholics" to "defend [either] the Church or their people," they cautioned Baptiste against timidity. "We will hang together or we will hang separately," the delegates warned.[1]

In the early 1970s, no issue was of greater concern to the African American Catholic community than the survival of the Black Catholic educational system. Before 1965, Church- and state-mandated school integration had closed or merged (with other with schools) several long-standing southern Black Catholic schools, many of which were led by the Black sisterhoods. Although members of the Black laity and sisters often protested these closures, the lack of a national Black Catholic apparatus left impacted communities with few options. However, the crisis of the late 1960s threatened the Black Catholic educational system with extinction. Between 1968 and 1969 alone, 637 US Catholic schools closed with schools in inner cities whose student bodies had transformed from white to predominantly Black or all Black following the Great Migrations and white Catholic withdrawal hit especially hard.[2] Because Catholic schools had historically been the primary vehicles for evangelization in Black communities, many observers viewed archdiocesan and diocesan decisions to close Black Catholic schools (almost always without consulting Black faculty or parents) as proof of a concerted Church effort to abandon African American communities. Some even understood it as part of massive white Catholic resistance to the civil rights movement and increasing demands for racial justice within the Church. As such, the nation's Black priests, sisters, and lay Catholics organized on local and national levels and fought back.

In a daring 1971 move, the leaders of the newly formed national Black Catholic religious and lay organizations, including Sister M. Martin de Porres Grey, the president of the National Black Sisters' Conference (NBSC), traveled to Vatican City to present their grievances to Pope Paul VI (figure 6.1). During their meeting with Vatican secretary of state Giovanni Bennelli, second in power only to the pope, the delegates argued that the Catholic Church was "dying" in the Black community, citing enduring racism in the Church, the interconnected crises of Black vocation losses and Black Catholic school closings, and the pressing need for Black leadership. In addition to recommending Black replacements for the retiring archbishop of Washington, DC, Patrick O'Boyle, the group presented Bennelli

FIGURE 6.1. The 1971 Black Catholic delegation to Vatican City. Standing from left to right: Charles Hammock, president of the board of directors of the National Office for Black Catholics; Joseph Dulin, president of the National Black Catholic Lay Caucus; Brother Joseph M. Davis, executive director of the National Office for Black Catholics; and Father Lawrence Lucas, president of the Black Catholic Clergy Caucus. Seated from left to right: Estelle Collins, a member of Baltimore's Black Catholic Lay Caucus; and Sister M. Martin de Porres (Patricia) Grey, president of the National Black Sisters Conference. Courtesy of the National Black Sisters' Conference.

with several Black Catholic publications, including the NBSC's *Celibate Black Commitment, Black Survival,* and *The Black Religious Woman as Part of the Answer,* and outlined the grave challenges facing the US Black Catholic community.[3] However, the meeting did not produce tangible results. Bennelli remained skeptical of the delegation's complaints, noting they were "in conflict with the reports from white American bishops." As a result, the Italian prelate advised the group to take a "slow and measured" approach to addressing their grievances.[4] In interviews given upon her return to the United States, however, Grey demurred. "The reality of the black Catholic situation in America is and has been one of separatism created by the domin[ant] culture of the American Catholic Church," she declared.[5] In addition to noting that Black Catholics had already demonstrated heroic patience with white Catholic racism, the NBSC president argued that the present crises demanded immediate action. "Within five years, most parochial schools in Black communities will be non-existent," Grey declared, adding, "It does not have to happen."[6]

This chapter chronicles Black sisters' efforts to preserve African American Catholic education and female religious life in the crucible of the 1970s. Like all sister leaders in 1971, the heads of the African American sisterhoods and the NBSC were knee-deep in an institutional crisis that few had predicted. After decades of steady exponential growth, the US Church was in distress. In the previous five years, thousands of religious men and women had departed their congregations. Among sisters, the figures were especially stark. In 1966, the national sister population had reached an all-time high of 181,421.[7] By 1971, that number had plummeted to fewer than 147,000, not including deaths.[8] Equally distressing was the state of the US Catholic educational system.[9] Between 1965 and 1971, over 1,500 Catholic elementary and secondary schools closed, and thousands more were threatened with extinction. Northern cities already experiencing massive white Catholic suburbanization, such as Milwaukee, Saint Paul, Chicago, Detroit, and Denver, recorded enormous one-year drops in Catholic school enrollment and closed scores of parochial schools, including some of the region's oldest.[10] Thus, as the 1970s began, most sister leaders, especially those whose congregations staffed Catholic schools, were faced with two herculean tasks: reversing the decline in their memberships and keeping their order's institutions viable.[11]

For the nation's Black sisters, however, these crises were substantially more acute. Not only was the rate of African American departures from religious life double that of white departures, but Catholic schools in predominantly Black inner-city communities were more likely to face closure or merger than their white suburban counterparts.[12] Most Black faithful had welcomed desegregation on principle. However, both Catholic and secular school desegregation had resulted in the closure of long-standing Black schools and the token integration of some Black students and a handful of Black teachers into previously all-white institutions. In many cases, Black parents voluntarily withdrew their children from Black Catholic schools to support government- and Church-mandated desegregation. However, thousands across the country, especially those skeptical of white-directed integration and wary of violent massive resistance to desegregation— remained committed to the survival of Black Catholic education, especially institutions led by Black nuns. In fact, many Black Catholic leaders of the 1970s viewed the dismantling of the Black Catholic educational system as part and parcel of the larger white Catholic backlash to the civil rights gains of the 1950s and 1960s—something Black Catholic activists felt had to be contested and stopped.

Without Black Catholic religious and schools, many Black faithful reasoned that the Church would lose all credibility and cease to function effectively, if at all, in the African American community. As one African American mother and delegate to a convention of Black Catholics held at the University of Detroit and sponsored by the National Black Catholic Lay Caucus explained in 1971, "Education is the most important thing for our children. We don't need drug centers or birth control centers as much as we need good schools."[13] Because Black Catholic schools had also played leading roles in the education of thousands of non-Catholic Black professionals, segments of the wider African American community also took notice and threw their support behind Black Catholic leaders struggling to preserve African American access to Catholic education. During the 1970s, Black sisters and their supporters employed a host of tactics, from strategic accommodation to direct-action protest, to keep surviving Black Catholic schools open. However, their efforts would be met with formidable resistance from forces bent on maintaining the racial status quo and evading the Church's moral responsibilities for equality and justice.

The Origins of the Black Catholic Educational Crisis

In 1965, the US Catholic Church operated the largest private school system in the world.[14] As early as the 1950s, though, a small contingent of Church officials questioned the wisdom of having expanded it so rapidly. Citing the common overcrowding of Catholic classrooms and the strain placed on teaching sisterhoods, a few clerics even argued that parish schools should begin limiting rather than increasing their enrollments. Otherwise, the quality of Catholic education would suffer. In 1956, Monsignor William McManus, the assistant director of the National Catholic Welfare Conference's Department of Education, surveyed twenty-eight archdiocesan and diocesan school systems and found them all strained beyond capacity, turning away hundreds of students annually. In "How Good Are Catholic Schools?" in the prominent Catholic weekly *America*, McManus wrote, "Our schools' rapid growth also explains the occasional awkwardness of Catholic education, e.g. overcrowded classrooms, temporary employment of poorly qualified teachers, 'hit or miss' procedures in selecting students for our limited high-school accommodations, clumsy supervision."[15] For

McManus and others, the Church's goal to have every Catholic child in a Catholic school was simply unrealistic. Even with peak enrollments in 1965, the system educated only 47 percent of the Church's children.[16]

With enrollments straining Church resources and forcing schools to turn away tens of thousands of students every year, lay observers also began to question the viability of the Catholic system. In her searing critique *Are Parochial Schools the Answer?* (1964), Mary Perkins Ryan, a white Catholic housewife and prominent voice in the liturgical reform movement, argued that the parochial school system had outlived its cultural and historical purposes. Ryan argued that the model failed to address the needs of adult Catholics and the life experiences of its diverse participants. Other lay critics cited the system's overcrowded classrooms and the lack of money, teachers, and space as proof of the need for reform and perhaps even downsizing.[17] Nonetheless, in 1965, the majority of Catholics, including the Black faithful, agreed that Catholic schools had to be sustained.

Between 1965 and 1970, though, enrollments in US Catholic primary and secondary schools dropped by over 21 percent, from 5.6 million to 4.4 million, and the number of schools declined from 13,1396 to 11,352.[18] While demand for Catholic education remained relatively high, especially among African Americans and white Catholic suburbanites, declining numbers of sisters translated into higher tuition rates, since schools had to hire lay teachers to supplement depleted teaching staffs. Unable and in many cases unwilling to pay the higher costs, thousands of middle- and working-class parents moved their children to public schools. This, combined with the steady white Catholic flight to suburban areas, where the parochial school system was much less developed, caused Catholic school enrollments to plummet. Between 1965 and 1968, elementary school enrollment alone dropped from 4.5 million to 3.9 million students.[19] In response, archdioceses and dioceses across the country began closing hundreds of schools. No area of the country was exempt, but Catholic schools in inner-city and predominantly Black communities were hit especially hard.[20]

New state laws banning federal aid to private education, on which many white Catholic schools depended, also drove the crisis. However, these factors alone do not adequately explain what happened with Black Catholic education. While white Catholic school enrollments plummeted between 1965 and 1970, African American enrollments increased. In 1965, for example, approximately 99,245 Black youths were enrolled in over 349 Catholic elementary and secondary schools. By 1970, Black enrollments reached an all-time high of 112,987, despite the increasing precarity of Black

Catholic schools.[21] Over the next five years, Black Catholic school enrollments would drop to 107,313, largely because of school closures and mergers, not declining Black support for Catholic education.[22] A 1970 study by the National Office for Black Catholics highlighted that support, revealing that African American parents, regardless of class background, consistently paid higher Catholic tuition rates than white Americans of the same class, an average annual tuition of $400 per child, while their white counterparts paid $160. The study also found that African American parents often paid more for one child's education than whites paid for five children, underscoring both how highly African Americans valued Catholic education and how unequal the Catholic school system was.[23]

In other ways detailed later, African American parents repeatedly demonstrated their dedication to Catholic education. That fact, and the insufficiency of other arguments to explain the crisis, suggest that it had an additional root: white Church leaders' long-standing, overtly racist opposition to substantial investment in Black Catholic education and evangelization.

While Black Catholic priests and sisters achieved a host of monumental firsts during the civil rights era, meaningful integration and racial justice proved elusive. Archdiocesan and diocesan plans (generally devised by white clerical and lay leaders) to integrate the Church's institutions, particularly its schools, almost always demanded closing Black schools and resulted in the token entry of a handful of Black youth into previously all-white Catholic schools with nonintegrated faculties.[24] For example, when St. Louis archbishop Joseph Ritter famously initiated desegregation in his diocese, he ordered the historically Black St. Joseph Catholic School closed in 1951 but made no formal provisions to ensure the admittance, protection, and retention of displaced Black students in the local white institutions. Moreover, across the nation, white Catholics mounted powerful campaigns against racial integration with the direct and indirect support of many Church leaders, prompting many Black Catholics to question publicly the sincerity of white Catholic commitment to racial justice. During a "confrontation group" at the 1969 meeting of the National Black Sisters' Conference in Dayton, Ohio, for example, participants pointed out that twenty-seven white priests from the city had written a paper "opposing desegregation of the school in the south."[25] Others noted that while members of the Episcopal hierarchy, other Protestant leaders, and some Catholic sisters and priests participated in the Selma protests of 1965, "the Roman Catholic Church in the form of its hierarchy neglected to commit itself during the freedom marches."[26] Such clear examples of individual and institutional fidelity to racial segregation in the Church were searing. So, too, was the pernicious resentment that some white sisters increasingly directed at Black sister-educators who began amplifying long-standing African American complaints about the detrimental impact of white sisters' educational ministries in Black communities.

At the first meeting of the NBSC in Pittsburgh, the sisters' small group discussions drew specific attention to the cultural incompetence and general unfitness of many white sisters teaching in Black schools. These discussions also emphasized the need for all sister educators of Black children to be able to instill Black pride in their pupils.[27] Speaking to a national group of white sisters ministering in the African American community at a Department of Educational Service conference in Chicago in 1969, a NBSC member explained how white-administered Catholic education often propagated white supremacy and enforced racial self-hatred in Black children. "You've done our children too much harm already with your stories of white angels and a white God," the sister declared. "And the devil's black isn't he, in the stories you've crammed down our children's throats? . . . I've heard you in and out of the convents, reassuring one another. 'The black children love the white nuns more than they do the black nuns.' . . . Because you've taught our children to love white and to hate black. . . . You've taught our children to love you and to hate themselves."[28] Speaking at the same meeting, School Sister of St. Francis Daniel Marie Myles testified about her gut-wrenching experiences of racism while desegregating her order, which was perceived to be a champion of racial equality. Myles also documented how the white members of her order who taught Black children with her in Chicago condemned her membership in the NBSC and continued to exclude her in explicitly hateful ways. "We're rejected, resented and hated, and we [Black nuns] know it," Myles stated.[29] While a few white sisters in attendance acknowledged their moral and educational failures in the Black community, one white nun told an observer, "Do you really think those black people in the ghetto could get along for one month or one week without our committed white sisters?"[30] The persistent of such paternalistic and racist attitudes among white sisters ministering in Black communities left many Black Catholics wondering if staying in the Church was worth the cost. While many Black Catholics opted to leave, others vowed to stay and fight. This was especially true of those who believed that preserving and transforming Black Catholic educational institutions was the key to dismantling white supremacy.

In the late 1960s, public protests against the mass closings and mergers of Catholic schools in inner-city and predominantly Black communities erupted across the nation. From New Orleans to Chicago, Charleston to New York, and Cincinnati to Detroit, African American Catholics demanded that Catholic schools not only remain open and accessible but also become true sites of Black educational liberation. Activists accused white ecclesiastical authorities, priests, sisters, and school boards of deliberately abandoning their professed commitments to Black Catholic education and giving in to massive white (Catholic) resistance to civil rights and demands for racial equality. While many Black (and some white) observers charged that the closures and mergers resulted from anti-Black racism, ecclesiastical and school board officials (overwhelmingly white and male) dismissed such claims. They cited instead the declining number of teaching sisters, increased operating costs, and the large presence of Black Protestants in formerly white Catholic urban neighborhoods as the chief catalysts, especially in the inner city.[31] However, ever-increasing African American Catholic school enrollments and the demonstrated willingness of African American parents to pay substantially higher tuition rates than their white and suburban counterparts belied claims that Black schools were no longer viable investments.[32] Simultaneously, white Church leaders directed substantial resources to building a new educational system to accommodate white Catholic suburbanization, itself in part an effort to circumvent racial integration. As a coalition of Black priests, sisters, and lay Catholics fighting proposed school closures in Detroit explained in 1970, "Education is liberation! And quality education is vital to the survival of the Black community. . . . The Catholic Church, if it is seriously interested in the survival of the Black community—the Black Catholic community—must take a stand in favor of our schools . . . in the inner city."[33]

Such marked differences in the Church's responses to Black and white communities were also apparent to those outside the Black community. "It is shocking to learn that the schools that are being 'phased out' are inner city schools which have the largest enrollment," William E. Brown, a white Catholic activist, wrote in 1970. "What message can possibly come through to these . . . people and the . . . communities among whom they live, except that the Church is not interested in them because they drain off too much energy and money? . . . The faith and courage of these . . . people . . . [fighting for] these schools holds up to shame before God and men the lack of charity and generosity of the people and their leaders who proclaim themselves to be the people of God, Christ present in the world."[34]

From the perspective of Black Catholic leaders, the decision to close inner-city and predominantly Black Catholic schools while steadily investing in suburban schools for richer white Catholic families was tantamount to racial genocide. As such, Black Catholic leaders took drastic measures to direct national and secular attention to the crisis. In Detroit, protesters led by NBSC member Sister M. Shawn Copeland and National Black Catholic Lay Caucus president Joseph Dulin responded to the archdiocese's 1970 proposal to close 75 percent of its schools, including its only Black Catholic high school, St. Martin de Porres, by seizing the all-Black Visitation Catholic Church on the Sunday after Thanksgiving. Adopting the tactics of the civil rights movement, the group sat in and blocked the church's entrance. "No schools, no churches!" the group proclaimed to reporters and the parishioners prevented from attending Visitation's three Sunday morning masses.[35] Because St. Martin de Porres High School had been established owing to the widespread exclusion of Black youth from most white Catholic schools in the archdiocese, protesters feared its closure would lead to "a systematic phasing out of Catholic education in the inner city."[36]

Such dramatic actions in Detroit brought Cardinal John Dearden to the table with three hundred Black Catholic leaders and parents in early December 1970. However, the meeting only exacerbated the tensions between the protesters and the white-led archdiocese. The group charged Dearden with addressing them in a cold, dismissive manner and giving evasive answers to their questions and demands. The archdiocese maintained its decision was driven by the new state law banning public aid to private schools and pointed out that it "took up a special collection [that] year to aid 21 financially troubled inner city schools," which were three-fourths Black.[37] The protesters argued that Church leaders who had unapologetically upheld segregation and exclusion could find the will to support Black Catholics in their "number one priority in the inner city ... EDUCATION."[38] "Blacks have demonstrated, picketed, protested, prayed, cried, and believed in the White racist Church in an unfruitful effort to become full human beings and total members of the Church," local Black sisters and lay leaders said in a statement. "This in itself is a failure on the part of the Church."[39] Across the country, Black Catholics kept the pressure up.

Since their institutions were usually the first targeted for closure by white-led archdiocesan and diocesan councils in the early years of desegregation, the leaders of Black teaching sisterhoods had been the earliest to recognize and confront the crisis. As the progenitors of Black Catholic education, these orders had built an impressive and mostly accredited network of seventy-five elementary and secondary schools across the United States during Jim Crow.[40] However, between 1954 and 1965 alone, five schools administered by the Oblate Sisters of Providence (OSP), including their St. Rita Academy in St. Louis, Missouri, and seven schools administered by the Sisters of the Holy Family (SSF) closed or merged.[41] While the SSF opened three new educational ministries, two of them in Los Angeles, during the period, in 1966 four SSF schools closed, and one in Klotzville, Louisiana, merged with another Black Catholic school, St. Augustine, in 1967.[42]

Because Black nun principals were among the earliest to decry racism in archdiocesan and diocesan decisions to close or merge Black Catholic schools, they were also among the first to experience the white clerical backlash to Black demands for the survival of Black Catholic education. White priests began pressuring Black leadership councils to remove "militant" Black sisters from leadership positions in Catholic schools. Most often, the sisters targeted were NBSC members who emphasized Black pride among their students, joined local protests, and revised their curricula to incorporate and champion Black studies. In 1969, Father André Bouchard, the white rector at Saints Paul and Augustine Catholic Church in Washington, DC, penned a letter scolding OSP leader Mother Mary of Good Counsel Baptiste for assigning Sister Majella Neal as the school's principal. Bouchard described Neal, a NBSC foundress, as "a woman who has no concern for the community or a willingness to understand it." While he admitted he was to blame for "a misunderstanding" at the beginning of their relationship, he nonetheless advised Baptiste "to advise and council [sic] Sister Mejella [sic] so that the experience [at Saints Paul and Augustine would] be a fruitful one both for the school and for this community."[43]

As detailed in earlier chapters, Black-administered Catholic schools were often attached to Black parishes led by white priests who held racially derogatory views of Black people and opposed Black leadership.[44] Historically, Black superiors had counseled their members to find ways to work with paternalistic and hostile white priests to ensure the survival of their schools.[45] However, by 1969, even the most cautious of Black superiors refused to let blatant disrespect for their members by offending white priests go unchallenged.

Baptiste, for example, took exception to Bouchard's characterization of Neal and her commitment to the Black community. She wrote, "You mention that Sister Mary Majella has no concern for the community or a willingness to understand it. It would be interesting to know the basis for this statement considering the fact that she has been there hardly a month. . . . There are several sides to every question, Father, and unless we are totally involved it is very difficult to sift the fact from personal opinion." Moreover, instead of heeding Bouchard's demand to get Neal in line, Baptiste suggested Bouchard "assist [the OSP] by a real spirit of communication and support."[46]

Despite Baptiste's efforts to assuage tensions, Bouchard and his successor, Father Leonard Hurley, continued to harass Neal, forcing her to transfer or risk termination in 1970. Such was also the case for Sister Marilyn Hopewell, who was forced to transfer from her teaching position at the historically Black Holy Comforter Catholic School in Washington, DC, after several run-ins with a white teacher (formerly a brother) during the same academic year. After Hopewell's removal and the forced transfers of all five OSP members assigned to Sts. Paul and Augustine for the 1969–70 academic year, Black lay Catholics in DC protested what they called "the politics of genocide being performed on . . . the Oblate Sisters by the white hierarchy of Washington, D.C." Black parents cited the "persistent, sinister pressure . . . constantly exerted on the black women of the Oblate Order to 'keep them in their place' and to 'whip them into line.'" They also championed the commitment of Neal and Hopewell to the Black community, noting that "those who come under the most merciless attack are the faithful, loyal women who have the courage and stamina to defend the rights and interests of black children."[47]

One month after members of Baltimore's Black Catholic Lay Caucus met with the OSP superior to express their concerns over the mistreatment of Black sister principals by white priests, the group held a sit-in at the Josephite headquarters in the city.[48] Since the Josephites' arrival in the United States, many white members had undermined the leadership of Black Catholic women—especially those whose influence could not be usurped by white religious—in the African American educational apostolate. By 1971, though, many in the Black Catholic community were steadily fighting back. In addition to calling for the Josephites to "make black priests and brothers more visible in black communities," the protesters demanded the order implement an antiracist and Black awareness training program for all Josephites through the National Office for Black Catholics, support programs for "the development of real Black leadership," and create a diaconate program "relevant to Black people."[49] This protest, combined with internal struggles within the Josephites, led to all-out revolt against white and Black faculty members regarded as "insensitive, irrelevant, white paternalists or as black Uncle Toms."[50] While some Josephite faculty members were transferred, the failure of the order's leaders to adopt an antiracist praxis prompted most of its Black seminarians and some white seminarians to defect from the order. Four Black ordained Josephites also resigned during the 1970s, leaving a significant void of Black clerical leadership when the Black community needed it most.[51]

Black lay Catholics also directed significant attention to the increasing retreat of white sisters from inner-city and predominantly Black schools, believing their decisions were racially motivated. While the experiences of Black youth in the increasingly Black inner-city Catholic schools of the North, Midwest, and West were never free of racism and paternalism, many upwardly mobile African American parents still preferred the Catholic system over the public one. This became even more true as select schools led by white sisters began to incorporate Black studies curricula and some orders stopped barring Black women and girls. However, when in the late 1960s and 1970s many white orders began closing their inner-city and predominantly Black schools and diverting resources to their increasingly suburban schools and academies for white Catholic families, Black Catholic parents protested.

In 1970, for example, Black Catholic parents supported by Father Edward McKenna, a white assistant pastor at St. Thomas Aquinas Catholic Church on Chicago's West Side, publicly charged the Religious Sisters of Mercy with racism after the order unexpectedly announced that it would soon close the parish's elementary school. While the Mercy leadership in Chicago initially denied the charge in letters to the editors of the city's newspapers, the evidence and the fight to keep St. Thomas Aquinas open over the next two years revealed that anti-Black racism was indeed the chief driving factor.[52] In a letter to the editor of the *News Journal* in Chicago, Father Michael Rochford, a pastor at Resurrection parish, not only outlined that "the Sisters of Mercy have not been open to, or attracted black vocations" but also pointed out that the order had withdrawn "from neighborhoods when they turned black." Regarding St. Thomas Aquinas, Rochford noted that "some white schools announced as withdrawal schools have made a 'deal' to keep the Sisters." He also noted that at the white sisters' initial meeting with Black Catholic parents, they "admitted . . . that they could not get their Sisters to teach at black schools," revealing it to be "the real reason" behind the proposed closure.[53] While there were notable cases of white sisters taking public stands against racism in white Catholic schools and unnecessary withdrawals from inner-city schools in the 1970s, white congregations by and large made minimal commitments to preserving Catholic schools in inner-city communities at a moment when Black parents regularly proved to be their most passionate champions.[54] In one highly publicized exception from 1971, ten Immaculate Heart of Mary sisters assigned to the all-white St. Raymond School in Detroit resigned in protest after the white parish council admitted that they did not want the school to close chiefly because it might lead to a decline in local property values, forcing people to leave and letting "undesirables . . . move in."[55]

In the face of declining white support for Black Catholic education, some Black superiors encouraged members to seek innovative ways to preserve Black Catholic schools and experiment with their apostolate. In 1969, the SSF released Sister Sylvia Thibodeaux from her teaching duties in Tulsa, Oklahoma, and permitted her to relocate to Boston to join the Association of Urban Sisters.[56] Founded in 1968 by local white sisters opposed to white flight, the association sought to coordinate efforts to maintain the city's urban Catholic schools and to be receptive to increasing demands for Black teachers and administrators.[57] Thibodeaux joined the teaching staff of the St. Joseph Community School, formerly a parish school, in 1969 and became the institution's principal one year later. Soon thereafter, Thibodeaux became a prominent figure in the local struggle for community control, arguing that if African Americans were to determine their own destiny, then "[they] must control areas [they] occupy—educationally, spiritually, economically, in every way."[58]

Such innovative approaches to the crisis were also reflected in the OSP's initial support of an attempt to transform their famed St. Frances Academy in Baltimore into a community school in 1969. Two years earlier, Sister Mary Paraclete Young, a twenty-two-year member of the community and a NBSC founding member, had assumed the leadership of St. Frances Academy and was charged with keeping the nation's oldest Black Catholic school open. Fearful that declining enrollment numbers and waning Church support might force it to close, Young and her staff devised a host of strategies. For example, in 1968, when she could not afford to pay $20,000 in lay teacher salaries, Young invested $2,000 in a car to transport seminarians from Woodstock College in suburban Baltimore to teach at St. Frances during the week. The following year, Young applied for a federal antipoverty grant to transform St. Frances into a community school. "St. Frances Academy will open in September if I have to crawl to Washington," the principal told local reporters in early 1969.[59] When her Model Cities grant application was rejected, Young was undeterred.

Soon thereafter, she began soliciting support from the Baltimore archdiocese to help actualize her proposed Brentwood-Forrest Community Center. Envisioned as "an oasis in the ghetto," the $16 million educational center was to be built on land adjoining St. Frances Academy and include a church, a library, a theater, residences, a language laboratory, a cafeteria, a child development center, a health center, and a research center. It "would educate every level of the family simultaneously," Young proclaimed.[60] Although the proposal received enthusiastic written endorsements from a host of community leaders and organizations—including the OSP leadership council, Baltimore mayor Thomas D'Alesandro III, US senator Joseph Tydings (Maryland), the Baltimore Archdiocesan Urban Commission, and even Baltimore's Cardinal Lawrence Shehan—the white-led archdiocesan finance committee flatly rejected it as "unrealistic, unfeasible, and impossible."[61] For Young and other proponents of Black Catholic education, the archdiocese's refusal to support the Black-led initiative while supporting the development of the suburban Catholic educational system was unacceptable and proof positive the Church opposed Black self-determination and leadership, prompting a host of protests in Baltimore.

On Wednesday, June 30, 1970, Young led approximately twenty-five local activists, including several Oblates, in a two-hour protest outside the administrative headquarters of the archdiocese of Baltimore. Carrying placards that read "Archdiocese Rejects Black Catholics," "the Cardinal is guilty," and "the Catholic Church is racist," the protesters sought to expose the Church's ongoing retreat from racial justice reform, most recently manifested in the archdiocese's refusal to support the Brentwood-Forrest Community Center.[62] The protesters did convince the Archdiocesan Finance Committee to subsidize St. Frances's operating and restoration costs for the next three years.[63] However, the protests also engendered a bitter divide between Black Catholic activists and the white-dominated Baltimore archdiocese, leaving the OSP leadership council in a contentious middle position. While seemingly capitulating to protesters' demands, white archdiocesan officials and other clerics increased their pressure on the OSP leadership council to get Young and her teaching staff under control.

Although Black congregations remained firmly committed to the survival of Black Catholic education, their institutions' financial vulnerability and their own legacy of strategic accommodation to white racism placed Black leadership councils in increasingly precarious positions. Faced with strident white opposition to Black self-determination and clerical pressure to clamp down on outspoken Black sisters, some Black superiors soon proved unwilling to support militant and creative struggles to preserve Black Catholic education. However, individual Black sisters kept up the pressure. Working within Black Catholic organizations and in alliance with white-led sister organizations opposed to white flight, Black sisters rallied to keep remaining inner-city and Black Catholic schools open by any means necessary. As the 1970s progressed, this increasingly meant advocating for community control.

The Struggle for Community-Controlled Black Catholic Education

From the first meeting of the NBSC, formal keynotes and small group discussions at the annual meetings of the NBSC included concerns about the state of Black Catholic education and called for a national plan of action to address it.[64] By 1970, discussions that members of Black sisterhoods led at NBSC regional and national board meetings prioritized the crisis of inner-city and Black Catholic school closings and emphasized the need for radical solutions developed within the Black community. Speaking at the third annual NBSC meeting, for example, Oblate Sister of Providence Marcellina Brooks pointed to education as an "open arena" for the nascent organization. "New areas of education need to be explored," Brooks declared. "Black sisters should be developing curricula, programs, and innovative projects that are positive examples of black leadership and cultural understanding." She also encouraged greater NBSC attention to "community action programs . . . aimed at the achievement of social, political, and economic black power. . . . We can be a tremendous influence in organizing sessions on understanding the dynamics and implementation of community action and control."[65] At the same meeting, NBSC leaders pledged their support for the recently established National Office for Black Catholics in Washington, DC, to coordinate "the redistribution of black religious women to better meet the demands of the black community," especially in "facilitating the achievement of Catholic schools in black communities."[66]

When established in 1970, the National Office for Black Catholics immediately created a department of educational services to gain a more accurate statistical profile of Black Catholic school enrollment and those Black and inner-city schools facing closure and merger.[67] One year later, the SSF in New Orleans released two sisters from their duties to join the National Office for Black Catholics' education staff and develop its plan of action to preserve the Black system.[68] By then, a growing segment of the Black Catholic community had concluded that the best way to save Catholic schools was to transform as many schools as they could into community-controlled institutions.

Black urban struggles for educational justice and dignity in white-led public school systems unwilling to embrace "quality integrated education" produced the first explicit calls for community control of inner-city and Black schools in the late 1960s.[69] From the beginning, these calls were especially attractive to Black parents and activists fighting to preserve the embattled Black Catholic educational system. During slavery and the immediate decades following emancipation, when most white Church leaders formally opposed Black Catholic education, Black nuns and lay Catholics were the first to erect Black Catholic parishes and schools in order to preserve Black Catholicism and create an educational infrastructure from which to launch an attack on segregation and white supremacy in the Church and wider society. Those foundational efforts produced powerful challenges to institutional anti-Black racism and exclusion in the Church through the Colored Catholic Congresses of the late nineteenth century, the Federated Colored Catholic movement of the 1920s and 1930s, and the national organization of Black priests, sisters, and lay Catholics (once again) by the late 1960s. Thus, by the early 1970s, many Black Catholic leaders, who began studying Black Catholic history, came to understand asserting community control over Black Catholic schools as a potential return to their roots in the Church. As Sister M. Martin de Porres Grey argued in December 1970, "If the Catholic Church is going to engage in the black revolution for the freedom of black people, her black constituency must decide whether the energy is for the revolution of inclusion or the revolution of separation."[70]

From April 13 to 15, 1971, seven NBSC members attended the annual convention of the National Catholic Educators' Association in Minneapolis to assess the state of integration in the parochial school system and its administration.[71] There, the delegation, which included Grey, staffed an exhibit booth to promote the NBSC's publications and "promote the image of black religious women deeply involved and concerned with Catholic schools in the black community."[72] While NBSC members felt that they made positive gains circulating their Black-oriented educational materials, they ultimately concluded that the association functioned mostly like a "peer-group operation." Specifically, there were no African Americans and only three women on the association's board, which they considered as demonstrating the organization's inability to address the crisis effectively.[73]

Two days later, the NBSC's board of directors met at the OSP motherhouse in Baltimore and endorsed community control. "The most viable survival strategy presently operative in the black community is the community controlled school," their press release declared. "The survival of the 400 black Catholic elementary and secondary schools in the U.S. will only exist with and under total black control." The NBSC board specifically rejected the National Catholic Educators' Association's push for integration and instead called for a "redistribution of black religious women educators and administrators." Black sisters working in predominantly white Catholic schools were especially urged to resign so that they could serve in predominantly Black schools, in direct conflict with the association's suggestion urging that "qualified minority teachers" be employed in the Church's predominantly white and all-white schools.[74] For NBSC leaders, like many community-control advocates in the 1970s and the leadership councils of the Black sisterhoods in the decades before, Black educational excellence could be ensured only in Black-controlled institutions that emphasized racial pride and rejected white supremacy in all of its manifestations.

At the fourth annual NBSC in Pittsburgh in August 1971, Sister Sylvia Thibodeaux hosted an institute on Black education, during which her fifty-plus workshop members adopted the NBSC's statement calling for Black control of all Catholic schools in predominantly Black communities and those serving a predominantly Black student body.[75] The following January, the NBSC launched Project DESIGN, an educational consulting agency to "facilitate the emergence and stabilization of community controlled schools."[76] DESIGN (Development of Educational Services in the Growing Nation) aimed to provide diagnostic evaluations of vulnerable Black schools; train parents in teacher evaluation and curriculum assessment; and offer in-service training for educators to help them develop Black studies curricula and foster more parental involvement and collaborative leadership. The brainchild of Thibodeaux and Sister of Notre Dame de Namur Dolores Harrall, who was then Boston's first Black nun principal, DESIGN also sought to halt the ongoing exodus of Black sisters from religious life by providing spiritual retreats and an institute for Black women's leadership development and by establishing more formal networks with the Black congregations.[77]

To put her full efforts behind the struggle for community control and "educational excellence in the black community," Grey resigned as the NBSC president in mid-1972 and became the executive director of DESIGN.[78] Then a PhD candidate in education at the University of Pittsburgh, Grey immediately began raising funds for the organization. Although unsuccessful in gaining support from Catholic philanthropic organizations, she received substantial support from Black women's organizations and Protestant-leaning foundations. In late 1972, the board of the Irwin-Sweeney-Miller Foundation in Columbus, Indiana, voted to fund DE-SIGN's first-year operational budget of $117,261 and 50 percent of the second year's projected budget, "with the expressed hope that the Catholic hierarchy would absorb the remainder."[79] The NBSC also received a $10,000 grant from the Black Women's Community Development Foundation to assist in recruiting and retaining Black female vocations to the Church.[80]

As the first agency organized explicitly to facilitate the transition of inner-city nonpublic schools to community-controlled institutions, DESIGN received an enthusiastic welcome from parents, administrators, and community organizations invested in the survival of Black Catholic education. In its first year, the DESIGN office received scores of requests for assistance from parents and faculties of schools threatened with closure. In response, DESIGN administrators under Grey organized a training laboratory, which introduced teachers and administrators to more effective teaching methods and innovative curricula designed to foster Black academic excellence. The program consisted of two four-week sessions held during the summer and included on-site observation and academic-year supervision by DE-SIGN's all-Black professional staff, made up of national educational specialists in curriculum development, politics, and psychology. Successful matriculation required the participation of a team of three to five teachers, including the respective school's principal. In its first year of work alone, DESIGN prevented the closures of two inner-city Catholic schools. [81] By 1973, NBSC members led three former Black Catholic schools turned community-controlled institutions in Boston and were deeply involved in similar struggles in Milwaukee and Baltimore.[82] Through DESIGN and in response to several Black sisters' desire to pursue graduate work previously denied to them, Grey also built relationships with several universities, including Antioch-Putnam Graduate School of Education, Carlow College (later University), and the University of Pittsburgh, to help Black sisters and other Black Catholic educators earn master's and doctoral degrees in education.[83]

Even before the violent anti-busing protests erupted in Boston in 1974, Project DESIGN leaders in Boston and Pittsburgh well understood the detrimental consequences of integrating Black children into white educational spaces where they were not wanted. As a result, they worked closely with early community-control advocate Dr. Kenneth Haskins of Harvard University's Graduate School of Education to preserve the inner-city Catholic schools that had experienced racial demographic shifts and to transform those institutions into sites of total Black liberation. Several of Haskins's Black graduate students worked with NBSC leaders to coordinate this effort. Among these students was twenty-three-year-old Patricia Hill, who went on to earn a PhD in sociology and author classic texts in Black feminist thought. Hill taught at the St. Joseph Community School led by Sister Sylvia Thibodeaux in the early 1970s, and the two worked to develop curricula that decolonized their students' minds, fostered academic excellence, and produced civically engaged graduates.[84] As Thibodeaux explained in 1970, "Every kid coming out of a black school ought to know how to organize a rent strike by the eighth grade." [85]

Despite its early successes, DESIGN faced challenges from the very beginning. Its full-time staff of only three people consistently received more requests than their resource-stretched office could answer. Declining numbers of Black sisters, financial uncertainty, and increasing African American frustration with the Church also limited DESIGN's efforts. Still, from 1972 to 1974, its training laboratory graduated thirty-four participants from fourteen different schools. However, the initiative did not survive 1974, which saw the abrupt and unexpected departure of NBSC chief architect Grey from religious life. Following a brief fight over control from 1974 to 1975, DESIGN collapsed.[86]

While many of the former Catholic schools that were transformed into community schools remained open and Black Catholic school enrollments rebounded as the 1970s progressed, Black-administered schools continued to close. Among the most devastating of these closures was that of Baltimore's St. Frances Academy for Girls. Citing financial difficulties, OSP superior and former St. Frances leader Mother Mary of Good Counsel Baptiste announced the congregation's decision in early January 1974.[87] Although the archdiocese had subsidized the institution for the previous three years, the congregation determined that ongoing costs would far exceed the proposed subsidy.[88] White clerics also surreptitiously continued to thwart the proposed Brentwood-Forrest Community Center and Sister Mary Paraclete Young's leadership at St. Frances. In a confidential memo apparently sent to the OSP council before the congregation's December vote to close St. Frances, white Josephite Henry J. Offer, a "professed" supporter of Black power, wrote that he did not think St. Frances should continue as it then existed. He stated that although he had "a great respect for Sister Paraclete and her dedication to the school and to the girls," he nonetheless felt that she should be removed as school principal. Offer, who noted that his relationship with the principal had been "strained in the past," also took the opportunity to criticize Young's proposed community center, characterizing it as "grandiose" and "too unreal." Cognizant of his racism, the Josephite priest also instructed the OSP leadership council to keep his memo "very confidential," noting that he would not be keeping a copy and that "all other evidence will be destroyed."[89]

While it is unclear whether Young knew of Offer's covert opposition, the decision to close St. Frances devastated her. Less than one month after the school officially closed, Young, a twenty-nine-year member of the congregation, requested and received an indult of exclaustration from the OSP.[90] One year later, she left the congregation permanently.[91]

Although several Oblates successfully mobilized to reopen St. Frances Academy as a coeducational institution in 1976, nationwide the Black-administered Catholic educational system lay largely in ruins after twenty years of school integration.[92] Black student enrollment in Catholic schools rebounded in the last half of the 1970s, but institutions operated by the OSP and SSF closed or merged at a frightening pace—twenty-nine between 1965 and 1975—leaving thousands of African American students displaced.[93] Because the merger of Black Catholic schools with white ones generally did not include the merger of the faculties or guarantee Black admission into those white schools, Black students often found themselves marginalized and targeted for grade demotion by white school administrators. However, Black sisters (when able) rallied for their students.

When the OSP's Immaculate Conception (IC) High School was forced to merge into Bishop England High School in Charleston, South Carolina, in 1968, for example, white administrators at Bishop England undermined the endeavor at every turn. Before the merger, IC was Charleston's premier Black high school; over 80 percent of its graduates matriculated at colleges and universities, including Harvard University, Xavier College of Louisiana, Columbia University, New York University, the University of Detroit, Howard University, Duquesne University, South Carolina State University, and Fisk University. By 1965, the Black Catholic school's alumni were also represented in a host of professions including medicine, law, dentistry, nursing, pharmacy, education, business, and religious life.[94]

However, in the first phase of the merger, IC students routinely faced harassment and open racism. Kendra Hamilton, an IC student who went on to earn her BA in English from Duke University and a PhD in English and American studies from the University of Virginia, attributed her "desire to be a writer and scholar" to a moment "when one of the German Catholic kids called me a liar to my face" after she stated that a Black man had invented the stoplight, a fact she had learned from her OSP instructors. "He said that was not true; the white teacher had no idea and remained silent," Hamilton recalled.[95]

Such indignities and hostilities continued for Black IC students after the school's full merger with Bishop England and the closure of their school. For example, white administrators at Bishop England, which still included the Sisters of Charity of Our Lady of Mercy, initially demoted IC transfer students by one or two grades, stating that the students were likely ill prepared to meet Bishop England's "rigorous" standards. Only after the protests of Sister Mary Immaculate Smith, IC's principal, who briefly served on Bishop England's staff, did administrators restore the former IC students to their proper grades.[96] However, severe challenges remained, and IC never became a truly integrated institution.

In cities and towns where Black Catholics made up a significant proportion of the population, the demand for Black-administered Catholic schools never diminished. During the Jim Crow era, the lack of Catholic schools open to Black youth had left an especially bitter taste in the mouths of African American Catholic parents seeking to fulfill their canonical duty to provide a Catholic education for their children. Despite months (and oftentimes years) of pleading with white Church officials and religious orders to establish a school for Black youth in their respective locales, parents could still come up empty-handed. Thus, when they were successful, many Black communities enthusiastically embraced the coming of the sisters and the building of the Catholic schoolhouse and church, throwing elaborate community celebrations and barbecues to welcome the sisters to their towns and cities and to support their institutions. So, when Black leadership councils were increasingly forced to withdraw from a school owing to lack of personnel in the late 1960s and 1970s or to close a school owing to desegregation, the order was often besieged with petitions and letters begging them to stay. In one striking example from 1971, Mrs. P. B. Parks, the president of the Parent-Teacher Organization at the Holy Trinity School in Orangeburg, South Carolina, pleaded with the OSP superior Mary of Good Counsel Baptiste not to withdraw her members.

Shortly after it was built in 1940, Holy Trinity had burned to the ground in suspected arson by the Ku Klux Klan. After the school was rebuilt in 1942, the local Black community, including faculty members at what became South Carolina State University, became especially protective of Holy Trinity and its Black sister administrators.[97] "Being a part of the community, the white here would like nothing better than for the school to close as we do not get any cooperation from them whatsoever," Parks wrote in 1971. "If we do not have any Sisters we will be at a los[s] as we feel the Sisters make the school and they are the ones the parents and students rally behind." As a result of Parks's pleas, the OSP remained in Orangeburg for another ten years.[98] However, declining OSP personnel and the detrimental effects of white-administered desegregation on Black Catholic schools made the leadership council's decision regarding Holy Trinity an exception, not the rule.

For the SSF, the story of Catholic school desegregation was similar, with eighteen of their schools and orphanages closed or merged as a result of integration from 1959 to 1970.[99] However, in 1971, the order scored a rare victory when they successfully mobilized to stop the closure of the elementary school attached to St. Francis Xavier Catholic Church, Baton Rouge's first Catholic parish for African Americans.[100] Under the leadership of the SSF since 1919, St. Francis Xavier Catholic Elementary School had thrived through the Jim Crow era. By 1943, the SSF educated six hundred students annually and in 1956 added a much-desired high school, the first Black Catholic secondary institution in Baton Rouge. Despite its marked successes, the school closed in 1962 after the federal government decided to run Interstate 10 through Baton Rouge's African American community; the six-year-old Black Catholic high school was in its direct path.[101] Although two white parishes had also been in the original path of the highway in Baton Rouge, local white Catholic legislators used their political connections to save those institutions and their schools. Despite repeated trips to Washington, DC, to plead for the survival of St. Francis Xavier High School, Black Catholics could not save it from destruction. Construction of the highway also severely damaged the church, eventually forcing its relocation, further angering Baton Rouge's Black Catholic community.[102]

Thus, when Bishop Richard Tracy indicated that he would close the elementary school at St. Francis Xavier in 1971 after a failed attempt to merge the institution with the desegregated St. Agnes School, Black Catholics revolted. Although white Catholics, including the St. Agnes pastor, had intentionally sabotaged the merger because they feared it would make the institution's youth and staff predominantly Black and they would lose control, St. Francis Xavier, which Black Catholics argued was the better facility, was punished. In a position paper sent to Bishop Tracy on September 14, 1971, the Holy Family Sisters stationed at St. Francis Xavier made it plain:

> Obviously, it is not Blacks who are uncooperative and openly defiant of Bishop Tracy's decrees regarding this situation; however, it is

equally obvious that, as usual, Blacks are expected to suffer the consequences of white defiance and hatred, even though we are attempting to fulfill our responsibility as cooperatively as possible. That spirit of blind obedience is rapidly coming to an end, especially in this situation.... This Sisters have emphatically stated, with approval of their Mother Superior, that they are tired of being kicked around and abused by religious tyrants who hide behind clerical collars and make pious statements about Christian charity and racial justice. We state emphatically that we are not espousing segregation, nor are we opposed to integration and an interparochial plan. We are insisting, however that if one facility is to be used to house the school, that the great St. Francis Xavier be accorded that honor.[103]

Although Bishop Tracy failed to respond, ssf members and Black parishioners at St. Francis Xavier kept writing and demanding a meeting with the prelate.

After Bishop Tracy rebuffed a third request to meet with the sisters and their supporters on September 21, 1971, the ssf, accompanied by two hundred to three hundred Black Catholic parents from St. Francis Xavier and Catholic Newman Club members at the historically Black Southern University, drove to the bishop's extravagant residence (nicknamed the Taj Mahal) and picketed on his front lawn. Because the group learned that the bishop had made an impromptu visit to a white school that day, they were fed up. However, it would take even more determined protesting, organizing, fundraising, and appeals before the prelate capitulated. Ultimately, Bishop Tracy decided to transform St. Agnes into a vocational rehabilitation center and keep St. Francis Xavier open, marking one of the few times that a white school was closed and a Black school survived during the era of desegregation.[104]

Even as white Catholics continued to revolt against integration, Black parents continued to invest in parochial schools, which they argued were preferable to the still often underresourced public schools in their communities and essential to the survival of the Black Catholic community. The National Office for Black Catholics held that all Catholic schools could be made to work, calling the ongoing closures a failure "by the total Catholic community, not just the particular parish concerned." The organization also pointed out that ecclesiastical opposition to non-Catholics attending Catholic schools (another prominent justification for closing inner-city schools) was in direct conflict with the Decree on Bishops' Pastoral Office proclaimed by

Pope Paul VI during the Second Vatican Council.[105] As such, the ongoing devaluation of Black and inner-city Catholic education by ecclesiastical authorities and the Church's waning commitment to racial justice eventually forced many Black Catholics to ponder their future in a church still bent on ignoring its moral responsibilities. And this crisis became even more acute as more Black sisters continued to depart religious life.

The Great Exodus

The departures of thousands of sisters from religious life in the late 1960s and 1970s forever transformed the Catholic educational system. Many who left, Black and non-Black, had struggled against racism and sexism within the Church and would have provided critical leadership as institutions navigated desegregation and the changing dynamics of the African American freedom struggle. Yet many leadership councils regularly discouraged sisters from engaging in antiracist activism or punished them when they did. This was especially true for Black junior members of congregations.

As early as 1969, NBSC leaders understood the steady departures of Black sisters from religious life combined with white institutional divestment as a crisis that threatened the long-term survival of the African American Catholic community. By September 1971, the NBSC established the Tribunal for Black Religious Affairs to assist Black sisters in temporary vows who were facing dismissal or forced departure from their congregations for their activism. On September 10, 1971, Grey, then still the NBSC president, announced the tribunal's creation at the Conference of Major Superiors of Women in Atlanta. Consisting of seven members (two sisters, one brother, one priest/canon lawyer, two secular attorneys, and one psychologist), the all-Black and Catholic tribunal aimed to function "when called upon by a sister to investigate, review and recommend courses of action to resolve differences between the Black sister and her congregation; to advise strategies the sister should employ to help her congregation to understand her viewpoint." The tribunal also proposed to arbitrate for the client with her congregation's leadership, if and when it became necessary.[106] In response, the leaders of the Adrian Dominican Sisters, the Pittsburgh Mercy community, and the Sisters of Notre Dame de Namur expressed their willingness to help Black sisters in tenuous situations transfer into their orders, which several soon did.[107]

Recognizing the need for cultural understanding and sensitivity among white superiors and novice directresses if Black sisters were to join and stay in white congregations, organization leaders also launched the National Black Sisters' Conference Formation Institute in 1971. Since 1968, NBSC members had been conducting formation workshops for white superiors and retreats for Black sisters to complement the nation's spiritual formation programs that lacked sensitivity to the plight of Black sisters in the white-dominated Church. However, it was clear that a formal apparatus, separate from the national Sister Formation Institute, was necessary to keep Black sisters in religious life. Forty white major superiors and members of vocation recruitment teams from across the nation attended the first NBSC Formation Institute, held at the Weber Center in Adrian, Michigan, on October 17–22, 1971. While less than 7 percent of the nation's religious communities of women were represented, most who attended were awakened to the plight of Black sisters and racism in the Church in a profound way. "The total experience was agonizing—searching—longing," one white participant stated. "Coming to a deeper awareness of what it is to be black—to be a black religious—and an understanding of how much we need your leadership and your uniqueness. My soul has been wrenched. I know I have died and have emerged a new woman."[108] Many left with the realization that, as one sister put it, "our biggest job is among ourselves—racism among whites—religious and lay."[109]

Despite the NBSC's efforts, mounting resistance to the Black Catholic movement and ongoing Black defections from religious life and the Church proved too much to overcome. The Tribunal for Black Religious Affairs was soon defunct owing to questions surrounding its authority. While the NBSC Formation Institute continued through the 1970s, eventually breaking into local units in cities across the Midwest and North, the continued departures of Black sisters left many white congregations without any Black members.[110]

The three surviving Black congregations also suffered monumental losses.[111] White backlash to the Black Catholic movement, the increasing refusal of priests to direct Black women to the Black sisterhoods in the name of integration, greater opportunities for women in the American workplace, and natural deaths all resulted in the steady decline of the national Black sister population.[112] However, the failure of Black congregations to fully support young Black sisters seeking transformative change in their ministries and battling racism in the Church also played a significant role in the losses. Black leadership councils sometimes accommodated white Catholic racism, believing that strategy could forestall the complete demise of the Black-administered Catholic educational system. However, the generational and ideological splits within Black congregations ultimately pushed some sisters to reconsider the utility of religious life in the changing society.

In the early 1970s, for example, early NBSC board member Sister Judith Therese Barial became disgusted with the enduring anti-Black animus of select members of historically Afro-Creole order in New Orleans. Emboldened by the Black consciousness movement and the spirit the NBSC had fostered, Barial began to challenge the conservatism and anti-Blackness of those peers. For example, after repeatedly witnessing some lighter-skinned Creole sisters publicly chastise students who wore Afros and expressed admiration for Black Power, Barial cut her hair into a short Afro. Although her act of protest engendered a significant backlash, Barial did not retreat. She also did not leave the congregation. Instead, she remained and hoped to be able to work for change within the SSF.[113]

Sister Sylvia Thibodeaux also opted to remain despite her congregation's increasing opposition to younger sisters' embrace of Black power. While working with the Association of Urban Sisters in Boston, Thibodeaux found some SSF members' resistance to her activism and to her decision to abandon her habit and wear a short Afro almost unbearable. After a bad experience at the order's chapter meeting in 1974, she resigned as principal of the St. Joseph Community School. The failures of Thibodeaux congregation's new leadership to rise fully to the occasion of Black power left her disillusioned. To "save" her vocation, Thibodeaux accepted an offer to relocate to Nigeria to assist in the formation of an indigenous community of women. Although Thibodeaux and Barial managed to remain in the SSF, many could not. Several young and older activist-oriented SSF members, including prominent NBSC leader Theresa Perry, departed the order in the 1970s. The order also lost members like Sister Sylvia Deconge, then a mathematics professor at Southern University, who left in 1976 owing to exhaustion from the increasing amounts of work required of local superiors.[114]

For those still committed to religious life, transferring to a different congregation sometimes proved a suitable alternative to defection. In many of these cases, sisters left congregations hostile to their participation in the Black Catholic movement. For example, in 1970, Sister Yvonne Tucker, a member of the Order of St. Francis and a teacher stationed in Green Bay, Wisconsin, left her community after several years to become a full-time staff member for the NBSC. That same year, she became an affiliate member of the Pittsburgh community of the Religious Sisters of Mercy and in 1972 professed her vows there, becoming the order's second African American member.[115] In 1973, Sister Teresita Weind completed a canonical transfer from the Sisters of Mary of the Presentation into the Ohio province of the Sisters of Notre Dame de Namur. Following her participation in the first NBSC meeting, Weind had relocated from North Dakota, where she was ministering as a nurse, to Chicago, where she began a parish ministry among the residents of the predominantly Black and economically impoverished Cabrini-Green housing projects. Soon thereafter, Weind decided to switch congregations to continue her ministry in the African American community. Although she had been barred admission to the Sisters of Notre Dame de Namur, her childhood educators, in 1960 owing to the order's racial quota system, Weind reapplied in 1970 as the order was dealing with the fallout from the defections of all three of their African American members in Ohio during the previous four years.[116]

The NBSC's executive director, Sister M. Shawn Copeland, also switched congregations to maintain her public commitment to the Black freedom struggle. Following her leading role in several Black Catholic protests against racism in Detroit in the early 1970s, Copeland opted to transfer from the Felician Sisters in Livonia, Michigan, to a congregation more accepting of her public activism. In 1974, she joined the Adrian Dominicans, a Michigan-based congregation whose African American members had been active in the Black Catholic movement from its earliest stages.[117]

Pioneering Black members in white congregations also continued to transfer to the Black sisterhoods. In 1976, for example, Sister Mary Joselinda (Mary Cecilia) Cummings, a twenty-one-year member of the Sisters of the Third Order of St. Francis, a nursing congregation in Peoria, Illinois, formally transferred to the Franciscan Handmaids of Mary. During the early 1950s, Cummings, a native of Birmingham, Alabama, and a former second lieutenant in the US Army, had volunteered as a nurse with the Handmaids at their Camp St. Edward for Black girls on Staten Island. Although Cummings reportedly had not faced severe resistance in her former congregation, she still "had a strong urge to be among African American sisters."[118]

For pioneering Black School Sister of Notre Dame Nathan Marie Adams, though, defection from religious life altogether was the only way to save her life. Despite the many challenges and overt acts of racism that Adams had previously faced in religious life, she had vowed to remain.[119] However, in 1976, the thirty-year-old Adams suffered a heart attack, which her doctor attributed solely to stress. When no member of her community visited her during her two-week stay in the intensive care unit at a local hospital, Adams decided it was finally time to go. Although Adams believed that some of the stress she suffered was also due to the conservatism of select Black priests in the Black Catholic movement, the failure of her community to offer any compassion or sympathy proved too much to bear. "It broke my heart," Adams recalled decades later. "They shredded my heart."[120]

In some cases, Black sisters—many of whom were NBSC members—were still dismissed from Black and white orders because of their activism. Others, though, left because they felt too constricted in their community roles. In a few instances, members of Black sisterhoods even transferred to more liberal white congregations where they were permitted to abandon their habits, take up new and innovative ministries, and engage more freely with the Black freedom struggle. In one case, Oblate Sister of Providence Josita Colbert, who became the principal of a Black Catholic school turned community-controlled institution in Boston in the early 1970s, transferred to the Sisters of Notre Dame de Namur, an order that had several Black members who were also NBSC leaders.[121] In other instances, members of Black orders departed religious life permanently, often in response to unrelenting white racism they faced in their assignments.

Among the most devastating of the OSP departures was that of former NBSC vice president Sister Marcellina Brooks. As principal of St. Cyprian-Holy Comforter School in Washington, DC, Brooks was one of most respected sisters in the Black Catholic community. However, like many of her counterparts, she became a target for harassment from white priests who felt threatened by Black Catholic demands for self-determination and Black leadership in their parishes. Although Black lay Catholics rallied for Brooks, taking the fight all the way to Archbishop William Baum in 1974, the unrelenting pressure and the opposition of Josephite John Lennon, who was supported by archdiocesan officials, ultimately proved too much for Brooks. In 1976, she requested a release from her vows, shocking the OSP leadership council. Although she would keep ties with her former order and remain a leader in Black education, eventually serving as the president of the historically Black Bowie State University, Brooks joined scores of NBSC leaders and other progressive sister activists in the secular realm.[122]

Undoubtedly, the most wrenching Black sister departure of the 1970s was that of NBSC chief architect Sister M. Martin de Porres Grey. Since 1968, Grey had been the undisputable face of the "new Black nun." However, Grey had also been the most prominent target of NBSC opponents, male and female, Black and non-Black. Although she had pressed forward with the organization through the early 1970s, the physical, emotional, and psychological labor of leading the NBSC while battling racism within her order, tensions within the NBSC, and the unyielding misogyny of select Black priests, brothers, and laymen at the joint meetings of the Black Catholic organizations began to take a major toll.[123] In 1973, Grey met a community activist while fundraising for DESIGN, fell in love, and decided to marry in 1974. Years later, the former nun noted, "If I had had some sort of sabbatical or break, I would have likely remained in religious life."[124] Upon choosing to marry, Grey left the Pittsburgh Mercy community, cutting its African American membership in half. Soon after her departure, Sister Yvonne Tucker also left religious life, ending the community's experiment in racial integration.[125]

Grey's departure from religious life had a lasting impact on the NBSC. For many, Grey had been the lifeblood of the organization. In the late 1960s and early 1970s, her writings and photographs of her had graced the pages of *Ebony*, *Time*, the *Black Scholar*, and most of the nation's leading Catholic periodicals.[126] Thus, her abrupt departure and the subsequent collapse of Project DESIGN left the NBSC struggling to find direction.

While the NBSC and the Black sisterhoods survived the 1970s, the vacuum created by the loss of so many talented young Black sisters left these entities refocusing their energies and scaling back their plans. At the same time, many Black Catholics continued to question whether it was possible to be Black and remain in a church seemingly bent on returning to white domination. Beyond the steady closings of Black Catholic schools and parishes despite Black demands and protests, the National Knights of the Ku Klux Klan's historic 1974 vote to admit (white) Catholics for the first time in its history proved consequential to Black Catholics. Once reviled and targeted by the nation's first domestic terrorist group, white Catholics had become worthy of Klan membership because of their widespread opposition to racial justice during the civil rights era. When the US Church hierarchy failed to immediately condemn the Klan's newfound interest in white Catholic members, many Black Catholics considered the Church's silence a clear indication of its stand on racial justice.[127]

Although African Americans were not the only Catholics to defect from the Church, the Black Catholic community experienced staggering losses. Some reports concluded that as many as 20 percent of Black Catholics stopped practicing between 1970 and 1975. A study published in 1980 estimated that over that same five-year period, 250 Black seminarians withdrew from their studies, 125 Black sisters left their congregations, and 25 of 190 Black priests left the ordained ministry.[128] Because Black Catholics already represented a marginal percentage of the national Catholic population, these departures signaled great uncertainty for the African American Catholic future. This was especially true for the nation's Black sisters, who, despite their best efforts, never had the numbers or support in the Church to dismantle white supremacy.

Writing for the *National Catholic Reporter* in 1975, NBSC executive director Sister M. Shawn Copeland warned about the future of US Black sisters if white and Black superiors failed to find new ways to support those fighting to remain in religious life. "Today's rising American Catholic conservatism is the kind of conservatism that spelled the end of the first black sisterhood," she wrote. "Only the most daring and determined options will prevail; new systems of formation and initiation are of necessity; the shape and shade of religious communities must change; new paradigms of communal living and organization must be explored."[129] Within a year, though, Copeland, exhausted and devastated by the losses of the previous six years, resigned from the NBSC, leaving a conspicuously smaller cadre of Black sisters to carry the struggle for racial justice forward during the last quarter of the twentieth century.

7. "The Future of the Black Catholic Nun Is Dubious"

AFRICAN AMERICAN SISTERS IN THE AGE

OF CHURCH DECLINE

The majority of priests, religious and lay ministers who serve the Black community in the United States still are not from the Black community and many of those people who attempt to serve among us . . . do not feel an obligation to learn or understand Black history or spirituality, or culture or life—Black tradition or ritual. They work for the people, but they have not learned to share life and love and laughter with the people. . . . Sometimes decisions are made that affect the black community for generations, and they're made in rooms by white people behind closed doors. —SISTER THEA BOWMAN, FSPA, 1989 Address to the USCCB

When Sister Thea Bowman took the stage at the semiannual meeting of the United States Conference of Catholic Bishops on June 17, 1989, she knew her time was short. As such, the fifty-one-year-old nun, then wheelchair bound and stricken with terminal cancer, did not hesitate to speak the "true truth," as she liked to say, about the beauty and pain of the African American experience to her nearly all-white audience. She began by singing the spiritual "Sometimes I Feel Like a Motherless Child" as a metaphor to describe the experiences of Black Catholics in the US Church. Bowman then transitioned into her formal address, in which she challenged her all-male audience to see the Black Catholic community as she saw it: unashamedly Black, authentically Catholic, and above all uncommonly faithful to their church. "What does it mean to be Black and Catholic?" she asked.

"It means that I come to my church fully functioning. . . . I bring myself, my Black self, all that I am. . . . I bring my whole history, my traditions, my experience, my culture, my African American song and dance and gesture and movement and teaching and preaching and healing and responsibility as gift to the Church."[1] In addition to rejecting dominant Catholic narratives that framed Black people as the passive recipients of white missionary efforts, Bowman scolded the prelates for routinely failing to include African Americans in decisions affecting their communities, offering lackluster support for Black Catholic education, dismissing the importance of Black culture and history, and making their Black constituents "feel like second and even third class citizens in the Holy City."[2]

In one especially poignant moment during the presentation, the dashiki-clad Bowman pointed to Catholicism's steady growth in Africa as a possible turning point for the African American Catholic community and the Church at large. "Do you folks realize that there are more Catholic Christians in Africa than in North America," she asked. "In Africa right now 300 people become Christian every day and 75% of them are becoming Roman Catholic. The Vatican's Central Office reports that in Africa the number of students for the priesthood increased by 88% between 1970 and 1988—while in North America the number dropped by 43%." Cognizant of the implications of the evolving global Church, Bowman was clear. "To be Black and Catholic means to be intensely aware of the changing complexion of the College of Cardinals," she declared. "I picked up your Catholic newspaper and I saw the picture Church—the World Church—a lot of folk look like me!" As she ended her presentation, Bowman asked the bishops to stand up, take each other's hands, and join her in singing "We Shall Overcome."[3] Nine months later, Bowman died, devastating those who loved her and leaving a conspicuous gap in Black Catholic leadership. Engraved on her headstone, per her request, were two simple words: "She tried."[4]

Like so many in the long African American Catholic freedom struggle, Bowman had tried. She had also stayed the course even when the road was treacherous. Despite the pivotal successes and leadership breakthroughs of the late 1960s and 1970s, the price of Black Catholic self-determination proved high. The combined forces of white resistance to Black civil rights gains, deindustrialization, and the institutional backlash against the Black Catholic movement manifested most acutely in the continued closings of high-achieving Black and inner-city Catholic schools as well as predominantly Black parishes through the 1980s. Declining interest in religious life fueled by the substantive gains of the civil rights movement and the departures of hundreds of Black priests, sisters, brothers, and seminarians from their institutes also jeopardized the long-term viability of the African American Catholic community. Yet all was still not lost from the perspective of Bowman and her peers who remained in religious life and continued to struggle against racism, sexism, and other forms of discrimination in the Church and wider society.

This chapter narrates the African American sisters' journey through the last quarter of the twentieth century and into the first decades of the twenty-first, when several African American nuns broke through the last remaining racial barriers in women's religious life and kept fighting to preserve and expand Black consecrated life and Black Catholic education in the United States—and increasingly in Africa. It also touches on the explosive growth of Catholicism in the Global South and the rising population of African sisters and priests, which has increasingly forced US Catholic leaders to confront the implications of the rising Black and Brown global Church.

The Pivot to Africa

Sister Thea Bowman's reflection on the revolutionary implications of the rising African presence in the global Church was prescient but not original. As early as 1969, members of the National Black Sisters' Conference (NBSC) discussed the steady growth of Catholic Africa and what it could mean for the embattled Black Catholic community in the United States. The earliest African American Catholic missionaries sent to Africa in the 1930s, 1940s, and 1950s had also recognized the transformative possibilities of the growing Black Catholic diaspora. Prior to that, though, save for the incorporation of African history in the Negro History Week celebrations of the Oblate Sisters of Providence (OSP), African American sisters—like much of the white world and the wider African American community educated in Western schools—viewed the African continent primarily as a missionary territory.[5] While several pioneering African American priests were sent to Africa as missionaries, the earliest efforts to convert Africans to Roman Catholicism were dominated by European and, later, white American Catholic priests and sisters.

The first four African American sisters known to have ministered in Africa arrived in the 1950s as decolonization campaigns began to sweep the continent.[6] Sister Peter Claver (Phenix) Grice, the "first Negro Medical Mission Nun" and the first African American sister reported to have ministered in Africa, departed from Philadelphia in 1953 to take up a nursing ministry in the British-controlled Gold Coast (now Ghana).[7] Two years later, Sister Demetria (Catherine) Smith, a native of Indianapolis, Indiana, and the first fully professed African American Missionary Sister of Our Lady of Africa, left the United States to complete her formation training and study French at the order's motherhouse in Lyons, France, and later in Algiers, Morocco, before beginning a nursing ministry in the British colony of Uganda.[8]

Because Grice departed the Medical Mission congregation in 1954, her experiences in the decolonizing Gold Coast are currently irrecoverable. However, Smith's experiences in colonial Africa and her own experiences of racial discrimination within the Missionary Sisters of Our Lady of Africa made her aware of the global realities of anti-Blackness and the need for pan-African unity in the struggle against white racism. Although Smith desired to become a registered nurse, her superiors initially only permitted her to enroll in training to become a licensed practical nurse. Like most of her Black counterparts in Uganda's segregated and subjugated Black orders, Smith had to fight with her white and European superiors to secure advanced nursing training, as they believed that Black nuns were "to remain beneath [white nuns]." Although her superiors repeatedly told her that her licensed practical nurse degree was "already too much," Smith protested for years, until they begrudgingly granted her permission to secure advanced training as a registered nurse and midwife.[9]

Maryknoll Sister Martin Corde (Jennieva) Lassiter (figure 7.1) was able to avoid the kind of opposition to her educational training that Smith faced. However, her struggles against racism also took on a global dimension when she began what became a seventeen-year ministry in Tanzania in 1958. Born in Cape Charles, Virginia, in 1925 and raised in Philadelphia, Pennsylvania, where she served as the vice president of her local National Association for the Advancement of Colored People (NAACP) youth chapter, Lassiter already held a bachelor's degree from the historically Black Central State University and a master's degree from Columbia University's School of Social Work when she became the second African American woman admitted into the Maryknoll congregation in 1956. Four years later, when Black college students launched sit-in protests against segregation throughout the South, Lassiter became the first of at least four African American Maryknoll Sisters to be sent on mission to Africa.[10]

In Tanzania, where she initially taught domestic and agricultural science and later African history at the first Catholic secondary school for girls in Morogoro, Lassiter witnessed the nation's independence from

FIGURE 7.1. Maryknoll Sister Martin Corde (Jennieva) Lassiter, standing to the immediate right of inaugural Tanzanian president Julius Nyerere, wears a traditional African dress at the groundbreaking ceremony of the Nangwa Girls Secondary School in 1976. Lassiter was a pioneering teacher at the institution, opened at Nyerere's request. She later worked with the Tanzanian government conducting leadership training and seminars for women and girls, training literacy teachers, and working in the Tanzanian Women's Union. Courtesy of the Maryknoll Mission Archives, Maryknoll, New York.

Great Britain in 1961.[11] She also played an active role in the building of the new nation. Because Pan-Africanist leader Julius Nyerere, Tanzania's first president, was a Roman Catholic with deep connections to the Maryknoll Fathers, he invited the Maryknoll Sisters stationed there to take part in the radical reconstruction of the nation built on the principle of Ujamaa or familyhood. In 1970, Nyerere even traveled to the United States to give a speech at the Maryknoll motherhouse in New York, outlining his vision for the former Tanganyika, where the congregation had ministered since 1948.[12] He declared that "until quite recently, the church was silent on the great issues of man in society, or even sided with those whose exclusive concern was their own power and the accumulation of riches."[13] Nyerere also argued that unless the Catholic Church participated "actively in the rebellion against those social structures and economic organizations which condemn men to poverty, humiliation and degradation, then the Church will become irrelevant to man and the Christian religion will degenerate into a set of superstitions accepted by the fearful."[14]

Although the Maryknoll Sisters welcomed Nyerere's invitation to support his vision for Tanzania, uprooting the missionary mentalities of some sisters proved a challenge. Reflecting on her work in Tanzania several years after her return to the United States, Lassiter confronted the colonizing attitudes that some of her white counterparts maintained following independence.[15] Ultimately, Lassiter, who joined the NBSC upon her return to the United States in 1978, developed antiracism workshops for her community to help alter their approach to their African ministries. "You go in [to Africa] saying we're going to learn something together [as opposed to saying] I'm just going to teach this ignorant person," Lassiter noted. "You then realize that person has a value and you both can learn things from each other."[16]

While the early missionary work of individual African American sisters in Africa had significant impacts both there and in the United States, the institutional responses of the Sisters of the Holy Family (SSF) and later the NBSC arguably established the most enduring connections between African American and African sisters struggling against white supremacy and exclusion in the modern Church. In 1964, for example, three founding members of the Handmaids of the Divine Redeemer (HDR) in Agomanya, Krobo, Ghana, arrived in Lafayette, Louisiana, to take up residence with the SSF and matriculate at their Holy Rosary Institute (figure 7.2).[17] A decade earlier, Bishop Joseph Oliver Bowers, Society of the Divine Word (SVD), a native of Dominica and a graduate of the Divine Word Seminary in Bay St. Louis, Mississippi, had initiated plans to establish a Ghanaian order in the diocese of Accra as one of his earliest acts as Ghana's first Black bishop (and the first Black bishop consecrated in the United States).[18] Although European and, later, white American sisterhoods had ministered in the former Gold Coast since the late nineteenth century, most refused to admit Africans into their ranks.[19] A few, however, founded separate, all-African auxiliary orders, whose members were often forced to work as the servants of white sisters and subjected to other humiliating abuses.[20] Thus, the HDR's successful establishment during Bowers's tenure was an important victory as the nation moved toward decolonization.

Join Hands With Sisters in Louisiana

Ghanaian Nuns Undertake Studies Here

LEARNING TO PLAY THE PIANO
. . . Sr. Consolata under guidance of Sr. Cornelia

ENJOYING GAME OF MONOPOLY
. . . Mother Benigna (left) with students and Sr. Marie Benedict (center) and Sr. Cornelia (right)

RECEIVING HOLY COMMUNION
. . . Rev. Francis Wade administers to Sr. Vincentia

MASTERING THE TYPEWRITER
. . . Miss Collison, Grail Missionary, teaches Sr. Vincentia and Sr. Consolata

FIGURE 7.2. On October 17, 1964, the *Pittsburgh Courier* reported on the educational partnership developed between the Sisters of the Holy Family and the Ghanaian Handmaids of the Divine Redeemer. In addition to noting the ancient "ties between the Catholic Church and Africa," the article reflected on the possibilities of the "growing communities of African priests and nuns" in decolonizing Africa. Courtesy of the Pittsburgh Courier Archives.

The first HDR members professed their vows in 1957, the year of Ghanaian independence from Great Britain. Although a white member of the Sisters of the Holy Spirit (SSpS) stationed in the diocese and appointed by Bowers had provided the initial spiritual training for the first HDR members, the African American bishop could not persuade local European sisterhoods to provide long-term education and formation training for the African sisters in Africa. In response, Bowers sought the educational expertise of the historically African American SSF, who provided it and supported Bowers's plan for the three sisters to "acquire college degrees."[21]

It is notable that the SSpS, the sister institute to the SVD priests, to which Bishop Bowers belonged, did not provide the HDR with college-preparatory education or admit indigenous African women into their ranks in Africa until 1988, though they arrived in German Togo in 1897 and in the British Gold Coast in 1946.[22] In comparison, the order accepted candidates from Asia as early as 1913, as well as non-Black Argentinians, Brazilians, and Chileans as soon as the order arrived in those areas. However, German and white American SSpS leaders steadfastly opposed the admission and equal treatment of African-descended women and girls through Vatican II with only five known exceptions.[23] Moreover, the earliest self-identified African-descended SSpS members faced entrenched anti-Black racism and overt bullying. Of the four African Americans known to have entered the SSpS between 1947 and 1967, only one, Sister Rose Martin Glenn of Chicago and Birmingham, Alabama, who entered in 1958, remained.[24]

Glenn's fight to be missioned in Africa became a part of her struggle against racism in the order and its imperial posture toward African-descended people. When in the mid-1960s her superiors kept extending her temporary vows, preventing her from becoming eligible for missionary work, Glenn threatened to leave and join the Peace Corps. In response, SSpS leaders granted Glenn permission to profess final vows in 1967 and soon commissioned her to Ghana, where she worked as a nurse until 1983. There, the white SSpS's refusal to admit indigenous African women and their public mistreatment of Glenn caused some Ghanaians to initially disbelieve that she was a nun because she was visibly Black. However, time and Glenn's nursing ministry eventually won her local acceptance.[25]

Because she was in Ghana, Glenn missed the first NBSC gathering in 1968, but two African sisters from the newly independent nations of Uganda and Kenya participated in the inaugural Pittsburgh meeting. As the Black power movement grew and more African religious studying in the United States began making contact with the African American Catholic community, select NBSC members' interest in developing deeper connections to their ancestral homeland expanded. In 1969, for example, charter member Sister Jayne Marie Simon, a Poor Clare nun and one of two Black contemplatives to attend the Pittsburgh meeting, began encouraging African American ministries in Africa through the NBSC's newsletter, *Signs of Soul.*[26] One year later, Simon joined a group of seven Poor Clares from the United States who accepted an invitation to establish an interracial monastery in Zambia and recruit local women into their ranks.[27]

Although the NBSC's primary focus was preserving Black religious life and Catholic education in the United States, in 1973 its leaders accepted an invitation to help establish the first Black-led indigenous congregation of sisters in Nigeria.[28] In November of that year, Bishop Patrick E. Epku, the first indigenous bishop of the diocese of Benin City and an Igbo survivor of the Nigerian Civil War, traveled to the United States and eventually met with NBSC leaders Sisters M. Martin de Porres Grey, M. Shawn Copeland, Sylvia Thibodeaux, and Elizabeth Harris to discuss his plans to develop a multiethnic order to minister to the educational, catechetical, and medical needs of the Benin City community, especially women.[29] Citing the inadequacy of white congregations active in the diocese, the increased desire among Nigerians for Nigerian sisters, and the diocese's desire "to comply with papal encouragement for native religious and priests," Bishop Epku believed the NBSC could provide prospective candidates with a healthy spiritual model that celebrated rather than denigrated Nigerian cultural traditions, which the European and white American sisterhoods in Nigeria had not done.[30] In 1974, Sister of the Holy Family Sylvia Thibodeaux relocated to Benin City to become formation directress of the Sisters of the Sacred Heart (SSH).[31] One year later, the NBSC donated 3,000 naira (4,870 US dollars) to the Sacred Heart Novitiate at Atani, Uromi, in Nigeria. In April 1975, NBSC executive director Sister M. Shawn Copeland traveled to Nigeria to observe the order's first procession ceremony and made a moving appeal to Nigerian parents to encourage their sons and daughters to become priests and nuns.[32]

With declining numbers of African American sisters, the NBSC leaders' shift to sub-Saharan Africa was strategic. African American leadership had been essential in the formation of the SSH, and these sisters' involvement could prove pivotal if struggling US congregations began turning to Catholic Africa in search of female vocations. In 1969, Jesuit theologian John C. Haughey thought the same. "At a time when vocations of service are growing impressively in the black community, black vocations to religious life are critically few in this country," he wrote. "Africa, by way of contrast, has many more young people who desire to follow a religious vocation than available facilities or trained personnel can cope with. Wouldn't it be one of history's ironies if black American nuns became an important factor in the reaping of that African harvest?"[33]

By 1975, NBSC leaders and Black Catholics in other areas of western and eastern Africa also embraced the potential of pan-African connections in female religious life. In April 1975, Reverend Dr. Peter Sarpong, archbishop of Kumasi in Ghana, requested the assistance of the NBSC in the training of "four young [Ashanti] women . . . seeking to serve God as sisters." Impressed with the development of the SSH in Benin City, Bishop Sarpong hoped that the NBSC's labors could be replicated in Kumasi.[34] That July, Benedict A. Karaimu, a Kenyan student studying at Saint Mary's College in Winona, Minnesota, also contacted the NBSC expressing hope that the organization could begin missionary work in Nairobi and eventually establish their headquarters there.[35] Although the lack of personnel and finances prevented realization of these proposals, the NBSC remained committed to building and sustaining partnerships in Catholic Africa and supporting the development of indigenous leadership. Although NBSC leader Thibodeaux initially committed to assisting the SSH for three years, she ultimately remained in Nigeria for nearly nineteen years as a guiding force and superior. The opposition she encountered from local white American and European nuns who regularly told her African women lacked the dedication and moral ability for religious life made her more determined to ensure the success of the SSH.[36] The desire to contest assertions that African people were incapable of leading their own churches and dioceses had also inspired Bishop Joseph Bowers to resign as the bishop of Accra in 1971 to make room for the first Ghanaian bishop.[37]

While other African American sisters also pursued long-term social service ministries in Africa through the end of the century, their numbers remained small.[38] Enduring challenges of racism and exclusion compelled most to remain focused on preserving Black female religious life and Catholic education on the American home front. This was especially true as an increasing number of African American sisters broke into new leadership positions in the Church.

The Continued Fight for Black Sisters

In response to the departures of Black sisters from religious life, the leaders of the three surviving Black US sisterhoods and the NBSC developed and expanded programs to nurture Black male and female vocations to religious life. The African American sisterhoods continued to host spiritual retreats to help Black laywomen discern a vocation to religious life, and NBSC members established (or helped to establish) the Sojourner Truth House of Prayer and Discernment in Detroit, the Mariama House in Philadelphia, and the Nia House in Brooklyn, New York, to do the same.[39] Mariama House produced at least five Black vocations to religious life in the Philadelphia area, including twin sisters Patricia and Lynn Marie Ralph.[40] Born into a cradle Catholic family in Jersey City, New Jersey, the Ralph sisters entered religious life in their early twenties, with Lynn Marie joining the Sisters of the Blessed Sacrament in 1983 and Patricia, despite initial resistance to her application, joining the Sisters of St. Joseph of Chestnut Hill, Pennsylvania, in 1985.[41]

African American sisters also worked to institutionalize the intellectual traditions of the Black Catholic community. In 1978, for example, the OSP leaders in Baltimore hosted the first meeting of the Black Catholic Theological Symposium, a scholarly organization established to support research and the professional development of Black Catholic scholars, at their motherhouse.[42] Two years later, NBSC founding members Sister Thea Bowman; Dr. Toinette M. Eugene, a former Sister of the Presentation of the Blessed Virgin Mary; Sister Dolores Harrall; and Sister Jamie Phelps played leading roles in establishing the Institute for Black Catholic Studies at Xavier University of Louisiana to support graduate education in Black Catholic history and theology.[43] Its courses aimed not only to provide Black Catholic leaders with a professionalized skill set to tackle racism and embrace African American intellectual and spiritual gifts but also to prepare members of the laity, Black and non-Black alike, for more leadership roles as the numbers of Black religious continued to decline.

Because revitalizing African American female religious life remained a core priority, founding NBSC members also emerged as powerful advocates for the younger Black women who entered religious life in the 1970s, 1980s, and 1990s. Select white vocational directors seeking to ensure that their formation programs met the needs of African American candidates consulted Black sisters who had desegregated their white orders. However, they sometimes did so in ways that reeked of racism or paternalism, prompting older African American sisters to intervene. For example, in 1974, the leaders of the Religious of the Sacred Heart of Jesus in San Francisco reached out to Sister Martin de Porres Coleman, California's first known Black nun, for advice on how to incorporate a young African American candidate into their community life, as they believed her to be too different in her ways.[44] Coleman's admission into the Sisters of Notre Dame de Namur in 1952 had been fiercely contested owing to white racism and ultimately required the powerful intervention of the province's younger and non-Black members of color. Thus, she moved quickly to defend the vocation of the Black Sacred Heart candidate.[45] Coleman instructed the white sisters to "leave [the young woman] alone" and let her progress as any other without trying to change her.[46] Ultimately, the Sacred Heart Sisters listened, and the candidate, Irma Dillard, the daughter of Louisiana migrants who had been active in the Catholic Youth Organization and supported the Black Panther Party's "survival programs," remained. When the Sisters of Notre Dame de Namur in California were asked to consider voting on a proposal to admit Kenyan women into the order's British province in the late 1970s, Coleman became outspoken again. Aware of her congregation's history of forming unequal African congregations to evade desegregation, Coleman joined a small chorus of sisters from Connecticut and Massachusetts led by Dolores Harrall, the first Black Sister of Notre Dame de Namur in the Northeast, who argued against participating in and even taking the vote at their general chapter meeting. Committed to the elimination of the formal barriers blocking African women from equal admission in their international order, the group believed that the nearly all-white US community with its own painful history and ongoing reality of racial exclusion should not influence the decision in any significant way.[47]

In white congregations with Black members, interventions to prevent the racist exclusion of a Black candidate were usually no longer necessary. However, the presence of Black nuns in leadership positions still proved invaluable. For Sister Patricia Chappell, who entered the Sisters of Notre Dame de Namur in Connecticut in 1977, the presence of her former teacher, Sister Dolores Harrall, made the difference in her decision to not only remain in religious life but also embrace her vocation to religious life.[48] Although Chappell's experience was not free from racism, she noted that she could always rely on Harrall and other older African American members of her order for mentorship and support. However, Chappell's experience was not common, even in the congregation's other US provinces.[49]

In the late 1960s and 1970s, many white congregations lost most or all of their African American members, leaving many Black sisters who subsequently entered these communities without critical support. Unwritten exclusionary admissions policies and practices also continued to bar Black women from membership in many white sisterhoods.[50]

Even when white congregations ended their racially based exclusionary admissions policies, the anti-Black animus of individual sisters and the failure of white superiors to institutionalize respect for cultural differences among members continued to jeopardize the perseverance of Black candidates. For Sister Larretta Rivera-Williams, who became the first self-identified African American accepted into the Religious Sisters of Mercy in the Deep South in 1982, the racial hostility of some white members of the order was not only mind-numbing but health-threatening. From her second week in the convent, Rivera-Williams noted that she was "confronted with off-colored jokes and words such as *nigger* and *pickaninny*." Beyond the verbal abuse, Rivera-Williams was also prohibited from professing her final vows in 1991 with the one other woman with whom she entered the order. When she inquired why, Rivera-Williams was told only that she needed "one more year of formation to learn humility." However, the same evening someone slipped a note under her door that read, "At least we didn't ask you to leave." Despite being permitted to profess her final vows in 1992, the challenges remained, and Rivera-Williams's health declined. At age forty-two, Rivera-Williams developed multiple sclerosis, which was regularly triggered by the racial stress she experienced in religious life. Yet, she opted to remain. With other Black Mercy sisters in other provinces, Rivera-Williams formed the congregation's first antiracism team to fight the discriminatory practices and attitudes deeply embedded in their order.[51]

Though Rivera-Williams ultimately found peace in her order, challenges like hers and others prompted several Black sisters to transfer to more progressive orders in the 1980s and 1990s. Among them was Sister Catherine Marie Lowe, a native of Birmingham, Alabama, who entered the Sisters of Notre Dame in Covington, Kentucky, in 1968. Although she was not the first African American admitted, the two Black women who entered before her both departed just as Lowe entered, leaving her to journey through formation in isolation. The Sisters of Notre Dame did not inform Lowe about the NBSC when she entered and forbade her from joining when she learned about it by chance in 1973. Although Lowe professed her final vows in 1976, the loneliness and conservatism of the order and the racial prejudices of the local community proved difficult to overcome. In 1981, she transferred to the Daughters of Charity, where she felt freer to exert more leadership in her ministries to the poor.[52]

Unyielding white racism also continued to drive Black women out of congregations. Sister Demetria Smith, for example, recalled that four to six African American women (at least two of whom were physicians) joined her congregation in the 1970s and 1980s. All left owing to the challenges of racism and the refusal of some white Missionary Sisters of Our Lady of Africa to treat them with respect as human beings and professionals, leaving Smith to lament that she would "live and die the only [African American Missionary Sister of Our Lady of Africa]."[53]

Early Black Sister of Notre Dame Phillis Marie (Deborah) Plummer also left religious life because of racism in the 1980s. Over the years, Plummer, who entered the congregation in Cleveland, Ohio, in 1969, had learned to ignore the open and private acts of racial hostility directed her way by members of her congregation. Whether it was initially being denied the opportunity to join the NBSC or having her superior try to undermine the success of a diocesan group for Black youth that she founded, Plummer, the daughter of Jamaican and Panamanian immigrants, countered the resistance with hard work and spiritual perfection. She also smuggled gospel music into the convent in an effort to maintain a connection to her spiritual and cultural foundations. Nevertheless, Plummer confessed that she was eventually consumed by the heavily German culture and European ethnic customs of her order, noting that she even learned to mispronounce words as her peers did and became culturally estranged from her family during rare visits home. But she desired to remain in the sisterhood, believing that she was making a difference.[54]

However, two episodes in the early 1980s hastened Plummer's departure from religious life. In the first, during a school trip to Washington, DC, a few of Plummer's students ran up to her complaining about having been grouped with students from another school on their tour of a government building. When Plummer asked what the problem was, her students, all white, stated almost in unison, "They put us in with two Black girls." Shocked, Plummer stood silent. When the depravity of their statements, especially to their Black nun teacher, finally dawned on Plummer's students, they apologized, repeating, "We love *you.*" However, the following year, while supervising two white male students after school, Plummer finally broke after she heard one loudly say "nigger." When the other student quickly shushed him and pointed to Plummer, the offending student laughed and said, "She's not really Black." That same day, Plummer "on impulse" marched to the office of her congregation's leaders and informed them she was leaving. Although her superiors maintained that racism was Plummer's "cross to bear," she departed the order. In so doing, Plummer joined three Black Sisters of Notre Dame who had departed the community in Cleveland before her.[55] Several other Black sisters then in their fifties and sixties—including former NBSC leaders Marie de Porres Taylor

FIGURE 7.3. The premature deaths of National Black Sisters' Conference charter members and education leaders Sisters Dolores Harrall (*left*) and Thea Bowman (*right*) rocked the Black Catholic community in 1988 and 1990, respectively. Both women had desegregated their Catholic high schools and white orders as teenagers in the 1950s, endured unconscionable racism in their communities, and gone on to earn doctorates. Harrall died from rectal cancer at age fifty-one, while Bowman died from breast and bone cancer at fifty-two. Courtesy of the New England Archives of the Sisters of Notre Dame de Namur, Ipswich, Massachusetts.

and M. Shawn Copeland—also left their white orders during this period, often in desperate attempts to save their very lives and minds.[56]

Before medical studies began documenting the health and emotional costs of white racism on Black and Brown people, many Black and white sisters pondered whether the early deaths of several pioneering Black sisters in white congregations—including Dolores Harrall, Mary Julian Griffin, Reginalda Polk, Jo Mary Davis, and Beatrice Jeffries—were directly related to their decisions to remain in religious life in the face of intractable bigotry.[57] The same could also be said of many pioneering Black bishops and priests, including founding National Office for Black Catholics leader Joseph Davis, who desegregated their seminaries and orders and/or were stationed in hostile white Catholic communities. While more research needs to be done on the health impact of white Catholic racism on African American religious, serious health conditions and premature deaths contributed to the decimation of the US Church's population of Black priests and sisters during the last quarter of the twentieth century. And no death had more impact than that of Sister Thea Bowman (figure 7.3).

By the time Bowman delivered her presentation to the US bishops in 1989, she was already one of the most famous Catholic nuns in the country. She had briefly pursued a career teaching English and African American literature after earning her PhD from the Catholic University of America in 1972. However, Bowman ultimately returned to her native Mississippi to teach African American youth and preserve the Catholic tradition that had brought her into the faith at age nine.[58] For Bowman, resurging racism in the nation could not be halted without dedicated Black religious men and women fighting against it. Thus, she turned her full attention and energy to achieving racial and educational justice in the Church.[59]

Though barred from the Catholic priesthood because of her sex, Bowman developed a ministry that combined African American storytelling, preaching, dancing, and singing. Through her innovative religious practices, she became what one contemporary called a "priest to the People of God."[60] Over the next fifteen years, Bowman's ministry took her into a diverse array of religious and educational institutions across the United States and around the world. As she frequently told her audiences, "Women can't preach in the Catholic Church. But I can preach in the streets. I can preach in the neighborhood. I can preach in the home. I can preach and teach in the family. And it's the preaching that's done in the home that brings life and meaning to the Word your priest proclaims in his official ministry in the pulpit."[61] And central to Bowman's ministry was championing the cultural, intellectual, and spiritual gifts of the African American community, which she believed would help break down barriers and heal racial divisions in the Church. As she explained in a 1984 interview, "[Black Catholics] are at the cutting edge of Catholicism: you know, the majority of the people in the world are not white Europeans!" While noting that white Catholics had "plenty of right ideas," Bowman concluded that "the expression comes across as incomplete, because a lot of churches try to do the head trip. . . . The nuns don't like clapping in church, so nobody claps. If you don't understand the importance of culture, you don't understand the importance of this."[62] For Bowman, reclaiming and practicing African American spiritual and cultural traditions in Catholic parishes was not only essential to the survival of the Black Catholic community but also inherently political.

After her ministry was featured on *60 Minutes*, during which she persuaded correspondent Mike Wallace to say, "Black is beautiful," on air in 1987, Bowman gained celebrity status in the secular world as well. The episode drew the attention of activist actors Harry Belafonte and Whoopi Goldberg, who aimed to make a documentary film about Bowman's life and created additional demand for African American novelist Margaret Walker's commissioned biography of Bowman.[63] Thus, Bowman's death at age fifty-two shook the Church to its core.

In his eulogy, Father John Ford, an African American Missionary Servant of the Most Holy Trinity, urged funeral attendees to reflect passionately on the life and suffering of his late friend.[64] He also urged emulation: "Even in the face of human suffering and anguish and death we must, this day, not only renew our belief that God will come, but we must also find ways to imitate this irreplaceable woman. There is no other Thea. None other will come in our lifetime. . . . We must . . . find a way, somehow, to imitate Thea, who took the psalmist's words literally. 'Wait for the Lord with courage. Be stouthearted and wait for the Lord.'"[65]

For many Catholics committed to racial justice and reconciliation, Bowman had been the hope of the US Church and its ongoing struggle to live up to the Catholic creed of universal humanity—especially in the wake of the controversial formation of an independent congregation of Black Catholics in Washington, DC, in 1989.[66] "At a time of much division in the Church, Sister Thea possessed the charismatic gifts to heal, to bring joy to the church," one cardinal stated. "She was poet, preacher, master teacher and blessed with an extraordinary voice. She challenged us to own our individuality, yet pleaded for us to be one in Christ."[67] At the conclusion of the funeral Mass, Bowman's body was escorted out of St. Mary's as the crowd sang an African American spiritual, one of the many Black intellectual and cultural gifts that Bowman championed in the Church.

While she did not fit the popular mold of a civil rights or Black power leader, Bowman played a critical role in the African American struggle for liberation. As a member of the generation of Black Catholic women and girls who desegregated the nation's white sisterhoods after World War II and a founding NBSC member, Bowman challenged her church to abide by its social teachings and welcome all persons equally into its fold. "Be woman. Be man. Be priest. Be Irish-American, be Italian-American, be Native-American, be African American, but be one in Christ," Bowman frequently stated.[68] In one of her final interviews, Bowman also made it clear where she stood on all forms of discrimination, especially misogyny and opposition to women's leadership in the Church. Specifically, Bowman declared, "I will never reconcile myself with injustice . . . racism . . . sexism, or classism . . . anything that is destructive."[69] Bowman's famed ministry of love had mixed results in the white-dominated and patriarchal Church, however. Indeed, many of Bowman's peers believed that she paid the ultimate price for her radical vision of freedom in a closed-minded world: unspeakable suffering and an untimely demise.[70]

Whether Bowman should be considered a martyr for human justice is debatable. What is clear is that in the weeks following her death, newspapers and magazines across the country printed obituaries and articles championing her life and legacy in the Church. *America*, the prominent Catholic weekly, for example, ran a full-page sketch of Bowman on April 28, 1990. It marked the first time in the Jesuit-owned magazine's eighty-one-year history that a Black woman graced its cover—a notable fact considering the Jesuits' mostly unreconciled history of brutalizing and economically exploiting Black women and girls during slavery.[71] A few weeks later, Bowman became the first African American to be awarded the Laetare Medal from the University of Notre Dame, the oldest and most prestigious service award given to American Catholics.[72] In 1992, Whoopi Goldberg starred in the smash hit film *Sister Act*, which was very loosely based on Thea's life and contributions to the Church.[73] In the hands of Hollywood, however, Bowman was transformed into a Black Reno lounge singer forced to pose as a nun in an all-white convent, while hiding from her white married mobster boyfriend. Such a gross departure from Bowman's actual identity suggests that mainstream American popular culture was still not ready to embrace the idea of a real Black nun, especially as a leading figure, in the 1990s. In 1993, however, the US Church began closely examining Bowman's life to assess her candidacy for sainthood, creating an opportunity to institutionalize her near-lifelong struggle against racism in the Church in a permanent and spiritual way.[74]

However, the movement to celebrate and preserve Bowman's legacy helped to limit the actualization of her dreams and efforts. As Bowman's supporters mobilized to canonize (and thus iconize) the late Black nun rather than the struggle that she personified, the long history of Black sisters in the fight for racial, educational, and gender equity in the United States was initially marginalized and disregarded and eventually forgotten. Thus, in its most devastating consequence, Bowman's death signaled another critical turning point in the history of African American sisters in the United States—one that left Black sisters' once-indisputable place within the spiritual leadership of the African American Catholic community uncertain.

In a controversy that rocked the US Church one year after Bowman's death, NBSC charter member Sister Teresita Weind was forced to resign as a pastoral associate at St. Catherine–St. Lucy Parish in Oak Park, Illinois (figure 7.4). In the preceding twelve years, Weind had been a charismatic member of the racially integrated church's leadership team, where she instructed converts, prepared liturgical services, led retreats, visited the sick, counseled the troubled, and preached once a month. In the three years before her departure, Weind also led Mass on Good Friday, during which she wore priestly vestments and was assisted by two male priests.[75] However, after witnessing Weind lead the Good Friday service in 1991, Father Edward K. Braxton, an African American priest seeking to become a bishop, issued a series of complaints to Chicago cardinal Joseph Bernandin in which he stated that Weind's "preaching alarmed [him] as a violation of canon law."[76] Soon thereafter, Cardinal Bernandin ordered Weind to cease her preaching at St. Catherine–St. Lucy and appointed Braxton as the parish's new pastor. After a series of political maneuvers designed to strip Weind of her previous spiritual duties, Braxton forced her to leave the parish that November— less than eight months after he launched his first complaint.[77]

For secular observers in Chicago, the widely publicized dispute between Braxton and Weind paralleled the then-recent Supreme Court confirmation hearing for one of the nation's most famous Black lay Catholics and a former seminarian, Clarence Thomas, whom law professor Anita Hill and at least two other former Black women employees had accused of sexual harassment.[78] For many Church observers, Weind's removal was emblematic of the Catholic Church's archaic position on the role of women in society and a direct attack on the movement for women's ordination. And in many ways it was.

Over the years, many Black sisters had felt called to preaching and had supported women's ordination to the priesthood.[79] At least two, former Oblate Sister of Providence Antoinette (Carol) Rodez and former Daughter of Charity Renee Fenner, left the Church to become Episcopalian priests.[80] While many NBSC members had initially been reluctant to join organizations pushing for women's ordination owing to the anti-Black attitudes of some of the movement's founding white sisters, Black nuns preaching had been an ever-present feature at NBSC meetings and joint meetings with Black priests and seminarians since 1970.[81] However, when several African American men became bishops in the 1980s, some Black sisters charged that some of these men increasingly became disconnected from the people.[82] Following one joint meeting when the Black bishops all arrived in separate limousines, to the vocal discontent of many attendees, Sister Irma Dillard also noted how some of these clerics increasingly began opposing Black sisters' leadership in the meetings.[83]

FIGURE 7.4. One of the most important leadership breakthroughs of the twenty-first century involved Sister Teresita (Helen) Weind, elected in 2006 to head the North American province of the Sisters of Notre Dame de Namur and then the worldwide order, becoming the first African American woman to lead a global congregation of women religious. Shortly after her election to serve a second term as her order's global leader, the parishioners of Oak Park's St. Catherine–St. Lucy Catholic Church invited Weind back into their pulpit, from which the Braxton debacle had removed her. Here, Weind preaches at the Oak Park parish in 2014 for the church's 125th-anniversary celebration. Courtesy of David Pierini.

Thus, for many Black sisters, Braxton's public mistreatment of Weind also represented a deep betrayal. For so long, Black Catholics had hoped that once Black men ascended to the episcopacy, they would serve as effective advocates and spokesmen for African American Catholics and articulate the community's unique trials, concerns, and needs. This hope was especially poignant for Black sisters, whose pioneering efforts had made embracing the religious state in the Church possible for African Americans. However, the historic ascendancy of sixteen African American men to the US episcopacy in the last quarter of the twentieth century did not entirely fulfill the hopes of their most loyal advocates and earliest champions. In fact, some of these men repeatedly proved that their desire for power within the white-dominated, male-controlled Church superseded the needs and best interests of the Black Catholic community—a fear first articulated by NBSC leaders in the late 1960s and 1970s.[84]

In 1990, a devastating scandal involving Archbishop Eugene Marino rocked the African American Catholic community again. On May 5, 1988, Marino, a Josephite priest, became the nation's first African American Catholic archbishop. However, the fifty-six-year-old Marino resigned two years later after he admitted to a two-year sexual relationship with a twenty-seven-year-old Black laywoman, Vicki Long. Marino had been counseling Long, who in 1987 successfully sued the Church over sexual abuse at the hands of at least two white priests and one white nun.[85] Upon Marino's resignation, James P. Lyke became Atlanta's and the nation's second African American archbishop. However, Lyke was soon diagnosed with cancer and died in 1991 at fifty-three, marking yet another early death among Black Catholic leaders.[86]

Although Braxton's tenure at St. Catherine–St. Lucy Parish was rocky following Weind's politically maneuvered exit, he was installed as an auxiliary bishop in the archdiocese of St. Louis in Missouri in 1995, as the second bishop of the diocese of Lake Charles in Louisiana in 2001, and as the bishop of the diocese of Belleville in Illinois in 2005.[87] Soon thereafter, Braxton became one of the Catholic prelates whose dioceses lost lawsuits over sexual abuse. Braxton also faced severe criticism as a "financial disaster" as bishop for misusing funds earmarked for the propagation of the faith and for repeatedly appealing an August 28, 2008, jury decision that found the diocese of Belleville guilty of fraudulent concealment in the case of a diocesan priest credibly accused of molesting youth in several parishes during the 1960s, 1970s, and 1980s.[88]

Devastating Losses, Monumental Triumphs, and New Beginnings

In the face of steady disappointments and setbacks, Black Catholic sisters continued to push their racial justice agendas forward and break long-standing racial and gender barriers in the Church. In the last two decades of the twentieth century, several Black sisters were elected into the leadership ranks of their predominantly white congregations, serving as local and national superiors as well as on their respective congregational leadership councils. In 1983, Good Shepherd Sister Barbara Beasley became the second self-identified Black woman to head a white congregation in the United States.[89] In 1985, Sister Juliana Haynes, the first professed African American Sister of the Blessed Sacrament, became her congregation's first Black president, a monumental achievement for an order still haunted by the legacy of racial segregation and exclusion.[90] Ten years later, legendary Benedictine Sister of Chicago Karen Bland became the first African American elected to lead a historically white sisterhood in the powerful midwestern archdiocese—a milestone that came more than seventy-five years after the first known Black nun from Chicago was forced to leave the city to enter a Black sisterhood owing to the anti-Black admissions policies of white congregations there.[91]

African American sisters also continued to break new ground in educational leadership. In 1990, three Black nuns (Sisters of the Blessed Sacrament Mary Norbert Moline and Marilyn Hopewell and Sister for a Christian Community Barbara Boynton) assumed the leadership of three predominantly Black Catholic schools in the Philadelphia archdiocese. Although the OSP had led Black Catholic schools in the city in the nineteenth and twentieth centuries, no Black member of a white congregation had served as a principal of a Catholic school until then.[92] In response to the historic reopening of eight previously shuttered Catholic schools and the building of one new school in inner-city Memphis by Bishop James Terry Steib, SVD, in 1999, several Black sisters stepped forward again.[93] Before the diocese of Memphis shuttered the Jubilee Schools in 2019, just three years after Steib's retirement, six Black nuns (five African American and one African) served as principals, teachers, and health service providers in the schools.[94] For former NBSC president Sister Donna Banfield, the opportunity to be a part of the "miracle in Memphis" was too good to pass up. "So often you hear about Catholic schools closing in urban areas," Banfield reflected. "I wanted to be a part of something different." Banfield, a Sister of the Blessed Sacrament, served as the principal of Memphis's Holy Names of Jesus and Mary Catholic School from 2006 to 2010.[95] Sister Rose Martin Glenn, SSpS, served as director of health services for the Jubilee Schools from 2009 to 2016.[96]

In the arena of pastoral leadership, current and former Black Catholic sisters also broke new ground. In 1990, Religious Sister of Mercy Cora Marie Billings became the first Black nun to lead a Roman Catholic parish in the nation when she was installed by the diocese of Richmond, Virginia, to serve as the pastoral administrator of the priestless St. Elizabeth's Catholic Church. Billings's official duties included delivering the liturgy, handing out Communion consecrated by a priest, and leading the parish's daily business affairs.[97]

Despite the enduring challenges of racism in religious life, African American women continued to enter orders. Among these candidates were older Black women like Sisters Jannette Pruitt, a member of the Franciscan Sisters of Oldenburg, Indiana, and Patricia Dual, a Dominican Sister of Peace, who had been called to religious life during their youth but did not enter for a host of reasons, including segregation.[98] In some instances, these women reintegrated white orders and made history. Sister Kathleen Smith, who entered the Sisters of Providence of St. Mary of the Woods in 1992 at the age of forty-nine, for example, became the congregation's first perpetually professed African American member in 2000.[99]

Black sisters also continued to forge new pathways in female religious life. In 1995, seventy-two-year-old Oblate Sister of Providence Wilhemina (Mary Elizabeth) Lancaster, a descendant of enslaved Black Catholics in St. Genevieve, Missouri, left her congregation after fifty-three years to establish the Benedictines of Mary, Queen of the Apostles. An interracial contemplative community whose primary duties center on praying for the sanctification of priests, the Benedictines of Mary were first established in the diocese of Scranton, Pennsylvania, and transferred to the diocese of Kansas City–St. Joseph, Missouri, in 2006.[100]

In the early twenty-first century, African American sisters, despite their ever-declining numbers, continued to push an inclusive human rights agenda in the US Church. They also turned greater institutional attention to issues of specific importance to Black Catholic women, religious and lay. In 2001, for example, the NBSC organized and sponsored the first National Gathering for Black Catholic Women, which drew more than eight hundred participants from across the country. There, attendees were encouraged to make their voices heard on issues such as racism and exclusion in the Catholic Church, the paucity of Black priests and nuns, the ongoing

closings of Black Catholic schools, disproportionately high Black imprison-
ment rates, poverty, and the devastating impact of HIV/AIDS in the African
American community.[101] In 2003, Sister Constance Phelps, a Sister of Charity of Leavenworth in Kansas, broke another important barrier when she became the first African American president of the Leadership Conference of
Women Religious, the nation's leading organization of women religious.[102]
So, too, did former NBSC president Sister Patricia Chappell when she assumed the executive directorship of Pax Christi USA, the leading Catholic
peace organization, in 2011 as its first African American leader. In pledging
to make antiracism work central to Pax Christi's efforts, Chappell stated,
"People really have to acknowledge that racism is a deep integral sin in our
country and we have to admit it continues to be an institutional sin."[103]

In the arena of public protest, Black sisters also continued to stand in the
vanguard of Catholic leadership on the matter of racial justice. At the dawn
of the era of #BlackLivesMatter, the nation's Black bishops, like their white
and Latino counterparts, remained collectively silent about the social, political, and economic challenges African American communities face as a
result of structural inequality, unchecked police violence, mass incarcera-
tion, and deindustrialization. Before 2020, no Catholic bishop even dared
proclaim the words "Black Lives Matter."[104] However, several Black sisters,
as directors of diocesan offices for Black Catholics, leaders in their congregations, and members of secular Black protest organizations aimed at elimi-
nating police violence, adopted the popular rallying cry in 2013 following
the acquittal of George Zimmerman for the murder of Trayvon Martin.[105]
In 2014, Selma march veteran Sister Mary Antona Ebo even went onto the
streets of Ferguson, Missouri, in protest of the police killing of Michael
Brown Jr. and the militarization of police forces against the predominantly
Black suburb's outraged citizens. Speaking to reporters, Ebo reminded
them, "You are not here to take a superficial picture. . . . You are going to
raise the rug up and look at what's under the rug."[106]

Six African American Sisters of St. Joseph of Carondelet (figure 7.5) also
responded prophetically to Brown's murder and openly chastised white
Catholics in St. Louis and the wider Church for their silence on the plight
of the African American community. In St. Louis for a meeting organized
by Selma march veteran Sister Barbara Moore before Brown's death, the
group drafted a statement denouncing the sin of racism and calling for
Catholic action. "In light of the times occurring in our country and our
world, it is timely for us to gather as women of color," Moore stated. "The
inciden[t]s that have happened in St. Louis are tragic. They are symptom-

FIGURE 7.5. The 2014 meeting of the nation's six African American Sisters of St. Joseph of Carondelet shortly after the police murder of Michael Brown Jr. in Ferguson, Missouri, marked the first gathering in their history. Seated from left to right: Sisters Barbara Moore, Ingrid Honoré-Lallande, and Clementine Lynch. Standing from left to right: Sisters Angelina Faustina, Gail Tripett, and Sharon Howell. Faustina, the granddaughter of Knights of St. Peter Claver founder Gilbert Faustina and the first African American admitted to the Sisters of St. Joseph of Carondelet in California, passed for white in the order until the early 1990s. Courtesy of the Sisters of St. Joseph of Carondelet, St. Louis, Missouri.

atic of what has been going on in many communities for many years."[107] In Sister Ingrid Honoré-Lallande's opinion, bearing witness to and speaking out against the conditions in Ferguson was something that all Sisters of St. Joseph of Carondelet should be doing, just not the Black members. "The Congregation Chapter of 2008 mandated that we address racism among ourselves so we can have an impact on the world in which we live," she wrote. "We have to ask the question and have honest, open and painful conversations around the issue of racism—and acknowledge that racism exists among us. It is in *every* institution: banking, education, health care, the Church. How can we as CSJs say we are exempt from racism? We are not. We *are* the Church."[108]

Despite Black sisters' steady calls to combat institutional racism within and outside of the Church, anti-Black racism remains a defining feature of

US and Catholic life. African American sisters in white orders still suffer acts of overt racism and unconscious bias.[109] While many opt to remain and fight, others have departed—among them Dr. Shawnee Daniels-Sykes, a former School Sister of Notre Dame and the nation's only Black Catholic woman health care ethicist.[110] Because African American vocations to religious life remain few and the average age of those who remain in white and Black orders is well over sixty, NBSC predictions that Africa held the key to the survival and transformation of African American female religious life are coming true.

"And Ethiopia Shall Stretch Forth Her Hands unto God"

The Church's declining numbers in North America combined with the steady growth of Catholicism in sub-Saharan Africa, which is supplying significant numbers of African sisters to Western ministries, has reversed the declining Black sister population in the United States.[111] In 2014, African-descended women constituted a significant 8 percent of women who had entered US religious formation programs in the previous ten years, even though African-descended people made up approximately 4 percent of the nation's Catholic population.[112] While African American women continue to enter religious life, African women have largely fueled this contemporary growth. According to a 2011 report, approximately a thousand African sisters were ministering in the country, with the majority having arrived since 1990.[113] And that number is steadily rising.

While most African candidates are entering the nation's historically white sisterhoods, several have entered the three surviving African American orders. Notably, in 2015, Sister Gertrude Lilly Jhenacho, a native of Nigeria who entered the Franciscan Handmaids of Mary in 2000, became the African American sisterhood's first non-American superior. Four years later, Jhenacho transferred the order's motherhouse to Nigeria, where vocations to religious life remain strong.[114]

African sisterhoods have also sent "reverse missionaries" to the United States to fill the voids created by the rapidly declining and aging sister population.[115] In a few cases, these African sisters have ensured the continuation of the nation's oldest Black Catholic ministries. In 2006, for example, three members of the Nigerian-based Handmaids of the Holy Child of Jesus assumed the administration of St. Augustine Catholic School in Washington, DC.[116] The OSP had led the St. Augustine school from 1908 until 1998, when personnel limitations forced the order to withdraw. Thus, the arrival of three Nigerian sisters restored the legacy of Black sisters' leadership at DC's oldest historically Black Catholic school.[117] Two years later, Sister Maria Babatunde, a member of the Nigerian-based Sisters of St. Michael the Archangel, became the principal of Tampa's St. Peter Claver School, Florida's oldest Black Catholic school.[118]

In 2006, the Nigerian-based Sisters of the Sacred Heart (SSH), established under NBSC leader and Sister of the Holy Family Sylvia Thibodeaux also expanded their ministries to the United States following Hurricane Katrina. The SSH superior, Sister Cecilia Dimaku, was visiting the SSF motherhouse in New Orleans when the hurricane hit and witnessed its devastation. Not only were most SSF properties in the city, including the motherhouse, St. Mary's Academy, and the order's nursing homes, destroyed, but also, for the first time in their history, the African American sisterhood, then under Thibodeaux's leadership, was homeless.[119] Dimaku answered Thibodeaux's request to remain and help the order rebuild. Since 2007, five SSH members have been missioned to New Orleans, where they have served on the teaching and administrative staffs at St. Mary's Academy.[120] The SSH's purchase of their first home in New Orleans in 2016 signified their intention to remain and help preserve the SSF's legacy.[121] From Thibodeaux's perspective, the presence of the SSH in New Orleans also brings the SSF's story full circle since records reveal that her order's chief foundress, Henriette Delille, was the great-great-granddaughter of an enslaved woman named Nanette who was born in West Africa.[122]

The national organization of the African Women Religious Conference has also cemented the growing place and influence of African sisters ministering in the United States. Meeting annually since 1997, the conference highlights issues regarding the welcoming and integration of African women religious into the US Church. It began one year before the African priests ministering in the country organized on the national level.[123] In 2000, the historic canonization of Canossian Sister Josephine Bakhita, an ex-slave Sudanese nun, gave a papal stamp of approval to the rising African sister population in the modern Roman Catholic Church. Bakhita's sainthood—the first for a Black woman in the modern era—has also helped mitigate some of the long-standing opposition to Black sisters' presence in the Western world.[124]

Despite their advances, African sisters are not protected from the historical legacies and toxic realities of anti-Blackness in the United States.[125] Heightened racism and nativism, especially in the wake of the 2016 presidential election and brief changes in immigration policies targeting African nations, like Nigeria, have threatened to reverse the growth of the African sister population in United States.[126] For the time being, though, the future of Black Catholic sisters in the nation remains viable. In fact, when one considers the Afro-Caribbean and African American roots of Black female religious life and Black Catholic education in the modern Church, it almost seems providential that Black sisters from the African continent, where religious life for women began, may carry the US tradition forward. And for the faithful, at least, that is an encouraging thought.

Conclusion

"THE CATHOLIC CHURCH WOULDN'T BE
CATHOLIC IF IT WASN'T FOR US"

I am a Black nun   No more begging,
Seeing, wondering, doubting,   No more cringing,
hoping and praying.   No more shaming,
I am a Black nun   Shaming no more,
Singing, talking, laughing,   no more, no more!
crying and dying.   I am a Black nun . . .
I am a Black nun—

—SISTER MARY ROGER THIBODEAUX, SBS,
A Black Nun Looks at Black Power

When Sister Mary Antona Ebo died on November 11, 2017, the US Catholic Church took notice. It had been fifty years since Ebo had openly sparred with the white leaders of her congregation and the National Catholic Conference for Interracial Justice (NCCIJ) for failing to understand and support Black sisters' leadership and expertise in the changing Black freedom struggle. In the decades that followed, the leaders of the Franciscan Sisters of Mary learned to refrain from intervening in Ebo's racial justice activism. The NCCIJ's influence in the Church and wider society also rapidly declined. Fueled by the larger white Catholic turn toward political conservatism, steady Church divestment from Black Catholic communities, and increasing Black Catholic demands for Black leadership in the Church, many white NCCIJ leaders and supporters proved incapable of fully reckoning with white Catholic culpability in America's racial crisis and steadily lost interest in the evolving Black freedom struggle as a result.[1] Sister Margaret Traxler, who ascended to the NCCIJ's top post in 1971, left in 1973 to focus her energies on the struggle for women's rights in the Church.[2] Her departure in the same year that Benedictine Sister Joyce Williams, a founding member of the National Black Sisters' Conference (NBSC), became the NCCIJ's first Black head of the Department of Educational Services confirmed many Black sisters in their suspicions that Traxler's commitment to racial justice was always conditional and simply a platform to grant her public credibility from which to launch a white women's campaign for ordination.[3] For Black sisters like Ebo and Williams, who also fought against clerical misogyny and supported women's calls to preaching, abandoning the fight for racial justice was never an option. Like most Black women leaders of their generation, Black sister activists understood that one had to battle the interconnected sins of racism and sexism simultaneously.

As the NCCIJ steadily faded into the background in the late 1970s and early 1980s (eventually shuttering its doors in Chicago in 2002), Ebo reemerged as one of the Church's most visible and durable links to the African American freedom struggle. In addition to her activism through the NBSC, which she headed from 1979 to 1981, Ebo served as a regular speaker on the Catholic lecture circuit, giving presentations related to the enduring sins of anti-Black racism and discrimination in the Church and American society.[4] Beginning in the 1980s, Ebo also began regularly traveling back to Selma, Alabama, to participate in the annual commemoration of the pivotal voting rights marches of 1965. During her first return to the city in 1985, the Black "Sister of Selma," as Ebo was then known, even met with Joseph Smitherman, who was still the city's mayor, and attempted a reconciliation. However, Smitherman, who once publicly referred to Dr. King as "Martin Luther Coon," reportedly told Ebo, "We often wondered what became of that little colored lady that they dressed up like a nun."[5] Despite Smitherman's enduring skepticism, the 2003 PBS film documentary *Sisters of Selma* introduced Ebo to a new generation of activists and students of history. So, too, did her surprise appearance on the streets of Ferguson, Missouri, in 2014 following the police murder of Michael Brown Jr.[6] Although hundreds of Catholic sisters and priests had participated in the Selma protests of 1965, only Ebo, then in her ninetieth year, found the courage to make the trip to the embattled St. Louis suburb and call for structural change before a crowd of reporters. As such, news of Ebo's death on Veteran's Day 2017

FIGURE CONC.1. The funeral Mass for Sister Mary Antona (Elizabeth Louise) Ebo, Franciscan Sister of Mary, was held at the historically Black St. Alphonsus "the Rock" Catholic Church in St. Louis, Missouri, on November 20, 2017. Here, Father Art Cavitt, a close friend, offers a farewell kiss to the famed Black "Sister of Selma." Photo by Lisa Johnston. Courtesy of the *St. Louis Review.*

sparked an outpouring of local and national tributes to her extraordinary life and legacy in the fight for racial justice (figure Conc.1). In an unprecedented move, even the powerful United States Conference of Catholic Bishops (USCCB) paid homage to Ebo as part of its annual commemoration of Dr. King's birthday in January 2018.[7]

Yet even as Church leaders, journalists, and everyday observers championed Ebo's legacy as a civil rights activist, aspects of her longer and more impactful history of activism and leadership in the broader African American freedom struggle, especially within Catholic boundaries, were minimized or altogether erased. Most of the published tributes to Ebo's life, for example, described her as a "reluctant convert" to the civil rights movement and characterized Ebo's historic participation in the 1965 Selma protests as the beginning of her racial justice activism.[8] Ironically, many of these same publications noted that Ebo was one of the first three African Americans to enter her Catholic sisterhood in 1946. A few obituaries even noted that Ebo suffered rejections from Catholic nursing schools in Illinois based on race before entering her congregation's all-Black nursing school in St. Louis in 1944.[9] Yet none of these tributes explicitly framed Ebo's Catholic firsts within the context of racial desegregation. They also failed to consider how Ebo's feats expanded the chronology of her racial justice activism. While employing the limiting language of "civil rights" to frame Ebo's story certainly contributed to these analytical failures, the writers' inability, and perhaps unwillingness, to engage with Ebo's longer history of struggle against white supremacy within Catholic boundaries is rooted in a much deeper problem.

Like Black Catholics' widely overlooked history in the long African American fight for civil and human rights, the history of white Catholic racism as manifested in 338 years of Church-sanctioned slavery in the land area that became the United States and more than 438 years of racial segregation and exclusion within Church boundaries remains largely unincorporated into the dominant narratives of the American and Catholic experiences. This is especially true within the history of female religious life. Popular and many scholarly narrations of women's religious life overwhelmingly still either minimize white sisters' histories as enslavers or segregationists or erase them altogether. Moreover, Black Catholics' lived experiences remain overlooked as essential sources for understanding and assessing the Church's place in the history of American racism and the global phenomenon of anti-Blackness. Consequently, the Church and society at large remain ill equipped to understand and appreciate just how extraordinary African American sisters' trailblazing feats were and continue to be—even as Black Catholic stories find a larger and more receptive audience in the twenty-first century.

Indeed, seven months before Ebo's death, Georgetown University, the nation's first Catholic institution of higher education, missed a prime opportunity to champion the foundational legacy of Black Catholic sisters in the Church and nation. In a formal ceremony on April 18, 2017, university officials renamed a building that had previously honored a Jesuit slaver after early Black Catholic educator and Oblate Sister of Providence Mary Aloysius (Anne Marie) Becraft (figure Conc.2).[10] Part of the Jesuit institution's long-term effort to investigate and make reparation for its extensive slaveholding past, the dedication of Anne Marie Becraft Hall brought unprecedented new attention to Becraft's remarkable presence in the early US Church. However, the official report of the Georgetown Working Group on Slavery, Memory, and Reconciliation and the various media articles related to the renaming of McSherry Hall not only presented Becraft's membership in the Oblate Sisters of Providence as an afternote to her story but also got Becraft's name in religion wrong.[11] While the report

FIGURE CONC.2. On April 16, 2018, members of the Oblate Sisters of Providence traveled to Georgetown University in Washington, DC, to participate in an Emancipation Day celebration honoring the life and legacy of their early member Sister Mary Aloysius (Anne Marie) Becraft. After the formal event, the sisters posed with university officials in front of Anne Marie Becraft Hall on campus. Courtesy of Georgetown University.

and officials acknowledged that Becraft "experienced both anti-Catholic and anti-black intimidation," none considered the deeper significance of the fact that Becraft established the nation's first Catholic school for Black children in the midst of the nation's and Church's slaveholding elite in 1820. The reports also did not explain (or even allude to) why Becraft—the only Catholic sister known to have a birthright to the early US Church and nation—ultimately had to turn over the leadership of her school and leave her hometown to enter religious life in Baltimore in 1831.[12] No statement acknowledged Becraft's blood connection to Georgetown's founder either.[13] This recognition would have not only helped to illuminate the revolutionary dimensions of Becraft's vocation to Catholic education and religious life but also silenced twenty-first-century detractors who opposed the renaming of McSherry Hall after Becraft by arguing that she had no direct connection to Georgetown.[14]

When the USCCB unanimously voted to open the sainthood cause for Sister Thea Bowman on November 13, 2018, they, too, minimized and even erased the dimensions of her journey that exposed anti-Black racism as a central feature of Church life.[15] To be sure, all official documents associated with Bowman's sainthood cause note that Bowman was the first (and to date only) African American member of her congregation. However, no statement plainly denotes that Bowman desegregated her historically white order, nor do any reference the gut-wrenching racism that Bowman experienced before and during her tenure in religious life. While all the USCCB's documents concerning Bowman's candidacy for sainthood cite her historic presentation to the bishops in 1989, none explicitly acknowledges her long history of activism against racism and sexism. Many of these public narratives also gloss over the glaring fact that Bowman, like many pioneering Black priests and sisters in white congregations, died young, at the age of fifty-two.[16] By contrast, the official Church narratives supporting the sainthood cause of Father Augustus Tolton, the nation's first self-identified Black priest, routinely incorporate his family's daring flight from slavery to freedom during the Civil War, his experience of racist rejection from US seminaries, and his death from exhaustion at age forty-three.[17] This not only serves to frame the victims of the most egregious forms of anti-Black racism in religious life as men but also privileges the struggle for Black priests in understandings of the Black Catholic freedom struggle—even though it was the pioneering successes of Black sisters that first helped to open the doors for the earliest generations of African American priests. While the canonization causes of Mary Lange, Henriette Delille, and Bowman have made African American sisters' existence visible in unprecedented ways, it remains nearly impossible to speak plainly about these holy women as Black freedom fighters and to illuminate the full significance of their journeys without public awareness of the centrality of white supremacy in the US Church, including women's religious life.

In offering the first full accounting of Black Catholic sisters in the long African American freedom struggle, *Subversive Habits* has recovered a consequential chapter in American and religious history. In illuminating Black sisters' foundational roots in the US Church, this book has made the visible the other (and ongoing) transatlantic story of North American Catholicism—the one beginning with Africans and African-descended people living in Europe and Africa in the sixteenth century. In telling Black sisters' stories of resistance and perseverance in the fight to make their church truly catholic and their nation truly democratic, *Subversive Habits* has also made the case for why scholars must center the experiences of Black women and girls in the history of US Catholicism, reconsider narratives that foreground white Catholics in struggles for racial, educational, and gender justice, and push back against characterizations of African American Catholics as politically complacent or conservative.[18]

While much remains to be said about African American sisters' journeys, this book has filled the historiographical gaps and silences that have obscured anti-Black racism as a defining feature of US Catholicism and women's religious life especially. The archival and oral history record reveals that rather than being an institution that absorbed, but diluted, the racist culture of secular society, the Catholic Church was never an innocent bystander in the construction and propagation of white supremacy in the United States. Catholic practices of slavery and segregation were no less evil or brutal that any other forms of these institutions. In fact, in the fifteenth century, with a series of papal bulls authorizing Portuguese and Spanish invasion of Africa (and later the Americas) and the perpetual enslavement of non-Christian Africans and Indigenous Americans, the Roman Catholic Church became the first global institution to declare that Black and Brown lives did not matter.

Yet, in the face of this brutal domination, something miraculous happened. Free, African-descended women living and laboring in the US slave South won approval to establish the modern world's first Roman Catholic sisterhoods for Black women and girls and some of the earliest Catholic social service institutions for Black people. In a society and an institution in which most Black people's bodies were legally not their own, these Black brides of Christ forced the Church to acknowledge the humanity of Black people and declare that their lives mattered in consequential ways. Their ministries also cemented the foundation of an antiracist and antisexist tradition of Catholicism rooted in the larger Black struggle against slavery, exclusion, and white domination. In the long-standing absence of an empowered African American clergy, Black sisters served as the most genuine and effective spiritual leaders of the African American community. As desegregation front-runners, Black sisters made possible generations of African American educational and professional achievement. Their pioneering efforts in preserving and teaching Black and Black Catholic history, art, and spirituality within Church boundaries also mattered. As educational and moral leaders, African American sisters instilled racial pride, molded community servants, and, most important, taught that racism and sexism had no place in the Church—long before the bishops and others collectively did so.

In restoring Black sisters to their rightful place as the vanguard of the Catholic fight for racial, educational, and sexual justice, this book has ultimately explained Sister Loretta Theresa Richards's 2009 summation of

Black sisters' greatest legacy. "The Catholic Church wouldn't be Catholic if it wasn't for us," declared the seventy-six-year-old leader of the Franciscan Handmaids of Mary.[19] From the earliest days of the United States, religious life was one of the fiercest strongholds of white supremacy and battlegrounds of the Black freedom struggle. As such, embracing the celibate religious state in the Catholic Church was always a spiritual *and* political act for anyone who did it. Through their existence, African American sisters upended the ideological foundation of white Christian supremacy: that Blackness was inherently evil, bad, and sexually deviant. They also embodied and taught the fundamental truth that Black history is and always has been Catholic history. This reality explains the great opposition that Black women and girls called to religious life have faced in their vocations and ministries over time as well as the many attempts to erase their footsteps in US history. It also illuminates why the African American sisterhoods and select Black members of white congregations—unlike most of their white counterparts—continue to wear the veil despite Vatican II reforms. "We fought so hard to have them [habits]," one Oblate Sister of Providence remarked in 2010. "We will never give them up."[20]

While the anti-Black admissions policies and practices of white congregations ensured that white sisters became a, if not the, dominant face and force of the US Church, these same commitments to white supremacy also ensured that the moral compass of the Church on matters of racism and other interconnected issues would never reside in white Catholic communities. Only when Black nuns and other Black people, Catholic and non-Catholic alike, dared the Church to live up to its core principles of universal humanity and acknowledge (however grudgingly) that the lives and souls of Black people mattered did the white-dominated Church reveal its capacity for becoming truly catholic. The same was also said for the nation at large. As NBSC founding member and early Black Sister of the Blessed Sacrament Mary Roger Thibodeaux put it in 1972, "American society can learn much from Black women. . . . Only insofar as Blacks have access to America will America have access to God."[21]

In the twenty-first century, the work of racial reckoning, justice, and reconciliation in the Catholic Church, as in much of American society, remains woefully incomplete. In many areas, this work has not even begun in any meaningful way. Despite continued condemnations of racism from the Black Catholic community, the USCCB, and select white congregations of men and women, white supremacy and racism remain ever-present realities in the Church, including in religious life.[22] Deeply segregated parishes persist across the country, as do white religious orders with few or no African American members, and most white Catholics, male and female, retain racially antagonistic voting patterns rooted in the backlash to the civil and equal rights gains of the 1950s and 1960s.[23] The teaching of Black and Black Catholic history outside of predominantly Black Catholic institutions also remains rare. However, important changes appear to be on the horizon. Beyond the growing number of Catholic institutions investigating their slaveholding roots and seeking to make reparation, a new generation of scholars and educators through diligent archival research and digital history projects are beginning to disabuse the nation and Church of the enduring myth of Catholic innocence during slavery and segregation.[24] The willingness of an increasing number of white sisterhoods to confront their communities' histories of white supremacy and segregation has also marked a crucial new turning point in the Church.[25] It also serves as the best testament to the ongoing power of Black sisters' historical truth telling.

In 2017, Sister Mary Pellegrino, the leader of the Sisters of St. Joseph (CSJ) of Baden, Pennsylvania, called for a racial reckoning at the annual meeting of the Leadership Conference of Women Religious.[26] The organization's outgoing president, Pellegrino challenged the congregational leaders present to confront their orders' discriminatory pasts and presents of denying Black and Brown vocations on the basis of race. "It is true that many of our congregations, including my own, and many of our Sisters, including my own, ministered in black communities and are committed to actively ensuring the dignity and rights of black people and people of other races," Pellegrino noted. "It is equally true that many congregations, including my own denied black women—and perhaps those of other races—entrance into our communities because they were black. . . . Let these truths humble us. Let them claim us. Let them mature us. And let them lead us to true conversion and repentance, not simply lamenting with words, but rooting out every trace of supremacy or exceptionalism."[27] In the previous two years, Pellegrino had coordinated a formal reconciliation with the NBSC's chief foundress, Dr. Patricia Grey, after learning that Grey had been denied admittance into her community in 1960 on the basis of race.[28] In July 2018, the CSJ of Baden invited Grey to their motherhouse to participate in a reconciliation conversation with the surviving eleven members with whom she would have entered the order in 1960 (figure Conc.3). During the meeting, CSJ leaders also presented Grey with the stole of the community's second admitted African American member, Sister Maria Harden, who died in 2016 at the age of fifty-four. Like Grey, Harden—who

FIGURE CONC.3. Dr. Patricia Grey at the motherhouse of the Sisters of St. Joseph of Baden in Pennsylvania, on July 12, 2018, with the eleven surviving CSJ members, who entered the community in 1960, the year Grey was rejected. Sister Sally Witt, who helped to facilitate the order's formal apology to and reconciliation with Grey, is standing, second from left. The congregation's leader, Sister Mary Pellegrino, is seated, second from right. Courtesy of the Sisters of St. Joseph of Baden, Pennsylvania.

entered the CSJ in 1989—had suffered a racist rejection from a white congregation as a teenager. According to one of Harden's obituaries, when she was enrolled at Pittsburgh's Ursuline Academy in the 1980s, a white member of that Ursuline congregation based in Kentucky responded to Harden's admission inquiry by stating that "she couldn't [enter] because she was black."[29] More than 250 years after the Ursulines arrived in New Orleans and inaugurated US female religious life, discriminatory policies still barred Black women and girls from entering branches solely on the basis of race. In fact, available records indicate that Ursulines in New Orleans have yet to admit a self-identified African American candidate. Even as Grey found unexpected healing with the CSJ of Baden, the searing realities of Harden's experiences of rejection, struggle, and early death were not lost on the NBSC foundress.[30]

Speaking at the fiftieth-anniversary celebration of the NBSC in New Orleans two weeks later, Grey reflected on the ongoing need for Black sisters' historical truth telling. "There are some things that happen in our lives that are literally defining, life changing and transformative," she declared.[31] Wearing Harden's stole, Grey described how the CSJ of Baden's rejection of her admission inquiry had haunted her for decades. She also encouraged those gathered, including the current president of the Leadership Conference of Women Religious, to continue confronting the enduring realities of anti-Black racism in religious life: "I believe that we, Black sisters and white sisters, have to look reality and its history SQUARELY in its face and call it EXACTLY what it is—WITHOUT excuses, in order to forgive and heal each other through the gift of God's grace." Grey also addressed those Black sisters present who were still reluctant to share the most difficult aspects of their journeys through religious life outside of NBSC circles. "**You** CANNOT *protect* your congregation's unchristian ways **conveyed through racism and white privilege**," she declared. "They happened. You have to acknowledge them. We all have to face and own our truths to be forgiven, healed, and transformed in order to reconnect and move forward in a mutual, new relationship *that is free from the past. . . .* **Jesus taught us to do this**."[32] It had been forty-four years since the stress of the NBSC's campaign to rid the Church of racism and her battles with Black clericalism and misogyny drove Grey out of religious life and into an era of strategic silence about her life as Sister M. Martin de Porres. Yet, like many Black freedom fighters and Church prophets, Grey never surrendered her belief in the emancipatory power of truth telling for the sake of justice, reconciliation, and peace. It is my hope that this book, in offering a more honest accounting of the US Catholic experience and the central place of Black sisters within it, can provide another pathway forward.

GLOSSARY

apostolate
mission and ministry to a specific field or community

apostolic community
group of religious engaged in public service ministries (e.g., teaching, nursing)

aspirant
a person who lives with a community before postulancy to determine her or his suitability for religious life and the community does the same

bride of Christ
another term for a Catholic sister or consecrated virgin who has taken public vows

canonization
the process by which a deceased person is declared a saint by the Catholic Church

charism
spirit of a community resulting from the founder's experience of God and ministry

cloister
enclosed building, buildings, or space that only members of a contemplative religious community may enter

congregation
community of religious with vows

contemplative community
congregation whose primary work is prayer and who maintain minimal contact with the outside world

convent
shared residence for a religious congregation

convert
a person who was not baptized into the Catholic Church as an infant but converted to the faith at another stage of his/her/their life

cradle Catholic
a person who was baptized into the Catholic Church as an infant

foundress
a woman who establishes a religious congregation

habit
the clothing signifying religious status worn by some communities

ministry
public services rendered by Church members

mother
title given in some religious communities to elected or appointed leaders

motherhouse
administrative headquarters of a religious community

novice
a person in training who is preparing to profess vows in a religious community

postulant
a person at the first step toward full membership in a religious community

religious
a person who pledges to live in accordance with a community's vows

superior
title given in some religious congregations to elected or appointed leaders

vocation
a calling toward a particular state of life or ministry

NOTES

Note on Terminology and Preface

1. This glossary supplemented the lcwr's *Women and Spirit: Catholic Sisters in America* exhibition, which toured the United States from 2009 to 2012, in a brochure titled "Nun 101." The author added definitions for *apostolate, aspirant, bride of Christ, canonization, convert,* and *cradle Catholic.*

2. "Black Sisters Weigh Contradictions in Christian and Secular Community: 200 Negro Nuns Attend First Nat'l Meet," *Pittsburgh Courier,* September 7, 1968.

3. C. Davis, *History of Black Catholics,* 98–155, 240–42. The entries on Black Catholic women in Darlene Clark Hine's *Black Women in America* were also invaluable at the start of the author's research.

4. Sister Mary Shawn Copeland, "Black Nuns: An Uneasy Story," *National Catholic Reporter,* March 7, 1975, 9.

5. Copeland, "Black Nuns"; Helen May, "Sister Shawn: Black Nun in the News," *Detroit Free Press,* December 13, 1970; and Dr. Shawn Copeland (formerly Sister M. Shawn Copeland, Congregation of Sisters of Saint Felix of Cantalice [cssf] and Dominican Sisters of Adrian, Michigan [op]), interview by author, March 5, 2007, telephone.

6. Copeland, interview.

7. Copeland, interview. See also Copeland, "Cadre."

8. Copeland, interview.

9. Copeland, "Cadre," 128. This was also a common theme in my archival, periodical, and oral history research.

10. Dr. Patricia Grey (formerly Sister M. Martin de Porres, Religious Sister of Mercy [rsm]), interview by author, Sewickley, PA, August 12, 2007. See also chapters 5 and 6.

11. Grey, interview, August 12, 2007.

12. The book I presented to Grey even misidentified the historically white Sisters of the Blessed Sacrament as a Black order.

13. Grey, interview, August 12, 2007.

Introduction

1. "Black Nuns Schedule Pittsburgh Caucus," *National Catholic Reporter*, July 3, 1968, 2; and Sister M. Martin de Porres Grey, "Follow-Up Letter for Upcoming First NBSC," ca. July 1968, in Ebo's personal collection.

2. Sister Mary Antona Ebo, Franciscan Sister of Mary (FSM), interview by author, March 26, 2007, telephone. Ebo recounted that her paternal grandfather, who had been born into slavery, adopted the surname Ebo upon emancipation. Ebo's father, Daniel, told her it was the only thing his father could remember about his African past. Decades later, a Black physician intrigued by the pronunciation of Ebo's surname explained to her that the Ibos, or Igbos, were a distinct West African ethnic group.

3. Ebo, interview.

4. Quoted and cited in Koehlinger, *New Nuns*, 13, 244n117.

5. Ebo, interview.

6. The film *Sisters of Selma* is one of the best accounts of the experiences of the sisters who traveled to Selma in 1965.

7. For two national examples, see John Herbers, "Mayor and Police Block 3 New Marches in Selma," *New York Times*, March 11, 1965; and Paul Good, "Selma's Mayor Blocks Another Attempt," *Washington Post*, March 11, 1965. For a local example, see "Nuns Join in Selma Protest Demonstrations," *Pittsburgh Catholic*, March 18, 1965.

8. Mary Peter Traxler, School Sister of Notre Dame (SSND), "After Selma Sister, You Can't Stay Home Again!," *Extension*, June 1965, 17.

9. Ebo, interview. See also Elaine Graybill, "From Orphanage to the History Books: Bloomington's Betty Ebo Has Made Her Place," *Pantagraph* (Bloomington, IL), February 15, 1990, 19.

10. Ebo, interview.

11. "Here and There," *Our Colored Missions*, December 1946, 179. See also "Colored Girl Accepted by Nursing Order," *Pantagraph* (Bloomington, IL), October 2, 1946, 3.

12. "Negro Nursing Sisters," *Colored Harvest*, December 1946–January 1947, 2–3.

13. Ebo, interview. See also Reverend William M. Drumm to the Most Reverend Joseph E. Ritter, November 23, 1946, Sisters of St. Mary/Franciscan Sisters of Mary File, Archdiocese of St. Louis Archives (ASL Archives), St. Louis, MO. Sister Joseph Marie Schuemann, novice mistress for the first Black Sisters of St. Mary, recalled in a 1977 interview that "the white Populants never did come out to the black Novitiate, and the black Postulants never came out to the Motherhouse." Quoted in Schadewald, "Remapping Race," 232.

14. During our interview, Ebo noted that the offending white sister had recently received a local award for her commitment to social justice but had yet to apologize for mistreating Ebo's father. Ebo also recounted the story of her father's mistreatment in an August 1983 joint interview of Ebo and Sister of St. Mary Thelma M. Mitchell con-

ducted by Sister Jean Derer, contained in Ebo's congregational file in the Archives of the Franciscan Sisters of Mary (FSM Archives), St. Louis, MO, and quoted in Schadewald, "Remapping Race," 229.

15. Quoted in Schadewald, "Remapping Race," 230.

16. The quoted characterization originates in Copeland, *Uncommon Faithfulness.*

17. Blum et al., "American Religion," 1.

18. For historiographical overviews of US female religious life, see McCauley, "Nuns' Stories"; and Coburn, "Historiography of Women Religious." Margaret McGuinness has noted that except for administering the sacraments and celebrating Mass, sisters for most of their history were "more actively involved in the everyday lives of Catholics than priests." McGuinness, *Called to Serve,* 8.

19. On slaveholding among US nuns, see Miller and Wakelyn, *Catholics*; Misner, *"Highly Respectable,"* 75–88; Clark, *Masterless Mistresses*; Doyle, *Pioneer Spirit*; and Jones-Rogers, *They Were Her Property.* In her seven-hundred-plus-page study of Catholic sisters in the West, Jo Ann Kay McNamara devotes less than two pages to slaveholding by European and white American sisterhoods. She also presents slavery as an institution forced on white sisters and erases their documented brutality. See McNamara, *Sisters in Arms,* 533, 579–80. For more on US sister saints and sainthood candidates involved in slavery, see O'Donnell, *Elizabeth Seton*; S. Curtis, *Civilizing Habits*; and "Report on the Commission." Despite copious materials documenting the life of Elizabeth Seton, the first US-born saint, evidence of her and her congregation's ties to slavery is curiously scarce. Seton scholar Marilyn Thei, for example, wrote that there is "no hard evidence establishing that Elizabeth and William [her husband] owned slaves, neither is there evidence to the contrary." See Thei, "The Woman," 252n94. In *Elizabeth Seton*, historian Catherine O'Donnell documents that Seton hailed from a slaveholding family and that her grandfather bequeathed an enslaved "boy, formerly named Brennus," to her in his will (22–23). O'Donnell also documents that enslaved people labored at Seton's first school in Emmitsburg, Maryland (263–64); that the early Sisters of Charity (SC) supervised the enslaved women of Mount St. Mary in Emmitsburg, where the order was established (385); and that Seton never embraced racial equality and abolitionism (385–86). Because the fate of the enslaved person willed to Seton is unknown (23), Seton's status as a slaveholder, if only briefly, seems clear. Seton's acceptance of the labor of enslaved people as tuition at her school (as noted by O'Donnell in Uva and Gotham Center, "The Life of Elizabeth Seton") also constitutes slaveholding, if only temporarily. Although O'Donnell maintains that the enslaved people who labored at Seton's school and Mount St. Mary were owned by the Sulpicians and members of the laity (*Elizabeth Seton,* 263, 290–92; and O'Donnell in Uva and Gotham Center, "The Life of Elizabeth Seton"), there is documented evidence that the SC in Emmitsburg owned and trafficked in enslaved people in the 1830s and that those who expanded the order's ministries into New Orleans in 1834 exploited enslaved labor until the Civil War. See Misner, *"Highly Respectable,"* 78–79; and Salvaggio, *New Orleans' Charity Hospital,* 68. Such realities necessitate deeper investigations into Seton's and her congregation's ties to slaveholding, especially in Emmitsburg, using the research methodologies outlined in Schmidt, "'Regulations.'" This is especially true since O'Donnell acknowledges that one of two boxes titled "Slavery at

the Mount" contained in the Archives at Mount St. Mary University was missing when she conducted her research in 2017 (*Elizabeth Seton*, 464n22).

20. Historians of Native American residential schools are notable exceptions. See Adams, *Education for Extinction*; and Churchill, *Kill the Indian*. See also chapter 2.

21. See Hannah Natanson, "An Elite D.C. Girls' School Thought Its Founding Nuns Taught Slaves to Read. Instead, They Sold Them Off for as Much as They Could," *Washington Post*, August 2, 2019; and Dawn Araujo-Hawkins, "Descendants of Enslaved People Find Their Roots in Sacred Heart Records," *Global Sisters Report*, September 12, 2019.

22. For classic and recent examples, see McGuinness, *Called to Serve*; Koehlinger, *New Nuns*; Hoy, *Good Hearts*; Cummings, *New Women*; Cressler, *Authentically Black*; Newman, *Desegregating Dixie*; and Carol K. Coburn, "The Selma Effect," *Global Sisters Report*, March 9, 2015.

23. This book examines the culture and practices of white supremacy in white and white ethnic sisterhoods. On the anti-Black and discriminatory policies of Catholic hospitals that white sisterhoods administered, see Wall, *American Catholic Hospitals*, 73–102. For a small sampling on the widespread mistreatment Black youth experienced in white-administered schools, parishes, and convents, see chapters 2 and 3.

24. Subsequent chapters examine these struggles and sufferings in detail.

25. Ebo, interview; and FSM *Chronicles Book #3-B: 1944–1953*, 481–82, FSM Archives.

26. Chapter 2 discusses these feats.

27. Ebo, interview. Because Ebo desired to become a nurse and serve the public, she preferred to enter the SSM. The OSP are a teaching order. See also "Pro Memoria," 1, SSM/FSM File, ASL Archives.

28. Chapters 4 through 6 discuss this history.

29. Chapters 3 through 5 cover sisters' specific stories.

30. Miller, "Failed Mission," 149.

31. McGreevy, *Parish Boundaries*, 62.

32. C. Davis, *History of Black Catholics*, 256.

33. Davis, a founding member of the Black Catholic Clergy Caucus, also failed to document Sister M. Martin de Porres Grey's presence at the Black priests' inaugural meeting and relegated the NBSC to a single mention on a timeline. See C. Davis, *History of Black Catholics*, 257–59, 262.

34. For two classic examples, see Landers, *Black Society*; and Clark and Gould, "Feminine Face."

35. Delle and Levine, "Excavations"; Wingert, *Slavery*; Schmidt, "Peter Hawkins"; Doyle, *Pioneer Spirit*, 168–70; and Thomas, *Question of Freedom*.

36. See Gatewood, "'Remarkable Misses Rollin'"; C. Davis, "Black Catholics"; Kelley, *Right to Ride*, 51–116; Wynn, "Diane Judith Nash"; "Interview of Lawrence Guyot," *History Makers*, November 9 and 17, 2004, https://www.thehistorymakers.org/biography/lawrence-guyot-40; Olivia B. Waxman, "'I Was Not Going to Stand': Rosa Parks' Predecessors Recall Their History-Making Acts of Resistance," *Time*, March 2, 2020; Davidson and Putnam, *Legendary Locals*, 94; K. Johnson, *One in Christ*; Neary, *Crossing Parish Boundaries*; and Newman, *Desegregating Dixie*.

37. See Ochs, *Desegregating the Altar*; and Cressler, *Authentically Black*.

38. Cressler, *Authentically Black*, 13.

39. For an introduction to Black women in the African American freedom struggle, see D. White, *Too Heavy a Load*; Shaw, *What a Woman*; Ransby, *Ella Baker*; Lee, *For Freedom's Sake*; Crawford, Rouse, and Woods, *Women*; Collier-Thomas and Franklin, *Sisters in the Struggle*; Giddings, *Ida*; Robinson, *Montgomery Bus Boycott*; and Farmer, *Remaking Black Power*.

40. See chapters 3 and 4 for a few specific examples of those who desegregated Catholic schools. Sister of the Blessed Sacrament Gilda Marie Bell is one of a few Black sisters who desegregated public schools. Bell integrated New Iberia High School in New Iberia, Louisiana, in 1969 and noted that she still bears the scars from the beatings that she received from the white men who attacked her classmates and her with chains as they departed their bus on the first day of school. Sister Gilda Marie Bell, SBS, interview by author, New Orleans, August 22, 2009.

41. On the two earliest Black lay protest movements, see Nickels, *Black Catholic Protest*; and Agee, *Cry for Justice*.

42. See Ochs, *Desegregating the Altar*; C. Davis, *History of Black Catholics*; R. Anderson, *Black, White, and Catholic*; Bennett, *Religion*; Southern, *John LaFarge*; Nickels, *Black Catholic Protest*; Copeland, "Cadre"; J. Davis and Rowe, "National Office"; Agee, *Cry for Justice*; and MacGregor, *Emergence*.

43. White prelates steadfastly refused to ordain most of the earliest generations of self-identified African American seminarians as priests. The few who were ordained were mostly denied leadership roles in US Black parishes until the late 1960s. Many were sent to the Caribbean or West Africa as missionaries. Others remained deliberately hidden as instructors or assistants in seminaries and predominantly white northern parishes. See Ochs, *Desegregating the Altar*, 2–5, 357–63; and Foley, *God's Men of Color*.

44. Ochs, *Desegregating the Altar*; and C. Davis, *History of Black Catholics*, 146–62, 203, 218–19, 233–34.

45. On white attitudes toward African Americans during and after slavery, see Kendi, *Stamped*; Jordan, *White over Black*; Frederickson, *Black Image*; Guy-Sheftall, *Daughters of Sorrow*; Morton, *Disfigured Images*; and Murphy, *Attitudes of American Catholics*.

46. On Black women's resistance to sexual, political, and economic exploitation during and after slavery, see D. White, *Ar'n't I a Woman*; Hine, "Rape"; Hunter, *To 'Joy My Freedom*; McGuire, *At the Dark End*; Feimster, *Southern Horrors*; Gilmore, *Gender and Jim Crow*; Hartman, *Scenes of Subjection*; Higginbotham, *Righteous Discontent*; Giddings, *When and Where*; Lindsey, *Colored No More*; B. Cooper, *Beyond Respectability*; and Blain, *Set the World*.

47. Two significant exceptions are found in Morrow, *Persons of Color*; and Detiege, *Henriette Delille*, but a more thorough historical examination of the radical and politically transformative dimensions of Black female religious life is needed. See also Estes-Hicks, "Henriette Delille."

48. See National Black Sisters' Conference, *Celibate Black Commitment*.

49. Sister Sylvia Thibodeaux, Sister of the Holy Family (SSF), interview by author, New Orleans, August 19, 2009. Her name in religion was Rita Francis.

50. Grey, interview, March 22, 2010.

51. For an introduction, see Landers, *Black Society*. Catholic records document that a free Black domestic servant from Spain married a Spanish soldier in St. Augustine, Florida, in 1565, inaugurating Christian marriage in what became the United States. See Sheldon Gardner, "Website Provides Details on Early St. Augustine Residents," *St. Augustine Record*, March 27, 2018.

52. For a few examples, see Lincoln and Mamiya, *Black Church*; Dolan, *American Catholic Experience*; and McGuinness, *Called to Serve*.

53. The phrase "minority within a minority" comes from Raboteau, *Fire in the Bones*, 117–40.

54. E. Curtis and S. Johnson, "Black Catholicism," 245.

55. This number was tallied from the available membership lists of the US Black sisterhoods and the NBSC as well as the obituaries of the women who persevered as Franciscan Handmaids of Mary. The exact number of Black women to enter white orders is unknown, and the congregational lists of the Black orders are missing the names of several early members. So the number of Black women who entered US religious orders is likely higher than 2,500.

56. See chapters 1 and 2 for these examples.

57. Greg Schaber, "Profile: Francesca Thompson, O.S.F.," *Xavier Magazine*, October 1, 2005.

58. "Mass Offered in Chicago for Sr. Mary Reginalda Polk, 58," *Jet*, February 5, 1990, 58.

59. A biography of Harrall was provided to the author by the Sister of Notre Dame de Namur archivist Sister Mary Ellen O'Keefe, email message to author, July 31, 2013.

60. See N. Davis, "Finding Voice," 45–46; Harris-Slaughter, *Our Lady of Victory*; and Missions Record Group (RG), box 39, folder 1, Archives of the Oblate Sisters of Providence (OSP Archives), Baltimore, MD.

61. Sister Gilda Marie Bell specifically cited the members of her parish's unit of the Ladies Auxiliary of the Knights of St. Peter Claver. Bell, interview.

62. Angela White (formerly Sister Mary Angela de Porres, Sister of Charity of Cincinnati [SC]), interview by author, Cincinnati, OH, October 23, 2013. White later married and took her husband's surname.

63. Adrian McCoy, "Obituary: Freda Ellis/August Wilson's Sister Served in Many Roles," *Pittsburgh Post-Gazette*, September 1, 2015. The author obtained the details on Ellis's entry into the Sisters of Divine Providence from Sister Bernie Duman, archivist of the Congregation of Divine Providence, email message to author, August 10, 2016. Ellis, who was Sister Edana in religion, departed the congregation in 1962. Thanks to Dr. Laurence Glasco for alerting me to Ellis's tenure in religious life.

64. Quoted in Dinah Livingston, "Cool August: Mr. Wilson's Red-Hot Blues" reprinted in Bryer and Hartig, *Conversations with August Wilson*, 45–46. Livingston interviewed Wilson and first published this article in the October 1987 edition of the *Minnesota Monthly*.

65. For another prominent example of the suppression and whitewashing of Black Catholic history, see Foley, "Adventures."

66. See Supan, "Dangerous Memory."

67. Supan, "Dangerous Memory," 65.

68. Supan, "Dangerous Memory," 65.

69. Historian Jay P. Dolan's 1992 supposition that by the 1950s, African American women and girls called to religious life were no longer tracked into Black congregations but instead welcomed in most white orders remains the standard narrative despite glaring contradictory evidence. See Dolan, *American Catholic Experience*, 370–71.

70. For the most extensive historical treatment of the SBS, see Lynch, *Sharing the Bread*, specifically the single-volume hardcover version published in 1998. The two-volume paperback edition published in 2001 under the same title is an abbreviated and significantly edited version.

71. Lynch, *Sharing the Bread* (1998), 407. See also Baldwin, *Call to Sanctity*, 94. Chapter 1 examines this story in detail.

72. The SBS's long-standing practice of attributing their anti-Black admissions policy to a request from Black female congregational leaders is documented in many Black sisters' oral testimonies and the 1998 hardcover edition of *Sharing the Bread* (407, 691n121). Sister Patricia Lynch specifically attributes this request to Mother M. Elizabeth Bowie, a leader of the Sisters of the Holy Family (SSF), and cites only an April 8, 1970, statement by Sister of the Blessed Sacrament Consuela Marie Duffy, an early Drexel hagiographer. Lynch also wrote, "No trace of a similar request from the Oblate Sisters of Providence has been found, but as many of their major superiors had been taught by the SBS, Mother Katharine probably believed they should have the benefit of the practice." Mother Bowie led the SSF order from 1909 to 1918 and from 1930 to 1946; the SBS vote to exclude African Americans and Native Americans was taken in 1893. See chapter 1 for this story. Interestingly, the 2001 paperback reprint of *Sharing the Bread* makes no mention of these alleged requests from the Black superiors to Drexel and erases the SBS's anti–Native American admissions policy on pp. 68–69. African American Catholics who supported Drexel's sainthood were seemingly unaware of the order's 1893 segregationist vote, and SBS leaders seemingly did not inform them. For documentation of Black Catholic support of Drexel's canonization, see Cummings, *Saint of Our Own*, 188–89, 208. Bowie's dates of leadership were obtained from New Orleans African American Museum of Art, Culture, and History (NOAAMACH), *Celebration of Faith*, 27. Finally, knowledge of the SBS's segregationist practices may not have disqualified Drexel for sainthood. White female congregational leaders Elizabeth Seton and Rose Philippine Duchesne, who exploited enslaved labor and practiced segregation, were canonized in 1975 and 1988 respectively. Cornelia Connelly, another enslaver and the US-born foundress of the Sisters of the Holy Child of Jesus (SHCJ), was declared venerable in 1992. See note 19 in this introduction and see chapters 1 and 5 for more on Seton's and Duschesne's ties to slavery and their respective congregations' segregationist practices in the US. Although the SHCJ began their ministries in Africa in 1930 and assisted in the formation of two separate African congregations—including the Handmaids of the Holy Child of Jesus in Nigeria (established in 1931)—the order did not admit its first African candidate until 1962. She did not remain, nor did the next two African-descended women admitted into the order. See "Report on the Commission," 5–6.

73. See Cummings, *Saint of Our Own*, 188–91, 208; Hughes, *Katharine Drexel*, 106–7; Baldwin, *Call to Sanctity*, 94; Bell, interview; and Sister Donna Banfield, SBS, interview by author, Memphis, TN, October 27, 2009.

74. See introduction, note 72; and chapter 1.

75. A member of the SBS leadership council who chose to remain anonymous read the minutes of the 1949 decision to the author over the telephone on October 17, 2016, and confirmed the details by email correspondence, October 19–24, 2016.

76. Sister Mary Clarence is believed to be loosely based on the life of Sister Thea Bowman, Franciscan Sister of Perpetual Adoration, whom Goldberg visited shortly before her death in 1990. See Smith and Feister, *Thea's Song*, 207–9, 269.

77. Sister Rose Martin (Kathryn) Glenn, Missionary Sister Servant of the Holy Spirit (SSpS), interview by author, Memphis, TN, November 20, 2009; and Glenn, public statement after a talk the author delivered on March 21, 2012, National Civil Rights Museum, Memphis, TN.

78. At the height of the US sister population in 1966, African American sisters barely numbered one thousand, or roughly 0.55 percent, of the approximately 181,451 Catholic nuns ministering in the country. See Berrelleza, Gautier, and Gray, *Population Trends*, 2; and "983 Negro Nuns in U.S., Catholic Magazine Reveals after Survey," *Chicago Daily Defender*, August 8, 1962, 10.

1. "Our Sole Wish Is to Do the Will of God"

1. On this apologist literature, see, for example, Miller, "Church in Cultural Captivity"; McGreevy, *Catholicism and American Freedom*, 49–56; Dolan, *American Catholic Experience*, 85–125; Ochs, *Desegregating the Altar*, 9; and Zanca, *American Catholics*, 111.

2. Misner, *"Highly Respectable,"* 75. On the slaveholding practices of the Ursulines, see Clark, *Masterless Mistresses*, 161–94.

3. See Farrelly, *Anti-Catholicism in America*. On the role of the Catholic Church in Latin American and Caribbean slavery, see Schwaller, *History*; Landers and Robinson, *Slaves*; and Klein and Vison, *African Slavery*. On Catholic slavery in Canada, see A. Cooper, *Hanging of Angélique*.

4. On the development of Spanish Catholic Florida, see Landers, *Black Society*.

5. On the development of Catholic Maryland, see J. Woods, *History*, 106–35, 141–74; and R. Hoffman, *Princes of Ireland*. On the role of the Catholic Calvert family in codifying race and legalizing slavery in Maryland, see Yentsch, *Chesapeake Family*; and Rodriguez, *Slavery*, 5. On the Calvert family's opposition to interracial marriage between free white women and enslaved Black men, but eventual role in overturning the 1664 anti-miscegenation statute, see Thomas, *Question of Freedom*, 24–25.

6. See, for example, C. Davis, *History of Black Catholics*, 35–37; J. Woods, *History*, 72–105, 175–214, 334–75; Ochs, *Black Patriot*, 22; Pasquier, *Fathers on the Frontier*; Janet, *In Missouri's Wilds*; Poole and Slawson, *Church and Slave*; Gollar, "Catholic Slaves and Slaveholders," 42; Agee, *Cry for Justice*, 7–9; and Curran, *Shaping American Catholicism*, 95–97. Catholic religious orders were often the largest and most influential slavers in Latin America as well. See Schwartz, *Sugar Plantations*, 96, 149; Burns, *Colonial Habits*, 1–4, 114–15; and R. O'Toole, "(Un)Making Christianity."

7. In his opinion in *Dred Scott v. Sandford* (1857), Roger B. Taney, the nation's first Catholic Supreme Court justice and a member of one of Maryland's most prominent slaveholding

families, infamously declared that Black people "had no rights which the white man was bound to respect." Quoted in Finkelman, *Supreme Injustice*, 8. On the Taney family's slave-holding and the *Dred Scott* decision, see again Finkelman, *Supreme Injustice*, 172–218.

8. The RSCJ was the sixth order of Catholic sisters to minister in the United States. See F. Woods, "Congregations of Religious Women," 100; and Curtis, *Civilizing Habits*, 58, 70. This offer is included in a letter from Rose Philippine Duchesne to Sophie Barat dated November 15, 1819, which is reproduced in Carreel and Osiek, *Philippine Duchesne*, 443. This letter also notes that the priest "offered several persons of color . . . to the Lazarist Fathers to be a kind of third order attached to them."

9. Curtis, *Civilizing Habits*, 58.

10. Quoted in Curtis, *Civilizing Habits*, 58–59. In multiple letters, Duchesne expresses her anti-Black animus and belief in the superiority of Native Americans over African Americans. In 1819, she wrote, "Indians are on a par with whites when they are not of mixed blood, but everyone agrees that the little girls must be taken in at four or five years of age before they have become incapable of learning." See Philippine to Mother Barat, February 15, 1819, in Carreel and Osiek, *Philippine Duchesne*, 402. See also Philippine to Mother de Charbonnel, 1818, Carreel and Osiek, *Philippine Duchesne*, 355. On Dubourg's slaveholding and leading efforts in expanding Catholic slavery in Missouri, see Curtis, *Civilizing Habits*, 56–57.

11. Quoted in Curtis, *Civilizing Habits*, 58.

12. For more on the desegregation of the RSCJ in 1948, see chapter 3. On the RSCJ's slaveholding past and the denied vocation of the order's former slave Eliza Nesbit, see Society of the Sacred Heart, "Enslavement," accessed August 10, 2020, https://rscj.org/history-enslavement.

13. Quoted in Curtis, *Civilizing Habits*, 59.

14. Clark and Gould, "Feminine Face"; and Clark, *Masterless Mistresses*, 134–35.

15. Clark, *Masterless Mistresses*, 161. The abbreviation SSF reflects the order's French name, Soeurs de Sainte Famille.

16. "To Thomas Jefferson from the Ursuline Nuns of New Orleans, 23 April 1804," *Founders Online*, National Archives, https://founders.archives.gov/documents/Jefferson/01-43-02-0250. See also Clark, *Masterless Mistresses*, 168. Notably, the Ursu-lines sent this letter seven years after they voted to exclude girls of color as day students at their academy and to separate the few girls of color who remained as boarders from white students. See chap. 1, note 76; and Clark, *Masterless Mistresses*, 168.

17. Saint Iphigenia (or Ephigenia), a Nubian virgin, reportedly established the world's first monastery for women in the first century. Despite questions about the veracity of this story, Saint Iphigenia became widely venerated among Black Catholic populations in the modern Iberian world. See Rowe, *Black Saints*, 30–31. On the female ascetics of fourth-century Egypt, see McNamara, *Sisters in Arms*, 61–88.

18. On the African noblewomen and nuns who drove the Portuguese Jesuits from Ethiopia in the seventeenth century, see Belcher, "Sisters Debating the Jesuits."

19. Pfann, *Short History*, 8.

20. For the only accessible English translation of "Dum Diversas," see "Dum Diver-sas," *Unam Sanctam Catholicam*, February 5, 2011, http://unamsanctamcatholicam

.blogspot.com/2011/02/dum-diversas-english-translation.html. For English translations of the other bulls that make up the Doctrine of Discovery, including *Inter caetera*, see "Document Directory," *Papal Encyclicals Online*, accessed July 13, 2021, https://www .papalencyclicals.net/document-directory. For a comprehensive examination of these bulls from an African perspective, see Adiele, *Popes*. On the impact of the Doctrine of Discovery in the Americas, see Newcomb, *Pagans*.

21. See Heng, *Invention of Race*; Ramey, *Black Legacies*; and Kaplan, *Figuring Racism*.

22. See Sweet, "Iberian Roots"; and Sweet, "Spanish and Portuguese Influences." On Black sisters in colonial Latin America and the exclusionary admissions policies of European and white orders there, see Lavrin, *Brides of Christ*; Van Deusen, *Souls of Purgatory*; and Burns, *Colonial Habits*. On the "blood purity" laws barring women of color in religious life, see, for example, Poole, "Politics of *Limpieza de Sangre*"; Lavrin, "Indian Brides of Christ"; Rowe, *Black Saints*, 206–10; and M. Martínez, *Genealogical Fictions*, 221.

23. For the first examination of the experiences of Black and Indigenous sisters in the Missioners of Jesus Christ in Brazil, see Beozzo, *Tecendo Memorias*.

24. See Iliffe, *African Poor*, 111; Foster, *Faith in Empire*, 27; and chapter 7.

25. For a recent examination of the Haitian Revolution and its Catholic dimensions, see Dubois, *Avengers*.

26. For one recent examination on this topic, see A. White, *Encountering Revolution*.

27. For two examples, see Zanca, *American Catholics*, 111; and McGreevy, *Catholicism and American Freedom*, 50.

28. A. White, *Encountering Revolution*, 124–202. For an English translation of this bull, see "In supremo apostolatus," *Papal Encyclicals Online*, accessed July 13, 2021, https:// www.papalencyclicals.net/greg16/g16sup.htm.

29. In the late eighteenth century, free white and enslaved Black Catholics from Maryland began settling in Kentucky's present-day Washington, Nelson, and Marion Counties. On the Church's development in Kentucky, see Crews, *American Holy Land*. See also Howlett, *Rev. Charles Nerinckx*, 259.

30. F. Woods, "Congregations of Religious Women," 100–101. Elizabeth Seton's Sisters of Charity is generally recognized as the first sisterhood with a US foundation, though Seton adapted the rule of the French Daughters of Charity, established in 1633, for her order.

31. The SL formally apologized for their slaveholding past in 2000. See Peter Smith, "Nuns Apologize for Slave Legacy," *Courier-Journal* (Louisville, KY), December 4, 2000.

32. Minogue, *Loretto Annals*, 96.

33. The author has a copy of the original rule provided by the Archives of the Sisters of Loretto (SL Archives).

34. Nerinckx quoted in Minogue, *Loretto Annals*, 96.

35. L. W. Reilly, "Negro Sisters of Loretto," *Colored Harvest*, October 1898, 54.

36. Gillard, *Colored Catholics*, 197.

37. Minogue, *Loretto Annals*, 78.

38. On the speculated African American origins of the early Loretto community, see J. Campbell, *Loretto*, 83–100, 212–15, 244–57. For most of the twentieth century, the SL

leaders adopted a strict code of silence about their order's slaveholding past—failing to teach their members about it and, according to Joan Campbell, censoring typed references to this history from 1929 to the early 1970s. Campbell credits the National Black Sisters' Conference and an unnamed Oblate Sister of Providence, who met Campbell at Jackson State University in 1970, with introducing her to the history of the SL's slaveholding and the congregation's early Black members. Campbell dedicated the rest of her life to researching this history. Her papers at the SL archive include a box of her correspondence with various archivists, scholars, librarians, and her editors documenting her attempts to reconstruct the SL's African American roots. This box also includes several "lost document" reports, in which she describes the disappearing of historical materials that she had previously used in the SL archives documenting proof of the SL's slaveholding and early black members in the 1990s. See Sister Joan Campbell, "Loretto Motherhouse Archives, Lost Document No. 3," August 8, 1997, and "Loretto Motherhouse Archives Lost Document No. 6," August 8, 1997, SL Archives, Nerinx, KY.

39. MacGregor, *Emergence*, 27.

40. Goodwin, "Schools and Education," 204.

41. G. Williams, *History*, 194–96. George Washington Williams cites the first national report on education. See Goodwin, "Schools and Education," 217–19.

42. Goodwin, "Schools and Education," 217–19. On the Visitation Sisters' slaveholding history, see Nalezyty, "History of Enslaved People." On the history of slavery at Georgetown, see Rothman and Mendoza, *Facing Georgetown's History*.

43. This is documented in D. Payne, *History*, 460–61. Early African Methodist Episcopal bishop Daniel Payne married Anne Becraft's sister Julia in 1847. See D. Payne, *Recollection of Seventy Years*, 92; "Married," *Baltimore Sun*, January 7, 1847; "Mrs. William Becraft, Bishop Payne's Mother-in-Law . . . at Georgetown, D.C.," *Christian Recorder*, June 16, 1866; and G. Williams, *History*, 196.

44. On Carroll's life, see Birzer, *American Cicero*.

45. Goodwin, "Schools and Education," 203–4. See also Wieneck, *Imperfect God*, 84–86, 284–85, 289.

46. Goodwin, "Schools and Education," 204–5. According to this record, the OSP order was "contemplating . . . [Becraft] . . . as its future Mother Superior" before her untimely death in 1833.

47. Morrow, *Persons of Color*, 4, 13–37, 39–44. The inaugural Oblates began their novitiate in 1828 and professed their first vows in 1829.

48. Morrow, *Persons of Color*, 39–40. On the role of the slaveholding Sulpicians, especially DuBourg, in the formation of the Sisters of Charity, see O'Donnell, *Elizabeth Seton*, 202–5, 220–21.

49. Morrow, *Persons of Color*, 19–20. For more on the Sulpicians history in the early US, see Kauffman, *Tradition*.

50. Although records indicate that Seton was asked to provide religious instruction to the Black people in Emmitsburg in 1809 and that her order may have briefly taught free Black girls in their school in Emmitsburg in the 1810s, their commitment to the formal education of Black children before the abolition of slavery was minimal. While the order administered a school for free girls of color in Mobile, Alabama, in the 1840s,

many of their other institutions explicitly excluded Black children. In Wilmington, Delaware, where the Sisters of Charity began ministering in 1830, for example, the order barred Black children from their school. As a result, the parents of early OSP members Marie Louise and Mary James Noel were forced to send their daughters to a Quaker school. See Morrow, *Persons of Color*, 63–64, 135–36; and chap. 1, note 79. Also, in 1853, a Black laywoman living New York City named Harriet Thompson sent a letter to Pope Pius IX documenting that the Sisters of Charity stationed there barred Black children from their schools. For a full transcript of Thompson's letter to Pope Pius IX, see Slattery, "Untold Story."

51. Quoted in Morrow, *Persons of Color*, 15.

52. Morrow, *Persons of Color*, 15–17.

53. Morrow, *Persons of Color*, 15.

54. Misner, "*Highly Respectable*," 12–41.

55. Herbermann, *Sulpicians*, 234.

56. Morrow, *Persons of Color*, 16–17.

57. Morrow, *Persons of Color*, 119.

58. Quoted in Morrow, *Persons of Color*, 139–40.

59. Morrow, *Persons of Color*, 53, 131.

60. Morrow, *Persons of Color*, 115–61, 265. See also Ochs, *Desegregating the Altar*, 25–26.

61. Morrow, *Persons of Color*, 125–27, 147–49.

62. See Goodwin, "Schools and Education," 211; Gerdes, "To Educate and Evangelize," 193–97; and Morrow, *Persons of Color*, 242–45.

63. Quoted in Morrow, *Persons of Color*, 27.

64. The names of the inaugural four SSF members in New Orleans first appear on sacramental records as godmothers to free and enslaved African-descended children baptized at St. Louis Cathedral—the nation's oldest Catholic Church—in 1829. See Deggs, *No Cross, No Crown*, xxxii.

65. For an overview of plaçage, see J. Martin, "*Plaçage*," 57–70.

66. Deggs, *No Cross, No Crown*, 40–41. According to Deggs, the sixth member of the order, Sister Anne Marie Fazende, was the daughter of "Miss A. L'Ange . . . of Baton Rouge and a granddaughter of the Pintados, one of the first Spanish families of that city" (40). Vicente Sebastian Pintado, originally from Spain, surveyed Spanish Louisiana and Spanish Florida for settlement in the late eighteenth and early nineteenth centuries.

67. Gaudin's unwed parents first fled to Cuba and settled in New Orleans by 1810. See C. Davis, *Henriette Delille*, 46. Deggs later clarifies that Gaudin was "of Cuba." See *No Cross, No Crown*, 13.

68. Gould, "Henriette Delille," 274; and Swanson, *Historic Jefferson Parish*, 88.

69. See Carol Glatz, "Mother Henriette Delille Declared Venerable," *Clarion Herald*, April 3, 2010.

70. Deggs, *No Cross, No Crown*, 42. See also Mother Mary Josephine Charles Haus Congregational file, Archives of the Sisters of the Holy Family (SSF Archives), New Orleans.

71. Fessenden, "Sisters," 204–5. See also Deggs, *No Cross, No Crown*, 46.

72. Deggs, *No Cross, No Crown*, 46.

73. Deggs, *No Cross, No Crown*, 73.

74. NOAAMACH, *Celebration of Faith*, 32–33.

75. Deggs, *No Cross, No Crown*, 23–24. See also "Mother Josephine: Death of the Founder of the Order of Sisters of the Holy Family," *Daily Picayune*, May 21, 1885. This obituary for Charles notes that she also received private instruction from a local woman. It also documents that she frequently attended "the religious ceremonies at the Carmelite convent" and as a young woman felt called to feeding the poor and catechizing the city's "neglected colored children."

76. Deggs, *No Cross, No Crown*, xxx, 10. In 1797, the Ursulines voted against admitting "mulatto" students into their academy as day students. While the order voted to retain their policy of admitting a few legitimate daughters of quadroon mothers and white fathers into their boarding academy, they agreed to do so "only if they [the girls of color] were kept separate." Clark, *Masterless Mistresses*, 134–35. Notably, also, Fontière's school began "with six small coins given by a black woman who was rather poor." Quote in C. Davis, *Henriette Delille*, 23.

77. Deggs, *No Cross, No Crown*, 10, 205n23. See also Curtis, *Civilizing Habits*, 70–71; and Foley, *God's Men of Color*, 150.

78. Deggs, *No Cross, No Crown*, xxx–xxxi, 22; C. Davis, *Henriette Delille*, 25; and Detiege, *Henriette Delille*, 14–25. It should be noted that Fontière's record of service to New Orleans's Black community is also marred by slaveholding. In 1829, the French nun purchased three enslaved persons, a mother and her daughters, to support the St. Claude School when it began to suffer financially. In 1831, Fontière's sold one of the daughters, aged thirteen, away from her family. See C. Davis, *Henriette Delille*, 23–26.

79. In 1830, two Sisters of Charity from Emmitsburg arrived in New Orleans to assist Fontière at her St. Claude School but according to one historian left upon learning she planned to establish a congregation dedicated to the education of African American girls and expected them to join her. See Hannefin, *Daughters of the Church*, 47. Hannefin misidentifies Fontière as Jeanne Marie Aliquot. Two other sources state that the Sisters of Charity departed the St. Claude School because its teachers, at least one of whom was African-descended, desired to join their order. See Deggs, *No Cross, No Crown*, 22; and C. Davis, *Henriette Delille*, 23.

80. Deggs, *No Cross, No Crown*, xxx–xxxii. See also Hart, "Violets," 7.

81. Deggs, *No Cross, No Crown*, xxxiii–xxxv.

82. Clark and Gould, "Feminine Face," 442. See also C. Davis, *Henriette Delille*, 36–40. The Ursulines in New Orleans adhered to Aliquot's stipulation until 1838 when they turned the St. Claude School over to the Sisters of Mt. Carmel and abandoned their formal educational ministries to African American youth in the city until the 1960s. The Ursulines seemingly continued to provide rudimentary religious instruction to their enslaved persons until 1865. See Baudier, *Catholic Church*, 364–65; Clark, *Masterless Mistresses*, 256; and chapter 2.

83. Deggs, *No Cross, No Crown*, xxxiii–xxxv.

84. Deggs, *No Cross, No Crown*, 10, 205n23. According to the second SSF historian, Sister Mary Borgia Hart, only Delille underwent formation training with the RSCJ in

St. James Parish in 1850. Delille reportedly returned to the SSF sometime in 1851 to provide formation for the other members.

85. Deggs, *No Cross, No Crown*, xxxiv.

86. Deggs, *No Cross, No Crown*, 46.

87. Fessenden, "Sisters," 188. See also Fichter, "White Church," 41.

88. Deggs, *No Cross, No Crown*, 206–7n37.

89. Gould, "'Chaos of Iniquity,'" 237. See also J. Martin, "*Plaçage*," 62.

90. Sister M. Borgia Hart states that the SSF received permission to wear habits in 1869, Virginia Meacham Gould and Charles E. Nolan have the date as 1872, and Deggs claims 1881. Hart, "Violets," 21; Gould and Nolan, *Henriette Delille*, 17; and Deggs, *No Cross, No Crown*, 14.

91. The SSF cared for the free and enslaved elderly from the start of their ministry. The local Church formally recognized the SSF's Old Folks Home in 1847, and a lay association supporting the order helped the sisters build the Hospice of the Holy Family in 1849. See NOAAMACH, *Celebration of Faith*, 30. See also Deggs, *No Cross, No Crown*, 36–38.

92. Deggs, *No Cross, No Crown*, xxxv.

93. On the OSP and SSF teaching white children during slavery, see Morrow, *Persons of Color*, 181; and Bennett, *Religion*, 144. On a few US white sisterhoods that provided religious instruction and some formal education to African-descended people but on a segregated basis during slavery, see Baudier, *Catholic Church*, 365; S. Curtis, *Civilizing Habits*, 70–71; Hannefin, *Daughters*, 36, 47, 82; and Clark, *Masterless Mistresses*, 134–36. On class-based segregation in white-led Catholic schools, see O'Donnell, *Elizabeth Seton*, 281–82.

94. Deggs, *No Cross, No Crown*, 12.

95. C. Davis, *Henriette Delille*, 55, 64–68. Gaudin's file in the SSF Archives contains a handwritten copy of entry #464 from volume 23 of the New Orleans archdiocese's *Baptismal Register of Negroes and Mulattoes*, denoting the November 23, 1830, baptism of Sean Baptiste Clement, "the son of Melania, Negro slave belonging to Mlle Juliette Gaudin of this parish." See also Deggs, *No Cross, No Crown*, 8, 10, 36.

96. Deggs, *No Cross, No Crown*, 8. Unlike Delille and Gaudin, there is no evidence that Charles ever owned enslaved people. In *Henriette Delille*, Cyprian Davis includes tables denoting the baptisms of free and enslaved people sponsored (and likely sponsored) by the three SSF cofoundresses at St. Augustine Church from 1845 to 1860 and at St. Mary's Church from 1834 to 1860. Notably, Josephine Charles sponsored the majority (44), not Delille (28). Gaudin sponsored only five. C. Davis, *Henriette Delille*, 132–36.

97. Deggs, *No Cross, No Crown*, 10, 36. There is one piece of evidence that suggests Delille and Gaudin may have been indirectly involved in the 1851 sale of an enslaved "mulatto boy" who was willed to an asylum funded by an association that supported the SSF. Although Delille and Gaudin were founding board members of the association in 1847, Father Cyprian Davis considers their involvement in the association by 1851 unlikely. See C. Davis, *No Cross, No Crown*, 50–52, 57n30.

98. On white Catholic support of the Confederacy, see Ochs, *Black Patriot*, 107.

99. C. Davis, *Henriette Delille*, 55, 64–68; see also 60n97.

100. Deggs, *No Cross, No Crown*, 10, 11, 13. Like Delille, Aliquot—who championed of the education and protection of girls of color until her death—also made plans to

emancipate her enslaved human property by 1850. See folder titled "Freedom to Her Slaves" in Aliquot's file in the SSF Archives.

101. Deggs, *No Cross, No Crown*, 29.

102. Deggs, *No Cross, No Crown*, 29, 43. See also Hart, "Violets," 49–53. The oral history of the SSF attributed the fight over Preval to anti-Black prejudice among the sisters, who, led by the Cuban-born Gaudin, objected to Preval's color, former slave status, and position as the archbishop's cook. The only three to vote for accepting her were Charles, "Wales," and Sister Marie Magdalene Alpaugh. While some have attempted to minimize the colorism and elitism behind the 1869 split, "Wales" (actually Wallace but also misidentified in SSF records as Elizabeth Brady and Elizabeth Bradley) wrote an account of the episode in her 1891 application to the OSP that confirms many important details of Hart's account, especially Gaudin's anti-Black animus and rancor. As an OSP member, Wallace was known as Sister Mary Ursula. See also Hart, "Violets," 49; Deggs, *No Cross, No Crown*, 5–7, 14, 25–28, 32–34, 144–46, 197; Sister Mary Alice Chineworth, OSP, to Sister Audrie Marie, SSF, July 26, 1972, Sister Mary Audrey Detiege file, SSF Archives; and copy of Wallace's handwritten account contained in Detiege's files in SSF Archives.

103. Morrow, *Persons of Color*, 18.

104. Morrow, *Persons of Color*, 69, 211. This enslaved woman, Harriet Reynolds, had been educated by the OSP as a youth and professed her vows as Sister Celestine in 1855.

105. In 1678, the Carmelites in Puebla, New Spain (now Mexico), permitted Juana Esperanza de San Alberto, a former slave of the order, to profess vows on her deathbed. See Lavrin, *Brides of Christ*, 169–70. For another early example of an ex-slave nun in the modern Roman Church, see Houchins and Fra-Molinero, *Black Bride of Christ*.

106. On the sexual vulnerability of Black women in the domestic slave trade, see W. Johnson, *Soul by Soul*; and E. Baptiste, "'Cuffy.'"

107. For these examples, see Clark, *Masterless Mistresses*, 137, 270–73; Morrow, *Persons of Color*, 261; and Ann Patrick Ware, "Loretto's Hispanic Tradition: Lights and Shadows," in Ware, *Naming Our Truth*, 53–89.

108. See Grimes, *Christ Divided*.

109. Bishop England to Dr. Cullen of the Irish College of Rome, February 23, 1836, in *Records of the American Catholic Historical Society* 8 (1897): 230–35.

110. Morrow, *Persons of Color*, 186–92.

111. Morrow, *Persons of Color*, 190.

112. M. Theresa Catherine (Sarah) Willigmann, OSP, "Memories of Sister Theresa Duchemin," typescript copy, n.d., 3–4, OSP Archives.

113. Morrow, *Persons of Color*, 187.

114. Supan, "Dangerous Memory," 41–60. For examples of the bishops' racist commentary about Maxis, see also Gannon, *Paths of Daring*.

115. "Memories," 4. See also Supan, "Dangerous Memory," 60–67.

116. Supan, "Dangerous Memory," 65.

117. Walsh, *Sisters of Charity*, 1:225–27.

118. Walsh, *Sisters of Charity*, 1:226.

119. Walsh, *Sisters of Charity*, 1:227–28.

120. M. Thompson, "Philemon's Dilemma," 6. See also Walsh, *Sisters of Charity*, 1:225–28.

121. The Healy siblings' mother, Eliza, was sixteen years old and enslaved by their father, Michael, then thirty-three years old, when he selected her to begin his family. This relationship reflects the variant forms of sexual abuse enslaved women and girls endured. See J. O'Toole, *Passing for White*, 5–22, 44.

122. J. O'Toole, *Passing for White*, 62–82, 105–71.

123. J. O'Toole, *Passing for White*, 172–76.

124. Sister Betty Ann McNeil, email correspondence with author, July 15, 2013; and Holloran, *Boston's Wayward Children*, 281n38. The story of two African American nuns at the deathbed of abolitionist Thaddeus Stevens also requires more scholarly attention beyond Scally's "Two Nuns and Old Thad Stevens."

125. Deggs, *No Cross, No Crown*, 8, 13. On pp. 60–61, Deggs also notes that early member Sister Marie Magdalene Alpaugh of Pointe Coupee, Louisiana, had a white half-sister who was a Mercy nun in New Orleans and who had nurtured her religious vocation. Deggs wrote on p. 60 that if the sisters' father had not died during the Civil War, "he might have taken [Alpaugh] to . . . New York and passed her for a German girl" as "there was no place in Pointe Coupee nor any other place where they believed she could enter."

126. Deggs, *No Cross, No Crown*, 13. As early as the 1600s, a few French sisterhoods opened their doors to African-descended candidates with elite connections established through blood or slavery. By the mid-nineteenth century, free French-speaking African-descended women and girls living in the United States, as well as those rescued as children from slavery in the French empire, could enter the Sisters of St. Joseph of Cluny on a segregated basis. See Sharpley-Whiting, *Bricktop's Paris*, 110–13; Harms, *Diligent*, 6–11; Curtis, *Civilizing Habits*, 203–8, 253; and Sisters of Saint Joseph of Cluny, *150 Years of Witness*.

127. For two sources on white Catholic support of the Confederacy and the rise of Jim Crow segregation in the New Orleans archdiocese, see Bennett, *Religion*, 136–228; and Collins, *Death and Resurrection*, 44, 51, 54, 69, 74.

128. Bennett, *Religion*, 136–228.

129. Deggs, *No Cross, No Crown*, 91.

130. Deggs, *No Cross, No Crown*, 91.

131. Deggs, *No Cross, No Crown*, 91. See also Nolan, *"Bayou Carmel,"* 14–24.

132. Deggs, *No Cross, No Crown*, 37, 210n34.

133. Deggs, *No Cross, No Crown*, 25, 41, 208n8. See also Hart, "Violets," 53.

134. Hart, "Violets," 54. See also Bennett, *Religion*, 152.

135. Hart, "Violets," 53.

136. Knecht, *Oblate Sisters of Providence*, 37. See also W. Campbell, *How Unsearchable His Ways*, 15–16, 172.

137. W. Campbell, *How Unsearchable His Ways*, 15–16, 172.

138. Gerdes, "To Educate and Evangelize," 190–93. See also Fialka, *Sisters*, 112; and W. Campbell, *How Unsearchable His Ways*, 172.

139. Gerdes, "To Educate and Evangelize," 190, 193.

140. Gerdes, "To Educate and Evangelize," 193.

141. Bennett, *Religion*, 167–70.

142. Miller, "Failed Mission," 168; and C. Davis, "Holy See," 175.

143. Southern, *John LaFarge*, 68.

144. Southern, *John LaFarge*, 68. See also Ochs, *Desegregating the Altar*, 39–42.

145. Southern, *John LaFarge*, 50.

146. Ochs, *Desegregating the Altar*, 38–45. See also J. Woods, *History*, 359.

147. Rosenkrans, "'Good Work,'" 141–49. See also Ochs, *Desegregating the Altar*.

148. Morrow, "'Undoubtedly a Bad State,'" 267–68.

149. Morrow, "'Undoubtedly a Bad State,'" 267–69. See also Rosenkrans, "'Good Work,'" 148–49; and Ochs, *Desegregating the Altar*, 45–85.

150. Morrow, "'Undoubtedly a Bad State,'" 267–69; and Rosenkrans, "'Good Work,'" 148–49.

151. Rosenkrans, "'Good Work,'" 141–49. The St. Frances Orphan Asylum, established by the OSP in 1866, was the only other Catholic orphanage for Black children in Baltimore at the time. See Knecht, *Oblate Sisters of Providence*, 99.

152. Morrow, "'Undoubtedly a Bad State,'" 269.

153. Rosenkrans, "'Good Work,'" 149–53. See also Gray and Barry, "Our Story," 47.

154. Rosenkrans, "Good Work," 151–53.

155. Rosenkrans, "'Good Work,'" 153.

156. Gray and Barry, "Our Story," 51–52, 72. See also "A Colored Nun: Sister Xavier, a Pioneer of Her Race in the Order of St. Francis," *Irish World and American Industrial Liberator*, October 7, 1894, 6.

157. Gray and Barry, "Our Story," 52. Mother Mary Paul, leader of the Franciscan Sisters of Mill Hill, frequently used racial derogatory language to describe the Black youth under the order's care in Baltimore. See Rosenkrans, "Good Work," 157–58, 216, 224.

158. "Colored Nun," 6. According to the Sister Celia Struck, the archivist of the Sisters of St. Francis of Assisi in St. Francis, Wisconsin, who currently maintain the archives of the Franciscan Sisters of Baltimore (formerly the Franciscan Sisters of Mill Hill), the Mill Hill Sisters admitted at least four Black women in the twentieth century, of whom the final three remained. However, Struck noted that the order directed most of their pupils and interested candidates to the OSP. Sister Celia Struck to author, email message, September 13, 2016; and image of Norma Lambert (Sister Mary Edward) as a child and an adult in *Josephite Harvest*, January–February 1964, 15.

159. SBS Annals, vol. 3, 1890, 20–21, Archives of the Sisters of the Blessed Sacrament (SBS Archives), Cornwells Heights, PA.

160. Hughes, *Katharine Drexel*, 195.

161. SBS Annals from 1896, 99–100.

162. *Official Catholic Directory* (1906), 734. The 1906 edition contains the statistics for the Church in 1905. "OSP Roster," provided to the author by OSP archivist Sharon Knecht, lists a sister's hometown when available. The OSP, which expanded its ministries to Cuba in response to an Afro-Cuban laywoman's pleas in 1900, also drew scores of Afro-Cuban women as the twentieth century progressed. See Sherwood, *Oblates'*, 245.

163. *Official Catholic Directory* (1906), 712. See also the SSF's "Matricula," n.d., which provides the names, hometowns, and dates of admission of most of the women who entered the order, SSF Archives.

164. See Hart, "Violets," 49–52; and Deggs, *No Cross, No Crown*, 5–7.

165. L. Brown, *Posing as Nuns*, 19.

166. L. Brown, *Posing as Nuns*, 19–24.

167. See Roger Baudier to Monsignor Plauche, July 28, 1950, SSF Archives. In this letter, Baudier confirms that the members of the Sisters of Our Lady of Lourdes "were Colored," noting that "Rt. Rev. Mgsr. F. M. Racine, the former Vicar-General" knew their story quite well. He also noted that "white congregations would not receive them, and they positively refused to join the ranks of the Sisters of the Holy Family. These young women were very fair, but mulatresses." Monsignor Francis M. Racine was the vicar general for the archdiocese of New Orleans under Archbishop Joseph Rummel.

168. L. Brown, *Posing as Nuns*, 39–49. See also C. Davis, *History of Black Catholics*, 109–10, 288n54.

169. The SSF perspective appears in "An Incident in Mother Magdalene's Administration" in Alpaugh Administration File, SSF Archives.

170. "Incident in Mother Magdalene's Administration," 1. See also Sister Teresa (Laurencia) Jacques Congregation Folder, SSF Archives.

171. "Incident in Mother Magdalene's Administration," 1–2.

172. "Incident in Mother Magdalene's Administration," 2–3.

173. Beyond scant records in the SSF, OSP, and Archdiocese of New Orleans archives, a lone letter from Fr. F. Coppin, Society of Mary (SM), to Mon. Rev. Pere, July 30, 1890, "regarding the sisters of color . . . received at the parish of St. Michael," exists in the Archives of the Society of Mary, Rome, Italy. Many thanks to Carlo Maria Schianchi, SM, the Marist Fathers' general archivist, for sending me this document.

174. Coppin to Pere, July 30, 1890.

175. Sister M. Teresa to Rev. Mother Superior, April 23, 1901, in Congregation RG: box 103, folder 6, OSP Archives. Jacques went by both M. Theresa (SSF) and M. Teresa (OSF) in religion.

176. "Incident in Mother Magdalene's Administration," 1–2.

177. See typed biographies in Mother Mathilda Beasley file, n.d., Archives of the Diocese of Savannah (DS Archives), Georgia. See also C. Davis, *History of Black Catholics*, 110–11; S. Taylor, *Reminiscences*, 6; Dannett, "Mother Mathilda Beasley," 144; and "Mathilda Beasley" Timeline, n.d., DS Archives.

178. McDonogh, *Black and Catholic*, 214.

179. For an account of Beasley's visit and the 1893 decision to bar African Americans and Native Americans, see a photocopy of the SBS Annals from 1896, 99–100, SBS Archives.

180. Baldwin, *Call to Sanctity*, 31–42; and Hughes, *Katharine Drexel*, 51–101.

181. McDonogh, *Black and Catholic*, 214.

182. SBS Annals from 1896, 99–100.

183. SBS Annals from 1896, 99–100.

184. SBS Annals from 1896, 99. See also McDonogh, *Black and Catholic*, 214.

185. See Lynch, *Sharing the Bread*, 407; Baldwin, *Call to Sanctity*, 94; and Herbes, *Histories*, 39–40.

186. Mother Mathilda Beasley, OSF, to Mother Kath[a]rine Drexel, July 3, 1893, SBS Archives.

187. McDonogh, *Black and Catholic*, 214. See also Ahles, *In the Shadow*, 138–53; and Rita H. DeLorme, "Frederica Law," *Southern Cross*, February 5, 2004, 3. Law, who took the name Sister Benedict of the Angels, was born into slavery, but secured her freedom before federal abolition, according to surviving relatives.

188. Mother Mathilda [Beasley] to V. Rev. J. R. Slattery, May 24, 1898, SBS Archives.

189. Mother Mathilda [Beasley] to V. Rev. J. R. Slattery, May 24, 1898.

190. According to *Mission Work among the Negroes and the Indians*, January 1905, 16–29, the Black and white Franciscan sisters still "live[d] together under the same roof, devoting themselves to the care of colored children." A typed copy of this report is in the Josephite Archives. According to "A Brief History of St. Benedict's Parish, 1874–1974," n.d., in the Mother Beasley file, DS Archives, one member of Beasley's community died soon after the white sisters took over St. Francis Home in 1899, while the youngest sister soon left Savannah to join the OSP.

191. "Colored," *Savannah Morning News*, December 8, 1901.

192. "St. Benedict's Church," *Savannah Tribune*, April 9, 1910.

193. "St. Benedict's Church," *Savannah Tribune*, April 9, 1910.

194. Lewis and Willis, *Small Nation of People*, 11–20, 203. See also Lewis, *W. E. B. Du Bois*, 248–51.

195. Deggs, *No Cross, No Crown*, 187–89.

196. Deggs, *No Cross, No Crown*, 180.

197. "Mother Mary Austin, Superioress of the Holy Family Convent: Dies at the Convent in Orleans Street," *Colored Harvest*, June 1909, 198.

198. "An Order of Negro Nuns," *Washington Post*, February 27, 1898; and Susan B. Anthony to the Superior of the Holy Family Convent, December 29, 1897, in Mother Austin Jones Administration File, SSF Archives.

199. "Mother Mary Austin."

200. "Mother Mary Austin." On Lafon's life, see Desdunes, *Our People*, 90–96.

201. For an examination of the SSF's missionary efforts in Belize and the discriminatory policies of the Jesuits and Religious Sisters of Mercy there, see Brett, *New Orleans Sisters*, 28–29.

202. "Mother Mary Austin," 198–99.

203. Lewis, *W. E. B. Du Bois*, 248–51.

204. Joseph Anciaux, "A Report to the Holy See on the Situation of African Americans in the United States, 1903," partially reproduced in C. Davis and Phelps, "Stamped," 88–89.

205. O'Toole, *Faithful*, 104–5. O'Toole notes that sisters outnumbered priests as early as 1820.

206. On the insults and opposition directed at white priests and sisters in the Black apostolate, see chapter 2.

207. Butler, *Across God's Frontiers*, 253–55. See also Hughes, *Katharine Drexel*, 126. Only one of several African American women to enter the Holy Ghost Sisters after World War II remained. She is Sister Martha Readore of Labeau, Louisiana.

208. Butler, *Across God's Frontiers*, 254.

209. Venable and Sisters of the Holy Spirit and Mary Immaculate, *Sisters of the Holy Spirit*, 18. Glenn professed her vows as Sister Mary Ludwina and remained in the order

until her death. Glenn's name in religion was gathered from the "OSP Roster," provided to the author by the OSP archivist on February 1, 2010. See also Butler, *Across God's Frontiers*, 253–55.

210. Sister Patricia Rogers, a Sinsinawa Dominican (OP), provided the author with biographical details about Sister Reynold Thompson and described the OP's discovery of Thompson's racial heritage at the National Black Sisters' Conference meeting in San Diego, California, on July 25, 2016. Lois Hoh, an OP archivist, confirmed Thompson's religious name and African heritage in email correspondence with the author, August 4, 2016. Hoh also provided a list of the African-descended women who entered the order.

211. In 1913, the Maryknoll Sisters, then known as the Teresians, admitted an African American woman who could pass for white as their fourteenth member. Elsie St. Clair Davis, who eventually took the name Sister M. Francis, opted not to hide her Black heritage. The congregation's early records document the "negro blood in her" and the leadership's admiration of Davis's refusal to be separated from her stepfather, famed orchestra director Walter Craig, and younger half-sister, both of whom were described as "black." See "Motherhouse Diary," November 1, 1914, and December 28, 1914, box 75, folder 1, Mission Diaries, Maryknoll Mission Archives. Davis's African American heritage was written out of Maryknoll histories and even the congregation's online database of deceased sisters until recently. Special thanks to Margaret Susan Thompson, who drew the author's attention to the documentation of Davis's racial heritage.

212. "The Life of Mother Mary Consuella Clifford, O.S.P.: Definitive Resume," typescript, n.d., in Congregation RG: box 41, folder 8, OSP Archives. Clifford was the 1905 valedictorian of the St. Frances de Sales School in Powhatan, Virginia, run by the SBS. See also S. M. Mercedes to My Dear Mother Teresa, August 17, 1937, in the same file. The opportunity came about after Rebecca's brother, Walter, desired to leave Virginia and pass for white but not abandon his sister. Walter, who "violently opposed" Rebecca's desire to the enter the OSP, consulted a priest who found a "white sisterhood" in Philadelphia willing to admit her. Opposition to Rebecca's call to religious life also came from a white Josephite priest, who curiously wanted her to return to Lynchburg and just "teach for him."

213. S. M. Mercedes to My Dear Mother Teresa.

214. J. O'Toole, *Passing for White*, 172–91. According to Marie-Josée Morin, the archivist for the Congregation of Notre Dame in Montreal, notes at the archive state that Eliza Healy, who became a local superior in Vermont, refused to be photographed owing to her darker color. The veracity of this claim is unclear. But no known images of the Healy sisters exist in Church archives. Marie-Josée Morin, email message to author, July 7, 2016.

2. "Nothing Is Too Good for the Youth of Our Race"

1. Bishop Emmet M. Walsh to Mother M. Consuella Clifford, July 25, 1933, and Mother Consuella to Bishop Walsh, July 28, 1933, in Administration RG: box 2, folder 33, OSP Archives.

2. J. Anderson, *Education of Blacks*, 186–237.

3. See Blose and Caliver, *Statistics*, 15. See also J. Anderson, *Education of Blacks*, 236.

4. While Avery became state accredited in 1935, the Colored Industrial School (later Burke High School) did not earn accreditation until 1949. See Powers, *Black Charlestonians*, 139. See also Richardson and Jones, *Education for Liberation*, 51; and Pyatt, *Burke High School*, 8.

5. Since the early nineteenth century, Charleston had had a notable Black Catholic population, enlarged by four waves of enslaved and free Black refugees from Saint-Domingue (later Haiti) from 1791 to 1809. See Gilkin, "Saint Dominguan Refugees," 59. See also Canon No. 1372 in Peters, *Pio-Benedictine Code*, 462.

6. See Carr, *Accredited Secondary Schools*, 99. See also McQueeney, *Sunsets over Charleston*, 96–97.

7. Sherwood, *Oblates' Hundred and One Years*, 256–58.

8. Walsh to Clifford, July 25, 1933; and Mother Consuella to Walsh, July 28, 1933.

9. On post–World War I Catholic teacher certification and school accreditation, see Brewer, *Nuns*; and Walch, *Parish School*, 134–51.

10. At the Third Plenary Council of Baltimore, US bishops promulgated educational legislation that directed the Church for the next half century, with the rallying cry, "Catholic schools for Catholic children." See Dolan, *American Catholic Experience*, 271–72. See also Canon No. 1374 in Peters, *Pio-Benedictine Code*, 462; and Pope Pius XI, *Divini Illius Magistri: On Christian Education*, December 31, 1929, https://www.papalencyclicals.net/pius11/p11rappr.htm.

11. Quoted in Agee, *Cry for Justice*, 47.

12. Agee, *Cry for Justice*, 149. See also Spalding, "Negro Catholic Congresses," 339–40.

13. Quoted in C. Davis, *History of Black Catholics*, 166. On Rudd and the Colored Catholic Congresses, see Agee, *Cry for Justice*.

14. C. Davis, *History of Black Catholics*, 173–75. See also Spalding, "Negro Catholic Congresses," 340–50.

15. See chapter 1. See also the story of Madame Bernard Couvent in Desdunes, *Our People*, 103–4; Sherwood, *Oblates' Hundred and One Years*, 209–65; M. Lucas, *History of Blacks*, 249–50; Alberts, "Black Catholic Schools," 81; and NOAAMACH, *Celebration of Faith*, 30–35.

16. MacGregor, *Emergence*, 34–91.

17. Erickson and Donovan, *Three R's*, 250–52. Figaro, a graduate of the SSF's St. Paul School in Lafayette, Louisiana, was the first formal teacher of Black Catholics in Lake Charles. In the 1920s, Figaro appealed to Katharine Drexel for additional financial support and sisters to help support the growing school. Under Figaro's leadership, Sacred Heart became an accredited elementary and high school and produced ten sisters and five priests, including two bishops.

18. See M. Lucas, *History of Blacks*, 249–50; Alberts, "Black Catholic Schools," 88; Gilmore, *We Came North*, 37; and the section "Schools for African Americans Staffed by SCN," in Sisters of Charity of Nazareth, "Empowering the Mind: Education Ministries," accessed August 10, 2020, https://scnfamily.org/archives/edu/.

19. Clark, *Masterless Mistresses*, 292; and Alberts, "Black Catholic Schools," 88. The order's Ursuline Academy in New Orleans did not admit its first Black students until 1966. See Maurent Mock Verderame, "Trailblazers of 1966: The Three Women Who Integrated Ursuline," *Ursulines*, November 1, 2016, 16–17. Although the Sisters of Charity administered a school for free girls of color in Mobile during slavery, the order withdrew from the African American apostolate in the diocese during Jim Crow. For example, in 1891, the Sisters of Charity staffed Mobile's Cathedral School, but a lay teacher taught the school's Black children. In fact, two of the three parochial schools for colored children in Mobile that year were led by lay teachers; the Religious Sisters of Mercy (RSM) administered the third school. See *Sadlier's Catholic Directory* (1891), 299. The Sisters of Charity's Providence Infirmary Training School in Mobile also excluded Black women. In one exception from the 1920s, an Afro-Creole woman who could pass for white enrolled and graduated. But the Sisters of Charity prevented Mildred Dolbear from receiving her diploma in public out of fear that her Black grandmother would attend the ceremony. This episode is referenced in a December 1929 letter from Mother M. Carmelita Hartman to Mother Provincial of St. Louis, RSM. See chap. 3, note 6.

20. A Member of the Order, "Southern Teaching Order," 253, 263. See also Morrow, *Persons of Color*, 123; and Misner, *"Highly Respectable,"* 51.

21. "Black Parishioners Write to Their Bishop, 1888," in C. Davis and Phelps, *"Stamped,"* 72–73.

22. A Member of the Order, "Southern Teaching Order," 263.

23. Sherwood, *Oblates' Hundred and One Years*, 252–58. See also St. Katherine (Charleston, SC) Convent Annals, 174, 176, Missions RG: box 105, folder 2. Both the SSF and the OSP also established Black Catholic schools in the Caribbean and Central America in the late nineteenth and early twentieth centuries in response to the anti-Black racism of white and European orders ministering there. See chapter 1; Brett, *New Orleans Sisters*, 13–16, 26–39, 58, 163–67; Sherwood, *Oblates' Hundred and One Years*, 245–51; and Knecht, *Oblate Sisters of Providence*, 86–95.

24. Ten of the first twenty-three self-identified African American men ordained to the Catholic priesthood were educated and mentored by the OSP or the SSF. Several also had aunts, sisters, and cousins who were Black nuns. See Foley, *God's Men of Color*, 125, 139, 149, 157.

25. Foley, *God's Men of Color*, 139–40. See also "Aunt Mary Eliza Smith Dead," *Lebanon (KY) Enterprise*, May 31, 1935; and "A Family Overtakes Christ," *Colored Harvest*, February 1951, 8–9. Because Foley's superiors and editors forced him to whitewash the overtly racist dimensions of the US Catholic past in his scholarship, it is plausible that Mary Eliza Smith's husband, Pius, was also enslaved prior to federal abolition. Foley only records that Pius Smith was a plasterer who "was employed by the Trappists to help in the construction of their monastery at Gethsemani." See Foley, *God's Men of Color*, 139; and "Adventures," 103–5, 116–18. Writer Dianne Aprile documents that the Trappist monks in Kentucky used enslaved Black labor to help construct the nation's oldest monastery in the 1850s and 1860s. See Aprile, *Abbey of Gethsemani*, 66–69.

26. Quoted in Foley, *God's Men of Color*, 89–90.

27. W. E. B. Du Bois, "The Catholic Church and the Negroes," *Crisis*, July 1925, 121.

28. Not until 1965 would Father Harold Perry, SVD, become the first self-identified Black bishop assigned to a US diocese. See C. Davis, *History of Black Catholics*, 256–57.

29. See chapter 1.

30. See Southern, *John LaFarge*, 81; and Fichter, "First Black Students," 537–39.

31. This figure is listed at the end of the monthly editions of *Our Colored Missions*. See also "The Privilege in Catholic America," *Our Colored Missions*, January 1931, back cover. That year, the CBMWCP paid the salaries of fifty-two SBS members, the most of any order.

32. US Office of Education, *Negro Education*, 1:303–4, 2:287.

33. *Our Negro and Indian Missions: Annual Report of the Secretary of the Commission for the Catholic Missions among Colored People and the Indians* (Washington, DC: Commission for Catholic Missions Among the Colored People and the Indians, 1920), 12, typed sheet in the Josephite Archives. Note that these numbers include only African American children in mostly Black Catholic schools, not in predominantly white schools.

34. *Our Negro and Indian Missions: Annual Report of the Secretary of the Commission for the Catholic Missions among Colored People and the Indians* (Washington, DC: Commission for Catholic Missions Among the Colored People and the Indians, 1941), 27, typed sheet in Josephite Archives and Gillard, *Colored Catholics*, 192–93. The 1941 school figures are from John T. Gillard, who indicates that archdiocesan and diocesan figures included 237 Black Catholic grade schools, 48 high schools, and 20 junior high schools. Because not all of the junior high and high schools were attached to the grade schools, it is unclear exactly how many Black Catholic schools there were in 1941. Also note that Black students enrolled in predominantly white Catholic schools are not generally included in these statistics before the civil rights movement. See Gillard, *Colored Catholics*, 204–11.

35. US Office of Education, *Negro Education*, 2:287. See also NOAAMACH, *Celebration of Faith*, 30. The SSF's St. Mary's Academy was also the first Black Catholic high school in the Deep South.

36. "Schools for African Americans Staffed by SCN," in Sisters of Charity of Nazareth, "Empowering the Mind: Education Ministries," accessed August 10, 2020, https://scnfamily.org/archives/edu/.

37. Typed text of Negro History Week talk delivered by Mother Marie Anselm Duffel in Detroit, Michigan, in "January 1958," but written by Sister Mary Esperance Collins according to handwritten notes on the sheet, 6–7, in Duffel Administration File, SSF Archives.

38. McNally, *Catholic Parish Life*, 188.

39. "Nuns at Negro Convent Ask Police to Protect Them from Neighbors: Trespasser on South Broadway Grounds Believed Near-By Resident," *St. Louis Daily Globe-Democrat*, August 23, 1921. See also "Neighbor Residents to Continue Efforts to Evict Negro Nuns," *St. Louis Daily Globe-Democrat*, August 24, 1921; "Welfare Association Formed to Fight Negro Encroachment: South Broadway Body Organized after Location of St. Rita's Convent," *St. Louis Daily Globe-Democrat*, September 4, 1921; Sister M. Henrietta Butler, OSP, "Pure Gold—Never Destroy," May 20, 1947, 8–9, in Missions RG: box 45, folder 2, OSP Archives. For more on Glennon, see chapter 3.

40. On Mayfield, see Alexander, *Ku Klux Klan*, 123–24, 192, 194–96. See also Rice, *Ku Klux Klan*, 24–25.

41. "Catholic Convent in Liberty County Where Whites and Blacks Mingle Freely: Reported That New York White Children and Southern Darkies Eat and Sleep Together in Catholic Schools," *Colonel Mayfield's Weekly*, March 25, 1922, 1.

42. See "Land of the Ku Klux Klan," *Colored Harvest*, July–August 1922, 13.

43. On white obsession with the Black mammy figure, see McElya, *Clinging to Mammy*.

44. "Death Claims Another Josephite Father," *Colored Harvest*, April–May 1947, 10–11.

45. Hart, *Violets*, 122.

46. "Land of the Ku Klux Klan," 13. See also Administrative File of Father Alexis Laplante and Ames, TX Mission File, Josephite Archives, Baltimore.

47. "Catholic Convent in Liberty County," 1. Mayfield also sought the cooperation of Black Protestants to stop the spread of Catholicism in the Black community.

48. Dolan, *American Catholic Experience*, 356. On US immigration policy during the 1920s, see Ngai, *Impossible Subjects*, 1–55. On anti-Catholic Klan violence during the 1920s, see Gordon, *Second Coming*; and Davies, *Rising Road*.

49. On violent white opposition to Black education, see Du Bois, *Black Reconstruction*; J. Anderson, *Education of Blacks*; and H. Williams, *Self-Taught*.

50. Rackleff, "Anti-Catholicism"; and Page, "Bishop Michael J. Curley," 101–17.

51. Florida's first Black-administered Catholic school, Holy Family School led by the SSF, opened in Apalachicola in 1920. It closed in 1968. The OSP administered St. Francis Xavier and Holy Redeemer Catholic Schools in Miami from 1961 to 1977 and 1960 to 1989, respectively. See NOAAMACH, *Celebration of Faith*, 31, 33; and the Holy Redeemer and St. Francis Xavier files in Mission RG: series 1 and 2, OSP Archives.

52. Page, "Bishop Michael J. Curley," 101–17. See also Landers, *Black Society*.

53. *Journal of the Senate of the State of Georgia*, 134, 247–48, 252, 272. The bill number was 17.

54. Quoted in Foley, *God's Men of Color*, 106.

55. Father Ignatius Lissner, "Handmaids of the Most Pure Heart of Mary (1916)," "The Franciscan Handmaids of Mary" folder, DS Archives, Savannah, Georgia. See also "Williams, Theodore" Cojourner File, Congregation RG: box 103, folder 6, OSP Archives.

56. Lissner, "Handmaids," 3–5. See also "Five Novices Take White Veil at St. Benedicts to Become Handmaids of the Most Pure Heart of Mary," *Savannah Tribune*, October 13, 1917.

57. Du Bois, "The Church." See also "Sister Mary Dorothy Hall, Former Superior General," *Catholic New York*, February 1, 1980, 36; and the unpublished necrologies of Mother Mary Charles (Alma) Wilson, Sister Mary Walburga (Margarita) Moralis, Sister Ann Theresa (Mary) Thibodeaux, and Sister Mary of the Presentation (Mary Christine) Gallavaga, provided to author from Sister Loretta Theresa Richards, FHM. Wilson, a native of Millville, New Jersey, entered from Philadelphia; Moralis entered from New York City; and Thibodeaux entered from Breaux Bridge, Louisiana. From their foundation in Havana, Cuba in 1700, the Carmelites required blood purity and

formally excluded candidates of African ancestry from admission. These anti-Black exclusionary practices seemly continued into the twentieth century. See Clune, *Cuban Convents*, 6, 12.

58. Lissner, "Handmaids," 4. See also McDonogh, *Black and Catholic*, 215.

59. Lissner's seminary soon failed, as white students vehemently opposed the presence of Black students there. See Ochs, *Desegregating the Altar*, 266, 257–60, 263–68; and McDonogh, *Black and Catholic*, 218–21.

60. McDonogh, *Black and Catholic*, 218–21.

61. *The History of the First Fifty Years of the Franciscan Handmaids of the Most Pure Heart of Mary* (New York: privately printed, 1967) in the SSF Archives. The pages in this source are not numbered. See also C. Moore, "Keeping Harlem Catholic."

62. Lissner,"Handmaids," 6. See also "Sister Mary Dorothy Hall," 36. The author has a photo of Hall.

63. Ochs, *Desegregating the Altar*, 273–74.

64. Ochs, *Desegregating the Altar*, 274–75.

65. Foley, *God's Men of Color*, 85–95. Josephite John T. Gillard documents that both Plantevigne and Father John Dorsey died "stark mad" in insane asylums because of the racism they faced. See Gillard to Rev. Wm. F. Markoe, Society of Jesus (SJ), August 28, 1930, Gillard Correspondence Folder, Josephite Archives.

66. For more on the 1903 lynching of Albert Plantevigne, see Foley, *God's Men of Color*, 83; and "The Death of Rev. L.A. Planving," *American Missionary* 57 (1903): 237–39. Albert Plantevigne was the brother of Josephite Father John Joseph Plantevigne. In 1918, W. E. B. Du Bois denotes that Mother Theodore was Plantevigne's cousin. See Du Bois, "The Church," *Crisis*, February 1918, 194–95.

67. Quote in Ochs, *Desegregating the Altar*, 274.

68. "FHM: A Chronology," typed sheet, ca. 1990, provided to author by Sister Loretta Theresa Richards, FHM. See also C. Moore, "Keeping Harlem Catholic." Though Moore notes that Handmaids affiliated with the Franciscans in 1929, the FHM Chronology states 1930.

69. Although Black Catholic Savannah would send several more vocations to religious life, the next Black nun to minister in Savannah, Sister Mary Julian (Norma Fae) Griffin, would not arrive until 1970. See Sister Mary Julian Griffin, Vincentian Sister of Charity (VSC) File, DS Archives, Savannah, Georgia.

70. On this case, see Abram, *Cross Purposes*.

71. Mattick, "Ministries," 46.

72. Mattick, "Ministries," 176–77.

73. Mattick, "Ministries," 178–82.

74. Frank A. Hall to Monsignor Brady, November 4, 1939, National Catholic Welfare Conference Collection, box 78, folder 24, Archives of the Catholic University of America (CUA Archives), Washington, DC.

75. "Life of Mother Mary Consuella Clifford," OSP Archives.

76. Saundra Ann Willingham (formerly Sister M. Melanie, Sister of Notre Dame de Namur [SNDdeN]), interview by author, June 29, 2012, telephone, and October 21, 2013, Cincinnati, OH.

77. On the sexual exploitation of Black women by white priests during and after slavery in Louisiana and the wider South, see Pasquier, *Fathers on the Frontier*, 79–87; Deggs, *No Cross, No Crown*, xxvii–xxviii; and Madeleine Davison, "Panel: Racism Compounds the Clergy Sex Abuse Crisis for Black Catholics," *National Catholic Reporter*, April 28, 2021. For two twentieth-century cases that have turned attention to the abuse of Black boys by white priests, see Michael Rezendes, "In Mississippi Delta, Catholic Abuse Cases Settled on Cheap," *Associated Press*, August 27, 2019. For one early example of the sexual exploitation of an enslaved Black woman by a Catholic priest in colonial Latin America, see McKinley, *Fractional Freedoms*, 1–4.

78. Quoted in C. Davis and Phelps, "Stamped," 63.

79. L. Lucas, *Black Priest/White Church*, 15.

80. Quadarella entered the SSND in Wilton, Connecticut, in 1963 and departed in 1976. Her mother, Anna, was African American and a descendant of people enslaved in Virginia. Carolyn Quadarella (formerly Sister Louis Mary, SSND), interview by author, December 29, 2015, telephone and email.

81. Foley, "Adventures," 105.

82. White, interview; Sister Melinda Pellerin, a Sister of St. Joseph of Springfield, Massachusetts (SSJ), interview by author, August 16, 2016, telephone; and Guidry, *Southern Negro Nun*. See also Mother Marie Anselm to Dear Reverend Pastor, typed copy, 1961 is handwritten at the top of the sheet, in Duffel Administration Files, SSF Archives.

83. For a few of the published examples documenting this abuse, see also C. Davis, *History of Black Catholics*, 204–6; Foley, *God's Men of Color*, 103; Southern, *John LaFarge*, 81; Joan Bird, "N.Y. Panther 21 Political Prisoner," *Black Panther*, June 27, 1970, 9; and Cora Marie Billings, "Saved by Grace: Striving for a More Racially Just and Equal Church," *America*, June 24, 2014, https://www.americamagazine.org/faith/2014/06/24/saved-grace-striving-more-racially-just-and-equal-church.

84. Cressler, *Authentically Black*, 32–33. Notably, Cressler's study of the rise of the Black Catholic Chicago in the twentieth century failed to include any discussion of the OSP, their decades-long ministry on the city's South Side, or the Black sisters' experiences of racist mistreatment from white missionary religious. On the verbal, physical, and sexual abuse of Black and Native American youth in white-led Catholic schools, see the rest of this chapter; Adams, *Education for Extinction*; and Churchill, *Kill the Indian*. For one published example of Black Catholic opposition to being treated like and referred to as "heathen" by white religious, see N. Davis, "Integration," 102–8.

85. Wynn, "Diane Judith Nash," 284.

86. Diane Nash, interview by author, November 13, 2015, telephone.

87. Ralph Wiley, "Darth Vader of G'Town," *ESPN*, accessed July 17, 2021, https://www.espn.com/page2/s/villains/wiley.html.

88. See also Terry Frei, "Schoolwork Comes First at Georgetown: Despite Success, John Thompson Isn't Running a Basketball Factory," *Los Angeles Times*, March 10, 1985; and Jesse Washington, "Georgetown's John Thompson Jr. Didn't Want to Be Boxed In," *Undefeated*, August 31, 2020.

89. Sister Charlotte (Rosa) Marshall, OSP, interview by author, Baltimore, MD, February 19, 2010. Marshall's vocation was saved because of the intervention of a white

laywoman, Victoria Chineworth, who worked with the BVM in Memphis. A decade before, Chineworth's African American daughter, Innocence, had been denied admission to the BVM (and soon thereafter the SBS) before being directed to the OSP. After the death of her husband, Victoria volunteered with the BVM and preserved the vocations of at least three Black girls rejected by the order by directing them to the OSP. Chineworth, interview.

90. Sister Josita Colbert, SNDdeN, interview by author, June 23, 2014, telephone. Colbert did not return to St. Peter Claver the next year.

91. Sister Gwynette Proctor, SNDdeN, interview by author, July 27, 2015, telephone.

92. Dr. Sheppard recounted this story at the 2012 Merle Jordan Conference at Boston University on October 7. On Sheppard's tenure in religious life, see Nancy Ryan, "HUD Settles Nuns' Race Discrimination Suit," *Chicago Tribune*, November 14, 1977.

93. Mason, *African Americans*, 148. See also Butler, *Across God's Frontiers*, 254–55.

94. The archival and oral history record of the anti-Black attitudes and practices of select Afro-Creole SSF members is extensive. For a couple of published sources, see Ochs, *Desegregating the Altar*, 150–53; and Delpit, "Act Your Age," 121–23.

95. Kathryn R. Goetz, "Founded in 1888, St. Peter Claver Church Was Minnesota's First African American Catholic Church," *Minneapolis Post*, December 18, 2017, https://www.minnpost.com/mnopedia/2017/12/founded-1888-st-peter-claver-church-was-minnesota-s-first-african-american-catholic/.

96. Earline Greenfield, interview by author, June 14, 2014, New Orleans, at the annual James Lyke Conference. Greenfield is her maiden name.

97. On the RSM's resistance to desegregation in St. Louis owing to the members' "Southern" sympathies, see chapter 3.

98. Greenfield, interview. A photo of Greenfield as the May Day queen is contained in the 1961 edition of *Mercian*, Mercy High School's yearbook. According to the yearbook, Sister M. Rosaria, RSM, was the head of the social studies department. See *Mercian*, 1961, in *U.S., School Yearbooks, 1900–1999* (Lehi, UT: Ancestry.com Operations, 2010).

99. Sister Mary Judith Therese Barial, SSF, interview by author, New Orleans, July 7, 2009.

100. See chapter 1 for one example involving Josephite priests.

101. John T. Gillard, SSJ, to Most Rev. Emmet Walsh, DD, August 18, 1933, John T. Gillard Papers, *Josephite Archives*.

102. Karen Katafiasz, "A New Voice for the New Black Sister," *St. Anthony Messenger*, April 1974, 38.

103. This is a common reflection by Black sisters in Black congregations. For one example, Sister Josita Colbert, a former OSP member, recalled that when she was stationed in Detroit, the OSP were excluded from most local events for sisters. She also remembered that some white Adrian Dominican nuns complained about Black nuns taking communion before white nuns at an interracial Mass. Sister Josita Colbert, SNDdeN, interview by author, telephone, June 23, 2014.

104. This is a common reflection by Black sisters in white orders. For published sources, see Ochs, *Desegregating the Altar*, 147; Saundra Willingham, "Why I Quit the Convent," *Ebony*, December 1968, 64–66, 68, 70, 72, 74; and S. Harris, *Sisters*, 267–82.

105. Sister Mary Alice Chineworth, OSP, interview by author, Baltimore, MD, February 1, 2010.

106. Roediger, *Working toward Whiteness*, 169.

107. For three published examples, see Bea Hines, "Neighbors in Religion: Catholic Nun Celebrates 75 Years of Service to Church, Community," *Miami Herald*, September 22, 2015, https://www.miamiherald.com/news/local/community/miami-dade/community-voices/article36098619.html; Jacques Kelly, "Sister Mary Paul Lee, 75, Oblate Sisters Treasurer," *Baltimore Sun*, December 8, 2004; and "St. Margaret's Gail Carter Says for 'Any Real Change We Must Be Sitting at the Table,'" *Catholic Standard*, March 10, 2021, https://cathstan.org/posts/black-catholic-voices-series-st-margaret-s-gail-carter-says-for-any-real-change-we-must-be-sitting-at-the-table.

108. Council Minutes: 1903–1932, 26, Administration RG: box 44, folder 5, OSP Archives.

109. Hayes, *Schools of Our Own*, 63.

110. Hayes, *Schools of Our Own*, 63. A 1946 program for the Negro History Week celebration at IC High School in Charleston features these performances. The program is contained in Missions RG: box 109, folder 85, OSP Archives.

111. A February 1939 edition of the *Ritagram*, a monthly publication of the students of St. Rita's Academy in St. Louis, features stories on these topics. See Administration RG: box 45, folder 15, OSP Archives.

112. Langston Hughes, "Poetry Buys a Ticket for Little Trip South during History Week," *Chicago Defender*, February 26, 1949, 6.

113. Hayes, *Schools of Our Own*, 62–63.

114. For one example, see Annals, April 22, 1944, Missions RG: box 46, folder 7, OSP Archives.

115. Michele Hemenway, educated at the School Sisters of Notre Dame's Immaculate Heart of Mary School in St. Louis, Missouri in the 1960s, noted that one of the order's earliest Black members, Sister Marie Stephen (Harriet) Miller, was her fourth-grade teacher and the first person to teach her Black history. However, the order removed Miller from the classroom soon after she taught her first Black history lesson. Michele Hemenway, interview by author, September 28, 2015, telephone. The SSND archivist provided the author with Miller's necrology in an email message on September 29, 2015. Miller was a former OSP pupil. See chapter 4 for additional examples.

116. C. Davis, *History of Black Catholics*, 254. See also Gillard, *Colored Catholics*, 214–15.

117. The SBS did not offer higher educational support to the SSF until 1925 and to the OSP until 1926.

118. Council Minutes: 1903–32, Administration RG: box 44, folder 5, OSP Archives.

119. The OSP General Council minutes, for example, note that the Black sisterhood appealed to Drexel as early as 1921. However, Drexel did not offer support until 1926 when the OSP entered Villanova and appealed to her for financial assistance. See Council Minutes: 1903–32, 61, Administration RG: box 44, folder 5, OSP Archives. The OSP appealed to Drexel again in 1931 to "permit two Sisters to come here and conduct a Summer Normal." See Annals, 1931, Motherhouse RG: box 35, no folder, OSP Archives.

120. In 1938 correspondence between Father John Gillard and Sister M. Honora Jack, president of the Immaculate Heart of Mary's Marygrove College in Detroit, Michigan, these policies are clear. After Marygrove rejected a Black female applicant, Gillard published an article detailing the situation titled "The Irony of It" in his order's *Colored Harvest*. See "The Irony of It," *Colored Harvest*, June–July 1938, 2; Sister M. Honora to Editor of *the Colored Harvest*, August 20, 1938; Rev. John Gillard to Rev. Sister M. Honora, IHM, August 24, 1938, Gillard Papers, Josephite Archives; and Albert S. Foley, "The Negro and Catholic Higher Education," *Crisis*, August–September 1957, 413–19, 455.

121. Quoted in Morrow, "'Making a Way,'" 26.

122. "Suggestions for the Sisters Attending College," n.d., Congregation RG: box 19, folder 21, OSP Archives.

123. Mother M. Consuella [Clifford] to Sr. M. Felix, OSP, July 31, 1931, Administration RG: box 3, folder 10, OSP Archives.

124. Fichter, "First Black Students," 539.

125. "Answers to Questions Asked in Letter to Reverend Mother Philip," for Roger Baudier, between 1946 and 1958, in Mother Philip Goodman Administration File, SSF Archives. See also Fichter, "First Black Students," 537–39.

126. See "History of the First Summer School," *Our Colored Missions*, September 1921, 130; and "The Colored Sisters: A Plea for Fair Play and Equal Opportunity," ca. 1921, prepared by the CBMWCP, Archives of the Sisters of Charity of Seton Hill (SCSH Archives), Greensburg, PA.

127. "Colored Sisters."

128. Fichter, "First Black Student," 537–38. See also 1920–21 correspondence for "Holy Family School," SCSH Archives; and Porter, "History of Negro Education."

129. Fichter, "First Black Students," 537–38.

130. "Summer School for the Sisters of the Holy Family, 1921–1957: Faculty Lists," n.d., SCSH Archives.

131. "History of the First Summer School," 130–31. Parts of this article were later reprinted in *America*. See "Seton Hill and the Negro Sisters," *America*, December 13, 1924, 213.

132. The summer school, which enrolled only SSF members, later became known as the Delisle Junior College and earned accreditation from the CUA.

133. Sister M. Eusebia to Sister Agnes Marie, September 29, 1929, SCSH Archives.

134. Fichter, "First Black Students," 547.

135. Mother M. Elizabeth to Reverend H. Gaudin, August 14, 1937; and Harold A. Gaudin, SJ, to Sister M. Elizabeth, August 17, 1937, SSF Archives. See also Fichter, "First Black Students," 543–47.

136. Fichter, "First Black Students," 542–43. Several SSF members noted that the agreement ended sometime in the 1990s.

137. Fichter, "First Black Students," 547.

138. "Here and There," *Our Colored Missions*, August 1944, 116.

139. Fichter, "First Black Students," 548. See also "Folder: Scholarship Program for Sisters of the Holy Family of New Orleans, Louisiana, at Seton Hill College, Greensburg, Pennsylvania," n.d., SCSH Archives.

140. Borgia, *Violets*, 116–17.

141. Gillard, *Colored Catholics*, 208–9.

142. Council Minutes: 1903–32, 28, Administration RG: box 44, folder 5, OSP Archives.

143. Sherwood, *Oblates' Hundred and One Years*, 193–96.

144. Sherwood, *Oblates' Hundred and One Years*, 194. Two additional Xavierian Brothers later took over leadership of the summer school. In 1924, Xavierian Brother Bede Rouse appealed to Father John Sparrow, Order of Saint Augustine (OSA), at Villanova College to help the OSP secure admission to the summer school there that same year.

145. Baptiste, "Study of the Foundation," 56. In 1923, or shortly thereafter, the Sisters of Charity of Leavenworth in Kansas, who administered St. Mary's College (now University of Saint Mary), also admitted OSP members stationed in Leavenworth into summer classes. See Sherwood, *Oblates' Hundred and One Years*, 193–94; and Sister M. Laurentia, OSP, "The Oblate Sisters of Providence and Higher Education," *Chronicle*, January 1932, 9.

146. Nuesse, "Segregation and Desegregation," 58–59.

147. Nuesse, "Segregation and Desegregation," 58–60, 64.

148. C. Davis, *History of Black Catholics*, 217–20. See also Nuesse, "Segregation and Desegregation," 59.

149. Quoted in Nuesse, "Segregation and Desegregation," 59.

150. Shields, "Need," 420.

151. Nickels, *Black Catholic Protest*, 42–60.

152. Nickels, *Black Catholic Protest*, 19–27. Turner, the first African American to earn a PhD in botany and the first to earn a doctorate from Cornell University, was the founding secretary of the NAACP's Baltimore branch.

153. "Platform of the Federated Colored Catholics," *St. Elizabeth's Chronicle*, September 1931, 549. See also Morrow, "'To My Darlings,'" 9.

154. See Laurentia, "Oblate Sisters of Providence," 8–9. See also Morrow, "'To My Darlings,'" 10–11; and Congregation RG: box 92, folder 13, OSP Archives.

155. Laurentia, "Oblate Sisters of Providence," 8.

156. Southern, *John LaFarge*, 129.

157. Southern, *John LaFarge*, 105–46. See also Ochs, *Desegregating the Altar*, 310–12.

158. Southern, *John LaFarge*, 105–213.

159. Gillard began a letter-writing campaign to his peers criticizing Turner's leadership as "self-appointed" and characterizing the FCC as representative of only a small northern faction with little support among southern Black Catholics. These missives are contained in Gillard's correspondence in the Josephite Archives. For one example, see Rev. John T. Gillard, SSJ, to Rev. L. J. Welbers, SSJ, May 5, 1932. See also Gillard to Most Rev. Michael Curley, DD, April 13, 1932, for documentation of the Josephite's opposition to an appeal made by "Miss Anita Williams," who sought Gillard's cooperation in the FCC's resurrection under Turner after the 1932 meeting. Although the FCC would be reorganized under Turner's leadership, it never regained its former influence or the significant support of white priests. See Southern, *John LaFarge*, 115–43.

160. Archbishop of Baltimore to Rt. Rev. Msgr. J. H. Ryan, June 6, 1932, Curley RGI, document R1646, Archives of the Archdiocese of Baltimore, AB.

161. Nickels, *Black Catholic Protest*, 42–60.

162. Archbishop of Baltimore to Dr. Deferrari, March 30, 1933, box 9, document D484, AB.

163. Mother Consuella to Bishop Walsh, August 8, 1933, Administration RG: box 2, folder 33, OSP Archives.

164. Mother Consuella to Bishop Walsh, August 8, 1933.

165. Following Bishop Walsh's approval, two recent Xavier College graduates were secured. See St. Katherine's Annals: 1917–1942, 150–53, Missions RG: box 105, folder 2, OSP Archives. See also Mother Consuella to Bishop Walsh, August 8, 1933.

166. The OSP motherhouse annals from June to September 1933 document the reintegration of the CUA by the order. See entries for June 12 and 19, August 3, and September 18, 1933, in Motherhouse RG: box 36, OSP Archives.

167. Annals entry for Wednesday, June 13, 1934, Motherhouse RG: box 36, OSP Archives.

168. See "Baptiste, Mary of Good Counsel (Mother Superior) Part 1" File, Congregation RG: box 37, folder 2, OSP Archives. See also "Catholic University Advisor Confirms Jim Crow Report," *Afro-American*, September 22, 1934; "Sisters at Catholic U.," *Afro-American*, February 2, 1935; and Nuesse, "Segregation and Desegregation," 64–68.

169. St. Katherine Convent Annals, 162–76, which includes a newspaper clipping from September 9, 1935, denoting that IC was an "accredited school," Missions RG: box 105, folder 2, OSP Archives. Richardson and Jones, *Education for Liberation*, 51.

170. Baptiste, "Study of the Foundation," 56. See also St. Rita's Annals (1934–45), Missions RG: box 46, folder 7, which denote the OSP members taking courses at Maryville; and "Chronicles," Missions RG: box 88, folder 1, which denote OSP members who took summer courses at Webster, OSP Archives. According to the St. Rita's Annals in September 1940, OSP members took Saturday courses at Maryville College beginning in the 1920s.

171. Gillard, *Colored Catholics*, 208–9.

172. Gillard, *Colored Catholics*, 208–9. See also May 16, 1945, entry in St. Rita's Annals, which denotes that the academy was "accredited by [the] University of Missouri, Columbia on May 16, 1945," Missions RG: box 46, folder 7, OSP Archives. Holy Epiphany, the fourth high school administered by the OSP in 1941, was the first Catholic high school for African Americans in Kansas.

173. In 1931, under Mother Mary Charles (Alma) Wilson, the FHM secured the educational assistance of four Dominican Sisters to help prepare them to enter Manhattan College Extension for Sisters, where many local sisters enrolled to earn their teaching credentials. See *History of the First Fifty Years*.

174. Gillard, *Colored Catholics*, 208–9.

175. A. J. Garvy, SJ, to Reverend and dear Mother, September 2, 1932, in Administration RG: box 4, folder 10, OSP Archives.

176. A. J. Garvy, SJ, to Reverend and dear Mother, September 2, 1932.

177. Hayes, *Schools of Our Own*, 53–58. The Black laywomen broke from the local branch of the National Catholic Interracial Federation, formerly the FCC, and organized under the new name of the Martin de Porres Guild after the future Black Peruvian saint.

178. Hayes, *Schools of Our Own*, 64–68.

179. Cressler, *Authentically Black*, 20–21.

180. McGreevy, *Parish Boundaries*, 182–92.

181. Baptiste, "Study of the Foundation," 54–56. See also Hayes, *Schools of Our Own*, 63.

182. Baptiste, "Study of the Foundation," 57.

183. Quoted in Hayes, *Schools of Our Own*, 63.

184. For more on another Catholic parish organized by Black laywomen and later staffed by Black nuns, see the discussion on Newark's Christ the King parish in Ward, *Mission for Justice*.

3. "Is the Order Catholic Enough?"

1. RSM General Council Minutes, February 25, 1946, Mercy Heritage Center Archives (RSM Archives).

2. On the RSM in the United States, see Sabourin, *Amalgamation*; and Werntz, *Our Beloved Union*. Also, the surnames of the RSM leaders referenced in this chapter were obtained from or confirmed in Werntz's *Our Beloved Union*.

3. Sister M. Bernardine, RSM, Mother General, to His Eminence Pietro Cardinal Fumasoni Biondi, May 21, 1946, RSM Archives.

4. Sister M. Bernardine to Fumasoni Biondi.

5. This chapter and chapter 1 detail nine cases involving the Sinsinawa Order of Preachers (OP), the Sisters of Notre Dame de Namur (SNDdeN), the Maryknolls, the School Sisters of St. Francis, the RSM, the Sisters of the Holy Family of Nazareth (CSNF), and the Bordentown Poor Clares. The Missionary Servants of the Most Blessed Trinity, or the Trinitarians, accepted two sisters Marion Brown (later Sister Mary Fabian) and Virginia Brown (later Sister Mary Virginia) from Brooklyn, New York, in 1927. They had a German mother and African American father, who passed for white. Sister Theresa Ahern, MBST, email message to author, May 2, 2018 and US Census records for Thomas Clark Lucas (later Thomas C. Brown, his mother Margaret's maiden name), who was born free in Washington, DC, in 1860 and eventually owned a dry-goods store in Brooklyn. Also, an unnamed US-born Black woman who could pass for white professed vows in a French order in Paris in the early twentieth century. See Sister Mary Ellen O'Hanlon, OP, "Two Little Stories: Two Lessons," *Our Colored Missions*, March 1949, 38–39.

6. Mother M. Carmelita Hartman to Mother Provincial of St. Louis, December 1929, RSM Archives. Attached to this letter is one dated December 2, 1929, from M. Ignatius to the Mother General of the Union, that references Dolbear and her experience of racism as a nursing student at the Sisters of Charity's Providence Infirmary Training School in Mobile, Alabama in the 1920s. Betsy Johnson, assistant archivist at the Mercy Heritage Center, email message to author, August 18, 2016; "Postulants Not Admitted to the Reception of the Habit since August 28, 1929," ca. 1934, Mildred Dolbear File; Sister Mary Bernardine Verlesen to Reverend Mother Provincial, RSM, August 7, 1930; and Mother Provincial to Rev. Mother (of the Visitation Holy Mary), n.d., Mildred Dolbear File, RSM Archives.

7. John T. Gillard, SSJ, to Dr. Carroll, April 30, 1941, NCWC Collection, box 104, folder 7, CUA Archives. Also Sister Miriam Varley, the Poor Clares' archivist, email message to

author, March 1, 2011; Louise S. Sherby, acting head of archives and special collections at Hunter College, email message to author, August 22, 2016; and Les Matthews, "District 5 Parents Agree on McBarnett?," *Amsterdam News* (New York), February 20, 1971.

8. Newman, *Desegregating Dixie*, x. The full text of *Encyclical Mystici Corporis Christi* is available on the Vatican's website at https://www.vatican.va/content/pius-xii/en /encyclicals/documents/hf_p-xii_enc_29061943_mystici-corporis-christi.html.

9. Ted Le Berthon, "Why Jim Crow Won at Webster College," *Pittsburgh Courier*, February 5, 1944. See also C. Denny Holland, *The St. Louis Story Retold*, March 19, 1961, pamphlet in Jesuit Archives Central United States, St. Louis, MO. The pamphlet relies on the firsthand account of Father John Markoe, SJ, who credited a Black Catholic mother and daughter with initiating the fight for school desegregation in the St. Louis archdiocese but noted they were subsequently erased from public retellings of the story.

10. Sister Mary Jordan, OP, emails to author from July 22, 2015, to January 18, 2016.

11. Sister Mary Dominic of the Rosary, OP, "Cloistered Dominicans Open Monastery for Colored Candidates," *Colored Harvest*, October–November 1944, 7.

12. See C. Davis, *History of Black Catholics*, 98–115. The all-Black Magdalens merged with the white Good Shepherd Sisters in the early 1960s. See Sister Nellie Hawkins, Religious of Our Lady of Charity of the Good Shepherd (RGS), interview by author, January 4, 2015, postal mail. Hawkins entered the all-Black Magdalens in 1955.

13. "Interracial Sisterhood," *Colored Harvest*, June–July 1946, 3.

14. In 1945, the Carmelite Nuns of Baltimore proposed to open a separate monastery for African American women and sent letters to the Black sisterhoods seeking prospective candidates, but the proposal was tabled by 1946. The formerly slave-holding order admitted its first Black member, Barbara Jean LaRochester, a former member of the Sisters of the Holy Family of Nazareth, in 1972. See "Letters to Mother Mary Magdalen Brunck re: the Proposed Carmel for Negro Nuns," box 1, folder 25, Archives of the Carmelite Monastery of Baltimore. See also LaRochester, "She Walked by Faith," 45.

15. For the best examination of the kneel-in protests to date, see Haynes, *Last Segregated Hour*.

16. See "Negro Nursing Sisters," *Colored Harvest*, December 1946–January 1947, 2–3. Although the SSM was the first white apostolic order to announce this step, the Daughters of the Heart of Mary (DHM) quietly admitted their first Black candidate, Frances Millicent Douglass, in 1945. Paulet Gaudet, DHM archivist, email message to author, September 29, 2015.

17. One exception: in St. Louis before the Civil War, the Sisters of Charity's hospital served Black patients during a cholera epidemic. See Schadewald, "Remapping Race," 210. See also Wall, *American Catholic Hospitals*, 73–102.

18. "An Interracial Role: Memoirs of Rev. William M. Markoe, SJ, 1900–1966," 42–44, typescript, Jesuit Archives Central United States, St. Louis, MO.

19. Wall, *American Catholic Hospitals*, 73–102.

20. Daniel Rudd, leader of the Colored Catholic Congresses, protested the refusal of Catholic hospitals led by white sisters to treat Black patients as early as 1887. See Agee, *Cry for Justice*, 75; and Schadewald, "Remapping Race," 179–98.

21. On the efforts of the National Association of Colored Graduate Nurses to desegregate military nursing ranks during World War II, see Hine, *Black Women in White*, 162–86.

22. The US Cadet Nursing Corps membership cards of the women who trained at St. Mary's Infirmary are available online on Ancestry.com. See Ancestry.com. *U.S., World War II Cadet Nursing Corps Card Files, 1942–1948* (Provo, UT: Ancestry.com Operations, 2011). See also Norman Parish, "Sister Antona Ebo: God's Work in Living Color," *Liguorian*, February 2010, 22.

23. Gleason, *Contending with Modernity*, 237. As chapter 2 recounts, members of the OSP had taken summer courses at Webster as early as 1940.

24. On Glennon's virulent anti-Black racism and efforts to thwart Black Catholic advancement, see Kemper, "Catholic Integration."

25. Le Berthon, "Why Jim Crow Won," 1. Foster was the 1942 salutatorian of the city's St. Joseph Catholic High School.

26. Holland, *St. Louis Story Retold*. Mrs. Williams and her daughter submitted their request to Jesuit John Markoe. This story is detailed in handwritten notes from Markoe on this pamphlet.

27. Gleason, *Contending with Modernity*, 237–38. See also "Missouri College Admits Race Girl," *Pittsburgh Courier*, October 13, 1945; and Ashley Westbrook, "Daughter of Webster University's First Black Student Shares Mother's Story," *Journal* (Webster University), December 7–13, 2011. The latter article details the racist opposition that Thomas faced from white students and at least one white nun while at Webster.

28. Valien, *St. Louis Story*. See also Kemper, "Catholic Integration"; and Clarence J. Howard, "Missouri Compromise No More," *St. Augustine's Messenger*, December 1946, 218–22.

29. Reverend William Drumm to Monsignor [Cody], March 14, 1945, SSM/FSM File, Archdiocese of Saint Louis Archives (ASL Archives), St. Louis, MO.

30. "Pro Memoria," 1, SSM/FSM File, ASL Archives.

31. Stepsis and Liptak, *Pioneer Healers*, 206–7. Sister Mary Antona Ebo noted that Brickus lived in an attic space during those years waiting to be admitted into the SSM. Ebo, interview.

32. Mother Mary Concordia, SSM, to Beloved and Most Holy Father, Eve of the Blessed Mother's Nativity, 1944 (stamped received February 27, 1945, chancery office), SSM/FSM File, ASL Archives.

33. Mother Mary Concordia, SSM, to Beloved and Most Holy Father, 1944. See also Mother Mary Concordia, SSM, to Most Holy Father, July 22, 1946 and Rev. William M. Drumm to Most Reverend Joseph E. Ritter, November 23, 1946, SSM/FSM File, ASL Archives.

34. Rev. William M. Drumm to Most Reverend Joseph E. Ritter, November 23, 1946.

35. Rev. William M. Drumm to Most Reverend Joseph E. Ritter, November 23, 1946.

36. Rev. William M. Drumm to Most Reverend Joseph E. Ritter, November 23, 1946. See also Mother Mary Concordia, SSM, to Most Reverend John J. Glennon, archbishop of Saint Louis, March 27, 1945, SSM/FSM file, ASL Archives.

37. Quoted in Schadewald, "Remapping Race," 210.

38. "A Call to the Missionary Life," *St. Augustine's Messenger*, October 1946, 179. Mary Dolores Allen of St. Louis entered the Missionary Sister Servants of the Holy Ghost (later Spirit) in 1947 but did not remain. See "Candidates for the Blue Sisters," *St. Augustine's Messenger*, March 1947, 56; and Glenn, interview.

39. "Good News!," *St. Augustine's Messenger*, October 1946, 169–70.

40. Although they are not included on the list, the Dominican Nuns of the Monastery of the Infant Jesus in Lufkin, Texas, accepted the application of Sister M. Ernestine Maughan, a SSF in New Orleans, in 1946. However, like the SSM, the Baltimore Carmelites in 1945, and the Poor Clare Sisters of Bordentown before them, the Lufkin Dominicans accepted Maughan only "with the intention of starting a foundation of colored cloistered sisters." Father John J. Roach to Mother M. Phillip Goodman, SSF, July 2, 1946, Goodman Administration File, SSF Archives.

41. On the Green Book and the perils of Black travel during Jim Crow, see Taylor, *Overground*.

42. Raymond Bernard, SJ, "Jim Crow Vocations," *Social Order* 2 (June 1949): 241–44, reprinted in *Interracial Review*, November 1949, 171.

43. "Sisters Receive First Colored Candidate," *St. Augustine's Messenger*, May 1947, 104. See also "Texas Gets First Race Catholic Nun," *Pittsburgh Courier*, November 27, 1948; "First Negro Joins Catholic Sisterhood," *New Journal and Guide* (Norfolk, VA), February 5, 1949; and Sister Mamie Jenkins, RSCJ, interview by Sister Irma Dillard, RSCJ, using author's interview guide, May 23, 2017.

44. For a scholarly overview of the Catholic Church's rampant anticommunism and its links to the fight against segregation and racism, see Southern, *John LaFarge*, 214–88.

45. Bernard, "Jim Crow Vocations," 241. See also Bernard, "Interracial Vocation Opportunities"; and Bernard, "More Vocation Opportunities."

46. See note 72 (introduction).

47. For an examination of these changes in Chicago, see Hoy, *Good Hearts*, 71–124.

48. "Report Shows 217,853 over 1950 Survey," *Chicago Defender*, March 26, 1960.

49. For one of many such examples, see George Hunton, "Communism and the Negro," *Interracial Review*, June 1937, 87.

50. Sister Magdala Marie Gilbert, OSP, "My Vocation Story," n.d., accessed August 10, 2020, http://www.oblatesistersvocations.com/SrMagdala.html.https://www.oblatesistersvocations.com/Sr-Magdala.html.

51. Rev. John F. O'Brien to Reverend Mother, n.d. [December 1946], RSM Archives.

52. Sister Mary Assumpta, RSM, Mother Provincial, to Mother M. Carmelita, Vicar General, December 6, 1946, RSM Archives.

53. RSM General Council Minutes from September 29, 1945, and November 12, 1945, RSM Archives.

54. Sister M. Carmelita, RSM, to Mother Provincial, Tarrytown, NY, December 9, 1946, RSM Archives.

55. Typed notes of RSM General Council Minutes from April 30, 1938, September 29, 1945, and November 12, 1945, RSM Archives.

56. Typed notes of RSM General Council Minutes from April 30, 1938, September 29, 1945, and November 12, 1945.

57. Watkins-Owens, *Blood Relations*, 4–5.

58. In 1944, the RSM's refusal to admit Maude Johnson, a Black laywoman suffering a life-threatening myocardial infarction, to their Chicago Mercy Hospital prompted the intervention of Cardinal Samuel Stritch, who eventually convinced local RSM leaders to lift their ban on Black patients after 1949. Wall, *American Catholic Hospitals*, 76.

59. "Our Colored Harvest in the Chicago Province," *Generalate Quarterly*, September 24, 1946, RSM Archives. See also Werntz, *Our Beloved Union*, 50.

60. Sister M. Bernardine to Fumasoni-Biondi.

61. Pietro Cardinal Fumasoni Biondi Protector to the Mother General, June 2, 1946, RSM Archives. In this letter, Fumasoni Biondi expressed that he preferred Black candidates still be directed to the Black orders. Fumasoni Biondi's preference is also cited in Sister M. Bernardine, RSM, to the Mother Provincial, RSM [Chicago, IL], July 9, 1946, and Sister Mary Genevieve Crane, RSM, to the Mother General, RSM, January 2, 1949, RSM Archives.

62. Sister Mary Genevieve Crane, RSM, to the Mother General, RSM, January 2, 1949, RSM Archives.

63. Mother Provincial [Griffin] to the Mother General, RSM, January 18, 1950, RSM Archives.

64. Mother Mary Domitilla, RSM, to the Mother General, RSM, November 16, 1950, RSM Archives.

65. Mother M. Bernardine, RSM, to the Mother Provincial [Chicago, IL], RSM, November 23, 1950, RSM Archives. Ultimately, Mother M. Bernardine Purcell advised Chicago leader M. Domitilla Griffin not to encourage Helen Mar, the interested Chinese American candidate, and instead to direct her to the "other communities that accept Chinese," where Purcell argued that she "would probably feel more at home."

66. Mother Mary Domitilla, RSM, to the Mother General, RSM, November 16, 1950, RSM Archives. Among those rebuffed were two unnamed African American girls in Portland, Oregon; a Loyola University Chicago graduate; and a Black laywoman of Brooklyn, New York. See the Mother Superior to Miss Pearl E. Tatem, July 24, 1960; Unknown to the Mother General, RSM, November 27, 1949; and Sister Mary Alberta, RSM, to Sister Mary Teresa Agnes, RSM, December 11, 1948, RSM Archives.

67. Sister Jean Marie Boyd, RSM, to Mother Mary Domitilla, RSM, October 21, 1950, RSM Archives.

68. [Mother Bernardine, RSM] to the Mother Provincial [Chicago, IL], RSM, January 17, 1951, RSM Archives.

69. Father Raymond Bernard, SJ, to Mother Superior, February 20, 1952, RSM Archives. Typed onto this letter is the following: "Answered 2/27/52; Policy to accept Negro Yes Policy in force about a year; Since, none have applied; Previously possible 5 have applied; Accepted –0."

70. Mother M. Hildegarde, RSM, to the Mother General, RSM, October 29, 1951, RSM Archives.

71. Mother M. Hildegarde, RSM, to the Mother General, RSM, October 29, 1951.

72. Mother M. Bernardine, RSM, to the Mother Provincial, RSM, November 1, 1951, RSM Archives.

73. RSM General Council Minutes, July 7, 1952, RSM Archives.

74. RSM General Council Minutes, February 28, 1953, RSM Archives.

75. Mother M. Bernardine, RSM, Mother General, to Mother Provincial and Sister Mistress, March 7, 1953, RSM Archives. Applicants and others were told there was no "policy for the acceptance or rejection of colored applicants."

76. Sister Cora Marie Billings, RSM, interview by author, July 6, 2010, telephone.

77. Billings, interview by author. On the expansion of Chicago's Black Catholic population, see Cressler, *Authentically Black*, 20–21.

78. Billings, interview. Billings mentored at least eight Black women who subsequently entered religious life in the Philadelphia area.

79. Massingale, *Racial Justice*, 53–55.

80. Raymond Bernard, SJ, "Sisterhoods and the Negro," *Interracial Review* (1995): 42–43; and Raymond Bernard, "Integration in the Convent," *America*, April 21, 1956, 83.

81. Bernard, "Integration," 83.

82. Bernard, "Some Anthropological Implications," 130.

83. This was mentioned in several Black sisters' testimonies.

84. See Hoy, *Good Hearts*, for an examination of these changes in Chicago.

85. Vocation Counselor to Sister Virginia Marie, January 8, 1955, Sister Marie Ann (Marjorie) Rideau, SL congregational file, Archives of the Sisters of Loretto (SL Archives), Nerinx, KY. Although Rideau was eventually admitted to the SL in Kentucky in 1956, additional correspondence contained in her file reveals that both the director in Kentucky and Rideau's former educators in Los Angeles attempted to dissuade Rideau from applying because they believed that Rideau might find the adjustment of being the only Black person in the community too daunting. The leaders of the SL also expressed concerns about Rideau's intellectual abilities and "Negro dialect." Rideau departed the SL in 1961 after she was not permitted to pursue a teaching vocation. See Rideau congregational file, SL Archives. The SL did not admit another Black candidate.

86. Sister Martin de Porres Coleman, SNDdeN, interview by author, September 4, 2013, telephone; Willingham, interview; Colbert, interview, August 9, 2016; and Sister Berchman of Mary to Sister Superior and Dear Sisters, February 28, 1953, Sr. Berchman of Mary Letters: 1952–1954, folder Cab2, B/A, Archives of the Sisters of Notre Dame de Namur, Cincinnati, OH. The latter letter documents the votes taken in California and Ohio regarding the "problem" of accepting "candidates, otherwise qualified, who ware wholly or partly of Negro blood." The vote in Cincinnati was taken in response to a written query from the archdiocesan vocational director, Rev. Charles F. Murphy.

87. Marie de Porres Taylor, interview by author, June 6, 2015, telephone. Taylor legally assumed her religious name.

88. Moore shared this story in a recorded panel discussion on antiracism at the CSJ motherhouse in St. Louis, Missouri, on September 21, 2019. The author also participated in this panel discussion. Moore, the only African American to remain in the CSJ in St. Louis, also recalled that the order rejected a Black candidate one year after her admission under suspicious circumstances. The candidate was later admitted into another local congregation.

89. The same was true of white seminaries and male religious orders. Historian Stephen J. Ochs reveals that the very few white seminaries and orders that would accept Black men generally admitted one "mulatto" man who could pass for white every few years to undermine the charge of racism in their admissions policies. See Ochs, *Desegregating the Altar*, 215, 244–45, 282, 293.

90. For example, in his 1945 letter of support for Daughter of the Heart of Mary Frances Douglass, Father Michael McLaughlin, pastor of Brooklyn's historically Black St. Peter Claver Church, emphasized her "light complexion," excellent diction, and position as a doctoral student at Fordham. He also noted that Douglass made good impressions "on the white people she deals with" and that the white Little Sisters of the Flower with whom Douglass interacted as a social worker had "expressed their willingness to accept her into their community should she desire to enter." Rt. Rev. Michael McLaughlin to Miss Miller, March 29, 1945, Archives of the Daughters of the Heart of Mary (DHM Archives), Holyoke, MA.

91. Joseph Donachie to Reverend and dear Mother Mary, April 6, 1956, in Loretta Hassell congregational file, Archives of the Sisters of Charity of New York (SCNY Archives), Bronx, NY. See also Sister Dolorita Maria to Mother Mary, March 3, 1956, Hassell file, SCNY Archives. Donachie had six biological sisters who were SCNY members, who helped advocate for Hassell's admission, despite the existence of an informal agreement among female superiors in New York City to dissuade and seemingly reject Black vocations according to the latter letter.

92. Rev. Michael J. Condon to Mother M. Felicitas, August 8, 1955, Rideau Congregational file, SL Archives.

93. For discussions of ethnic conflict among white sisters, see M. Thompson, "Sisterhood and Power."

94. Sister Sandra Smithson, School Sister of St. Francis (SSSF), interview by author, Nashville, TN, June 11, 2015; and "Sister Lourene Holley: Longtime Alvernia Faculty Member Dead at 54," *Just for You: A Newsletter for Parents of Alvernians*, Spring 1975, 1. Holley's and Smithson's religious names were Mary Lourene and Maria Cruces, respectively. Smithson reverted to her baptismal name after Vatican II.

95. The case of the Sisters of Charity of the Blessed Virgin Mary (BVM) is a good example. Although the BVM taught thousands of African American children, several of whom became nuns, the order accepted only one or two Black women. The BVM archivist, for example, noted that the order's only Black member entered in 1951 and left in 1971. Jennifer Head, BVM archivist, email message to author, September 28, 2016. However, the records of the National Black Sisters' Conference indicate that there were two African American BVM sisters. They were Sister Nancy Cross, who appears on the NBSC Members' Directory in 1968, and Sister Margaret Coleman, who helped draft the NBSC's position paper in 1969. See NBSC Members' Directory, December 1968 in series 6, box 1, folder 8, NBSC Papers, Department of Special Collections and University Archives, Raynor Memorial Libraries, Marquette University, hereafter MUSCA; and "The Survival of Soul: National Black Sisters' Conference Position Paper" in National Black Sisters' Conference, *Black Survival*, 159.

96. "Racism: Will We Ever Overcome?," *U.S. Catholic Magazine,* July 13, 2016, https://uscatholic.org/articles/201607/racism-will-we-ever-overcome/. This staff interview originally appeared in the magazine in March 1983.

97. Council Minutes, 1960, 98, Administration RG: box 45, folder 4, OSP Archives.

98. Proving the existence and use of racial quotas by white congregations is difficult without full archival access. For example, the Sisters of St. Mary in St. Louis, Missouri, admitted nine Black women between 1946 and 1949. However, the order curiously did not admit any Black candidates from 1950 to 1954 or from 1957 to 1962. Of the seventeen African American women who entered the SSM before 1965, only five remained, with most departing within one to three years of their admission. "African American Membership in SSM/OSF/FSM," typed sheet compiled by Sister Marylu Stueber, archivist of the Franciscan Sisters of Mary, August 4, 2010, for author during visit to archives.

99. See chapter 1.

100. Lois Wheeler, interview by author, June 25, 2017, Southfield, Michigan. Wheeler is Sister Marie Lutgarde (Phillis Rae) Johnson's biological sister.

101. Wheeler, interview. See also "Professed as Carmelite," *Colored Harvest,* January 1957, 1; and "Woman Becomes First Negro Nun in Magdalens," *Los Angeles Sentinel,* October 14, 1948.

102. Wheeler, interview.

103. Current and former Black sisters shared the details of Dr. Yvonne Irvin's story, as she died shortly before her scheduled interview with the author. Sherrill Adams (formerly Sister Nathan Marie, SSND), interview by author, July 24, 2014; and Colbert, interview, August 9, 2016. Irvin's dates of entrance, vow professions, and religious name were obtained from her former congregation in Secrétaire Générale, Congregation of Divine Providence (CDP), email message to author, December 19, 2016.

104. Bernard, "Integration in the Convent," 83. Bernard's date of departure from the Society of Jesus (SJ) was provided by Ann N. Rosentreter, associate archivist, Jesuit Archives, Central United States in St. Louis, Missouri, in her email message to author, April 20, 2017.

105. For two examples, see White, interview; and Bell, interview. This is apparent in most Black sisters' testimonies.

106. Mother M. Bernardine, OP, to Reverend Mother M. Bernardine, RSM, December 27, 1946, RSM Archives.

107. Davis, interview.

108. Smith and Feister, *Thea's Song,* 55. Sister Charlene Smith, Franciscan Sister of Perpetual Adoration (FSPA), recounted some of the mistakes the order made when Bowman entered in *Sr. Thea: Her Own Story.* The quote is Smith's.

109. Quoted in S. Harris, *Sisters,* 279. The date of Myles's entrance and biographical information were obtained in a phone conversation with an SSSF archivist on August 17, 2011, and follow-up postal correspondence.

110. Quoted in S. Harris, *Sisters,* 280.

111. Harrall died in 1988. However, in formal and informal discussions with the author, Black and white Sisters of Notre Dame de Namur, including Sisters Patricia Chappell,

Josita Colbert, and Mary Johnson, have shared details about Harrall's experiences in religious life. Colbert also noted that Harrall's mother met with SNDdeN leaders before her daughter's admission and requested that they not make Dolores a maid. Colbert, interviews, June 23, 2014 and August 9, 2016. The order did admit an African-descended woman from Jamaica who could pass for white in 1903. Sister Marie Eugénie Lecesne taught at Trinity College (now Trinity Washington University) and remained until her death in 1966. See "Information Sheet" for Lecesne provided by Sister Kim Dalgarn, SNDdeN archivist, email message to author, May 26, 2017.

112. Smith and Feister, *Thea's Song*, 104–5. See also M. Francesca, OSF, "Thrice Called." The first African American Sister of St. Francis of Oldenburg was Sister Vincent de Paul (Sarah) Page. "African American Women Who Entered Oldenburg OSFS," typed sheet, provided by Sister Jannette Pruitt, OSF, email message to author, June 8, 2015.

113. Sister Rosella Marie Holloman, Sister of Charity of St. Augustine (SCA), interview by author, Richfield, OH, June 19, 2014. Holloman did note that one additional Black woman entered the SCA. This woman professed vows but faced racist opposition from white patients. She eventually departed the order. Holloman also noted that Bishop Friend's intervention made possible the admission of Juanita Shealey (later Sister Nativa), the first and only African American Sister of St. Joseph of Cleveland, in 1951.

114. Grey (August 12, 2007), Davis, Glenn, and Ebo, interviews. See also Willingham, "Why I Quit"; and S. Harris, *Sisters*, 243–91.

115. Adams, interview. After OSP leaders learned that Adams entered the SSND in Baltimore, two members began regularly visiting her at the SSND motherhouse. Adams credited these OSP members' support with helping her to remain in religious life for as long as she did.

116. On the hostile reception of Latina women in white US sisterhoods, see Medina, *Hermanas*.

117. Grey, interview, August 12, 2007; Sister Barbara Jean LaRochester, a Carmelite nun (OCD), interview by author, June 4, 2015, telephone; and John C. Haughey, "Black Sisters Become Soul Sisters," *America*, August 2, 1969, 67.

118. Quoted in S. Harris, *Sisters*, 251.

119. Grey, interview, August 12, 2007.

120. White, interview.

121. White, interview; and Holloman, interview.

122. Sister Barbara Beasley, RGS, interview by author, July 24, 2015, telephone. See also chap. 4, note 142.

123. For two examples, see S. Harris, *Sisters*, 247–48; and "Black Bismarck, ND," *Jet*, May 9, 1968, 43.

124. Sister Mary Ann Henegan, Missionary Sister of the Most Blessed Trinity (MSBT), interview by author, October 29, 2016, telephone.

125. This is a common theme in my oral interviews with early Black sisters in white congregations and Black sisters who desegregated the faculties of traditionally white Catholic institutions, especially White, interview; Sister Sylvia Thibodeaux, SSF, interview by author, New Orleans, August 19, 2009; and Sister Jamie Phelps, OP, interview by author, New Orleans, July 22, 2009.

126. "Catholic Students Condemn Racism in American Life," *Chicago Daily Defender*, May 1, 1962, 11. Sister Jamie Phelps, OP, recalled that this happened to an Afro-Puerto Rican Adrian Dominican Sister in Chicago. It may be the same case. Phelps, interview.

127. "Catholic Students Condemn Racism," 11.

128. McNamara, *Sisters in Arms*, 598.

129. McNamara, *Sisters in Arms*, 598.

130. Billings, interview. See also Cora Marie Billings, "Saved by Grace," *America*, June 24, 2014.

131. Billings, interview.

132. LaRochester, interview; and "Adopted by Our Foundress and Cared for by Mother Lauretta Lubowidzka," sheet prepared by Sister Rebecca Sullivan, CSNF archivist, and emailed to author on September 26, 2016. Sister Mary Ann (Stella) Charleston, born in Chicago, entered the community in Rome, Italy, in 1898; served as a superior in France; and died in Rome in 1962. Sister Miriam (Alma) Mosley entered in 1916 and died in 1965. Sister Izmaela (Julia) Dorsey entered in 1914 and died in 1963.

133. Mother M. Getulia, CSFN, Provincial Superior, to Reverend Mother M. William [Hundley], OSP, March 27, 1965, in Congregation RG: box 103, folder 4, OSP Archives.

134. Mother M. Getulia to Mother M. William.

135. See Sister Mary Angela Wade, OSP, to Mother William [Hundley], March 15, 1965 and Sister Mary Angela Wade, OSP, to Rev. Mother Mary William [Hundley], OSP, July 8, 1965, in Congregation RG: box 103, folder 4, OSP Archives.

136. Quotes in "Direction, 65?," *Josephite Harvest*, November–December 1964, 20. See also "To Discuss Catholics and Race," *National Catholic Reporter*, November 4, 1964, 9.

137. Quoted in "Direction, 65?," 20.

4. "I Was Fired Up to Go to Selma"

1. For one scholarly examination of the Selma protests, see Garrow, *Protest at Selma*.

2. *Sisters of Selma*, 25:51 to 26:01. Ouellet is generally credited as being the only white Selma resident to support the local Black civil rights movement. See Murray, "'Most Righteous White Man.'"

3. Quoted in Sexuaer, "Well-Behaved Woman," 43.

4. Ebo, interview.

5. Quoted in Rev. Robert Reicher, "The Clergy Witness—How and Why?," *Community*, April 1967, 9.

6. Ebo, interview. See also *Sisters of Selma*, 26:08 to 26:56 and 50:09 to 50:19.

7. Ebo, interview. Ebo noted that she made this statement at Brown AME Chapel and to several reporters in Selma. See also Stepsis and Liptak, *Pioneer Healers*, 210.

8. *Sisters of Selma*, 29:09 to 29:40.

9. *Sisters of Selma*, 29:06 to 29:08.

10. Quoted in Edward B. Fiske, "Finding Identity, Black Nuns Put Soul into Religious Life," *New York Times*, August 15, 1971.

11. Massingale, *Racial Justice*, 53–55.

12. Massingale, *Racial Justice*, 55.

13. Poché, "Catholic Citizens' Council." See also R. Anderson, "Prelates,"; McGreevy, *Parish Boundaries*; and P. Jones, *Selma*.

14. Sexauer, "Well-Behaved Woman," 50.

15. See chapter 3; and Foley, "Adventures," 104–5.

16. King, *Why We Can't Wait*, 78; and "Survey Shows Pattern Varies in College Desegregation," *Southern School News*, December 1959, 1. See also Padgett, "'Without Hysteria,'" 180.

17. On this underresearched history, see Critchley-Mentor, "Jim Crow SJ," 26, 32–35. Like several white sisterhoods, the Jesuits admitted racially ambiguous African-descended men and Black men born outside of the United States in select US provinces long before they admitted US-born men who were visibly Black. The first African American admitted into the Jesuits in the Deep South entered the New Orleans Province in 1956, but he did not remain. Available oral history suggests that the Jesuits may have also utilized a racial quota system to keep their African American membership low. For example, the Jesuits in Missouri admitted Carle W. Shelton in 1946. However, Earline Greenfield reported that her cousin, Albert Xavier Vaughn, unsuccessfully applied for admission to the Jesuit province in Missouri from 1952 to the late 1980s. After Vaughn suffered a nervous breakdown owing to these rejections, a white Jesuit visited him at the hospital and confessed that white racism had blocked Vaughn's admittance. Vaughn was ordained a deacon in the Catholic Church in 1991. Greenfield, interview and Joseph A. Brown, SJ, interview by author, telephone and email, June 20, 2014.

18. Clarence J. Howard, SVD, "Progress in the Negro Apostolate in 1950: Great Strides on All Fronts," *St. Augustine Messenger*, January 1950, 4–7, 21. Before this, the Benedictine Sisters in Guthrie, Oklahoma operated Claver College, the first and only Catholic college for African Americans west of the Mississippi River. See Gillard, *Colored Catholics*, 192, 215.

19. NOAAMACH, *Celebration of Faith*, 32 and Lauren Beach, "Faith in Action: Tulsans Remember a School That Touched Their Lives," *Tulsa People*, December 19, 2013, https://www.tulsapeople.com/faith-in-action/article_38eb5848-767f-52e8-abb4-240dfoa39778.html.

20. Brett, *New Orleans Sisters*, 72.

21. See convent annals from Chicago, Minneapolis, and Detroit, Missions RG: boxes 15–18 and 41–42, and box 38, folders 6–7; and "Education for OSP Sisters" subgroup for Congregation RG: box 18, folders 13, 16, and box 19, folders 1–3, OSP Archives. See also *Oblates in Action*, Fall 1967, 2.

22. Fichter, "First Black Students," 548–49. Sometime between 1950 and 1953, a Sister of the Holy Family also desegregated Ursuline College, an unaccredited liberal arts institution, administered by the Ursulines in New Orleans. Newman, *Desegregating Dixie*, 27; and R. Anderson, *Black, White and Catholic*, 214n4. In 1959, Senegal became Loyola's second African American graduate and the first person of color to earn an undergraduate degree from the institution.

23. R. Anderson, *Black, White and Catholic*, 98–110.

24. Dr. Norman Francis, interview by author, September 11, 2009, telephone. A SSF member had also nurtured his brother, Joseph Abel Francis's, vocation to religious life. See Foley, *God's Men of Color*, 276.

25. N. Smith, interview by author.

26. "A Family Overtakes Christ," *Colored Harvest*, February 1951, 8–9.

27. "Negro Nuns Serve 1,000 Guests at Annual Fund-Raising Dinner," *New York Times*, May 28, 1962. The FHM also operated and staffed a day nursery, a community center for elderly women, and a summer camp for underprivileged girls in the New York archdiocese. "The FHM Mission Statement and a Chronology," ca. 2008, provided to the author by Sister Loretta Theresa Richards, former congregational leader of the Franciscan Handmaid of Mary.

28. Beito and Beito, *Black Maverick*, 45.

29. Rev. John W. Bowman, SVD, to Reverend Mother Teresa, OSP, June 4, 1953, Missions RG: box 43, folder 1, OSP Archives.

30. "Silver Jubilee: St. Gabriel's Church," program, December 15, 1974, copy in Missions RG: box 43, folder 1, OSP Archives; and Colbert, interview, June 23, 2014. Colbert noted that OSP members stationed in Mound Bayou also created a study booklet on voting to support the city's registration efforts. On Mound Bayou's relationship to the civil rights movement, see Beito and Beito, *Black Maverick*.

31. Council Minutes: 1956–1968, 16, 23, 74, Administration RG: box 45, folder 4, OSP Archives.

32. See Knecht, *Oblate Sisters of Providence*, 80.

33. "FHM Mission Statement and a Chronology."

34. Knecht, *Oblate Sisters of Providence*, 80–81.

35. Quoted in Clarence M. Zens, "Teacher Convention Stresses Better Racial Understanding," *N.C.W.C. News Service*, April 19, 1950, 2.

36. See example of Shirley Snead in chapter 3. In a Negro History Week talk delivered by Mother Marie Anselm Duffel in 1958, the SSF superior also references the vocations her order sent into "integrated communities." Copy contained in Duffel's Administration file, SSF Archives.

37. Council Minutes, 1959, 65, Administration RG: box 45, folder 4, OSP Archives. Details about Humphrey's background were gathered from her file in Congregation RG: box 56, folder 3, OSP Archives.

38. Humphrey remained until her death.

39. Linell Smith, "Ordered Lives: Oblate Sisters Serve God by Teaching Black Children," *Baltimore Sun*, February 20, 1944. The second white OSP member was Sister John Schilling.

40. Council Minutes, August 10, 1955, Administration RG: box 45, folder 3, OSP Archives. See also entries in the General Council Minutes, 1960, 98; and September 8, 1964, 172–74, Administration RG: box 45, folder 4, OSP Archives.

41. "Council Minutes for June 21, 1962, 125; and November 15, 1963, 169, Administration RG: box 45, folder 4, OSP Archives. Educated by the Mission Helper Sisters as a child in Trenton, New Jersey, White entered the OSP order in 1934 after suffering a racist rejection from a white Franciscan community one year earlier. In 1961, a white Dominican priest concluded that White had a contemplative vocation, and over the next two years, White with the support of her superiors "wrote to every Carmelite cloister in the U.S. and three in Canada." After enduring rejections from each community, White "began trying other

contemplative orders," to no avail. In 1963, the contemplative Franciscans in Cleveland, Ohio admitted White stating that they were willing to "try" her vocation. See "My Poustinia, August 11–September 11, 1973," 3–4, in Congregation RG: box 103, folder 1 OSP Archives.

42. Quoted in Lindblad, "Sister Joyce Williams," 6.

43. For more on the history of lynchings in Minnesota, see Bessler, *Legacy of Violence*.

44. White, interview.

45. White, interview.

46. White, interview.

47. Smith and Feister, *Thea's Song*, xv, xvi, 42–43, 64–65. Bowman desegregated the order's Saint Rose High School in 1953 and the order in 1956 and was the first Black patient treated at River Pines Sanitorium in Stevens Point, Wisconsin, in 1955.

48. Smith and Feister, *Thea's Song*, 9.

49. Smith and Feister, *Thea's Song*, 28–29.

50. *Sr. Thea: Her Own Story*.

51. Dr. Patricia Grey, "Personal and Unfinished," National Black Sisters' Conference 50th-Anniversary Address given on July 30, 2018, in New Orleans, typescript, 15–16, copy in author's possession.

52. For more on the "Till generation," young African American activists radicalized by Till's lynching and the acquittal of his murders, see C. Payne, *I've Got the Light*, 54.

53. Grey, interview, June 21, 2009.

54. S. Harris, *Sisters*, 245.

55. NOAAMACH, *Celebration of Faith*, 32.

56. Sister Doris Goudeaux, SSF, interview by author, New Orleans, August 18, 2009.

57. See "The Josephite Fathers Make an Appeal to Catholics!," January 1961 (date handwritten on the copy), 3; and "The Sisters of the Blessed Sacrament Issue a Call to Catholic New Orleans," *Catholic Action: Official Organ of the Archdiocese of New Orleans*, February 12, 1961, 13, in "Catholic Action" Folder, Xavier University of Louisiana Archives. The SBS's statement was also published in the *Times-Picayune*, the *New Orleans States-Item*, and the *Louisiana Weekly*.

58. "Sisters of the Blessed Sacrament Issue a Call." Writer John Steinbeck famously described the "demented cruelty" of the white housewives and mothers who protested the four African American girls who desegregated New Orleans's public elementary schools in 1960 as "a kind of frightening witches' Sabbath." See Brückmann, *Massive Resistance*, 90–91.

59. Jed Lipinski, "When Freedom Rang; How Norman Francis Made Xavier a Shelter from a Storm of Violence in 1961," *Times-Picayune*, July 5, 2015.

60. White opponents to desegregation issued several bomb threats to the administrators of Catholic schools scheduled to integrate in 1962 and eventually bombed Our Lady of Good Harbor Parochial School, an integrated Catholic school, in 1963. See "Blast Severely Damages Buras Parochial School," *Times-Picayune*, August 28, 1963, 1, 12. Although also subject to racial segregation laws, many in Louisiana's Afro-Creole population had long maintained an identity separate from both white and Black people and

retained certain privileges in the state's social structure. In 1962, Afro-Creoles in Buras, Louisiana, protested the admission of "Negro" children into their separate parish school after Our Lady of Good Harbor Church closed its school owing to threats of violence. See Newman, *Desegregating Dixie*, 171–78.

61. "New Orleans Street Scene," *New York Times*, April 24, 1962.

62. "3 Racists Excommunicated by Louisiana Archbishop: Perez, Mrs. Gaillot, and Ricau Ousted for Opposing School Integration—Vatican Voices Support," *New York Times*, April 17, 1962. See also Henry A. Cabirac to C. Ellis Henican, July 18, 1963, Catholic Council on Human Relations of the Archdiocese of New Orleans Records, 1961–64, box 1, Tulane Amistad Research Center, New Orleans. In this letter, Cabirac, the council's executive director, responds to recent statements made by white Catholic segregationist leader Una Gaillot on the "station WWOM" in which she opposed calls for local white businessmen to employ "negros" [*sic*] outside of a menial capacity when the archdiocese of New Orleans did not. Subsequent documents in this folder include council proposals to induce local Catholic leaders to hire Black workers in Catholic construction projects and in non-menial jobs.

63. Typed notes detailing this episode and dated 1959 are contained in Mother Marie Anselm Duffel's Administration File, SSF Archives.

64. "Mother Marie Anselm to Dear and Reverend Fathers," August 13, 1959, Duffel Administration File, SSF Archives.

65. McCarthy, *Catholic Tradition*, 62–64.

66. O'Malley, *Tradition and Transition*, 17. See Abbott, *Documents of Vatican II*.

67. For an English translation of "Pacem in terris," see John XXIII, "Pacem in terris," April 11, 1963, Vatican, accessed August 23, 2021, https://www.vatican.va/content/john -xxiii/en/encyclicals/documents/hf_j-xxiii_enc_11041963_pacem.html.

68. "De Porres Canonization Victory of Church over Bigotry, Negro Nun Says," *Catholic Standard and Times*, June 15, 1862. See also "Catholics' Silence Is Seen Aiding Racial Injustice," *Catholic Transcript*, June 28, 1962; and "Nun Warns of 'Creeping Fog,'" *Catholic Transcript*, October 22, 1964.

69. K. Harris, "Missa Luba," 1–2.

70. For one example, see "Not Even Religious Garb Can Protect: Negro Nun Tells of Heartaches, Frustration Caused by Prejudice," *Catholic Standard and Times*, August 7, 1964.

71. For more on this protest, see Hoy, *Good Hearts*, 139–42.

72. Sister Patricia Haley, SCN, interview by author, March 30, 2012, telephone. See also Kelly McDaniels, "Sister Patricia Haley: An Interview," Sisters of Charity of Nazareth, November 28, 2018, https://scnfamily.org/sister-patricia-haley-an-interview/.

73. Quoted in Hiley H. Ward, "Negro Nuns Criticize Books," *Detroit Free Press*, February 9, 1963.

74. MacGregor, *Emergence*, 342–44. Former OSP member Josita Colbert remembered that OSP members stationed in Washington, DC, participated in the march. March participants from St. Augustine also confirmed OSP participation decades later. Colbert, interview by author, June 23, 2014; and Mark Zimmermann, "'It Was Like a Homecoming, Everybody Coming Together,'" *Catholic Standard*, August 14, 2013.

75. Annal entry for Wednesday, August 28, 1963, Motherhouse RG: box 44, OSP Archives.

76. "Negro Nun Named Mother General," *Catholic Transcript*, November 5, 1964, 8.

77. See "Frances M. Douglass," typed biography, Daughters of the Heart of Mary Archives.

78. "Negro Is Appointed DePaul Unit Chief," *Chicago Sun-Times*, September 13, 1956.

79. Rev. John G. Barnett, SSJ, "The March on Washington," *Josephite Harvest*, September–October 1963, 16–17. See also "God's People on the March," *Josephite Harvest*, January–February 1964, 12–13.

80. Koehlinger, *New Nuns*, 75, 78.

81. See Sister Barbara Moore, CSJ, interview by author, April 30, 2007, telephone. Moore's name in religion was Ann Benedict. She reverted to her baptismal name after Vatican II.

82. "Remembering Selma 50 Years Later," KSDK *News*, March 9, 2015, accessed on August 20, 2020, https://www.ksdk.com/article/news/local/stltogether/remembering -selma-50-years-later/63-211103274. The video of Sister Moore referencing the ride from the airport and armed white men who came out on their porches is no longer available online.

83. Quote is from *Sisters of Selma*, 37:11.

84. Philip Benjamin, "15,000 March through Harlem to Protest the Racial Strife in Selma," *New York Times*, March 15, 1965.

85. Photos of the FHM marching are included in the New York *Amsterdam News*, March 20, 1965, box 61, folder 4, Catholic Interracial Council of New York Collection, CUA Archives.

86. "FHM Mission Statement and a Chronology."

87. Mary Bertha Alexander (formerly Sister Mary Concepta, FHM) and Barbara Ann Johnson (formerly Sister Jacinta Marie, FHM), joint interview by author, New York, June 8, 2017. Both Alexander and Johnson later married and assumed their husband's surnames.

88. "'Osservatore' Deplores Selma Conflict," *Pittsburgh Catholic*, March 18, 1965.

89. Grey, interview, August 12, 2007.

90. "Two Sisters Leave for Selma," photograph in Congregation RG: box 49, folder 2, OSP Archives.

91. Annal Entry, March 25, 1965, Motherhouse RG: box 44, OSP Archives.

92. Handwritten notes from Sister M. Virginie Fish, OSP, interview by author, Baltimore, MD, March 11, 2010. Fish said this before the recording began.

93. See Holy Name Convent Annals beginning February 1965, Mission RG: box 17, folder 3, OSP Archives.

94. Council Minutes: 1903–1932, Administration RG: box 44, folder 5, OSP Archives.

95. "Selma, Alabama: Typed Transcript of Father Maurice Ouellet Speech to UAS at St. Joseph School, Chicago," April 5, 1965, Mary Benet Papers, folder 4/01: [UAS] Urban Apostolate '63–65, University of Notre Dame Archives (UND Archives).

96. "Selma, Alabama: Typed Transcript," 2, 3.

97. "Selma, Alabama: Typed Transcript," 4. The underlined text has been preserved from this transcript.

98. Holy Name of Mary Convent Annals, Wednesday, April 7, 1965, Mission RG: box 17, folder 3, OSP Archives.

99. This letter is cited in Sexauer, "Well-Behaved Woman," 50.

100. Very Rev. Maurice F. Ouellet, SSE, to Rev. Mother William, OSP, April 21, 1965, Administration RG: box 10, folder 9, OSP Archives.

101. Colbert, interview, June 23, 2014. See also Very Rev. Matthew J. O'Rourke, SSJ, "Dramatizing a Need: Open Housing," *Josephite Harvest*, November–December 1965, 8. On November 6, 1965, two Oblates participated an opening housing march through downtown Baltimore organized by the city's Federation of Civil Rights Organizations. In both instances, the members who participated in these campaigns were lightly reprimanded by their superiors.

102. Koehlinger, *New Nuns*, 53.

103. Traxler, "After Selma Sister," 17.

104. On this phenomenon, see Borromeo, *Changing Sister*; and Traxler, *New Works*.

105. Becker, "Operation Mississippi," 69–70.

106. See curriculum vitae and biography in Sister Mary Julian Griffin VSC, file, DS.

107. Koehlinger, *New Nuns*, 80.

108. Koehlinger, *New Nuns*, 85.

109. Koehlinger, *New Nuns*, 63.

110. Koehlinger, *New Nuns*, 15, 17, 64–123, 176–225.

111. Koehlinger, *New Nuns*, 47.

112. Knecht, *Oblate Sisters of Providence*, 31; "Administration of the Reverend Mother Marie Anselm, June 17, 1958–June 17, 1970," 3, SSF Archives; and P. Lucas, "Diary of Change," 176.

113. Rev. Mother Marie Anselm, SSF, "New Dimensions for New Demands," *Divine Word Messenger*, March 1968, 59–62.

114. "Outline of Michigan Missions and Dates," n.d., Missions RG: subgroup 9, OSP Archives. See also "Three Rivers," *Oblates in Action: Newsletter*, Fall 1967, 1.

115. "Sister M. Virginie" and "Sister Concepta Marie," *Oblates in Action: Newsletter*, Fall 1967, 1.

116. "Sister M. Monica," *Oblates in Action: Newsletter*, Fall 1967, 1.

117. "Administration of the Reverend Mother Marie Anselm," 3.

118. "News Release," March 30, 1967 Faculty Exchange Program File, SCSH Archives. See also "Administration of the Reverend Mother Marie Anselm," 3.

119. Sister Louise Grundish, SCSH archivist, email message to author, April 30, 2018.

120. Bill McClinton, "Five Negro Nuns Serving Here in a Unique Teacher Exchange," *Pittsburgh Catholic*, January 12, 1968, 1.

121. Anselm, "New Dimensions," 61.

122. Anselm, "New Dimensions," 61.

123. "Scholarly Sister," *Jet*, June 24, 1965, 27. See also "Administration of the Reverend Mother Marie Anselm," 4; and Mrs. Roger L. (Caroline) Putnam to Most Reverend William G. Connare, August 10, 1965, SCSH Archives.

124. See also "Administration of the Reverend Mother Marie Anselm," 4; and "Mary Lovinia [*sic*] Deconge-Watson," in Warren, *Black Women Scientists*, 82–83. In 1943, Euphemia Lofton Haynes, an African American Catholic laywoman, educator, and civil rights activist, became the first Black woman to earn a PhD in mathematics. Haynes earned her doctorate from the Catholic University of America. See Kelly, Shinners, and Zoroufy, "Euphemia Lofton Haynes."

125. Chineworth, interview. See also Baptiste, "Study of the Foundation," 56. A faculty list from Mount Providence Junior College notes that Sister Mary Josephita Larrea Melgares, OSP, held a PhD in Spanish from the University of Havana, earned in 1960.

126. "Negro Catholic School to Open," *New York Times*, September 6, 1966. See also Knecht, *Oblate Sisters of Providence*, 113. From 1959 to 1967, the SSF operated Delisle Junior College as a part of the order's juniorate and formation program. This institution, open only to SSF members and aspirants, was accredited by the Catholic University of America. Brett, *New Orleans Sisters*, 72–73.

127. Archdiocese of Milwaukee, "Milestones in Black Catholic History: 'Our Story,'" n.d., accessed July 22, 2021, http://www.archmil.org/ArchMil/Resources/Milestones inBlackCatholicHistory07.pdf. See also Burroughs, "Being Black Isn't All That Makes This Nun Stand Out," *Hyde Park Herald*, October 14, 1987; and "Deaths: Sister Mary Reginalda Polk, School Principal," *Milwaukee Journal*, January 13, 1990.

128. Stepsis and Liptak, *Pioneer Healers*, 210. In 1968, Ebo stated that this appointment may have resulted from her growing complaints about the rising rates of Black infant mortality rate in St. Louis, which she attributed partially to the transition of her order's St. Mary's Infirmary "from a general hospital for Negroes to a center for alcoholics" during the era of desegregation. Ebo was making plans to create a mobile unit from the formerly all-white St. Mary's Hospital that would serve in the city's highest impacted areas when she was sent to Wisconsin. See Sister Mary Antona Ebo, "Contemporary Opportunities and Limitations of the Black Sister in a White Community to Promote Racial Solidarity," n.p., n.d., but August 20, 1968, typed transcript, NBSC series 5, box 4, folder 1, MUSCA.

129. Smith and Feister, *Thea's Song*, 99–103.

130. Donald Janson, "Clergymen Join Wisconsin March," *New York Times*, September 17, 1967. On Catholic engagement with the Black freedom movement in Milwaukee, see P. Jones, *Selma of the North*.

131. Ebo, "Contemporary Opportunities and Limitations."

132. Ebo, interview. See also Ebo, "Contemporary Opportunities and Limitations." Charges of white paternalism and racism plagued the NCCIJ through the 1960s and 1970s. See K. Johnson, *One in Christ*, 218–27.

133. Quoted in Lindblad, "Sister Joyce Williams," 9.

134. Biography, Sister Mary Julian Griffin, VSC File, DS.

135. On the racist caricatures of African Americans, see Bogle, *Toms*, 29–88.

136. Saundra Willingham, "Why I Quit the Convent," *Ebony*, December 1968, 65.

137. Willingham, "Why I Quit," 68.

138. Willingham, "Why I Quit," 74.

139. Willingham, interview. A young white boy turned a water hose on Willingham while she was participating in the DES-sponsored Summer in Suburbia program,

conducting a door-to-door race-relations survey in an all-white Catholic neighborhood with a group of white sisters. The incident is also reported in Albin A. Gorisek, "Nun's Story Is Study of Racial Split," *Plain Dealer* (Cleveland, OH), March 9, 1969.

140. Willingham, "Why I Quit," 68, 72.

141. Cited in Branch, *At Canaan's Edge*, 705–6.

142. Sister Mary Schultz, Home Visitor of Mary (HVM), to Mother M. Omer and the Conference of Major Superiors of Women Executive Committee, February 13, 1968, Leadership Conference of Women Religious Papers, box 31, folder 33, University of Notre Dame Archives.

143. Sister Mary Schultz, HVM, to Mother M. Omer and the Conference of Major Superiors of Women Executive Committee.

5. "Liberation Is Our First Priority"

1. "Nun Helps Her People in Ghetto: Only American Negro in Order," *Plain Dealer*, April 26, 1969.

2. Lindblad, "Sister Joyce Williams," 7. Joyce is Williams's baptismal name. She did not take a religious name. Before Vatican II, she was known as Sister Mary Joyce.

3. Lindblad, "Sister Joyce Williams," 7–11.

4. Lindblad, "Sister Joyce Williams," 7.

5. "Nun Helps Her People," 3-B. See also Berg, "Sisters," 5.

6. Quoted in "Nun Helps Her People," 3-B; and Berg, "Sisters," 5.

7. "Nun Helps Her People," 3-B.

8. "The Survival of Soul: National Black Sisters' Conference Position Paper" in National Black Sisters' Conference, *Black Survival*, 156.

9. Quoted in Smith and Feister, *Thea's Song*, 103.

10. Sister Teresita Weind, "A Black Nun Thinks Black," *America*, September 21, 1968, 214.

11. Weind, "Black Nun," 215.

12. "Racism: Will We Ever Overcome?"

13. Holy Name of Mary Convent Annals, April 4–5 and April 9, 1968, Missions RG: box 18, folder 1, OSP Archives. See also C. Davis, *History of Black Catholics*, 257; and "Negroes Criticize Daley Order to Shoot Arsonists," *New York Times*, April 17, 1968. Young white athletic clubs, largely Catholic, and their informal policing of urban spaces were cited as leading causes of the Chicago Race Massacre of 1919. Daley was then a member of the Hamburg Social and Athletic Club, which was at the center of much of the violence; he later served as the president of the club. See Royko, *Boss*, 31; and Chicago Commission on Race Relations, *Negro in Chicago*, 12–17, 42.

14. MacGregor, *Emergence*, 358.

15. St. Joseph School and Convent Annals, April 7, 1968, Missions RG: box 1, folder 5, OSP Archives. As a part of a delegation of local activists, M. Loyola Holley also met with the mayor of Mobile, Alabama, and two city commissioners on April 15, 1968, to discuss ways to combat discrimination against Black citizens in employment, housing, education, and media coverage, especially in wake of the Mobile *Press-Register*'s offensive reporting on King's assassination. See Sister Marilyn Keen, SL, Sister Susan

Ardoyno, SL, Sister M. Loyola Holley, OSP, Sister August Reilly, RSM, and Sister Danita Wren, OP, to Sisters, April 24, 1968, Missions RG: box 1, folder 7, OSP Archives.

16. See "Eight Holy Family Sisters Participate in Final Rites for Dr. Martin Luther King, Jr.," *Contact: Holy Family Newsletter*, May 22, 1968.

17. Sister Mary Deborah Johnson, OSP, "The Plea of a Negro Sister: 'Give Testimony to the Gospel,'" *Catholic Review*, ca. May 1968, in Congregation RG: box 91, folder 8, OSP Archives.

18. Glapion, *Seeing the Face*, 14. Glapion is Floyd's married name.

19. Rosaria Floyd Glapion (formerly Sister Mary Florence, FSP), interview by author, August 18, 2015, telephone. Floyd later married and assumed her husband's surname.

20. Adams, interview.

21. For a classic examination of the Tulsa massacre, see Ellsworth, *Death*.

22. Phyllis Coons, "Parochial School Run as Community Enterprise Is Success," *Boston Globe*, May 20, 1973; and Cynthia Bellamy, "Black Sister with Mission," *Boston Globe*, July 27, 1974.

23. Thibodeaux, interview, August 19, 2009. See also Arthur Jones, "Holy Family Mission: Local Schools, Africa and Belize," *National Catholic Reporter*, March 5, 1999, 1.

24. Thibodeaux, interview, August 19, 2009.

25. Thibodeaux, interview, August 19, 2009.

26. Grey, interview, August 12, 2007.

27. Grey, interview, August 12, 2007.

28. Grey, interview, August 12, 2007. See also Sister M. Martin de Porres Grey, RSM, "Action, Discernment, and Response to the Spirit," ca. 1969, series 2, box 2, folder 4, National Black Sisters' Conference (NBSC) President Papers, Marquette University Special Collections and University Archives (MUSCA), Milwaukee, WI; and Rosemary Gemperle, interview by author, South Bend, IN, August 1, 2010. Gemperle is Carroll's niece. As president of Mount Mercy, Carroll defended the college's decision to permit Bayard Rustin, organizer of the 1963 March on Washington, to deliver a lecture in the face of white backlash. A news clipping in the author's possession, "For Doubting Opponents," n.p., n.d., recounts the episode Gemperle described.

29. Grey, interview, August 12, 2007.

30. Grey, interviews, August 12, 2007, and August 25, 2019.

31. See C. Davis, *History of Black Catholics*, 257.

32. Richard Philbrick, "U.S. Negro Priests Set First Meeting," *Chicago Tribune*, April 3, 1968. In February 1968, Black Episcopalians formed the Union of Black Clergymen and Laymen of the Episcopal Church. The Methodists named their group Black Methodists for Church Renewal.

33. Philbrick, "U.S. Negro Priests." See also C. Davis, *History of Black Catholics*, 257.

34. "St. Rita's Catholic Church Conducts Holy Week Revival: Rev. Fr. John N. Labauve, SVD," *Indianapolis Recorder*, March 21, 1964. See also Grey, interview, August 12, 2007.

35. Grey, interview, August 12, 2007.

36. Grey, interview, August 12, 2007. See also J. Davis and C. Rowe, "National Office for Black Catholics," 269. In Davis and Rowe's article, Davis omits his and Grey's initial rejection from the Detroit meeting in 1968.

37. Rev. Lawrence E. Lucas, "Ejection of Whites from Black Sisters' Conference," ca. August 1968, but unpublished, series 2.1, box 1, folder 18, NBSC Papers, MUSCA. This name of the author of this unpublished source is partially cut off, but Lucas's authorship seems clear.

38. Grey, interviews, August 12, 2007, and August 25, 2019.

39. "Negro Priests Assail Catholic Church as Racist," *New York Times*, April 19, 1968.

40. Grey, interview, August 12, 2007.

41. Quoted in S. Harris, *Sisters*, 255.

42. Grey, interview, August 12, 2007. See also Grey, "Action, Discernment." In the case of George Clements, who in 2019 was credibly accused of abusing a minor at Chicago's Holy Angels Catholic Church in 1974, Clements noted in a 2012 interview with scholar Matthew Cressler that he "definitely wanted to become a monsignor and . . . eventually . . . an auxiliary bishop" before becoming active in the Black Catholic movement. Clements, who later adopted four African American boys, specifically characterized his former self as a "clergy prostitute." Quoted in Cressler, *Authentically Black*, 116, 223n1–2. See also David Struett and Sam Charles, "Retired Celebrity Priest George Clements Accused of Sex Abuse in 1970s," *Chicago Sun-Times*, August 8, 2019, https://chicago.suntimes.com/2019/8/8/20794180/retired-priest-george-clements-accused-sex-abuse-1970s.

43. Grey, interview, August 25, 2019.

44. "Black Nuns Schedule Pittsburgh Caucus," 2.

45. "Black Nuns Schedule Pittsburgh Caucus," 2. See also Grey, interview, August 12, 2007.

46. Quoted in "Black Nuns Schedule Pittsburgh Caucus," 2.

47. Quoted in "Black Nuns Schedule Pittsburgh Caucus," 2.

48. Mary Lou Berger, "Denies Black Nuns' Meeting a 'Caucus,'" *Pittsburgh Catholic*, July 26, 1968.

49. Grey, "Follow-Up Letter."

50. Grey, "Follow-Up Letter."

51. Grey, interview, August 12, 2007. See also Haughey, "Black Sisters Become Soul Sisters," 67; Bryan, "*History*," 6; and S. Harris, *Sisters*, 252–53.

52. Haughey, "Black Sisters Become Soul Sisters," 67.

53. M. Mary Florence to Sister M. Martin de Porres, RSM, June 21, 1968, NBSC President Correspondence, 1968, series 2, box 1, folder 1, NBSC Papers, MUSCA.

54. Sister Mary Daniel, SNDdeN, to Sister M. Martin de Porres, RSM, June 26, 1968, NBSC President Correspondence, 1968, series 2, box 1, MUSCA.

55. Sister M. Catalina to Sister M. Martin de Porres, June 21, 1968, NBSC President Correspondence, series 2, box 1, MUSCA.

56. Sister Eulalia to Sister M. Martin de Porres, R.S.M., July 1, 1968, and Mother Mary Helena Barnes, S.H.C.J. to Sister M. Martin de Porres, R.S.M., July 8, 1968, NBSC President Correspondence, series 2, box 1, MUSCA.

57. Coleman, interview.

58. "Negro Nuns in the U.S.A.," *Divine Word Messenger*, June 1962, 184–85.

59. Alexander and Johnson, joint interview.

60. "Necrology of Mother Miriam Cecelia Cormier," n.d., from Sister Loretta Theresa Richards. See also Lucas, "Diary of Change," 176.

61. P. Lucas, "Diary of Change," 176.

62. Sister Loretta Theresa Richards, FHM, interview by author, New York, December 28, 2009.

63. Barial, interview and Thibodeaux, interviews, August 19, 2009, and August 4, 2016.

64. Goudeaux, interview; and Barial, interview. See also Fr. James F. LaChapelle, SVD, to Sister M. Martin de Porres, July 1, 1968; Edwin Cabey to Sister M. Martin de Porres, July 8 and 22, 1968; Richard F. Wagner, SSJ, to Sister Martin de Porres, July 8 and 15, 1968; and Mother Marie Anselm, SSF, to Sister Martin de Porres, RSM, June 25, 1968, NBSC President Correspondence, series 2, box 1, folders 12, MUSCA.

65. Grey, interview, August 12, 2007. See also Sister M. Martin de Porres Grey's curriculum vita and itineraries, series 2, box 2, folders 2–3; and Grey's program for "The Changing Negro Mood" workshop, series 6, box 4, folder 8, NBSC Papers, MUSCA.

66. Grey, interview, August 12, 2007. See also Koehlinger, New Nuns, 80, 100; and James R. Sena, "'Nun Power'—New Course Charted," National Register, July 21, 1968, n.p., copy in NBSC President's Correspondence, series 2, box 1, MUSCA.

67. See chapter 4.

68. Grey, interview, August 12, 2007.

69. Sena, "'Nun Power.'"

70. Sena, "'Nun Power.'" Traxler specifically called the audience's sympathetic reaction to Grey's comments "odd."

71. Sister M. Martin de Porres, RSM, to Editors of the Denver Catholic Register, July 23, 1968, NBSC President's Correspondence, series 2, box 1, MUSCA.

72. Sister Mary Peter Traxler, SSND, to Editor, Denver Catholic Register, July 22, 1968, NBSC President's Correspondence, series 2, box 1, MUSCA. It remains unclear if the quote misrepresenting Grey's comments came from Traxler. However, the reporter, James Sena, did not attend the conference, and Traxler "passed on" to Sena all the other quotes from the conference's sister speakers contained in the article.

73. Sister Christina Marie, "RSM Memo Re: July 21 Article Denver Register," July 24, 1968; Sister Stella Maria, SBS, to Sister Martin de Porres, July 22, 1968; and Mother M. Claudia to Sister M. Martin de Porres, RSM, August 5, 1968, NBSC President's Correspondence, series 2, box 1, MUSCA.

74. Sister Anita Baird, DHM, interview by author, July 24, 2016, and March 3, 2017, telephone. Baird had a brief tenure in the SBS in the 1960s.

75. Quoted in Bryan, "History," 5.

76. Quoted in Bryan, "History," 5.

77. Copeland, "Cadre," 129. Though Copeland states that 155 sisters attended the first NBSC meeting, other sources, including the first membership directory, suggest as many as 168 sisters attended the conference.

78. "1968 NBSC Directory," series 6, box 1, folder 8, NBSC Papers, MUSCA.

79. Mary Lou Berger, "Most of Meetings Limited to Blacks," Pittsburgh Catholic, August 23, 1968. Also "Conference Highlights," ca. September 1968, and "Negro Nuns Hold National Conference: Whites Are Ejected; Speaker Urges Strength in Unity,"

St. Louis Review, ca. early September 1968, in personal collection of Sister Mary Antona Ebo.

80. Lucas, "Ejection of Whites." See also *Crux of the News*, June 24, 1968, copy in NBSC Newspaper Clippings File, MUSCA.

81. "Most of Meetings Limited to Blacks"; and "Negro Nuns Hold National Conference," 10.

82. Lucas, "Ejection of Whites." See also "Conference Highlights"; and "First National Black Sisters' Conference, August 17–24, 1968," program, NBSC Papers, series 5, box 1, folder, 1, MUSCA.

83. Mary Lou Berger, "Black Nuns Ponder Their Responsibilities," *Pittsburgh Catholic*, August 23, 1968, 3.

84. Grey, interview, August 12, 2007.

85. "Promoting the Black Sister's Voice," *Crosswinds*, November 1968, copy in NBSC Newspaper Clippings File, MUSCA.

86. "Promoting the Black Sister's Voice."

87. Reactors to 'The Contemporary Opportunities and Limitations of the Black Sister in a White Community to Promote Racial Solidarity"; NBSC series 5, box 4, folder 1, MUSCA.

88. Lucas, "Ejection of Whites."

89. "First National Black Sisters' Conference: Projected Membership," program, August 17–24, 1968, NBSC series 5, box 1, folder 7, MUSCA; and Ebo, interview.

90. Grey, interview, August 12, 2007. See also S. Harris, *Sisters*, 256; and Bryan, *All along the Way*, 102–6.

91. Thibodeaux, interview, August 19, 2009. See also Sister Sylvia Thibodeaux to S. M. Martin de Porres Grey, RSM, ca. February 20, 1969, NBSC President's Correspondence, series 2, box 1, MUSCA.

92. Richards, interview.

93. Richards, interview.

94. Grey, interview, August 12, 2007; and Colbert, interview, June 23, 2014.

95. Bryan, "History," 5.

96. Ebo, interview. See also handwritten notes titled "Black Sisters Conference, Small Group Discussions, 8-20-1968," NBSC series 5, box 4, folder 1, MUSCA.

97. NBSC press release, August 26, 1968, personal collection of Sister Mary Antona Ebo.

98. NBSC press release.

99. Quoted in "Promoting the Black Sisters' Voice," 81.

100. A video clip of Burns stating this is included in *The Way We Were: NBSC 50th Anniversary Commemorative Video*, independently produced by Valerie Shields, 2018. This video was distributed to attendees at the NBSC's fiftieth anniversary celebration in New Orleans, held from July 30 to August 2, 2018.

101. "An Awakening of Black Nun Power: Catholic Sisters Caucus at Pittsburgh Confab," *Ebony*, October 1968, 44–48. See also typed transcript of talk by Johnny Clark on "Thursday Panel," n.d., but August 22, 1968, NBSC Papers, series 5, box 4, folder 1 MUSCA.

102. Sister Deborah Johnson, OSP, "The Contemporary Opportunities and Limitations of the Black Sister in a Black Community to Promote Racial Solidarity," August 20, 1968, typed transcript, NBSC series, 5, box 4, folder 1, MUSCA.

103. Grey, interview, August 12, 2007, and Colbert, interview, June 23, 2014. These are Grey's and Colbert's recollections, not their personal feelings.

104. See handwritten notes titled "Black Sisters Conference, Small Group Discussions, 8-20-1968"; Ebo, "Contemporary Opportunities and Limitations of the Black Sister in a White Community to Promote Racial Solidarity"; and "Reactors to 'The Contemporary Opportunities and Limitations of the Black Sister in a White Community to Promote Racial Solidarity,'" August 20, 1968, NBSC series 5, box 4, folder 1, MUSCA. See also Anthony Calypso, "The Real 'Sister Act': Black Nuns in America," *Grio*, August 26, 2009.

105. Grey, interview, August 12, 2007. Again, these are Grey's recollection, not her personal feeling. This is also confirmed in several Black sisters' testimonies.

106. "Reactors to 'The Contemporary Opportunities and Limitations of the Black Sisters in a White Community to Promote Racial Solidarity' Panel." See also Lindblad, "Sister Joyce Williams."

107. Sister M. Veronica to Sister [M.] Martin [de Porres], January 27, 1969, NBSC President's Correspondence, series 2, box 1, MUSCA. Sister M. Veronica's surname was obtained from the NBSC Members' Directory.

108. Quoted in "A Nun Probes Negro's Needs: Avila Nursing Instructor Tells of Black Sisters' Meeting: Talk at Home-Coming," *Kansas City Times*, October 7, 1968, copy in NBSC Papers, MUSCA. See also "Negro Nun's View: White Racism Caused Black Power," copy, n.d., NBSC Papers, MUSCA.

109. Quoted in "Nun Says: 'I Really Believe in Black Front,'" *Afro-American* (Washington, DC), December 12, 1968, n.p., copy in NBSC Papers, MUSCA.

110. "Black Boycott in Alabama: Project Blackout," *Signs of Soul*, December 1969, 3.

111. R. Williams, "Black Women, Urban Politics," 86. The SOUL (Society of United Liberators Inc.) School was founded by the Baltimore chapter of the Congress of Racial Equality in 1966. See also Al Rutledge, "Militant Nun Leaves Convent," *Afro-American* (Baltimore), February 1, 1969.

112. "Negro Nun among 23 Arrested at Sit-In," *Anchor* (Diocese of Fall River, MA), May 29, 1969.

113. Sister Mary Kimberley Clark, RSM, to Sister Re: The Detroit Archdiocesan Black Sisters' Committee, September 10, 1968, NBSC series 6, box 3, folder 10, MUSCA; "Black Sisters Convene," *Mercy Detroiter*, October 1968, 1; and Reverend Kimberley Edmond (formerly Sister Mary Kimberley Clark, RSM), interview by author, November 20, 2015, telephone. Clark was the first African American accepted into the RSM in Detroit. The only other Black person to enter in Michigan did so in 2000. Like Edmond, this candidate did not remain.

114. "Community Unites against 'Stress,' Detroit's New Kill Squad," *Black Panther*, October 9, 1971, 7; and Sister Elizabeth Harris, HVM, interview by author, July 14, 2014, telephone. The STRESS unit operated from 1971 to 1974. In its three-and-a-half-year existence, it killed twenty-four men, twenty-two of whom were African American, before

Black protest forced its dismantling. On STRESS, see H. Thompson, *Whose Detroit*, 81–204.

115. Sister Anita Robinson, OSB, to Sister M. Martin de Porres, January 6, 1969, NBSC President's Correspondence, series 2, box 1, NBSC Papers, MUSCA.

116. Typed transcript of address by "Miss Saundra Willingham" at the first NBSC Meeting, n.d., but August 20, 1968, series 5, box, 1, folder 4, NBSC Papers, MUSCA.

117. Sister Anna [Cox], SBS, "The Black Candidate," 43. Date of Cox's entrance and last name from SBS archivist, email message to author, September 26, 2011. See also "Sister Anna Cox," *Des Moines Register*, February 2, 1975.

118. Grey, interview, August 12, 2007. See also handwritten "NBSC Steering Committee Minutes, August 24, 1968"; and handwritten notes titled "Black Sisters Conference, Small Group Discussions, 8-20-1968," NBSC series 5, box 4, folder 1, MUSCA.

119. Grey, interview, August 25, 2019; and Copeland, interview. See also Lucas, "Ejection of Whites"; and handwritten "NBSC Steering Committee Minutes, August 24, 1968."

120. Quoted in "Black Sister Says Racism Is a White, Not Black Problem," *Catholic Transcript*, April 18, 1969.

121. Grey, interview, March 22, 2010. These conversations continued after the 1968 meeting. See also S. Harris, *Sisters*, 258–66; and H. Christian, "Psychological Implications," 81.

122. Emery, "Experiment," 43–44.

123. See also Thibodeaux, *Black Nun*, 70.

124. Quoted in "Anyone for Africa?" *Signs of Soul*, December 1969, 3.

125. Sister Jayne Marie Simon, "Black Contemplative," *Contemplative Review*, August 1969, 8.

126. NBSC to "Our Black Sisters in Christ," August 25, 1968, Administration RG: box 12, folder 2, OSP Archives.

127. "Black Is Beautiful: An Open Forum on Black Power: Given by Oblates for Oblates," packet, Administration RG: box 12, folder 2, OSP Archives.

128. Johnson, Purcell and Richards, interviews.

129. Johnson, interview.

130. P. Lucas, "Diary of Change," 176–77. Sister Patricia Lucas, Daughter of the Heart of Mary (formerly Sister Mary Immanuel, FHM), March 22, 2010, telephone.

131. Johnson, interview.

132. Handwritten "NBSC Steering Committee Minutes, August 24, 1968, "series 1, box 1, folder 4, NBSC Papers, MUSCA. Barial, interview.

133. S. M. Martin de Porres Grey, RSM, to Mother Marie Anselm, SSF, February 19, 1969, NBSC President's Correspondence, MUSCA. See also Grey, interview, August 12, 2007; and S. M. Martin de Porres Grey, RSM, to Sister Sylvia Thibodeaux, February 26, 1969, NBSC President's Correspondence, series 2, box 1, folder 3, MUSCA.

134. Thibodeaux to Grey, ca. February 20, 1969.

135. Thibodeaux to Grey. See also Thibodeaux, interview, August 19, 2009; and Bryan, "History," 8.

136. National Black Sisters' Conference, *Black Survival*, x–1.

137. Sister Jayne, "Role of the Black Contemplative," 8.

138. "Survival of Soul," 154–59.

139. "Survival of Soul," 157–58.

140. "Survival of Soul," 156.

141. Quoted in "Nun Who Stayed for Black Power," *Baltimore Afro-American*, February 8, 1969.

142. Sister M. Martin de Porres Grey, RSM, "An Overview of the National Black Sisters' Conference," *Sisters Today*, November 1970, 138.

143. Rutledge, "Militant Nun Leaves Convent," 1.

144. See Sister Marijo Lynch, SP, Sister Joan Gannon, CHM, Sister Shirley Ostholm, IHM, Sister Mary Ann McCauley, SP, and Sister Helen Margaret Cullen, SC to Mother Mary of Good Counsel, August 14, 1969, in Congregation RG: box 103, folder 4, OSP Archives. Also Grey, interview, August 12, 2007.

145. See also Sister Elizabeth Harris, HVM, "The Survival of the Black Sister," *Sisters Today*, March 1970, 402.

146. Laura A. Kiernan, "Nun Takes Vows 9 Years Late," *Washington Post*, July 29, 1972.

147. Grey, interview, August 25, 2019.

148. Grey, interview, August 25, 2019. See also "Arise, Search, Embrace: Ceremony of the Final Procession of Sister M. Martin de Porres Grey," series 2, box 2, folder 4, NBSC Papers, MUSCA.

149. Sister Mary Julian Griffin, VSC file, DS.

150. Sister Cecilia Abhold, FCSP, to Sister M. Martin de Porres, RSM, January 23, 1970, and completed "Survey of Black Sisters," 24a, series 2.13, box 1, folder 8, NBSC Papers, MUSCA.

151. Many Black sisters and priests cite the impact of James Cone's *Black Theology and Black Power* (1969) on the development of Black Catholic theology.

152. Two notable exceptions were the work of Father Clarence Rivers in Cincinnati, Ohio, beginning in the late 1950s and Mary Lou Williams's 1964 recording of "Black Christ of the Andes" to honor Martin de Porres's canonization. See Rivers, "Freeing the Spirit"; and Murchison, "'Black Christ of the Andes.'" See also chapter 2.

153. Grey, interview, August 25, 2019.

154. Grey, interview, August 25, 2019.

155. Grey, interview, August 25, 2019. See also Floyd, *Power of Black Music*.

156. National Black Sisters' Conference, *Black Survival*, table of contents.

157. Dr. Vincent Harding, "Toward a Black Theology," in National Black Sisters' Conference, *Black Survival*, 70.

158. Reverend C. T. Vivian, "Black Spirituality and Revolution," in National Black Sisters' Conference, *Black Survival*, 1–2.

159. "Survival of Soul," 155.

160. Sister Elfreda Chatman, "Credo," ca. 1969, 85, series 2.1, box, 1, NBSC Papers, MUSCA.

161. Quoted in "Nun Helps Her People." See also Albin A. Gorisek, "Black Nun Describes Her Work in Inner-City," *Plain Dealer* (Cleveland, OH), July 11, 1970.

162. Ford, *Liberated Threads*, 9.

163. Grey, interview, August 25, 2019. For images from the conference, see National Black Sisters' Conference, *Celibate Black Commitment*.

164. Brooks, "The Future of the National Black Sisters' Conference," in National Black Sisters' Conference, *Celibate Black Commitment*, 11.

165. René, "Psychological Implications"; and Perry, "Overview of Celibate Black Commitment."

166. Perry, "Overview of the Celibate Black Commitment," 36.

167. Grey, "The National Black Sisters' Conference Is Because," in *Celibate Black Commitment*, 95–96.

168. Sister Gloria Graciela Gallardo to Sister M. Martin de Porres, March 5, 1971, NBSC Series 2.10, box 1, folder 98, MUSCA. See also "Chicano Nuns Organize Caucus," *National Catholic Reporter*, April 16, 1971; and "Black Seminarians Meet in D.C.," *Signs of Soul*, May 1971, 7. On Chicano priests' struggle for rights and equity in the Church, see R. Martinez, *Padres*.

169. Grey, "National Black Sisters' Conference Is Because," 97.

6. "No Schools, No Churches!"

1. "Black Lay Caucus Meeting with Reverend Mother, Baltimore, MD, Monday, April 5, 1971," typed statement, Administration RG: box 12, folder 16, OSP Archives.

2. "Black Lay Caucus Meeting with Reverend Mother."

3. "Blacks Lobby for Papal Interview," *Signs of Soul*, January 1972, 13. See National Black Sisters' Conference, *Celibate Black Commitment*; National Black Sisters' Conference, *Black Survival*; and Grey, *Black Religious Woman*.

4. "Blacks Lobby for Papal Interview," 13.

5. Quoted in "Blacks Lobby for Papal Interview," 13, 15.

6. Quoted in Herbert G. Stein, "A Brief Interview with Sister Martin de Porres," ca. 1971, personal collection of Dr. Patricia Grey. Author has a copy of article.

7. Dolan, *American Catholic Experience*, 438.

8. "Information Sheet," *National Black Sisters' Conference In/Search Workbook* (1973), 23–24, NBSC series 2.4, box 1, folder 16, MUSCA.

9. Fialka, *Sisters*, 172.

10. Walch, *Parish School*, 180.

11. On this phenomenon, see Ebaugh, *Women*.

12. "Information Sheet," 23. See also National Office for Black Catholics, "The Crisis of Catholic Education in the Black Community," January 15, 1976, National Office for Black Catholics (NOBC) Papers, Saint Thomas University Archives, Miami, FL; Walch, *Parish School*, 169–87; and W. Brown and Greeley, *Can Catholic Schools Survive?* 47–191.

13. Quoted in George Vecsey, "Black Catholics Weigh a Break with Church at Detroit Meeting," *New York Times*, August 21, 1971.

14. Fialka, *Sisters*, 172.

15. Very Rev. Msgr. William E. McManus, "How Good Are Catholic Schools?" *America* 95 (September 8, 1956): 523.

16. Cited in Walch, *Parish School*, 180.

17. Walch, *Parish School*, 170–77.

18. In 1965, 5.6 million youth were enrolled in 13,396 Catholic primary and secondary schools. By 1970, there were only 4.408 million youth enrolled in 11,352 Catholic primary and secondary schools. See Rosten, *Religions of America*, 514; and Center for Applied Research in the Apostolate, "Frequently Requested Church Statistics," accessed July 24, 2021, https://cara.georgetown.edu/frequently-requested-church-statistics.

19. Walch, *Parish School*, 177–78.

20. Walch, *Parish School*, 178.

21. These numbers were gathered from the *Our Negro and Indian Missions* reports for January 1965, 21–22, and for January 1970, 21–22, typed sheets, Josephite Archives.

22. *Our Negro and Indian Missions*, January 1975, 21–22, typed sheets, Josephite Archives.

23. NOBC, "Crisis of Catholic Education."

24. For a general overview of Catholic and public school desegregation, see Newman, *Desegregating Dixie*; and Fairclough, *Class of Their Own*. See also NOBC, "Crisis of Catholic Education."

25. "Is the Catholic Church Really a Racist Institution? A Confrontation Group," n.p., series 5, box 1, folder 9, NBSC Papers, MUSCA.

26. "Is the Catholic Church?"

27. Handwritten notes titled "Black Sisters Conference, Small Group Discussions, 8-20-1968."

28. Quoted in S. Harris, *Sisters*, 274. See also Koehlinger, *New Nuns*, 115. S. Harris identified this "dark-brown" NBSC member as "Sister Joyce of the Order of Mercy based in Cincinnati." However, the RSM in Cincinnati did not have a sister by that name or description in 1969. This may have been Sister Joyce Williams, OSB, who was by then affiliated with the Department of Educational Services in Chicago.

29. S. Harris, *Sisters*, 281–82. Note Myles's congregation, the School Sisters of St. Francis, is routinely lauded in US Catholic history for picketing the Illinois Club for Catholic Women on Loyola University Chicago's campus in 1963. See chapter 4 for that discussion and chapter 3 for Myles's specific experiences of racism from her white counterparts.

30. Quoted in S. Harris, *Sisters*, 275.

31. Walch, *Parish School*, 169–87. See also NOBC, "Crisis of Catholic Education."

32. NOBC, "Crisis of Catholic Education."

33. Press release from Detroit Black Catholics for Action, December 5, 1970, series 6, box 3, folder 11, NBSC Papers, MUSCA.

34. W. Brown and Greeley, *Can Catholic Schools Survive?*, 53.

35. May, "Sister Shawn," 83.

36. Gene Golz, "Black Protesters Bar Catholics from Church," *Detroit Free Press*, November 30, 1970.

37. Mary Ann Weston, "Dearden Rapped by Black Catholics," *Detroit Free Press*, December 7, 1970.

38. Quoted in Weston, "Dearden Rapped," 4.

39. Press release from Detroit Black Catholics for Action. See also Susan Holmes, "Black Catholics Seize Church: Dearden Sees 75% of Schools Shut," n.d.; "'No School,

No Church': 200 Protesters Shout"; and Joseph Dulin et al. to His Eminence John Cardinal Dearden, November 29, 1970, all in folder "Black Catholic Movement in Detroit," NBSC series 6, box 3, folder 5, MUSCA.

40. Rector, "Black Nuns as Educators," 240–52.

41. These numbers were gathered from the Missions RG in the OSP Archives and NOAAMACH, *Celebration of Faith*, 32–33.

42. NOAAMACH, *Celebration of Faith*, 39.

43. Father André Bouchard to Mother Mary of Good Counsel, September 3, 1969, Administration RG: box 18, folder 11, OSP Archives.

44. See chapters 2 and 4.

45. For two notable examples, see Hayes, *Schools*, 64–68; and Morrow, "'To My Darlings.'"

46. Mother Mary of Good Counsel to Rev. Andre Bouchard, September 13, 1969, Administration RG: box 18, folder 11, OSP Archives.

47. "An Open Letter Re: Father Hurley's Destruction of Black Women (The Oblate Sisters of Providence)," ca. 1970, in Administration RG: box 18, folder 11, OSP Archives.

48. Newman, *Desegregating Dixie*, 242–43.

49. Quoted in Ochs, *Desegregating the Altar*, 448.

50. Quote is Ochs's in *Desegregating the Altar*, 449.

51. Ochs, *Desegregating the Altar*, 449–50.

52. David Sutton, "Withdrawal of Nuns Perils Future of West Side School," *Chicago Tribune*, December 17, 1970. See also "Letter to the Editor: Mercy Sisters Deny Charges of 'Racism,'" December 30, 1970, Mercy Heritage Center Archives.

53. Rev. Michael Rochford, "Letter to the Editor: Much Soul Searching among Mercy Sisters," *News Journal* (Chicago), January 27, 1971.

54. For two examples, see "Nuns' Racial Stand in South Is Hailed," *New York Times*, January 25, 1970; and Sister Patricia Flinn, SNDdeN, "I Teach in a Racist School," *America*, September 26, 1970, 201–3.

55. See "Nuns Quit School over Pupils' Parents' Racism," *Jet*, February 25, 1971, 18.

56. "Administration of Reverend Mother Marie Anselm, June 17, 1958, to June 17, 1970, typed report, n.d., Duffel Administration file, SSF Archives.

57. Koehlinger, *New Nuns*, 14.

58. Quoted in "Blacks Must Control Black Schools," *Pittsburgh Catholic*, August 20, 1971.

59. Quoted in "Academy Seeks Federal Aid: St. Frances Fights to Stay Open," *Catholic Review*, February 7, 1969, n.p., copy in Congregation RG: box 104, folder 6, OSP Archives.

60. Quoted in Patrick Joyce, "Thirty Stage March at Catholic Center," *Catholic Review*, July 3, 1970, A7.

61. Sister Mary Paraclete Young, "The Brentwood Forrest Community Center Proposal: An Oasis in the Ghetto," 1969, Motherhouse RG: box 15, folder 3, OSP Archives. See also Joyce, "Thirty Stage March."

62. "25 Picket Archdiocese Offices: East Baltimore Group Charges Failure to Back Ghetto Plan," *Sun* (Baltimore), July 1, 1970. Young had already raised eyebrows earlier that year after she bailed a local Black activist, John A. Dixon, out of jail using St. Frances

Academy funds. See Council Minutes, March 14, 1970, Administration RG: box 45, folder 5, OSP Archives.

63. "25 Picket Archdiocese Offices." See also Sister Mary Paraclete Young and Staff of Saint Frances Academy to the Oblate Sisters of Providence, December 2, 1971, Administration RG: box 18, folder 5, OSP Archives.

64. Reverend Harold Salmon, "Catholic Education: Crisis in Black and White," typed transcript, n.d. but August 22, 1968; handwritten notes from "Black Sisters Conference Small Group Discussions, 8-20-1968"; and handwritten "NBSC Steering Committee Minutes, August 24, 1968," NBSC series, 5, box 4, folder 1, MUSCA.

65. Brooks, "Future of the National Black Sisters' Conference," 11.

66. Grey, "An Overview of the National Black Sisters' Conference," 140.

67. J. Davis and Rowe, "National Office for Black Catholics."

68. NOAAMACH, Celebration of Faith, 33. See also "Focus: Department of Educational Services," Impact, July 1972, 1.

69. For an excellent treatment of the Black struggle for community-controlled education, see Rickford, We Are an African People.

70. Grey, "Church, Revolution," 23.

71. NBSC Central Committee Meeting Minutes, August 20, 1971, NOBC Papers, Saint Thomas University Archives (STUA).

72. "Black Sisters Exhibit at the NCEA Convention," Signs of Soul, May 1971, 5.

73. Minutes of NBSC Board Meeting, ca. April 19, 1971, NOBC Papers, STUA.

74. "Press Release: Black Nuns Opt for Community Controlled Schools," April 17, 1971, series 6, box 3, folder 2, NBSC Papers, MUSCA.

75. "Blacks Must Control Black Schools."

76. Copeland, "A Cadre," 139.

77. "Development of Educational Services in the Growing Nation," Signs of Soul, January 1972, 4. See also Copeland, "Cadre," 139–40.

78. Sister Helen M. Christian, RSM, to Sisters, October 9, 1972, series 2, box 2, folder 5, NBSC Papers, MUSCA. Christian was the new NBSC president.

79. "DESIGN," Signs of Soul, January 1973, 13.

80. Minutes of the (NBSC) Central Committee Meeting, January 6, 1973, NOBC Papers, STUA. See also Grey, interview, August 12, 2007.

81. Copeland, "Cadre," 139–40.

82. In Boston, Sister Sylvia Thibodeaux led the St. Joseph Community School; Sister Dolores Harrall led St. Francis de Sales School, and Sister Josita Colbert led St. John's School. In 1975, Sister Callista (Nancy) Robinson, a Franciscan Sister of Little Falls, Minnesota, joined the staff of the Harambee Community School (formerly St. Elizabeth School) in Milwaukee as a teacher and eventually served as its principal for over a decade. Colbert, interview, June 23, 2014.

83. Grey, interview, August 12, 2007.

84. Copeland, "Cadre,"139–40. See also Formisano, Boston; Thibodeaux, interview, August 4, 2016. Patricia Hill became Dr. Patricia Hill Collins. A photo of Hill teaching at the St. Joseph Community School is included in Signs of Souls, January 1973, 17.

85. Fiske, "Finding Identity," 27.

86. Copeland, "Cadre," 140. See also Sister Nathan Marie Adams, SSND, to Attorney Ricardo Calvin Jackson, March 20, 1975, series 8, box 3, folder 13, NBSC Papers, MUSCA.

87. Mother Mary of Good Counsel to Every Oblate Sister of Providence, January 21, 1974, Administration RG: box 18, folder 5, OSP Archives.

88. Mother Mary of Good Counsel to Every Oblate Sister of Providence.

89. Henry J. Offer, "Strictly Confidential Memo Regarding Sister Paraclete," in Administration RG: box 18, folder 4, OSP Archives. When stationed at St. Francis Xavier Parish, the city's oldest Black Catholic Church, in 1958, Offer first voiced his unfavorable opinion of Black nuns. The council minutes read: "Rev. Mother related to the Councilors a few remarks made by Rev. Henry Offer, SSJ . . . he does not want any old Sisters, nor sick Sisters. He doesn't seem to care about having colored Sisters. This is his first experience with them." See Council Minutes: 1956–68, 40, Administration RG: box 45, folder 4, OSP Archives. See also Offer, "Black Power."

90. Sister Mary of Good Counsel Baptiste, OSP, to Most Rev. George R. Evans, JCD (Juris Canonici Doctor), May 1, 1974, in Congregation RG: box 104, folder 6, OSP Archives.

91. Sister Mary Paraclete Young to Reverend Mother Mary of Good Counsel Baptiste and General Council, April 18, 1975, in Congregation RG: box 104, folder 6, OSP Archives. Young did not abandon religious life but joined family members who had migrated to Denver, Colorado, where she became and ministered as a consecrated virgin in the archdiocese until her death. See "Obituaries and Memorials: Sister Mary Paraclete Young," *Denver Post*, June 27, 2004.

92. Frank P. L. Somerville, "State's Oldest Black School Reborn," *Sun* (Baltimore), July 18, 1979; and "12 Nuns, 6 Houses Form an 'Oasis in the Ghetto,'" *Boston Sunday Globe*, December 16, 1979.

93. These numbers were gathered from the Mission Records contained in the OSP Archives and NOAAMACH, *Celebration of Faith*, 32–33. In the case of the OSP, all five of the order's schools in Cuba also closed in June 1961 following the failed Bay of Pigs invasion and Fidel Castro's nationalization of the island's schools. The order's Mount Providence Junior College closed in 1972. Knecht, *Oblate Sisters of Providence*, 92–93, 112.

94. Hadrick, "Contributions," 66.

95. Dr. Kendra Hamilton, email message to author, February 1, 2020.

96. M. Smith, interview.

97. Knecht, *Oblate Sisters of Providence*, 71.

98. Mrs. P. B. Parks to Mother Mary of Good Counsel Baptiste, June 3, 1971, Missions RG: box 102, folder 2, OSP Archives.

99. NOAAMACH, *Celebration of Faith*, 32–33.

100. See Delpit, "Act Your Age," 116–18; and NOAAMACH, *Celebration of Faith*, 30–33.

101. For an introduction to how the federal interstate highway system disrupted and often decimated Black communities and business districts, see Brundage, *Clash*, 227–68.

102. Delpit, "Act Your Age," 116–18. See also Erickson and Donovan, *Three R's*, 102–13.

103. Quoted in Erickson and Donovan, *Three R's*, 116–21.

104. Erickson and Donovan, *Three R's*, 122–28. See also Newman, *Desegregating Dixie*, 243–45; and George Morris, "Celebrating 100 Years, St. Francis Xavier Church Proves Its Resilience," *Advocate* (Baton Rouge, LA), December 21, 2018.

105. NOBC, "Crisis of Catholic Education."

106. NBSC press release, September 9, 1971, 1–2, series 6, box 3, folder 2, NBSC Papers, MUSCA. See also Copeland, "Cadre."

107. Colbert, interview.

108. "NBSC Formation Institute: Total Black Experience," *Signs of Soul*, January 1972, 11.

109. "NBSC Formation Institute," 10.

110. These decimated communities included the Sisters of Charity of the Blessed Virgin Mary, the Sisters of Charity of Cincinnati, and various provinces of the Religious Sisters of Mercy and the School Sisters of Notre Dame.

111. According to *The Official Catholic Directory* published by P. J. Kenedy and Sons in 1965 and 1975, the three surviving African American sisterhoods lost a combined total of 230 sisters between those years. Specifically, the OSP membership declined from 337 to 224, while the SSF membership declined from 359 to 273. The Franciscan Handmaids of Mary lost nearly half of its membership, dropping from 76 sisters in 1965 to 45 sisters in 1975. These volumes were consulted in the AB.

112. Handwritten notes titled "Black Sisters Conference, Small Group Discussions, 8-20-1968" detail the NBSC foundresses' concern "regarding priests' attitudes toward Black communities," specifically priests' increasing refusal to direct Black candidates to them.

113. Barial, interview.

114. Thibodeaux, interview, August 19, 2009; and Lovenia Deconge-Watson (formerly Sister Mary Sylvester, SSF), interview by the History Makers, June 9, 2010, https://www.thehistorymakers.org/biography/lovenia-deconge-watson-41.

115. "Asante Yvonne!," *Signs of Soul*, January 1972, 12.

116. "Founding Board Member Teresita Weind"; "Racism: Will We Ever Overcome?"; Cheryl Varner (formerly Sister Ruth, SNDdeN), interview by author, November 15, 2013, telephone; and Willingham, interview. In 2006, Weind would become the first African American to lead the Sisters of Notre Dame de Namur, in the United States and globally. See "Local Sister Elected Leader of Worldwide Sisters of Notre Dame," *Catholic Telegraph*, August 22, 2008.

117. Copeland, interview.

118. "In Memory of Sister Mary Joselinda Cummings, FHM on the Anniversary of Her Death, December 4, 1993," typed sheet provided to author by Sister Loretta Theresa Richards, FHM.

119. Laura A. Kiernan, "Nun Takes Vows 9 Years Late," *Washington Post*, July 29, 1972.

120. Adams, interview.

121. Sister Josita Colbert, OSP, to Sister Marie Infanta, OSP, July 21, 1978, in Congregation RG: box 84, folder 9, OSP Archives.

122. Richard W. Saxton to the Very Reverend William W. Baum, Archbishop, November 2, 1974; Sister Marcellina Brooks to Mother Mary of Good Counsel, January 31, 1976; Mother Mary of Good Counsel to Sister Marcellina, February 17, 1976, Congregation RG: box 83, folder 3, OSP Archives.

123. For an explosive episode in which Grey documents "irrational and spontane-ously deliberate attacks on [her] physical and emotional person" at a 1971 meeting of the National Black Catholic Lay Caucus, see Grey to Bro. Joseph Davis, CDAV Folder 2/02, Joe Davis Papers, UND Archives.

124. Grey, interview, August 12, 2007.

125. Grey, interview, August 12, 2007.

126. For three examples, see "Awakening of Black Nun Power"; "The New Nuns," *Time*, "The American Woman" (special issue), March 20, 1972, 64; and Grey, "Church, Revolution."

127. Edward P. Jones, "Baum Repudiates KKK, Kathlix," *Impact!*, April 1977, 1, 3. See also "Klan to Let Catholics and Immigrants Join," *New York Times*, December 16, 1974.

128. Ochs, *Desegregating the Altar*, 447.

129. Copeland, "Black Nuns," 9.

7. "The Future of the Black Catholic Nun Is Dubious"

1. "Sr. Thea Bowman's Address to the U.S. Bishop's Conference, June 1989," typed transcript, n.d., 1, 3, accessed on July 20, 2021, https://www.usccb.org/issues-and-action /cultural-diversity/african-american/resources/upload/Transcript-Sr-Thea-Bowman -June-1989-Address.pdf.

2. "Sr. Thea Bowman's Address," 3–5.

3. "Sr. Thea Bowman's Address," 5.

4. Smith and Feister, *Thea's Song*, 284.

5. Chapter 2 mentions the OSP's celebration of African Catholic history in their Negro History Week celebrations.

6. "Photo Standalone 10," *Amsterdam News* (New York), September 12, 1964. This section features the photographs of four Black Maryknoll Sisters (Mary Agneta, Sister Mary Deporres, Martin Corde, and Maria Lisa) and a short caption. Although the caption identifies Martin Corde as "the first American Negro Sister of the Maryknoll Sisters of the Roman Catholic Church to be assigned to a foreign mission," that desig-nation belongs to Sister Francis (Elsie St. Clair) Davis, who began a ministry in China in the 1920s. See chapter 1 for more on Davis. The caption also notes that Sister Martin de Porres (also identified as Mary Deporres in the text) had been serving in Africa since 1946, suggesting that she was not and/or did not identify as an "American Negro."

7. "Notable News Photos," *Colored Harvest*, April 1953, 4. Sister Peter Claver's secular name comes from email with the congregation's executive secretary, April 25, 2018.

8. Sister Demetria Smith, MSOLA, interview by author, June 13, 2015, telephone.

9. D. Smith, interview.

10. "Sister Jennieva Lassiter, MM," *Maryknoll Mission Archives*, n.d., accessed August 10, 2020, https://maryknollmissionarchives.org/?deceased-sisters=sister-geneva-lassiter -mm. Many sources misspell Lassiter's first name as Geneva. Her legal name was Jennieva. See also Martha S. Wright, "Philadelphia Youth Council Active," *Crisis*, May 1944, 154.

11. "Sister Jennieva." See also Sister Rose M. McCormick, "My Black Sister," *Luguor-ian*, July 1970, 37.

12. In 1948, Tanganyika had become the first African nation to receive the Maryknoll Sisters. See Lernoux, *Hearts on Fire,* 200–201.

13. Quoted in Lernoux, *Hearts on Fire,* 200–201.

14. Nyerere, "Church's Role in Society," 111.

15. Unlike most of her white counterparts, Lassiter emphasized the agency of Tanzanians in their pursuit of education in the era of decolonization in her recollections of the order's ministry there. "Our educational efforts affirmed what students already had," she noted. See *Buffaloes,* 107.

16. Quoted in Terri Heard, "For Nuns of Color, Their Mission Doesn't End at the Convent Walls," *Philadelphia Tribune,* March 22, 1994. Lassiter specifically noted the resentment that many of her white counterparts directed at her for being "so in tune with them [the Africans]."

17. "Ghanaian Nuns Undertake Studies Here," *Pittsburgh Courier,* October 17, 1964.

18. "Consecrate First Negro Catholic Bishop in U.S.," *Jet,* April 30, 1953, 30. A 1952 attempt by a SVD priest and a Missionary Sister of the Holy Spirit, both white, to establish an indigenous order had failed. See "Foundation History," n.d., accessed on July 14, 2021, https://hdrsisters.org/foundation-history.html; and Brandewie, *In the Light,* 242–43.

19. Pfann, *Catholic Church in Ghana,* 27–31.

20. Stornig, *Sisters Crossing Boundaries,* 372. For another examination of this under-researched history in Africa, see P. Martin, *Catholic Women,* 108–16.

21. "Ghanaian Nuns," 9.

22. The SSpS were expelled from Togo in 1918, and the order did not return to the west Africa until 1946 with the arrival of sisters in what is now Ghana. During the SSpS's time in Togo, the sisters raised and educated Julia Althoff, the daughter of a German trader and indigenous African woman from the Gold Coast. Althoff eventually moved to Germany and entered the SSpS in 1923. She took the name Sister Virginie and ministered in Argentina and Ghana. Stornig, *Sisters Crossing Boundaries,* 362–72.

23. Stornig, *Sisters Crossing Boundaries,* 341–42, including notes 1, 4, and 5–8.

24. Glenn, interview.

25. Glenn, interview. Glenn never mentioned Althoff, suggesting that they may have been kept apart. Glenn also did not know about the first African American woman admitted into the SSpS in 1947 before the author told her.

26. "Anyone for Africa?," 3.

27. "7 Cloistered Nuns Leaving U.S. for Africa," *Guardian: Official Publication of the Diocese of Little Rock,* June 26, 1970, 1.

28. "A Proposal for the Organization and Formation of an Indigenous Religious Congregation in Nigeria, West Africa," 1974, NBSC series 2.4, box 2, folder 2, MUSCA.

29. Thibodeaux, interview, August 19, 2009. See also *Journey of Faith.*

30. "Proposal for . . . Indigenous Religious Congregation."

31. Thibodeaux, interview, August 19, 2009. See also Jones, "Holy Family Mission."

32. Ignatius Ohi, "Gift from U.S.," *Independent* (Nigeria), April 27, 1975, copy in NBSC series 5, box 1, folder 3, MUSCA.

33. Haughey, "Black Sisters Become Soul Sisters," 67.

34. Sister Mary Shawn Copeland, OP, to Right Reverend Dr. Peter Sarpong, April 24, 1975, and Sarpong to Copeland, May 9, 1975, NBSC series 2.4, box 2, folder 2, MUSCA.

35. Benedict A. Karaimu to Sister Copeland, July 4, 1975, NBSC series 2.4, box 2, folder 2, MUSCA.

36. Thibodeaux, interview, October 8, 2018. See also Jones, "Holy Family," 1.

37. See Brandewie, *In the Light,* 350–51.

38. "Sister Sylvia Elaine Postles," Maryknoll Sisters, n.d., accessed August 10, 2020, https://www.maryknollsisters.org/sisters/sister-sylvia-elaine-postles/; Daly, "Call Me Sister"; Sister Patricia Lucas, DHM (formerly Sister Mary Immanuel, FHM), interview by author, March 22, 2010, telephone; and Harris, interview.

39. Copeland, "Cadre," 141. See also Glose, "Take the Blinders," 63–73.

40. Henegan, interview; and Sister Patricia Ralph, SSJ, interview by author, August 7, 2015, telephone. See also Maureen Daly, "Call Me Sister," *VISION Vocation Network,* accessed August 10, 2020, https://vocationnetwork.org/articles/show/224.

41. Ralph, interview.

42. "The Institute for Black Catholic Studies: History," Xavier University of Louisiana, n.d., accessed September 10, 2019, https://www.xula.edu/ibcs-history.

43. "Institute for Black Catholic Studies."

44. Coleman, interview.

45. Sister Irma Dillard, RSCJ, interview by author, April 14, 2017, telephone and email.

46. Dillard and Coleman, interviews.

47. Coleman, interview. On the segregationist practices of the Sisters of Notre Dame de Namur in Africa, see Clevenger, *Unequal Partners.*

48. Sister Patricia Chappell, SNDdeN, interview by author, May 14, 2017, telephone.

49. Patricia Hamilton, a native of Washington, DC, entered the SNDdeN in Baltimore in 1978 and endured pernicious racism from several white members until she left in 1993. She was the only Black SNDdeN member in Baltimore until Gwynette Proctor entered in 1980. Patricia Hamilton, interview by author, June 14, 2014, New Orleans.

50. One example is cited in the conclusion. See also Glose, "Take the Blinders," 88–243.

51. Sister Larretta Rivera-Williams, RSM, interview by author, August 8, 2016, telephone and email.

52. Sister Catherine Marie Lowe, DC, interview by author, August 27, 2016, telephone.

53. D. Smith, interview.

54. Dr. Deborah Plummer Bussey (formerly Sister Phillis Marie, SND), interview by author, October 23, 2013, telephone. Plummer later married and added her husband's surname.

55. Bussey, interview. Only one, Sister Mary Kendra (Patricia) Bottoms, a descendant of Mary Eliza Spalding Smith (see chapter 2), remains in the Sisters of Notre Dame in Cleveland. Sister Mary Kendra Bottoms, SND, interview by author, November 18, 2017, email.

56. Copeland, interview; and Taylor, interview.

57. Douglas Jacobs, "We're Sick of Racism, Literally," *New York Times,* November 11, 2017; and Chappell, interview. At Harrall's wake, Sister Josita Colbert, then a SNDdeN,

recalled that a white sister approached her and remarked, "We should have never let her [Harrall] in." Colbert, interview, June 23, 2014.

58. Smith and Feister, *Thea's Song*, 99–193.

59. Smith and Feister, *Thea's Song*, 135–281.

60. B. Johnson, "Thea Bowman: Priest to the People of God," in Koontz, *Thea Bowman*, 51.

61. Cepress, *Sister Thea Bowman*, 76.

62. Quoted in Smith and Feister, *Thea's Song*, 181.

63. Smith and Feister, *Thea's Song*, 199–203, 242. See also Mary Queen Donnelly, "In Memoriam," *America*, April 28, 1990, 420–21.

64. Donnelly, "In Memoriam," 420.

65. Quoted in Smith and Feister, *Thea's Song*, 284.

66. In 1989, Father George Stallings, a Black priest, established the Imani Temple African American Catholic Congregation in Washington, DC, after calling for a separate, semiautonomous status for Black Catholics in the United States. After the Imani Temple announced that it would separate from Rome and Church mandates, such as priestly celibacy, prohibition of abortion and birth control, and the exclusion of women and married men from the priesthood, Stallings, then under investigation for sexual abuse, was excommunicated from the Catholic Church. See "D.C. Priest Splits from Catholic Church, Black Bishops Decry the Act," *Jet*, July 10, 1989, 12. See also C. Davis, *History of Black Catholics*, 260; and Laura Session Stepp and Bill Dedman, "Concerns about Stallings's Lifestyle Fueled Conflict," *Washington Post*, April 30, 1990.

67. Donnelly, "In Memoriam," 240–41.

68. Quoted in Smith and Feister, *Thea's Song*, 283.

69. Quoted in Pramuk, *Hope Sings*, 151.

70. M. Neal, "She Made the Bishops Dance," in Koontz, *Thea Bowman*, 56. Chappell, interview.

71. Smith and Feister, *Thea's Song*, 283. For more on the Jesuits' brutal mistreatment and exploitation of enslaved people in the United States, including their practice of whipping enslaved women naked, see Schmidt, "Peter Hawkins"; and Thomas, *Question of Freedom*, 157–91.

72. Lyke, "On Receiving the Laetare Medal," in Koontz, *Thea Bowman*, 30–32. Lyke, who was then the Apostolic Administrator of the Archdiocese of Atlanta accepted the award on Bowman's behalf.

73. Smith and Feister, *Thea's Song*, 207–9, 269.

74. Ervin Dyer, "Black Nun Being Examined for Sainthood," *Pittsburgh Post-Gazette*, November 28, 2010.

75. Robert McClory, "A Silenced Woman," *Chicago Reader*, January 2, 1992, https://www.chicagoreader.com/chicago/a-silenced-woman/Content?oid=878903.

76. Sister Agnes Arvin, SP, Sister Barbara Batista, SP, and Sister Judith Birgen, SP, "Show Nun Charity," *Chicago Tribune*, September 21, 1991.

77. McClory, "Silenced Woman."

78. For more on the hearing and Thomas's other women accusers, see Mayer and Abramson, *Strange Justice*. On Thomas's brief tenure as a Catholic seminarian, see

Brady, *Fraternity*, 7–10. Thomas was educated by the historically white Missionary Franciscan Sisters of the Immaculate Conception (MFIC) in Savannah, Georgia. See chapters 1 and 2 for more on the order.

79. See Sue Hively, "Sister Juanita," *Plain Dealer* (Cleveland, OH), May 13, 1973. In the article, NBSC founding member Sister Juanita Shealey states, "If they ever have women priests, I want to be one of the first. I hope there will be women priests."

80. Lightfoot, *I've Known Rivers*, 195–288. See also "New Call for Renee L. Fenner."

81. Grey, interview, August 25, 2019. See also Dillard, interview and William McClinton, "Black Nuns Reaffirm Dedication to Freedom," *Pittsburgh Catholic*, August 20, 1971. This article features a photograph of Sister Teresita Weind at the annual NBSC meeting giving "a major homily at the Black Unity Mass" presided over by Bishop Harold Perry, SVD.

82. Chappell, interview.

83. Dillard, interview.

84. Grey, interview, August 25, 2019; and Adams, interview.

85. See "Archbishop Eugene Marino Resigns after Relationship with Young Georgia Woman," *Jet*, August 20, 1990, 4–6. See also Ochs, *Desegregating the Altar*, 1; Lauran Neergaard, "Woman at the Center of Catholic Church Scandal Takes Paternity Suit to Trial," *Associated Press*, December 8, 1991; and "Vicki Long Claims She Was Seduced by Nun, Newspaper Says," Associated Press, August 8, 1990.

86. "James Lyke Dies at 53; Archbishop of Atlanta," *New York Times*, December 28, 1992.

87. "About Bishop Emeritus Braxton," n.d., accessed July 14, 2021, https://www .diobelle.org/bishop-emeritus/biography. See also Lydialyle Gibson, "Recalling a Prickly Pastor," *Wednesday Journal* (Oak Park, IL), updated February 11, 2021, https:// www.oakpark.com/2005/07/05/recalling-a-prickly-pastor/.

88. Robert McClory, "Braxton Battles on Against Abuse Suit," *National Catholic Reporter*, July 22, 2011, 13–14; and Robert McClory, "Belleville Bishop Finally Surrenders," *National Catholic Reporter*, August 12, 2011, https://www.ncronline.org/blogs/ncr-today /belleville-bishop-finally-surrenders.

89. Beasley, interview.

90. Lynch, *Sharing the Bread*, 578, 602. Sister Juliana Haynes served as the president of the Sisters of the Blessed Sacrament from 1985 to 1990.

91. Shirley Salemy, "Benedictine Nuns Choose a Leader," *Chicago Tribune*, October 13, 1995. In 2003, Sister Diane Marie Collins, a Franciscan Sister of Chicago, became the second African American nun to lead a white congregation in Chicago. According to the OSP roster, the first member from Chicago entered in 1920. Because the roster is incomplete, there could be a Chicago native who entered earlier. For example, one source notes that Father Augustus Tolton and his mother, Mary Jane Chisley Tolton, nurtured the vocation of a young girl in Chicago and eventually directed her to the OSP in the 1890s. See Duriga, *Augustus Tolton*, 43–44.

92. Martha Woodall, "Hailing Black Nuns as Principals: Appointment of 3 Sets Archdiocese Milestone," *Philadelphia Inquirer*, November 9, 1990. The article overlooks that the OSP led the Blessed (later St.) Peter Claver School in the nineteenth century and the Bambino Gesu Child Development Center and Montessori School from 1964 until the mid-1990s. See Knecht, *Oblate Sisters of Providence*, 84–85.

93. Michael Humphrey, "Miracle in Memphis," *National Catholic Reporter*, April 4, 2008; and Bishop J. Terry Steib, SVD, interview by author, Memphis, TN, October 19, 2009.

94. Bill Dries, "Catholic Diocese Ending Jubilee Schools after 2018–2019 School Year," *Daily News* (Memphis), January 24, 2018, https://www.memphisdailynews.com /news/2018/jan/24/catholic-diocese-ending-jubilee-schools-after-2018-2019-school -year/. Some local white Catholics had opposed the Jubilee Schools from the beginning. See Ashley Fantz, "A Gift from God?," *Memphis Flyer*, August 19–25, 1999, http:// www.memphisflyer.com/backissues/issue548/cvr548.htm.

95. Banfield, interview. See also Barbara Bradley, "Quiet Revolution: New Research Spotlights Role of Black Catholic Nuns in Desegregation," *Commercial Appeal* (Memphis), May 22, 2011.

96. Glenn, interview.

97. "Cora Billings Named 1st Black Catholic Nun to Pastor Church in the United States," *Jet*, October 15, 1990, 8.

98. Sister Jannette Pruitt, Sister of St. Francis of Oldenburg, Indiana, interview by author, June 2, 2015, telephone and email; and Sister Patricia Dual, Dominican Sister of Peace, interview by author, June 20, 2014, telephone.

99. Sister Kathleen Smith, SP, interview by author, July 8, 2014, telephone.

100. Sister M. Wilhelmina Lancaster, "Starting Over," in *The Good Sisters*, n.p., ca. March 1996, copy in Congregation RG: box 92, folder 13, OSP Archives. See also John Heuertz, "'Wondrous Love' Moves Five Sisters to Next Step in Vocation," *Catholic Key* (Kansas City, MO), January 16, 2009.

101. Collier-Thomas, *Jesus, Jobs, and Justice*, 485.

102. See list of LCWR presidents in Leadership Conference of Women Religious, "LCWR Officers," n.d., accessed February 12, 2019, https://lcwr.org/about/officers.

103. Quoted in Dennis Sadowski, "Sister Patricia Chappell Named Executive Director of Pax Christi," *Catholic News Service*, October 24, 2011.

104. Bishop Mark J. Seitz, "El Paso's Bishop Mark Seitz: Black Lives Matter," *National Catholic Reporter*, June 4, 2020. Seitz used the phrase in response to the global protests over the police murders of George Floyd and Breonna Taylor and systemic racism. See also Tia Noelle Pratt, "There Is Time for the Church to Support Black Catholics—If It Has the Will to Do So," *America*, September 18, 2019. On #BlackLivesMatter, see Alicia Garza, "A Herstory of the #BlackLivesMatter Movement," *Feminist Wire*, October 7, 2014, https://thefeministwire.com/2014/10/blacklivesmatter-2/.

105. For one of several examples, see Proctor, "What We've Seen." Proctor's reflection was originally published in Baltimore's *Catholic Review*.

106. Quoted in Dave Luecking, "Sister Antona Ebo Encourages 'Looking under the Rug' in Ferguson," *St. Louis Review*, October 15, 2014, copy in author's possession.

107. Quoted in Sister Mary Flick, "CSJ African American Sisters Gather," *Sisters of St. Joseph of Carondelet, St. Louis Province: Newsletter*, September 20, 2015, copy in author's possession.

108. Quoted in Flick, "CSJ African American Sisters."

109. Baird, interview.

110. Three African American women under age thirty-five who have entered US religious life in the twenty-first century are Sister Nicole Trahan, the first African American Marianist Sister; Sister Desire-Anne Findlay, a Felician Sister of North America; and Megan Graves, a former candidate in the Sinsinawa Dominicans. While Trahan and Findlay have remained in religious life, Graves, who became active in local campaigns against police violence while stationed in Minneapolis, departed in 2016. Sister Nicole Trahan, FMI, interview by author, October 10, 2015, telephone; Sister Desire-Anne Findlay, CSSF, interview by author, August 29, 2015, telephone; and Megan Graves, interview by author, August 11, 2015, telephone. See also Dr. Shawnee Daniels-Sykes (formerly SSND), interview by author, September 22, 2016, email.

111. J. J. Ziegler, "Nuns Worldwide," *Catholic World Report,* May 12, 2011, https://www.catholicworldreport.com/2011/05/12/nuns-worldwide/. See also Sr. Bibiana M. Nugundo and Jonatha Wiggins, "Women Religious in Africa," *Center for Applied Research in the Apostolate* (Summer 2017): 1–8.

112. Berrelleza, Gautier, and Gray, *Population Trends,* 1–8.

113. Okure, "African-Born," 7.

114. Dawn Araujo-Hawkins, "Q & A with Sr. Gertrude Lilly Ihenacho, a Centenary of Revitalization," *Global Sisters Report,* February 25, 2016, https://www.globalsistersreport.org/blog/q/q-sr-gertrude-lilly-ihenacho-centenary-revitalization-37841. See also Dartunorro Clark, "Harlem Order of Black Nuns Selling W. 124th Street Headquarters," *DNAInfo,* June 19, 2017, https://www.dnainfo.com/new-york/20170619/central-harlem/the-franciscan-handmaids-harlem-black-nuns-building-sale/.

115. NCR Staff, "African Sisters Journey to US for Education, Mission," *National Catholic Reporter,* July 18, 2012, https://www.ncronline.org/news/african-sisters-journey-us-education-mission. See also Elise Harris, "Tanzanian Nuns in America's Paradise Capture Catholic Shift from North to South," *Crux,* November 19, 2019, https://cruxnow.com/church-in-the-usa/2019/11/tanzanian-nuns-in-americas-paradise-capture-catholic-shift-from-north-to-south/.

116. See St. Augustine Catholic School, "Our History," accessed August 10, 2020, https://staug-dc.org/our-history; and MacGregor, *Emergence,* on the history of St. Augustine Catholic School.

117. St. Augustine, "Our History."

118. Elisabeth Parker, "Sister Maria Wields No Ruler, She Uplifts Her 'Kids,'" *Tampa Bay Times,* March 25, 2012.

119. Thibodeaux, interview, October 8, 2016.

120. Thibodeaux, interview, October 8, 2016. See also Fritz Esker, "St. Mary's Academy Celebrates 150 Years," *Louisiana Weekly,* August 14, 2017, http://www.louisianaweekly.com/st-marys-academy-celebrates-150-years/.

121. Sister Cecilia Dimaku, SSH, interview by author, October 20, 2016, New Orleans.

122. Thibodeaux, interview, October 8, 2016. See also Deggs, *No Cross, No Crown,* xxxvi.

123. Sister Joanna Okereke, Handmaid of the Holy Child of Jesus, "History of the African Conference of Catholic Clergy and Religious in the United States (ACCCRUS)," African Conference of Catholic Clergy and Religious in the United States, accessed August 10, 2020, https://www.acccrus.org/index.php/about-acccrus/history.

124. On Bakhita's life, see Zanini, *Bakhita*.

125. Okure, "African-Born," 7.

126. Okure, "African-Born." See also Gina Christian, "Local Nigerian Catholics Stunned by New Travel Ban," *Catholic Philly*, February 11, 2020, https://catholicphilly .com/2020/02/news/local-news/local-nigerian-catholics-stunned-by-new-travel-ban/.

Conclusion

1. K. Johnson, *One in Christ*, 219–27.

2. Koehlinger, *New Nuns*, 234–35.

3. Lindblad, "Sister Joyce Williams, 11; Grey, interview, August 12, 2007; and Koehlinger, *New Nuns*, 234. Koehlinger's narration of the NCCIJ's decline and how "the resources, staff, and loyal following of the DES became those of NCAN [National Coalition of American Nuns]" in the early 1970s includes no discussion of Sister Joyce Williams's historic appointment as the DES head in 1973 or consideration of its implications.

4. Graybill, "From Orphanage," 19. See also Ebo's "Presidential File," series 2, box 2, folder 7, NBSC Papers, MUSCA.

5. Paul Murray, "Selma March at 50: 'This Is the First Time in My Life I Am Seeing a Negro Nun,'" *National Catholic Reporter*, March 13, 2015, https://www.ncronline.org /blogs/ncr-today/selma-march-50-first-time-my-life-i-am-seeing-negro-nun. See also Makani Themba-Nixon, "Notorious Racist Mayor Challenged: Selma's Unfinished March to Freedom," *Colorlines*, August 25, 2000, https://www.colorlines.com/articles /notorious-racist-mayor-challenged-selmas-unfinished-march-freedom.

6. Luecking, "Sister Antona Ebo Encourages."

7. United States Conference of Catholic Bishops, "USCCB President Calls for Courage and Commitment on Martin Luther King Jr. Day," January 10, 2018, http://www .usccb.org/news/2018/18-005.cfm.

8. Gloria S. Ross, "Obituary: Sister Mary Antona Ebo, One of the 'Sisters of Selma,'" *St. Louis Public Radio*, November 13, 2017, https://news.stlpublicradio.org/government -politics-issues/2017-11-13/obituary-sister-mary-antona-ebo-one-of-the-sisters-of -selma.

9. Ross, "Obituary." See also "Antona Ebo, F.S.M.: 1924–2017," *St. Louis University Newsroom*, accessed August 20, 2020, https://www.slu.edu/news/2017/november /sister-antona-ebo-obit.php; Denise Hollinshed, "Sister Antona Ebo, Civil Rights Leader and Nun for 71 Years, Dies at 93," *St. Louis Post-Dispatch*, November 11, 2017; and "Franciscan Sr. Mary Antona Ebo, Civil Rights Leader, Dies at 93," *Catholic News Service*, November 17, 2017.

10. "Building to Be Renamed for Pioneer Black Educator Anne Marie Becraft," Georgetown University, April 13, 2017, https://www.georgetown.edu/news/anne -marie-becraft-hall. See also Mark Zimmermann, "Georgetown Renaming of Buildings Reflects Shared Journey with Slave Descendants," *Crux*, April 20, 2017, https://cruxnow .com/church-in-the-usa/2017/04/georgetown-renaming-buildings-reflects-shared -journey-slave-descendants/; Melanne Verveer, "Viewpoint: Celebrating Anne Marie

Becraft," *Hoya*, April 18, 2017, https://thehoya.com/viewpoint-celebrating-anne-marie
-becraft/; and Ian Simpson, "Georgetown University Renames Building to Atone for
Slavery Ties," *Reuters*, April 18, 2017, https://www.reuters.com/article/us-washingtondc
-georgetown-slavery/georgetown-university-renames-buildings-to-atone-for-slavery
-ties-idUSKBN17K2AR. In the *Reuters* article, Becraft's life as a nun is not mentioned.

11. "Building to Be Renamed"; Verveer, "Viewpoint"; Simpson, "Georgetown University"; and "Report of the Working Group."

12. "Building to Be Renamed."

13. Chapter 1 discusses Becraft's genealogical origins.

14. See comments under Verveer, "Viewpoint."

15. "Canonization Cause for Sister Thea Bowman Approved," *Catholic News Service*,
November 20, 2018.

16. Although the biography on the official website for Bowman's sainthood cause
notes that she had a "short lifetime," it omits her battles with cancer. See "Biography,"
Sister Thea Bowman: Cause for Canonization, accessed August 8, 2020, https://www
.sistertheabowman.com/biography/.

17. For one example, see Bishop Joseph N. Perry, Postulator, "Father Augustus
Tolton, 1854–1897," Archdiocese of Chicago, accessed July 15, 2021, https://tolton
.archchicago.org/documents/1604561/1604725/Tolton+Biography+-+PDF/d8d2f8ac
-b0c6-4180-b474-0ea68b4849ba

18. According to the Pew Research Center's report "Faith among Black Americans,"
published in 2021, the vast majority of US Black Catholics state that "fighting racism
and sexism is essential to their faith." Black Catholics in the United States are also more
likely than their Black Protestant counterparts to state that "opposing racism is essential
to being Christian." See "Faith among Black Americans," 66; and Madeleine Davison,
"Panel: Social Justice Is Essential to Black Catholics' Faith," *National Catholic Reporter*,
March 4, 2021, https://www.ncronline.org/news/parish/panel-social-justice-essential
-black-catholics-faith.

19. Calypso, "Real 'Sister Act.'"

20. Sister Mary Alice Chineworth said this to the author during an informal conversation at the motherhouse of the Oblate Sisters of Providence on February 1, 2010.
Variations of this statement have also been made to the author by several members of
the African American sisterhoods and select Black members of white sisterhoods.

21. Thibodeaux, *Black Nun*, 42, 80. Note: Sisters Mary Roger Thibodeaux, sbs and
Sylvia Thibodeaux, ssf are different people. They are cousins.

22. Rhina Guidos, "Speakers Prompt Young Adults to Help Heal Injustices and Sin
of Racism," *Catholic News Service*, November 10, 2017. See also USCCB, *Open Wide Our
Hearts*; Pratt, "There Is Time"; Rhina Guidos, "Bishops Urge Closer Look at COVID
Deaths in Black Communities," *Catholic News Service*, May 5, 2020; and Olga Segura,
"Do US Bishops Really Believe Black Lives Matter?," *National Catholic Reporter*, May 8,
2020, https://www.ncronline.org/news/coronavirus/do-us-bishops-really-believe
-black-lives-matter.

23. John Gehring, "White Christians' Voting Patterns Are an Indictment of
Churches," *National Catholic Reporter*, November 23, 2020, https://www.ncronline

.org/news/opinion/white-christians-voting-patterns-are-indictment-churches. See also Christopher White, "Major Catholic Funders and Power Brokers Spearhead Voter Suppression Efforts," *National Catholic Reporter*, April 8, 2021, https://www.ncronline .org/news/justice/major-catholic-funders-and-power-brokers-spearhead-voter -suppression-efforts; Jessica Martinez and Gregory A. Smith, "How the Faithful Vote: A Preliminary 2016 Analysis," *Pew Research Center—Fact Tank*, November 9, 2016; and Michael Pasquier, "White Catholics Have to Talk about Race and to Admit Their Racism," *America*, July 27, 2016, https://www.americamagazine.org/politics-society/2016 /07/27/white-catholics-have-talk-about-race-and-admit-their-racism.

24. Araujo-Hawkins, "Descendants of Enslaved People." See also Smith, "Nuns Apologize"; Sean Salai, SJ, "Meet the Researchers Helping the Jesuits Address Their History of Slaveholding," *America*, January 6, 2020; and Miranda Bryant, "Catholic Order Pledges $100m in Reparations to Descendants of Enslaved People," *Guardian*, March 16, 2021, https://www.theguardian.com/world/2021/mar/16/jesuit-conference -canada-us-catholic-reparations-descendants-enslaved-people.

25. Araujo-Hawkins, "Reckoning: White Sisters Respond to Their Own Racism, to One Historian's Call for Justice," *Global Sisters Report*, January 8, 2018, https://www .globalsistersreport.org/news/trends-equality/reckoning-white-sisters-respond-their -own-racism-one-historians-call-justice. See also Pamela Schaeffer, "'Ouch' Moments Discomfit, Challenge Sisters at Convocation on Racism," *Global Sisters Report*, April 3, 2019, https://www.globalsistersreport.org/news/equality/ouch-moments-discomfit -challenge-sisters-convocation-racism-56042?gsr_redirect=1.

26. Soli Salgado, "LCWR Assembly Reaffirms Commitment to Address 'the Sin of Racism,'" *Global Sisters Report*, last modified August 10, 2018, https://www .globalsistersreport.org/news/equality/lcwr-assembly-reaffirms-commitment -addressing-sin-racism-55278.

27. Mary Pellegrino, CSJ, "The Future Enters Us Long Before It Happens: Opening Space for an Emerging Narrative Communion," 2017 LCWR Presidential Address delivered on August 10, 2017, in Orlando, Florida, typed copy in author's possession.

28. Araujo-Hawkins, "A Sisters' Community Apologizes to One Woman Whose Vocation Was Denied," *Global Sisters Report*, last modified January 8, 2018, https://www .globalsistersreport.org/news/trends-equality/sisters-community-apologizes-one -woman-whose-vocation-was-denied-51191.

29. Matthew Santoni, "Devout Sister Became Ideal Teacher, Role Model," *Pittsburgh Tribune and Review*, September 25, 2016, https://archive.triblive.com/news/obituaries /devout-sister-became-ideal-teacher-role-model/.

30. Grey, "Personal and Unfinished." See also Maria Harden, CSJ, "Just Call Me Maria," *Giving Voice*, March 2000, 2–3.

31. Grey, "Personal and Unfinished," 3. The author was present at this celebration.

32. Grey, "On Forgiveness and Reconciliation: Closing Remarks," address delivered on July 30, 2018, at the NBSC's fiftieth anniversary celebration meeting held at the New Orleans Downtown Marriott at the Convention Center hotel, New Orleans, copy in the author's possession. The capitalized, underlined, and boldfaced text has been preserved from the original.

BIBLIOGRAPHY

Archives and Manuscript Collections

Amistad Research Center, Tulane University, New Orleans
  Catholic Council on Human Relations Papers
American Catholic History Research Center and University Archives at Catholic University of America, Washington, DC (CUA Archives)
  Catholic Interracial Council of New York Collection
  National Catholic Welfare Conference Collection
Archives of the Archdiocese of Baltimore, Baltimore (AB Archives)
Archives of the Archdiocese of St. Louis, St. Louis, MO (ASL Archives)
Archives of the Diocese of Savannah, Savannah, GA (DS Archives)
Archives of the Carmelite Monastery of Baltimore
Archives of the Daughters of the Heart of Mary, Holyoke, MA (DHM Archives)
Archives of the Franciscan Sisters of Mary Archives, St. Louis, MO (FSM Archives)
Archives of the Oblate Sisters of Providence, Baltimore (OSP Archives)
Archives of the Sisters of Charity of Seton Hill, Greensburg, PA (SCSH Archives)
Archives of the Sisters of Charity of New York, Bronx, NY (SCNY Archives)
Archives of the Sisters of Loretto at the Foot of the Cross, Nerinx, KY (SL Archives)
Archives of the Society of Mary, Rome, Italy
Archives of the Sisters of the Blessed Sacrament, Cornwells Heights, PA (SBS Archives)
Archives of the Sisters of St. Francis of Assisi, St. Francis, WI
Archives of the Congregation of the Sisters of the Holy Family, New Orleans (SSF Archives)
Archives of the University of Notre Dame, Notre Dame, IN (UND Archives)
  Leadership Conference of Women Religious Papers

Joseph M. Davis Papers

Archives of the Ursuline Sisters of the Eastern Province, New Rochelle, NY

Department of Special Collections and University Archives, Raynor Memorial Libraries, Marquette University, Milwaukee, WI (MUSCA)

National Black Sisters' Conference Papers

Georgia Historical Society, Savannah, GA

Jesuit Archives and Research Center, St. Louis, MO (JARC)

Josephite Archives, Baltimore, MD

Maryknoll Mission Archives, Maryknoll, NY

Mercy Heritage Center Archives, Belmont, NC (RSM Archives)

National Archives, Washington, DC

New England Archives of the Sisters of Notre Dame de Namur, Ipswich, MA

Ohio Archives of the Sisters of Notre Dame de Namur, Cincinnati, OH

Pittsburgh Courier Archives

Saint Thomas University Archives, Miami Gardens, FL

National Office for Black Catholics (NOBC) Papers

Sisters, Servants of the Immaculate Heart of Mary Archives, Monroe, MI

Xavier University of Louisiana Archives and Special Collections, New Orleans (XULA
Archives)

Periodicals and Newsletters

Advocate (Baton Rouge, LA)

Afro-American (Baltimore)

Afro-American (Washington, DC)

America

American Catholic Tribune

American Missionary (New York)

Amsterdam News (New York)

Anchor (Diocese of Fall River, MA)

Associated Press

Baltimore Sun

Black Panther

Boston Globe

Boston Sunday Globe

Catholic Action of the South (New Orleans)

Catholic Key (Kansas City, MO)

Catholic News Service

Catholic New York

Catholic Philly

Catholic Review (Baltimore)

Catholic Standard and Times (Washington, DC)

Catholic Telegraph (Cincinnati, OH)

Catholic Transcript (Hartford, CT)

Catholic World Report
Chicago Daily Defender
Chicago Defender
Chicago Reader
Chicago Sun-Times
Chicago Tribune
Christian Recorder
Chronicle: Official Organ of the Federated Colored Catholics of the United States (formerly
    the *St. Elizabeth's Chronicle*, later the *Interracial Review*)
Clarion Herald (New Orleans)
Colonel Mayfield's Weekly (Houston, TX)
Colored Harvest (later *Josephite Harvest*)
Colorlines
Commercial Appeal (Memphis, TN)
Community (New York)
Contact: Holy Family Newsletter
Contemplative Review
Courier-Journal (Louisville, KY)
Crosswinds
Crux
Daily News (Memphis, TN)
Daily Picayune (New Orleans)
Denver Post
Des Moines Register
Detroit Free Press
DNAInfo
Ebony
Extension (Chicago)
Feminist Wire
Generalate Quarterly
Giving Voice: A Newsletter for Women Religious Under 50
Global Sisters Report
Grio
Guardian (Manchester, UK)
Guardian: Official Publication of the Diocese of Little Rock (Arkansas)
Hoya
Hyde Park Herald
Impact!: Newsletter of the National Office for Black Catholics
Independent (Nigeria)
Indianapolis Recorder
Interracial Review
Irish World and American Industrial Liberator
Jet
Josephite Harvest (formerly the *Colored Harvest*)

The Journal (Webster University)

Just for You: A Newsletter for Parents of Alvernians

Kansas City (MO) Times

Lebanon (KY) Enterprise

Liguorian

Los Angeles Sentinel

Los Angeles Times

Louisiana Weekly

Mercy Detroiter

Miami Herald

Milwaukee Journal

Minneapolis Post

Morning Star (New Orleans)

National Catholic Reporter

National Catholic Register (formerly the *Denver Catholic Register*)

N.C.W.C. *News Service*

New Journal and Guide (Norfolk, VA)

New Orleans States-Item

News Journal (Chicago)

New York Times

Oblates in Action: Newsletter

Our Colored Missions

Pantagraph (Bloomington, IL)

Pew Research Center—Fact Tank

Philadelphia Inquirer

Philadelphia Tribune

Pittsburgh Catholic

Pittsburgh Courier

Pittsburgh Post-Gazette

Pittsburgh Tribune and Review

Plain Dealer (Cleveland)

Reuters

Savannah (GA) Morning News

Savannah (GA) Tribune

Signs of Soul: Newsletter of the National Black Sisters' Conference

Sisters of St. Joseph of Carondelet, St. Louis Province: Newsletter

Sisters Today

St. Anthony Messenger

St. Augustine's Messenger (later the *St. Augustine's Catholic Messenger* and the *Divine Word Messenger*)

St. Augustine (FL) Record

St. Louis Daily Globe-Democrat

St. Louis Globe and Democrat

St. Louis Post-Dispatch

St. Louis Review
Tampa Bay Times
Time Magazine
Times-Picayune (New Orleans)
Undefeated
U.S. Catholic Magazine
Washington (DC) Informer
Washington Post
Washington Post and Times-Herald
Wednesday Journal (Oak Park, IL)
Xavier Magazine

Cited Interviews

Interviews are by author unless otherwise noted.

Adams, Sherrill (formerly Sister Nathan Marie, SSND), July 24, 2014.

Alexander, Mary Bertha (formerly Sister Mary Concepta, FHM), New York, June 8, 2017.

Baird, Sister Anita, DHM, July 24, 2016, and March 3, 2017. Telephone.

Banfield, Sister Donna, SBS, Memphis, TN, October 27, 2009.

Barial, Sister Mary Judith Therese, SSF, New Orleans, July 7, 2009.

Beasley, Sister Barbara, RGS, July 24, 2015. Telephone.

Bell, Sister Gilda Marie, SBS, New Orleans, August 22, 2009.

Billings, Sister Cora Marie, RSM, July 6, 2010. Telephone.

Bottoms, Sister Mary Kendra, SND, November 18, 2017. Email.

Brown, Dr. Joseph A., SJ, June 20, 2014. Telephone and email.

Bussey, Dr. Deborah Plummer (formerly Sister Phillis Marie, SND), October 23, 2013. Telephone.

Chappell, Sister Patricia, SNDdeN, May 14, 2017. Telephone.

Chineworth, Sister Mary Alice, OSP, Baltimore, February 1, 2010.

Colbert, Sister Josita, SNDdeN (formerly OSP), June 23, 2014, and August 9, 2016. Telephone.

Coleman, Sister Martin de Porres, SNDdeN, September 4, 2013. Telephone.

Copeland, Dr. M. Shawn (formerly Sister M. Shawn Copeland, CSSF and OP), March 5, 2007. Telephone.

Daniels-Sykes, Dr. Shawnee (formerly SSND), September 22, 2016. Email.

Deconge-Watson, Lovenia (formerly Sister Mary Sylvester, SSF), June 9, 2010. Interview by *The HistoryMakers*.

Dillard, Sister Irma, RSCJ, April 14, 2017. Telephone and email.

Dimaku, Sister Cecilia, SSH, New Orleans, October 20, 2016.

Dual, Sister Patricia, OP, June 20, 2014. Telephone.

Ebo, Sister Mary Antona, FSM, March 26, 2007. Telephone.

Edmond, Reverend Kimberley Clark (formerly Sister Mary Kimberley, RSM), November 20, 2015. Telephone.

Fasutina, Sister Mary Angela, CSJ, October 30, 2015. Telephone.

Findlay, Sister Desire-Anne, CSSF, August 29, 2015. Telephone.

Fish, Sister M. Virginie, OSP, Baltimore, March 11, 2010.

Francis, Dr. Norman, September 11, 2009. Telephone.

Gemperle, Rosemary, South Bend, IN, August 1, 2010.

Glapion, Rosaria Floyd (formerly Sister Mary Florence, FSP), August 18, 2015. Telephone.

Glenn, Sister Rose Martin, SSpS, Memphis, TN, November 20, 2009.

Goudeaux, Sister Doris, SSF, New Orleans, August 18, 2009.

Graves, Megan, August 11, 2015. Telephone.

Greenfield, Earline. New Orleans, June 14, 2014.

Grey, Dr. Patricia (formerly Sister M. Martin de Porres, RSM), Sewickley, PA, August 12, 2007, June 21, 2009, March 22, 2010, and August 25, 2019.

Haley, Sister Patricia, SCN, March 30, 2012. Telephone.

Hamilton, Patricia (former SNDdeN), July 14, 2014, New Orleans.

Harris, Sister Elizabeth, HVM, July 15, 2014. Telephone.

Hawkins, Sister Nellie, RGS, January 4, 2015. Postal mail.

Hemenway, Michele, September 28, 2015. Telephone.

Henegan, Sister Mary Ann, MSBT, October 29, 2016. Telephone.

Holloman, Sister Rosella Marie, SCA, Richfield, OH, June 19, 2014.

Jenkins, Sister Mamie, RSCJ, May 23, 2017. Conducted by Sister Irma Dillard, RSCJ, using author's interview guide.

Johnson, Barbara Ann (formerly Sister Jacinta Marie, FHM), New York, June 8, 2017.

LaRochester, Sister Barbara Jean, OCD, June 4, 2015. Telephone.

Lowe, Sister Catherine Marie, DC, August 27, 2016. Telephone.

Lucas, Sister Patricia, DHM (formerly Sister Mary Immanuel, FHM), March 22, 2010. Telephone.

Marshall, Sister Charlotte, OSP, Baltimore, February 19, 2010.

Moore, Sister Barbara, CSJ, April 30, 2007. Telephone.

Nash, Diane, November 13, 2015. Telephone.

Pellerin, Sister Melinda, SSJ, August 16, 2016. Telephone.

Phelps, Sister Jamie, OP, New Orleans, July 22, 2009.

Proctor, Sister Gwynette, SNDdeN, July 27, 2015. Telephone.

Pruitt, Sister Jannette, OSF, June 2, 2015. Telephone and email.

Quadarella, Carolyn (formerly Sister Louis Mary, SSND), December 29, 2015. Telephone and email.

Ralph, Sister Patricia, SSJ, August 7, 2015. Telephone.

Richards, Sister Loretta Theresa, FHM, New York, NY, December 28, 2009.

Rivera-Williams, Sister Larretta, RSM, August 8, 2016. Telephone and email.

Smith, Sister Demetria, MSOLA, June 13, 2015. Telephone.

Smith, Sister Kathleen, SP, July 8, 2014. Telephone.

Smith, Sister Naomi, OSP, Baltimore, May 5, 2010.

Smithson, Sister Sandra, SSSF, Nashville, TN, June 11, 2015.

Steib, Bishop J. Terry, SVD, Memphis, TN, October 19, 2009.

Taylor, Marie de Porres (formerly SNJM), June 6, 2015. Telephone.

Thibodeaux, Sister Sylvia, SSF, New Orleans, August 19, 2009, August 4, 2016, and October 8, 2016.

Trahan, Sister Nicole, FMI, October 10, 2015. Telephone.

Varner, Cheryl (formerly Sister Ruth, SNDdeN), November 15, 2013. Telephone.

Wheeler, Lois, Southfield, MI, June 25, 2017.

White, Angela (formerly Sister Mary Angela de Porres, SC), Cincinnati, OH, October 23, 2013.

Willingham, Saundra Ann (formerly Sister M. Melanie, SNDdeN), June 29, 2012, telephone, and October 21, 2013, Cincinnati, OH.

Film Documentaries

Sisters of Selma: Bearing Witness for Change. Directed by Jaysari Majumdar Hart. Los Angeles, CA: Hartfilms, 2006. DVD.

Sr. Thea, Her Own Story: A Video Autobiography. Florissant, MO: Oblate Media and Communication, 1991. VHS.

The Way We Were: NBSC 50th Anniversary Commemorative Video. Produced by Valerie Shields. Washington, DC: National Black Sisters' Conference, July 30, 2018. DVD.

Unpublished Papers, Blog Posts, Theses, and Dissertations

Baptiste, Mary of Good Counsel, OSP. "A Study of the Foundation and Educational Objectives of the Congregation of the Oblate Sisters of Providence and of the Achievements of These Objectives as Seen in Their Schools." Master's thesis, Villanova University, 1939.

Critchley-Mentor, William. "Jim Crow, SJ: Segregation and White Supremacy in the American Society of Jesus." Master's thesis, St. Louis University, 2021.

Daly, Maureen. "Call Me Sister." *VISION Vocation Network Blog*, October 4, 2009. https://vocationnetwork.org/en/blog/spiritcitings_blog/2009/10/finding_her _way_through_racism.

Davis, Nancy. "Integration, the 'New Negro,' and Community Building: Black Catholic Life in Four Catholic Churches in Detroit, 1911 to 1945." PhD diss., University of Michigan, 1996.

Gilbert, Sister Magdala Marie, OSP. "My Vocation Story." n.d. Accessed August 10, 2020, http://www.oblatesistersvocations.com/SrMagdala.html.

Gilkin, Margaret Wilson. "Saint Dominguan Refugees in Charleston, South Carolina, 1791–1822: Assimilation and Accommodation in a Slave Society." PhD diss., University of South Carolina, 2014.

Glose, Georgianna. "Take the Blinders from Your Vision, Take the Padding from Your Ears." PhD diss., City University of New York, 1996.

Gray, Sister Mary, OSF, and Sister Barbara Barry. "Our Story: The Franciscan Sisters of Baltimore, 1868–2000." Unpublished, n.d. Archives of the Sisters of St. Francis of Assisi, St. Francis, WI.

Hadrick, M. Emma, OSP. "Contributions of the Oblate Sisters of Providence to Catholic Education in the USA and Cuba, 1829–1922." Master's thesis, Catholic University of America, 1964.

Hart, Sister M. Borgia, SSF. "Violets in the King's Garden: A History of the Congregation of the Sisters of the Holy Family in New Orleans." Bachelor's thesis, Xavier College, 1931.

Herbes, Sister Emily Ann, OSF. "Histories of the Sisters of St. Francis of Philadelphia in Wyoming since 1892." Philadelphia, PA, 2005. https://dioceseofcheyenne.org /documents/2020/6/SistersofStFrancis.pdf.

Mattick, Barbara. "Ministries in Black and White: The Catholic Sisters of St. Augustine, Florida, 1859–1920." PhD diss., Florida State University, 2008.

"A New Call for Renee L. Fenner '05." *General Theological Seminary Blog*, May 23, 2019. https://general-seminary-test.squarespace.com/general-news/2019/5/23/a-new-call -for-renee-l-fenner-05.

Okure, Aniedi, OP. "The African-Born and the Church Family in the United States." Unpublished paper for the Institute for Policy Research and Catholic Studies at the Catholic University of America, 2011.

Proctor, Sister Gwynette. "What We've Seen and Heard . . . Black Lives Matter." *Sister of Notre Dame de Namur Justice, Peace and Integrity of Creation Blog*, March 7, 2016. https://SNDdeNjpic.org/2016/03/07/what-weve-seen-and-heardblack-lives-matter.

"Report of the Working Group on Slavery, Memory, and Reconciliation to the President of Georgetown University." Washington, DC, June 3, 2016. https://georgetown .app.box.com/s/nz01tx4elaerg13akjwxuve3pv9sb03a.

"Report on the Commission for the Legacy of Slavery at Rosemont College." Rosemont, PA, updated in December 2019. https://corneliaconnellylibrary.org/library -materials/Report%20on%20Legacy%20of%20slavery%20updated.pdf.

Rosenkrans, Amy. "'The Good Work': Saint Frances Orphan Asylum and Saint Elizabeth Home, Two Baltimore Orphanages for African Americans." PhD diss., Notre Dame of Maryland University, 2016.

Schadewald, Paul John. "Remapping Race, Religion, and Community: William Markoe and the Legacy of Catholic Interracialism in St. Louis, 1900–1945." PhD diss., Indiana University, 2003.

Schmidt, Kelly L. "'Regulations for Our Black People': Reconstructing the Experiences of Enslaved People in the United States through Jesuit Records." Paper presented at the Fifth Annual International Symposium on Jesuit Studies, Engaging Sources: The Tradition and Future of Collecting History in the Society of Jesus, Boston College, Boston, June 11–13, 2019. https://jesuitportal.bc.edu/publications/symposia /2019symposium/symposia-schmidt/. DOI:10.51238/ISJS.2019.12.

Slattery, John. "The Untold Story of Harriet Thompson in the Battle for Racial Equality in Catholicism." *Daily Theology*, January 23, 2014. https://dailytheology.org/2014 /01/23/the-untold-story-of-harriet-thompson-in-the-battle-for-racial-equality-in -catholicism-tbt.

Sweet, James H. "Spanish and Portuguese Influences on Racial Slavery in British North America, 1492–1619." Paper presented at the Fifth Annual Gilder Lehrman Center

International Conference, Collective Degradation: Slavery and the Construction of Race, Yale University, New Haven, CT, November 7–8, 2003. https://glc.yale.edu/sites/default/files/files/events/race/Sweet.pdf.

Uva, Katie, and Gotham Center for New York City History. "The Life of Elizabeth Seton: An Interview with Catherine O'Donnell." *Gotham Center for New York City History Blog*, November 13, 2018. https://www.gothamcenter.org/blog/the-life-of-elizabeth-seton-an-interview-with-catherine-odonnell.

Weind, Teresita, SNDdeN. "Founding Board Member Teresita Weind, SNDdeN." *Mary's Pence Blog*, accessed August 19, 2021. https://www.maryspence.org/stories/founding-board-member-teresita-weind-snden.

Published Sources

Abbott, Walter, SJ, ed. *The Documents of Vatican II*. New York: Herder and Herder, 1966.

Abram, Paula. *Cross Purposes: Pierce v. Society of Sisters and the Struggle over Compulsory Public Education*. Ann Arbor: University of Michigan Press, 2009.

Adams, David Wallace. *Education for Extinction: American Indians and the Boarding School Experience, 1875–1928*. Rev. ed. Lawrence: University Press of Kansas, 2020.

Adiele, Pius Onyemechi. *The Popes, the Catholic Church, and the Transatlantic Enslavement of Black Africans, 1418–1839*. Hildesheim: Georg Olms, 2017.

Agee, Gary B. *A Cry for Justice: Daniel Rudd and His Life in Black Catholicism, Journalism, and Activism, 1854–1933*. Fayetteville: University of Arkansas Press, 2011.

Ahles, Sister Mary Assumpta, OSF. *In the Shadow of His Wings: A History of the Franciscans*. Saint Paul, MN: North Central Publishing, 1977.

Alberts, John B. "Black Catholic Schools: The Josephite Parishes during the Jim Crow Era." *U.S. Catholic Historian* 12, no. 1 (1994): 77–99.

Alexander, Charles C. *The Ku Klux Klan in the Southwest*. Lexington: University Press of Kentucky, 1965.

Anderson, James D. *The Education of Blacks in the South, 1860–1935*. Chapel Hill: University of North Carolina Press, 1988.

Anderson, R. Bentley. *Black, White, and Catholic: New Orleans Interracialism, 1947–1956*. Nashville: Vanderbilt University Press, 2005.

Anderson, R. Bentley. "Prelates, Protest, and Public Opinion: Catholic Opposition to Desegregation, 1947–1955." *Journal of Church and State* 46 (2004): 617–44.

Aprile, Dianne. *The Abbey of Gethsemani: Place of Peace and Paradox*. Louisville, KY: Trout Lily Press, 1998.

Baldwin, Lou. *A Call to Sanctity: The Formation of the Life of Mother Katharine Drexel*. Philadelphia: Catholic Standard and Times, 1988.

Baptiste, Edward E. "'Cuffy,' 'Fancy Maids,' and 'One-Eyed Men': Rape, Commodification, and the Domestic Slave Trade in the United States." *American Historical Review* 106, no. 5 (December 2001): 1619–50.

Baudier, Roger. *The Catholic Church in Louisiana*. New Orleans: Hyatt, 1939.

Becker, Sister Johanna, OSB. "Operation Mississippi: An American Mission." *American Benedictine Review* 17 (1966): 68–74.

Beito, David T., and Linda Royster Beito. *Black Maverick: T. R. M. Howard's Fight for Civil Rights and Economic Power*. Urbana: University of Illinois Press, 2009.

Belcher, Wendy Laura. "Sisters Debating the Jesuits: The Role of African Women in Defeating Portuguese Proto-Colonialism in Seventeenth-Century Abyssinia." *Northeast African Studies* 13, no. 1 (2013): 121–66.

Bennett, James B. *Religion and the Rise of Jim Crow in New Orleans*. Princeton, NJ: Princeton University Press, 2005.

Beozzo, José Oscar. *Tecendo memórias, gestando futuro: História das irmãs negras e indígenas Missionárias de Jesus Crucificado, MJC*. São Paulo: Paulinas, 2009.

Berg, Carol, OSB. "Sisters and the Civil Rights Movement." *Benedictine Sisters and Friends*, Spring–Summer 2015, 5.

Bernard, Raymond, SJ. "Interracial Vocation Opportunities: Supplemental List of Seminaries and Novitiates." *Social Order*, o.s. 2 (December 1949): 454–55.

Bernard, Raymond, SJ. "Jim Crow Vocations?" *Social Order*, o.s. 2 (June 1949): 241–44.

Bernard, Raymond, SJ. "More Vocation Opportunities." *Social Order*, o.s. 3 (October 1950): 368.

Bernard, Raymond, SJ. "Some Anthropological Implications of the Racial Admission Policy of the U.S. Sisterhoods." *American Catholic Sociological Review* 19, no. 2 (June 1958): 124–33.

Berrelleza, Erick, SJ, Mary L. Gautier, and Mark M. Gray. *Special Report: Population Trends among Religious Institutes of Women*. Washington, DC: Center for Applied Research in the Apostolate, 2014.

Bessler, John D. *Legacy of Violence: Lynch Mobs and Executions in Minnesota*. Minneapolis: University of Minnesota Press, 2006.

Birzer, Bradley J. *American Cicero: The Life of Charles Carroll*. Wilmington, DE: Intercollegiate Studies Institute, 2010.

Blain, Keisha N. *Set the World on Fire: Black Nationalist Women and the Global Struggle for Freedom*. Philadelphia: University of Pennsylvania Press, 2018.

Blose, David T., and Ambrose Caliver. *Statistics of the Education of Negroes, 1933–34 and 1935–36*. Washington, DC: US Government Printing Office, 1939.

Blum, Edward J., Tracy Fessenden, Prema Kurien, and Judith Weisenfeld, eds. "Forum: American Religion and 'Whiteness.'" *Religion and American Culture* 19, no. 1 (Winter 2009): 1–35.

Bogle, Donald. *Toms, Coons, Mulattoes, Mammies, and Bucks: An Interpretive History of Blacks in American Films*. New York: Bloomsbury Academic US, 2015.

Borromeo, Sr. M. Charles, CSC, ed. *The Changing Sister*. Notre Dame: Fides, 1965.

Brady, Diane. *Fraternity*. New York: Spiegel and Grau, 2012.

Branch, Taylor. *At Canaan's Edge: America in the King Years, 1965–1968*. New York: Simon and Schuster, 2006.

Brandewie, Ernest. *In the Light of the Word: Divine Word Missionaries of North America*. Maryknoll, NY: Orbis Books, 2000.

Brett, Edward T. *The New Orleans Sisters of the Holy Family: African-American Missionaries to the Garifuna of Belize*. Notre Dame, IN: University of Notre Dame Press, 2012.

Brewer, Eileen Mary. *Nuns and the Education of American Catholic Women, 1860–1920.* Chicago: Loyola University Press, 1987.

Brooks, Sister Marcellina, OSP. "Future of the National Black Sisters' Conference." In *Celibate Black Commitment: Report of the Third Annual National Black Sisters' Conference,* 10–13. Pittsburgh: National Black Sisters' Conference, 1971.

Brown, Lisa Marie. *Posing as Nuns, Passing for White: The Gouley Sisters.* New Orleans: Pel Hughes, 2010.

Brown, William E., and Andrew M. Greeley. *Can Catholic Schools Survive?* New York: Sheed and Ward, 1970.

Brückmann, Rebecca. *Massive Resistance and Southern Womanhood: White Women, Class and Segregation.* Athens: University of Georgia Press, 2020.

Brundage, William Fitzhugh. *The Southern Past: A Clash of Race and Memory.* Cambridge, MA: Belknap Press of Harvard University Press, 2005.

Bryan, Sister Louis Marie, SC, DSW. *All along the Way: Gifts, Blessings, and Graces from Our Loving God.* Clifton Corners, NY: Jubilee Studio, 2010.

Bryan, Sister Louis Marie, SC, DSW. "History of the National Black Sisters' Conference." In *Celibate Black Commitment: Report of the Third Annual National Black Sisters' Conference,* 2–9. Pittsburgh: National Black Sisters' Conference, 1971.

Bryer, Jackson R., and Mary C. Hartig, eds. *Conversations with August Wilson.* Oxford: University Press of Mississippi, 2006.

The Buffaloes: A Story Commemorating Maryknoll Society's 50 Years in Tanzania, 1946–1996. Maryknoll, NY: Privately printed, 1997.

Burns, Kathryn. *Colonial Habits: Convents and the Spiritual Economy of Cuzco, Peru.* Durham, NC: Duke University Press, 1999.

Butler, Anne. *Across God's Frontiers: Catholic Sisters in the American West, 1850–1920.* Chapel Hill: University of North Carolina Press, 2012.

Campbell, Joan, SL. *Loretto: An Early American Congregation in the Antebellum South.* St. Louis, MO: Bluebird, 2015.

Campbell, William. *How Unsearchable His Ways: One Hundred Twenty-Fifth Anniversary, Saint Patrick's Church.* Philadelphia: Privately printed, 1965.

Carr, Margaret J. S. *Accredited Secondary Schools in the United States.* Washington, DC: US Government Printing Office, 1930.

Carreel, Marie-France, RSCJ, and Carolyn Osiek, RSCJ, eds. *Philippine Duchesne: Pioneer on the American Frontier (1769–1852): Complete Works.* Translated by Frances Gimber, RSCJ. Vol. 1. Turnhout, Belgium: Brepols, 2019.

Cepress, Celestine, FSPA, ed. *Sister Thea Bowman: Shooting Star.* Winona, MN: Saint Mary's Press, 1993.

Chicago Commission on Race Relations. *The Negro in Chicago: A Study of Race Relations and a Race Riot.* Chicago: University of Chicago Press, 1922.

Christian, Sister Helen Marie, RSM. "Psychological Implications of the Celibate Black Commitment." In *Celibate Black Commitment: Report of the Third Annual National Black Sisters' Conference,* 78–89. Pittsburgh: National Black Sisters' Conference, 1971.

Churchill, Ward. *Kill the Indian, Save the Man: The Genocidal Impact of American Indian Residential School.* San Francisco, CA: City Lights Publishers, 2004.

Clark, Emily. *Masterless Mistresses: The New Orleans Ursulines and the Development of a New World Society, 1727–1834.* Chapel Hill: University of North Carolina Press, 2007.

Clark, Emily, and Virginia Meacham Gould. "The Feminine Face of Afro-Catholicism in New Orleans, 1727–1852." *William and Mary Quarterly* 59 (April 2002): 409–48.

Clevenger, Case Ritchi. *Unequal Partners: In Search of Transnational Catholic Sisterhood.* Chicago: University of Chicago Press, 2020.

Clune, John J. *Cuban Convents in the Age of Enlightened Reform, 1761–1807.* Gainesville: University Press of Florida, 2008.

Coburn, Carol. "An Overview of the Historiography of Women Religious: A Twenty-Five-Year Retrospective." *U.S. Catholic Historian* 22, no. 1 (2004): 1–26.

Collier-Thomas, Bettye. *Jesus, Jobs, and Justice: African-American Women and Religion.* New York: Alfred A. Knopf, 2010.

Collier-Thomas, Bettye, and V. P. Franklin, eds. *Sisters in the Struggle: African American Women in the Civil Rights-Black Power Movement.* New York: New York University Press, 2001.

Collins, Donald E. *The Death and Resurrection of Jefferson Davis.* Lanham, MD: Rowman and Littlefield, 2005.

Cone, James H. *Black Theology and Black Power.* 1969. Reprint, Maryknoll, NY: Orbis, 2019.

Connolly, Mary Beth Fraser. *Women of Faith: The Chicago Sisters of Mercy and the Evolution of a Religious Community.* New York: Fordham University Press, 2014.

Cooper, Afua. *The Hanging of Angélique: The Untold Story of Canadian Slavery and the Burning of Old Montreal.* Athens: University of Georgia Press, 2007.

Cooper, Brittany. *Beyond Respectability: The Intellectual Thought of Race Women.* Urbana: University of Illinois Press, 2017.

Copeland, M. Shawn. "A Cadre of Women Religious Committed to Black Liberation: The National Black Sisters' Conference." *U.S. Catholic Historian* 14, no. 1 (1996): 121–44.

Copeland, M. Shawn. *The Subversive Power of Love: The Vision of Henriette Delille.* New York: Paulist Press, 2009.

Copeland, M. Shawn, ed. *Uncommon Faithfulness: The Black Catholic Experience.* Maryknoll, NY: Orbis Books, 2009.

[Cox], Sister Anna, SBS. "The Black Candidate." In *Prayer and Renewal: Proceedings and Communications of Regional Meetings of the Sister-Formation Conferences 1969,* edited by Sister Mary Hester Valentine, SSND, 40–45. New York: Fordham University Press, 1970.

Crawford, Vicki L., Jacqueline Anne Rouse, and Barbara Woods, eds. *Women in the Civil Rights Movement: Trailblazers and Torchbearers, 1941–1965.* Brooklyn, NY: Carlson, 1990.

Cressler, Matthew J. *Authentically Black and Truly Catholic: The Rise of Black Catholicism in the Great Migration.* New York: New York University Press, 2017.

Crews, Clyde F. *An American Holy Land: A History of the Archdiocese of Louisville.* Wilmington, DE: Michael Glazier, 1987.

Cummings, Kathleen Sprows. *New Women of the Old Faith: Gender and American Catholicism in the Progressive Era.* Chapel Hill: University of North Carolina Press, 2009.

Cummings, Kathleen Sprows. *A Saint of Our Own: How the Quest for a Holy Hero Helped Catholics Become American*. Chapel Hill: University of North Carolina Press, 2019.

Curran, Robert Emmett. *Shaping American Catholicism: Maryland and New York, 1805–1815*. Washington, DC: Catholic University of America Press, 2012.

Curtis, Edward, and Sylvester A. Johnson. "Black Catholicism." *Journal of Africana Religions* 2, no. 2 (2014): 244–45.

Curtis, Sarah A. *Civilizing Habits: Women Missionaries and the Revival of the French Empire*. Oxford: Oxford University Press, 2010.

Dannett, Sylvia G. L. "Mother Mathilda Beasley (1834–1903): The First Negro Nun in Georgia." In *Profiles of Negro Womanhood*, 1:144–45. Yonkers, NY: Educational Heritage, 1964.

Davidson, June Davis, and Richelle Putnam. *Legendary Locals of Meridian, Mississippi*. Charleston, SC: Arcadia, 2013.

Davies, Sharon L. *Rising Road: A True Tale of Love, Race, and Religion in America*. Oxford: Oxford University Press, 2010.

Davis, Cyprian, OSB. "Black Catholics in the Civil Rights Movement in the Southern United States: A.P. Tureaud, Thomas Wyatt Turner, and Earl Johnson." *U.S. Catholic Historian* 24, no. 4 (2006): 69–81.

Davis, Cyprian, OSB. *Henriette Delille: Servant of Slaves, Witness to the Poor*. New Orleans: Archdiocese of New Orleans in Cooperation with the Sisters of the Holy Family, 2004.

Davis, Cyprian, OSB. *History of Black Catholics in the United States*. New York: Crossroad, 1990.

Davis, Cyprian, OSB. "The Holy See and American Black Catholics: A Forgotten Chapter in the History of the American Catholic Church." *U.S. Catholic Historian* 7, nos. 2–3 (1988): 157–81.

Davis, Cyprian, OSB, and Jamie Phelps, OP, eds. *"Stamped with the Image of God": African Americans as God's Image in Black*. Maryknoll, NY: Orbis Books, 2003.

Davis, Joseph M., SM, and Cyprian S. Rowe. "The Development of the National Office for Black Catholics." *U.S. Catholic Historian* 7, nos. 2–3 (1988): 269–75.

Davis, Nancy M. "Finding Voice: Revisiting Race and American Catholicism in Detroit." *American Catholic Studies* 114, no. 3 (Fall 2003): 39–58.

Deggs, Sister Mary Bernard. *No Cross, No Crown: Black Nuns in Nineteenth-Century New Orleans*. Edited by Virginia Meacham Gould and Charles E. Nolan. Bloomington: Indiana University Press, 2001.

Delle, James A., and Mary Ann Levine. "Excavations at the Thaddeus Stevens and Lydia Hamilton Smith Site, Lancaster, Pennsylvania: Archaeological Evidence for the Underground Railroad?" *Northeast Historical Archaeology* 33 (2004): 131–52.

Delpit, Lisa. "Act Your Age, Not Your Color." In *Growing Up African American in Catholic Schools*, edited by Jacqueline Jordan Irvine and Michele Foster, 116–25. New York: Teachers College Press, 1996.

Desdunes, Rodolphe Lucien. *Our People and Our History: Fifty Creole Portraits*. Translated by Sister Dorthea Olga McCants. 1911. Reprint, Baton Rouge: Louisiana State University Press, 1973.

Detiege, Sister Audrey Marie. *Henriette Delille, Free Woman of Color: Foundress of the Sisters of the Family.* New Orleans: Sisters of the Holy Family, 1976.

Dolan, Jay P. *The American Catholic Experience: A History from Colonial Times to the Present.* Garden City, NY: Doubleday, 1992.

Doyle, Mary Ellen, SCN. *Pioneer Spirit: Catherine Spalding, Sister of Charity of Nazareth.* Lexington: University Press of Kentucky, 2006.

Dubois, Laurent. *Avengers of the New World: The Story of the Haitian Revolution.* Cambridge, MA: Harvard University Press, 2009.

Du Bois, W. E. B. *Black Reconstruction in America, 1860–1880.* 1935. Reprint, New York: Free Press, 1997.

Duriga, Joyce. *Augustus Tolton: The Church Is the True Liberator.* Collegeville, MN: Liturgical Press, 2020.

Ebaugh, Helen Rose Fuchs. *Women in the Vanishing Cloister: Organizational Decline in Catholic Religious Orders in the United States.* New Brunswick, NJ: Rutgers University Press, 1993.

Ellsworth, Scott. *Death in a Promised Land: The Tulsa Race Riot of 1921.* Baton Rouge: Louisiana State Press, 1992.

Emery, Sister Andree. "Experiment in Counseling Religious." *Review for Religious* 28 (1969): 35–47.

Erickson, Donald A., and John D. Donovan. *The Three R's on Nonpublic Education in Louisiana: Race, Religion, and Region; A Report to the President's Commission on School Finance.* Chicago: US Department of Health, Education, and Welfare Office of Education, 1972.

Estes-Hicks, Onita. "Henriette Delille: Free Woman of Color, Candidate for Roman Catholic Sainthood, Early Womanist." In *Perspectives on Womanist Theology,* edited by Jacquelyn Grant, 41–54. Black Church Scholars Series 7. Atlanta, GA: Interdenominational Theological Center Press, 1995.

Fairclough, Adam. *A Class of Their Own: Black Teachers in the Segregated South.* Cambridge, MA: Belknap Press of Harvard University Press, 2007.

Farmer, Ashley D. *Remaking Black Power: How Black Women Transformed the Era.* Chapel Hill: University of North Carolina Press, 2017.

Farrelly, Maura Jane. *Anti-Catholicism in America, 1620–1860.* New York: Cambridge University Press, 2018.

Feimster, Crystal L. *Southern Horrors: Women and the Politics of Rape and Lynching.* Cambridge, MA: Harvard University Press, 2009.

Fessenden, Tracy. "The Sisters of the Holy Family and the Veil of Race." *Religion and American Culture* 10, no. 2 (Summer 2000): 187–224.

Fialka, John J. *Sisters: Catholic Nuns and the Making of America.* New York: St. Martin's, 2003.

Fichter, Joseph H., SJ. "First Black Students at Loyola University: A Strategy to Obtain Teacher Certification." *Journal of Negro Education* 56, no. 4 (Autumn 1987): 535–49.

Fichter, Joseph H., SJ. "The White Church and the Black Sisters." *U.S. Catholic Historian* 12, no. 1 (1994): 31–48.

Finkelman, Paul. *Supreme Injustice: Slavery in the Nation's Highest Court.* Cambridge, MA: Harvard University Press, 2018.

Floyd, Samuel A. *The Power of Black Music: Interpreting Its History from Africa to the United States*. Oxford: Oxford University Press, 1995.

Foley, Albert S., SJ. *God's Men of Color: The Colored Catholic Priests of the United States, 1854–1954*. New York: Farrar, Straus, 1955.

Foley, Albert S., SJ. "Adventures in Black Catholic History: Research and Writing." *U.S. Catholic Historian*. 5, no. 1 (1986): 103–18.

Ford, Tanisha C. *Liberated Threads: Black Women, Style, and the Global Politics of Soul*. Chapel Hill: University of North Carolina Press, 2015.

Formisano, Ronald P. *Boston against Busing: Race, Class, and Ethnicity in the 1960s and 1970s*. Chapel Hill: University of North Carolina Press, 1991.

Foster, Elizabeth A. *Faith in Empire: Religion, Politics, and Colonial Rule in French Senegal, 1880–1940*. Stanford, CA: Stanford University Press, 2013.

Frederickson, George M. *The Black Image in the White Mind: The Debate on Afro-American Character and Destiny, 1817–1914*. New York: Harper and Row, 1971.

Gannon, Margaret, IHM, ed. *Paths of Daring, Deeds of Hope: Letters by and about Mother Theresa Maxis Duchemin*. Scranton, PA: Sister Servants of the Immaculate Heart of Mary, 1992.

Gatewood, Willard B. "The Remarkable Misses Rollin': Black Women in Reconstruction South Carolina." *South Carolina Historical Magazine* 92, no. 3 (July 1991): 172–88.

Garrow, David J. *Protest at Selma: Martin Luther King, Jr., and the Voting Rights Act of 1965*. Rev. ed. New Haven, CT: Yale University Press, 2015.

Gerdes, Sr. M. Reginald, OSP. "To Educate and Evangelize: Black Catholic Schools of the Oblate Sisters of Providence, 1828–1880." *U.S. Catholic Historian* 7, nos. 2–3 (1988): 183–99.

Giddings, Paula J. *Ida: A Sword among Lions; Ida B. Wells and the Campaign against Lynching*. New York: HarperCollins, 2008.

Giddings, Paula J. *When and Where I Enter: The Impact of Black Women on Race and Sex in America*. New York: William Morrow, 1984.

Gillard, John T. *Colored Catholics in the United States*. Baltimore: Josephite Press, 1941.

Gilmore, Glenda. *Gender and Jim Crow: Women and the Politics of White Supremacy in North Carolina, 1896–1920*. Chapel Hill: University of North Carolina Press, 1996.

Gilmore, Sister Julia, SCL. *We Came North: A History of the Sisters of Charity of Leavenworth*. St. Meinrad, IN: Abbey Press, 1961.

Glapion, Rosie [Floyd]. *Seeing the Face of God: Memoirs of a Light-Skinned Black Woman*. Nashville: WestBow, 2014.

Gleason, Philip. *Contending with Modernity: Catholic Higher Education in the Twentieth Century*. New York: Oxford University Press, 1995.

Gollar, C. Walker. "Catholic Slaves and Slaveholders in Kentucky." *Catholic Historical Review* 84, no. 1 (January 1998): 42–62.

Goodwin, Moses B. "Schools and Education of the Colored Population." In *Special Report of the United States Commissioner of Education on the Condition and Improvement of Public Schools in the District of Columbia*, by the Department of Education, 193–300. Washington, DC: US Government Printing Office, 1871.

Gordon, Linda. *The Second Coming of the KKK: The Ku Klux Klan of the 1920s and the American Political Tradition*. New York: Liveright, 2017.

Gould, Virginia Meacham. "'A Chaos of Iniquity and Discord': Slave and Free Women of Color in the Spanish Ports of New Orleans, Mobile, and Pensacola." In *The Devil's Lane: Sex and Race in the Early South*, edited by Catherine Clinton and Michele Gillespie, 232–45. Oxford: Oxford University Press, 1997.

Gould, Virginia Meacham. "Henriette Delille, Free Women of Color, and Catholicism in Antebellum New Orleans, 1727–1852." In *Beyond Bondage: Free Women of Color in the Americas*, edited by David Barry Gaspar and Darlene Clark Hine, 271–85. Urbana: University of Illinois Press, 2004.

Gould, Virginia Meacham, and Charles E. Nolan. *Henriette Delille: "Servant of Slaves."* New Orleans: Sisters of the Holy Family, 1998.

Grey, Sister M. Martin de Porres. *Black Religious Women as Part of the Answer*. Pittsburgh: National Black Sisters' Conference, 1971.

Grey, Sister M. Martin de Porres. "The Church, Revolution, and Black Catholics." *Black Scholar* 2, no. 4 (December 1970): 20–26.

Grey, Sister M. Martin de Porres, RSM. "The National Black Sisters' Conference Is Because." In *Celibate Black Commitment: Report of the Third Annual National Black Sisters' Conference*, 90–100. Pittsburgh: National Black Sisters' Conference, 1971.

Grimes, Katie Walker. *Christ Divided: Antiblackness as Corporate Vice*. Minneapolis, MN: Fortress Press, 2017.

Guidry, Sister Mary Gabriella, SSF. *The Southern Negro Nun: An Autobiography*. New York: Exposition Press, 1974.

Guy-Sheftall, Beverly. *Daughters of Sorrow: Attitudes toward Black Women, 1880–1920*. Brooklyn, NY: Carlson, 1990.

Hannefin, Sister Daniel, DC. *Daughters of the Church: A Popular History of the Daughters of Charity in the United States, 1809–1987*. Brooklyn, NY: New City, 1989.

Harding, Vincent. "Toward a Black Theology." In *Black Survival: Past, Present, Future; A Report of the Second National Black Sisters' Conference*, 69–78. Pittsburgh: National Black Sisters' Conference, 1970.

Harms, Robert W. *The Diligent: A Voyage Through the Worlds of the Slave Trade*. New York: Basic Books, 2002.

Harris, Kim R. "Missa Luba, an American Mass Program, and the Transnationalism of Twentieth-Century Black Roman Catholic Liturgical Music." *Journal of Africana Religions* 9, no. 1 (2021): 1–20.

Harris, Sara. *The Sisters: The Changing World of the American Nun*. Indianapolis: Bobbs-Merrill, 1970.

Harris-Slaughter, Shirley. *Our Lady of Victory: The Saga of an African-American Catholic Community*. Privately printed, 2014.

Hartman, Saidiya V. *Scenes of Subjection: Terror, Slavery, and Self-Making in Nineteenth-Century America*. New York: Oxford University Press, 1997.

Hayes, Worth Kamili. *Schools of Our Own: Chicago's Golden Age of Black Private Education*. Evanston, IL: Northwestern University Press, 2020.

Haynes, Stephen R. *The Last Segregated Hour: The Memphis Kneel-Ins and the Campaign for Southern Church Desegregation*. Oxford: Oxford University Press, 2012.

Heng, Geraldine. *The Invention of Race in the European Middle Ages*. Cambridge: Cambridge University Press, 2018.

Herbermann, Charles George. *The Sulpicians in the United States*. New York: Encyclopedia Press, 1916.

Higginbotham, Evelyn Brooks. *Righteous Discontent: The Women's Movement in the Black Baptist Church, 1880–1920*. Cambridge, MA: Harvard University Press, 1993.

Hine, Darlene Clark, ed. *Black Women in America: An Historical Encyclopedia*. Rev. ed. New York: Oxford University Press, 2005.

Hine, Darlene Clark. *Black Women in White: Racial Conflict and Cooperation in the Nursing Profession, 1890–1950*. Bloomington: Indiana University Press, 1989.

Hine, Darlene Clark. "Rape and the Inner Lives of Black Women in the Middle West: Preliminary Thoughts on the Culture of Dissemblance." *Signs* 14, no. 4 (Summer 1989): 912–20.

Hoffman, Ronald. *Princes of Ireland, Planters of Maryland: A Carroll Saga, 1500–1782*. Rev. ed. Chapel Hill: University of North Carolina Press, 2002.

Holloran, Peter C. *Boston's Wayward Children: Social Services for Homeless Children, 1830–1930*. Rutherford, NJ: Farleigh Dickinson University Press, 1989.

Houchins, Sue E., and Ballasar Fra-Molinero, eds. *Black Bride of Christ: Chicaba, an African Nun in Eighteenth-Century Spain*. Translated by Sue E. Houchins and Ballasar Fra-Molinero. Nashville: Vanderbilt University Press, 2018.

Howlett, Rev. William J. *Life of Rev. Charles Nerinckx*. Techny, IL: Mission Press, SVD, 1915.

Hoy, Suellen. *Good Hearts: Catholic Sisters in Chicago's Past*. Urbana: University of Illinois Press, 2006.

Hughes, Cheryl C. D. *Katharine Drexel: The Riches-to-Rags Story of an American Catholic Saint*. Grand Rapids, MI: Wm. B. Eerdmans, 2014.

Hunter, Tera W. *To 'Joy My Freedom: Southern Black Women's Lives and Labors after the Civil War*. Cambridge, MA: Harvard University Press, 1997.

Iliffe, John. *The African Poor: A History*. Cambridge: Cambridge University Press, 1987.

Janet, Richard J. *In Missouri's Wilds: St. Mary's of the Barrens and the American Catholic Church, 1818 to 2016*. Kirksville, MO: Truman State University Press, 2017.

Johnson, Brigid. "Thea Bowman: Priest to the People of God." In *Thea Bowman: Handing on Her Legacy*, edited by Christian Koontz, RSM, 51–53. Kansas City, MO: Sheed and Ward, 1991.

Johnson, Karen Joy. *One in Christ: Chicago Catholics and the Quest for Interracial Justice*. New York: Oxford University Press, 2018.

Johnson, Walter. *Soul by Soul: Life inside the Antebellum Slave Market*. Cambridge, MA: Harvard University Press, 1999.

Jones, Patrick D. *The Selma of the North: Civil Rights Insurgency in Milwaukee*. Cambridge, MA: Harvard University Press, 2009.

Jones-Rogers, Stephanie E. *They Were Her Property: White Women as Slave Owners in the American South*. New Haven, CT: Yale University Press, 2019.

Jordan, Winthrop. *White over Black: American Attitudes toward the Negro, 1550–1812.* Chapel Hill: University of North Carolina Press, 1968.

Journal of the Senate of the State of Georgia, Regular Session. Atlanta, GA: Chas. P. Byrd, State Printer, 1915.

A Journey of Faith: The History of the Sisters of the Sacred Heart of Jesus (1975–2000). Privately printed, 2000.

Kaplan, Lindsay. *Figuring Racism in Medieval Christianity.* Oxford: Oxford University Press, 2019.

Kauffman, Christopher. *Tradition and Transformation in Catholic Culture: The Priests of Saint Sulpice in the United States from 1791 to the Present.* New York: Macmillan, 1988.

Kelley, Blair L. M. *Right to Ride: Streetcar Boycott and African American Citizenship in the Era of* Plessy v. Ferguson. Chapel Hill: University of North Carolina Press, 2010.

Kelly, Susan E., Carly Shinners, and Katherine Zoroufy. "Euphemia Lofton Haynes: Bringing Education Closer to the 'Goal of Perfection.'" *Notices of the American Mathematical Society* 64, no. 9 (2017): 995–1003.

Kemper, Donald J. "Catholic Integration in St. Louis, 1935–1947." *Missouri Historical Review* 73 (October 1978): 1–22.

Kendi, Ibram X. *Stamped from the Beginning: The Definitive History of Racist Ideas in America.* New York: Nation Books, 2016.

King, Martin Luther, Jr. *Why We Can't Wait.* 1963. Reprint, New York: Signet Classic, 2000.

Klein, Herbert S., and Ben Vison. *African Slavery in Latin America and the Caribbean.* 2nd ed. Oxford: Oxford University Press, 2007.

Knecht, Sharon C. *Oblate Sisters of Providence: A Pictorial History.* Virginia Beach, VA: Donning, 2007.

Koehlinger, Amy L. *The New Nuns: Racial Justice and Religious Reform in the 1960s.* Cambridge, MA: Harvard University Press, 2007.

Landers, Jane G. *Black Society in Spanish Florida.* Urbana: University of Illinois Press, 1999.

Landers, Jane G., and Barry M. Robinson, eds. *Slaves, Subjects, and Subversives: Blacks in Colonial Latin America.* Albuquerque: University of New Mexico Press, 2006.

LaRochester, Barbara Jean. "She Walked by Faith and Not by Sight." In *Thea Bowman: Handing on Her Legacy,* edited by Christian Koontz, RSM, 45–50. Kansas City, MO: Sheed and Ward, 1991.

Lavrin, Asunción. *Brides of Christ: Conventual Life in Colonial Mexico.* Stanford, CA: Stanford University Press, 2008.

Lavrin, Asunción. "Indian Brides of Christ: Creating New Spaces for Indigenous Women in New Spain." *Mexican Studies* 15, no. 2 (1999): 225–60.

Lee, Chana Kai. *For Freedom's Sake: The Life of Fannie Lou Hamer.* Urbana: University of Illinois Press, 1999.

Lernoux, Penny. *Hearts on Fire: The Story of the Maryknoll Sisters.* Maryknoll, NY: Orbis Books, 2011.

Lewis, David Levering. *W. E. B. Du Bois, 1868–1919: Biography of a Race.* New York: Henry Holt, 1994.

Lewis, David Levering, and Deborah Willis. *A Small Nation of People: W. E. B. Du Bois and African-American Portraits of Progress*. New York: Amistad, 2003.

Lightfoot, Sara. *I've Known Rivers: Lives of Loss and Liberation*. New York: Basic Books, 1994.

Lincoln, C. Eric, and Lawrence H. Mamiya. *The Black Church in the African American Experience*. Durham, NC: Duke University Press, 1990.

Lindblad, Sister Owen, OSB. "Sister Joyce Williams: A Voice for Interracial Justice." *Crossings* 35 (March 2009): 3–13.

Lindsey, Treva. *Colored No More: Reinventing Black Womanhood in Washington, D.C.* Urbana: University of Illinois Press, 2017.

Lucas, Lawrence. *Black Priest/White Church: Catholics and Racism*. New York: Random House, 1970.

Lucas, Marion B. *A History of Blacks in Kentucky from Slavery to Segregation, 1760–1891*. 2nd ed. Lexington: University Press of Kentucky, 2003.

Lucas, Patricia. "Diary of Change." In *Midwives of the Future: American Sisters Tell Their Story*, edited by Ann Patrick Ware, 171–79. Kansas City, MO: Leaven, 1985.

Lyke, James P. "On Receiving the Laetare Medal." In *Thea Bowman: Handing on Her Legacy*, edited by Christian Koontz, RSM, 30–32. Kansas City, MO: Sheed and Ward, 1991.

Lynch, Sister Patricia, SBS. *Sharing the Bread: Sisters of the Blessed Sacrament, 1891–1991*. Bensalem, PA: Sisters of the Blessed Sacrament, 1998.

Lynch, Sister Patricia, SBS. *Sharing the Bread: Sisters of the Blessed Sacrament, 1891–1991*. 2 vols. Bensalem, PA: Sisters of the Blessed Sacrament, 2001.

MacGregor, Morris J. *The Emergence of a Black Catholic Community: St. Augustine's in Washington*. Washington, DC: Catholic University of America Press, 1999.

Martin, Joan. "*Plaçage* and the Louisiana *Gens de Couleur Libre*: How Race and Sex Defined the Lifestyles of Free Women of Color." In *Creole: The History and Legacy of Louisiana's Free People of Color*, edited by Sybil Keil, 57–70. Baton Rouge: Louisiana State University Press, 2000.

Martin, Phillis M. *Catholic Women of Congo-Brazzaville: Mothers and Sisters in Troubled Times*. Bloomington: Indiana University Press, 2009.

Martínez, María Elena. *Genealogical Fictions: Limpieza de Sangre, Religion, and Gender in Colonial Mexico*. Stanford, CA: Stanford University Press, 2008.

Martinez, Richard Edward. *Padres: The National Chicano Priest Movement*. Austin: University of Texas Press, 2005.

Mason, Kenneth. *African Americans and Race Relations in San Antonio, Texas, 1867–1937*. New York: Garland, 1998.

Massingale, Bryan N. *Racial Justice and the Catholic Church*. Maryknoll, NY: Orbis Books, 2010.

Mayer, Jane, and Jill Abramson. *Strange Justice: The Selling of Clarence Thomas*. Boston: Houghton Mifflin, 1994.

McCarthy, Timothy. *The Catholic Tradition: Before and after Vatican II, 1878–1993*. Chicago: Loyola University Press, 1994.

McCauley, Bernadette. "Nuns' Stories: Writing the History of Women Religious in the United States." *American Catholic Studies* 125, no. 4 (Winter 2014): 51–68.

McDonogh, Gary Wray. *Black and Catholic in Savannah, Georgia.* Knoxville: University of Tennessee Press, 1993.

McElya, Micki. *Clinging to Mammy: The Faithful Slave in Twentieth-Century America.* Cambridge, MA: Harvard University Press, 2007.

McGreevy, John T. *Catholicism and American Freedom: A History.* New York: W. W. Norton, 2003.

McGreevy, John T. *Parish Boundaries: The Catholic Encounter with Race in the Twentieth-Century Urban North.* Chicago: University of Chicago Press, 1996.

McGuinness, Margaret M. *Called to Serve: A History of Nuns in America.* New York: New York University Press, 2013.

McGuire, Danielle L. *At the Dark End of the Street: Black Women, Rape, and Resistance; A New History of the Civil Rights Movement from Rosa Parks to the Rise of Black Power.* New York: Alfred A. Knopf, 2010.

McNally, Michael J. *Catholic Parish Life on Florida's West Coast, 1860–1968.* Madison, WI: Catholic Media Ministries, 1996.

McNamara, Jo Ann Kay. *Sisters in Arms: Catholic Nuns through Two Millennia.* Cambridge, MA: Harvard University Press, 1996.

McQueeney, W. Thomas. *Sunsets over Charleston: More Conversations with Visionaries, Luminaries and Emissaries of the Holy City.* Charleston, SC: History Press, 2012.

Medina, Lara. *Las Hermanas: Chicana/Latina Religious-Political Activism in the U.S. Catholic Church.* Philadelphia: Temple University Press, 2004.

A Member of the Order. "A Southern Teaching Order. The Sisters of Mercy of Charleston, S.C.A.D. 1829–1904." *Records of the American Catholic Historical Society of Philadelphia* 15, no. 3 (1904): 249–65.

Miller, Randall M. "A Church in Cultural Captivity: Some Speculations on Catholic Identity in the Old South." In *Catholics in the Old South: Essays on Church and Culture,* edited by Randall M. Miller and Jon Wakelyn, 11–52. Macon, GA: Mercer University Press, 1983.

Miller, Randall M. "The Failed Mission: The Catholic Church and Black Catholics in the Old South." In *Catholics in the Old South: Essays on Church and Culture,* edited by Randall M. Miller and Jon Wakelyn, 149–70. Macon, GA: Mercer University Press, 1983.

Miller, Randall M., and Jon Wakelyn, eds. *Catholics in the Old South: Essays on Church and Culture.* Macon, GA: Mercer University Press, 1983.

Minogue, Ann C. *Loretto Annals of the Century.* New York: America Press, 1912.

Misner, Barbara, SCSC. *"Highly Respectable and Accomplished Ladies": Catholic Women Religious in America, 1790–1850.* New York: Garland, 1988.

Moore, Cecilia A. "Keeping Harlem Catholic: African-American Catholics and Harlem, 1920–60." *American Catholic Studies* 114, no. 3 (2003): 3–22.

Morrow, Diane Batts. "'Making a Way Out of No Way': The Oblate Sisters of Providence Pursue Higher Education under Jim Crow." *Journal of the Black Catholic Theological Symposium* 12 (2019): 19–42.

Morrow, Diane Batts. *Persons of Color and Religious at the Same Time: The Oblates Sisters of Providence, 1828–1860*. Chapel Hill: University of North Carolina Press, 2002.

Morrow, Diane Batts. "'To My Darlings, the Oblates, Every Blessing': The Reverend John T. Gillard, S.S.J., and the Oblate Sisters of Providence." *U.S. Catholic Historian* 28, no. 1 (2010): 1–26.

Morrow, Diane Batts. "'Undoubtedly a Bad State of Affairs': The Oblate Sisters of Providence and the Josephite Fathers, 1877–1903." *Journal of African American History* 101, no. 3 (2016): 261–87.

Morton, Patricia. *Disfigured Images: The Historical Assault on Afro-American Women*. New York: Praeger, 1991.

Murchison, Gayle. "Mary Lou Williams's Hymn 'Black Christ of the Andes (St. Martin de Porres)': Vatican II, Civil Rights, and Jazz as Sacred Music." *Music Quarterly* 86, no. 4 (2002): 591–629.

Murphy, John C. *An Analysis of the Attitudes of American Catholics toward the Immigrant and the Negro, 1825–1925*. Washington, DC: Catholic University of America Press, 1940.

Murray, Paul T. "'The Most Righteous White Man in Selma': Father Maurice Ouellet and the Struggle for Voting Rights." *Alabama Review* 68, no. 1 (2015): 31–73.

Nalezyty, Susan. "History of Enslaved People at Georgetown Visitation." *U.S. Catholic Historian* 37, no. 2 (2019): 23–48.

National Black Sisters' Conference. *Black Survival: Past, Present, Future; A Report of the Second National Black Sisters' Conference*. Pittsburgh: National Black Sisters' Conference, 1970.

National Black Sisters' Conference. *Celibate Black Commitment: Report of the Third Annual National Black Sisters' Conference*. Pittsburgh: National Black Sisters' Conference, 1971.

Neary, Timothy B. *Crossing Parish Boundaries: Race, Sports, and Catholic Youth in Chicago, 1914–1954*. Chicago: University of Chicago Press, 2016.

Newcomb, Steven. *Pagans in the Promised Land: Decoding the Doctrine of Christian Discovery*. Golden, CO: Fulcrum, 2008.

Newman, Mark. *Desegregating Dixie: The Catholic Church in the South and Desegregation, 1945–1992*. Jackson: University Press of Mississippi, 2018.

New Orleans African American Museum of Art, Culture, and History. *A Celebration of Faith: Henriette Delille and the Sisters of the Holy Family*. New Orleans: New Orleans African American Museum of Art, Culture, and History, 2008.

Ngai, Mae M. *Impossible Subjects: Illegal Aliens and the Making of Modern America*. Princeton, NJ: Princeton University Press, 2005.

Nickels, Marilyn. *Black Catholic Protest and the Federated Colored Catholics, 1917–1933: Three Perspectives on Racial Justice*. New York: Garland, 1988.

Nolan, Charles E. *"Bayou Carmel": The Sisters of Mount Carmel of Louisiana, 1833–1903*. Kenner, LA: Privately printed, 1977.

Nuesse, C. Joseph. "Segregation and Desegregation at the Catholic University of America." *Washington History* 9, no. 1 (1997): 54–70.

Nyerere, Julius. "The Church's Role in Society." In *A Reader in African Christian Theology*, edited by John Paratt, 111–28. London: Society for Promoting Christian Knowledge, 1987.

Ochs, Stephen J. *A Black Patriot and a White Priest: André Cailloux and Calude Paschal Maistre in Civil War New Orleans*. Baton Rouge: Louisiana State University Press, 2000.

Ochs, Stephen J. *Desegregating the Altar: The Josephites and the Struggle for Black Priests, 1871–1960*. Baton Rouge: Louisiana State University Press, 1990.

O'Donnell, Catherine. *Elizabeth Seton: American Saint*. Ithaca, NY: Cornell University Press, 2018.

Offer, Henry J., SSJ. "Black Power—a Great Saving Grace." *American Ecclesiastical Review* 49 (September 1968): 193–201.

The Official Catholic Directory and Clergy List for the Year of Our Lord 1906. Milwaukee, WI: M. H. Wiltzius Co., 1906.

O'Malley, John. *Tradition and Transition: History Perspectives on Vatican Council II*. Wilmington, DE: Michael Glazier, 1989.

O'Toole, James M. *The Faithful: A History of Catholics in America*. Cambridge: Harvard University, 2008.

O'Toole, James M. *Passing for White: Race, Religion, and the Healy Family, 1820–1920*. Boston: University of Massachusetts Press, 2002.

O'Toole, Rachel Sarah. "(Un)Making Christianity: The African Diaspora in Slavery and Freedom." In *The Oxford Handbook of Latin American Christianity*, edited by Virginia Garrard, Susan Fitzpatrick-Behrens, and David Thomas Orique, 101–19. Oxford: Oxford University Press, 2020.

Padgett, Charles S. "'Without Hysteria or Unnecessary Disturbance': Desegregation at Spring Hill College, Mobile, Alabama, 1948–1954." *History of Education Quarterly* 41, no. 2 (2001): 167–88.

Page, David. P. "Bishop Michael J. Curley and Anti-Catholic Nativism in Florida." *Florida Historical Quarterly*, 45, no. 2 (1966): 101–17.

Pasquier, Michael. *Fathers on the Frontier: French Missionaries and the Roman Catholic Priesthood in the United States, 1789–1870*. Oxford: Oxford University Press, 2010.

Payne, Charles M. *I've Got the Light of Freedom: The Organizing Tradition and the Mississippi Freedom Struggle*. Berkeley: University of California Press, 2007.

Payne, Daniel Alexander. *History of the African Methodist Episcopal Church*. Edited by C. S. Smith. Nashville: Publishing House of the A.M.E. Sunday School Union, 1891.

Payne, Daniel Alexander. *Recollections of Seventy Years*. Nashville: A.M.E. Sunday School Union, 1888.

Perry, Sister Theresa, SSF. "An Overview of the Celibate Black Commitment." In *Celibate Black Commitment: Report of the Third Annual National Black Sisters' Conference*, 34–39. Pittsburgh: National Black Sisters' Conference, 1971.

Peters, Edward N., trans. *The 1917 or Pio-Benedictine Code of Canon Law*. San Francisco: Ignatius Press, 2001.

Pew Research Center. "Faith among Black Americans." Washington, DC. Accessed on July 28, 2021. https://www.pewforum.org/2021/02/16/faith-among-black -americans.

Pfann, Hélè M. *A Short History of the Catholic Church in Ghana*. 2nd ed. Cape Coast, Ghana: Catholic Mission Press, 1970.

Poché, Justin D. "The Catholic Citizens' Council: Religion and White Resistance in Post-war Louisiana." *U.S. Catholic Historian* 24, no. 4 (2006): 47–68.

Poole, Stafford. "The Politics of *Limpieza de Sangre*: Juan Ovando and His Circle in the Reign of Philip II." *Americas* 55, no. 3 (1999): 359–89.

Poole, Stafford, and Douglas J. Slawson. *Church and Slave in Perry County, Missouri, 1818–1865.* Lewiston, NY: Edwin Mellen, 1986.

Porter, Betty. "The History of Negro Education in Louisiana." *Louisiana Historical Quarterly* 25 (July 1942): 728–821.

Powers, Bernard E. *Black Charlestonians: A Social History, 1822–1885.* Fayetteville: University of Arkansas Press, 1994.

Pramuk, Christopher. *Hope Sings, So Beautiful: Graced Encounters across the Color Line.* Collegeville, MN: Liturgical Press, 2013.

Pyatt, Sherman E. *Burke High School, 1894–2006.* Charleston, SC: Arcadia, 2007.

Raboteau, Albert J. *A Fire in the Bones: Reflections on African-American Religious History.* Boston: Beacon Press, 1995.

Rackleff, Robert B. "Anti-Catholicism and the Florida Legislature, 1911–1919." *Florida Historical Quarterly* 50, no. 4 (1972): 356–64.

Ramey, Lynn T. *Black Legacies: Race and the European Middle Ages.* Gainesville: University Press of Florida, 2016.

Ransby, Barbara. *Ella Baker and the Black Freedom Movement: A Radical Democratic Vision.* Chapel Hill: University of North Carolina Press, 2005.

Rector, Theresa A. "Black Nuns as Educators." *Journal of Negro Education* 51, no. 3 (1982): 238–53.

René, Sister Antoinette, SCSC. "The Woman in the Nun." In *Celibate Black Commitment: Report of the Third Annual National Black Sisters' Conference,* 64–69. Pittsburgh: National Black Sisters' Conference, 1971.

Rice, Arnold S. *The Ku Klux Klan in American Politics.* New York: Haskell House, 1972.

Richardson, Joe M., and Maxine D. Jones. *Education for Liberation: The American Missionary Association and African Americans, 1890s to the Civil Rights Movement.* Tuscaloosa: University of Alabama Press, 2009.

Rickford, Russell J. *We Are an African People: Independent Education, Black Power, and the Radical Imagination.* Oxford: Oxford University Press, 2016.

Rivers, Clarence J. "Freeing the Spirit: Very Personal Reflections on One Man's Search for the Spirit in Worship." *U.S. Catholic Historian* 19, no. 2 (2001): 95–143.

Robinson, Jo Ann Gibson. *The Montgomery Bus Boycott and the Women Who Started It: The Memoir of Jo Ann Gibson Robinson.* Knoxville: University of Tennessee Press, 1987.

Rodriguez, Junius, ed. *Slavery in the United States: A Social, Political, and Historical Encyclopedia.* Santa Barbara, CA: ABC Clio, 2007.

Roediger, David R. *Working toward Whiteness: How America's Immigrants Became White: The Strange Journey from Ellis Island to the Suburbs.* New York: Basic Books, 2005.

Rosten, Leo, ed. *Religions of America: Ferment and Faith in an Age of Crisis.* Rev. ed. New York: Simon and Schuster, 1975.

Rothman, Adam, and Elsa Barraza Mendonza, eds. *Facing Georgetown's History: A Reader on Slavery, Memory, and Reconciliation*. Washington, DC: Georgetown University Press, 2021.

Rowe, Erin Kathleen. *Black Saints in Early Modern Global Catholicism*. Cambridge: Cambridge University Press, 2019.

Royko, Mike. *Boss: Richard J. Daley of Chicago*. New York: E. P. Dutton, 1971.

Ryan, Mary Perkins. *Are Parochial Schools the Answer? Catholic Education in the Light of the Council*. New York: Holt, Rinehart, and Winston, 1964.

Sabourin, Justine. *The Amalgamation: A History of the Union of the Religious Sisters of Mercy of the United States of America*. Saint Meinrad, IN: Abbey, 1976.

Salvaggio, John. *New Orleans' Charity Hospital: A Story of Physicians, Politics, and Poverty*. Baton Rouge: Louisiana State University Press, 1992.

Scally, Sister Anthony. "Two Nuns and Old Thad Stevens." *Biography* 5, no. 1 (1982): 66–73.

Schmidt, Kelly L. "Peter Hawkins and the Enslaved Community of St. Stanislaus." *Florissant Valley Quarterly* 38, no. 3 (2020): 3–5.

Schwaller, John Frederick. *The History of the Catholic Church in Latin America: From Conquest to Revolution and Beyond*. New York: New York University Press, 2011.

Schwartz, Stuart B. *Sugar Plantations in the Formation of Brazilian Society, Bahia, 1550–1835*. Cambridge: Cambridge University Press, 1985.

Sexauer, Cornelia F. "A Well-Behaved Woman Who Made History: Sister Mary Antona's Journey to Selma." *American Catholic Studies* 115, no. 4 (2004): 37–57.

Sharpley-Whiting, T. Denean. *Bricktop's Paris: African American Women in Paris between the Two World Wars*. Albany: State University of New York Press, 2015.

Shaw, Stephanie J. *What a Woman Ought to Be and to Do: Black Professional Women Workers during the Jim Crow Era*. Chicago: University of Chicago Press, 1996.

Sherwood, Grace. *The Oblates' Hundred and One Years*. New York: Macmillan, 1931.

Shields, Thomas Edward. "The Need of the Catholic Sisters College and the Scope of Its Work." *Catholic Educational Review* 17 (September 1919): 420–29.

Sisters of Saint Joseph of Cluny. *150 Years of Witness and Worship: The Sisters of St. Joseph of Cluny in the Caribbean, 1836–1986*. Port of Spain, Trinidad: Privately printed, 1986.

Smith, Charlene, and John Feister. *Thea's Song: The Life of Thea Bowman*. Maryknoll, NY: Orbis Books, 2009.

Southern, David W. *John LaFarge and the Limits of Catholic Interracialism, 1911–1963*. Baton Rouge: Louisiana State University Press, 1996.

Spalding, Thomas. "The Negro Catholic Congresses, 1889–1894." *Catholic Historical Review* 55, no. 3 (1969): 337–57.

Stepsis, M. Ursula, and Dolores Ann Liptak. *Pioneer Healers: The History of Women Religious in American Health Care*. New York: Crossroad, 1989.

Stornig, Katharina. *Sisters Crossing Boundaries: German Missionary Nuns in Colonial Togo and New Guinea, 1897–1960*. Bristol, CT: Vandenhoeck und Ruprecht, 2013.

Supan, Marita-Constance, IHM. "Dangerous Memory: Mother M. Theresa Maxis Duchemin and the Michigan Congregation of the Sisters, IHM." In *Building*

Sisterhood: A Feminist History of the Sisters, Servants of the Immaculate Heart of Mary, Monroe, Michigan, 31–68. Syracuse, NY: Syracuse University Press, 1997.

Swanson, Betsy. *Historic Jefferson Parish: From Shore to Shore*. Gretna, LA: Pelican, 2003.

Sweet, James H. "The Iberian Roots of American Racist Thought." *William and Mary Quarterly* 54, no. 1 (1997): 143–66.

Taylor, Candacy. *Overground Railroad: The Green Book and the Roots of Black Travel in America*. New York: Abrams, 2020.

Taylor, Susie King. *Reminiscences of My Life in Camp: An African American Woman's Civil War Memoir*. Athens: University of Georgia Press, 2006.

Thei, Marilyn, SC. "The Woman Elizabeth Bayley Seton, 1793–1803." *Vincentian Heritage Journal*, 14, no. 2 (1993): 227–66.

Thibodeaux, Sister Mary Roger, SBS. *A Black Nun Looks at Black Power*. New York: Sheed and Ward, 1972.

Thomas, William G., III. *A Question of Freedom: The Families Who Challenged Slavery from the Nation's Founding to the Civil War*. New Haven, CT: Yale University Press, 2020.

Thompson, Heather Ann. *Whose Detroit? Politics, Labor, and Race in a Modern American City*. Ithaca, NY: Cornell University Press, 2001.

Thompson, Margaret Susan. "Philemon's Dilemma: Nuns and the Black Community in Nineteenth-Century America; Some Findings." *Records of the American Catholic Historical Society of Philadelphia* 96, nos. 1–4 (1985): 3–18.

Thompson, Margaret Susan. "Sisterhood and Power: Class, Culture, and Ethnicity in the American Convent." *Colby Library Quarterly* 25, no. 3 (September 1989): 149–75.

[Thompson], Sister M. Francesca, OSF. "Thrice Called." In *Twice Called: The Autobiographies of Seventeen Convert Sisters*, edited by George L. Kane, 91–102. Milwaukee, WI: Bruce Publishing Company, 1959.

Traxler, Margaret, ed. *New Works of New Nuns*. St. Louis, MO: B. Herder, 1968.

US Office of Education. *Negro Education: A Study of the Private and Higher Schools for Colored People in the United States: Prepared in Cooperation with the Phelps-Stokes Fund under the Direction of Thomas Jesse Jones, Specialist in the Education of Racial Groups, Bureau of Education*. Washington, DC: Government Printing Office, 1917.

Valien, Bonita H. *The St. Louis Story: A Study of Desegregation*. New York: Anti-Defamation League of B'Nai B'rith, 1956.

Van Deusen, Nancy, ed. *The Souls of Purgatory: The Spiritual Diary of a Seventeenth-Century Afro-Peruvian Mystic, Ursula de Jesus*. Translated by Nan van Deusen. Albuquerque: University of New Mexico Press, 2004.

Venable, Cecilia Gutierrez, and the Sisters of the Holy Spirit and Mary Immaculate. *The Sisters of the Holy Spirit and Mary Immaculate*. Charleston, SC: Arcadia, 2018.

Vivian, Reverend C. T. "Black Spirituality and Revolution." In *Black Survival: Past, Present, Future; A Report of the Second National Black Sisters' Conference*, 1–14. Pittsburgh: National Black Sisters' Conference, 1970.

Walch, Timothy. *Parish School: American Catholic Parochial Education from Colonial Times to the Present*. New York: Crossroad, 1996.

Wall, Barbara Mann. *American Catholic Hospitals: A Century of Changing Markets and Missions*. New Brunswick, NJ: Rutgers University Press, 2011.

Walsh, Marie de Lordes. *The Sisters of Charity of New York, 1809–1959.* 3 vols. New York: Privately printed, 1960.

Ward, Mary. *A Mission for Justice: The History of the First African American Catholic Church in Newark, New Jersey.* Knoxville: University of Tennessee Press, 2002.

Ware, Ann Patrick, ed. *Naming Our Truth: Stories of Loretto Women.* Inverness, CA: Chardon, 1995.

Warren, Wini. *Black Women Scientists in the United States.* Bloomington: Indiana University Press, 1999.

Werntz, Mary Regina. *Our Beloved Union: A History of the Sisters of Mercy of the Union.* Westminster, MD: Christian Classics, 1989.

White, Ashli. *Encountering Revolution: Haiti and the Making of the Early Republic.* Baltimore: Johns Hopkins University Press, 2010.

White, Deborah Gray. *Ar'n't I a Woman? Female Slaves in the Plantation South.* New York: W. W. Norton, 1999.

White, Deborah Gray. *Too Heavy a Load: Black Women in Defense of Themselves, 1894–1994.* New York: W. W. Norton, 1999.

Wieneck, Henry. *An Imperfect God: George Washington, His Slaves, and the Creation of America.* New York: Farrar, Straus and Giroux, 2004.

Williams, George Washington. *History of the Negro Race in America from 1619 to 1880.* New York: G. P. Putnam's Sons, 1882.

Williams, Heather Andrea. *Self-Taught: African American Education in Slavery and Freedom.* Chapel Hill: University of North Carolina Press, 2005.

Williams, Rhonda Y. "Black Women, Urban Politics, and Engendering Black Power." In *The Black Power Movement: Rethinking the Civil Rights-Black Power Era,* edited by Peniel E. Joseph, 79–104. New York: Routledge, 2006.

Wingert, Cooper H. *Slavery and the Underground Railroad in South Central Pennsylvania.* Cheltenham, UK: History Press, 2016.

Woods, Frances Jerome, CDP. "Congregations of Religious Women in the Old South." In *Catholics in the Old South: Essays on Church and Culture,* edited by Randall M. Miller and John L. Wakelyn, 99–123. Macon, GA: Mercer University Press, 1983.

Woods, James M. *A History of the Catholic Church in the American South: 1513–1900.* Gainesville: University Press of Florida, 2011.

Wynn, Linda T. "Diane Judith Nash: A Mission for Equality Justice and Social Change." In *Tennessee Women: Their Lives and Times,* edited by Sarah Wilkerson Freeman and Beverly Bond, 1:281–304. Athens: University of Georgia Press, 2009.

Yentsch, Anne E. *A Chesapeake Family and Their Slaves: A Study in Historical Archaeology.* Cambridge: Cambridge University Press, 1994.

Zanca, Kenneth J., ed. *American Catholics and Slavery: 1789–1866.* Lanham, MD: University Press of America, 1994.

Zanini, Roberto Italo. *Bakhita: From Slave to Saint.* San Francisco: Ignatius Press, 2013.

INDEX

Page numbers in italic indicate figures.

Bishop Kelley High School (Tulsa, Oklahoma), 173

Black Catholic Clergy Caucus, 170, 174–76, 183, 185, 199, 276n33

Black Catholic Lay Caucus (Baltimore), 200, 211

Black Catholics, xv–xvi; active opposition to white supremacy, 64; armed men's protection of schools, 71; exodus from Church, 21, 47–48, 66–67, 192–94, 203, 242–44; increased rates of conversion, post-World War II, 115, 120; independent congregation, Washington DC, 247, 338n66; as "minority within a minority," 13; and racial pride, 94, 101, 106, 188, 192, 195, 197–98, 207, 210, 217, 265; refusal to abandon faith, 17–18; rejection of survival tactics, 200–201; rethinking religious experiences of, 12–17. *See also* Black sisterhoods; Black sisters; education, Black Catholic; education, Black Catholic, late twentieth century; history, Black; priests, Black; teachers, Black

Black Catholic Theological Symposium, 241

Black consciousness movement, 192, 226

#BlackLivesMatter, 254

Black Nun Looks at Black Power, A (Thibodeaux), 259

Black Panther Party, 189, 192

Black Power, 20–21, 167–99, 185; and African religious, 238–39; Afro-Creole Catholic opposition to, 179–80, 226; Christian aspects of, 188; historical continuity of, 194; masculinist ethos of, 12; white sisters' opposition to, 166. *See also* National Black Sisters' Conference (NBSC)

Black Religious Woman as Part of the Answer, The (NBSC), 202

Black sisterhoods: and choice not to pass, 59–60; as college founders and administrators, 162; growth of, 51–58; organized in protest of Jim Crow, 72–76, 73; service focus of, 160–66; subversive and emancipatory nature of, 30. *See also* future of Black sisters; National Black Sisters' Conference (NBSC)

Black sisters, 278n55, 280n78; African sisters in United States, 256; aid efforts during 1968 rebellions, 171–72; enslaved, 40, 40–41; exodus 1960s through 1980s, 192–95, 224–30,

242–44; forgotten Till generation, 142–49; as formative for Catholic Church, 265–66; health issues related to racist-induced stress, 227–28, 242, 245, 264; internalization of racism, 127–28, 170, 178–79, 184, 186; marginalization and erasure of, xvi–xviii, 33, 45, 298n84; "new Black nuns," xvii, 158, 169, 187–88; nurses, 3, 108–12, 130, 233–34; post-emancipation religious life, 46–56; resignation from teaching white students, 168–69; Southern experiences of, 142–43; temporary vows extended, 194–95, 224, 238, 242; visual record of, 6, 17; white opposition to idea of, 12, 24, 27–29, 33, 38, 47–52, 59. *See also* candidates, Black; departures of Black sisters; future of Black sisters; teachers, Black; vocations

Black Survival (NBSC), 202

Black theology, 195, 196

Black United Front (Pittsburgh), 180

Black Women's Community Development Foundation, 218

Blanc, Antoine (bishop, New Orleans), 37, 38

Bland, Sister Karen, 252

Blessed Sacrament Elementary School (Baltimore), 80–81

Blessed St. Peter Claver School (San Antonio, Texas), 59

blood purity, notions of, 27, 296n57

Bloody Sunday (Selma, Alabama), 2, 8, 134–35

Boegue, Sister Rose, 33

Bolton Act (1943), 109

Bonzano, Giovanni Vincenzo Cardinal, 93

Boston College, xvi

Bottoms, Sister Mary Kendra (Patricia), 337n55

Bouchard, Father André (priest), 210–11

Bowers, Joseph Oliver (bishop, Accra, Gold Coast), 236, 238, 240

Bowie, Mother M. Elizabeth, 279n72

Bowie State University, 228

Bowman, Father John (priest), 140

Bowman, Sister Thea (Bertha Elizabeth), 21, 127, 143–44, 233, 245, 280n76; *60 Minutes* episode, 246–47; address to US Conference of Catholic Bishops, 231–32, 246; awards for service, 248; and Institute for Black Catholic Studies, 241; untimely death of, 245–48, 264

school founded by, 43; at NBSC conference, 184, 192; Oblate Institute, 162; Philadelphia school, 47; releases of sisters from traditional duties, 160–61; and school closures, 210; stands against discrimination, 150–51; St. Augustine School (Washington, DC), 85; St. Francis Academy, 33, 101, 213–14, 219–20; St. Gabriel's Mission School (Mound Bayou, Mississippi), 139–40; Benedictines of Mary Queen Apostles, 253; and Third Order of Saint Francis, 53; transfer requests to, 141–42; white candidates, 141; white opposition to, 33, 47

O'Boyle, Patrick (archbishop, Washington, DC), 151, 201–2

O'Brien, Father John F. (priest), 116–17

O'Donnell, Catherine, 275–76n19

Offer, Father Henry J. (priest), 219–20, 332n89

Oliver, Sister Maria Mercedes (Aurelia), 132–33, 150

Operation Mississippi, 158, 164

Order of Saint Benedict (Covington, Kentucky), 52

Order of St. Benedict (St. Joseph, Minnesota), 167–68

Order of St. Francis, 142, 226

ordination, women's, 21, 190–91, 246, 249, 260

Ouellet, Father Maurice (priest), 134, 137, 156–57, 313n2

Our Colored Missions (CBMWCP), 89–90

Our Lady of Perpetual Help School (Washington, DC), 80

Our Lady of Victory (storefront Catholic mission, Detroit), 14

Our Lady of Victory Catholic School (Detroit), 150

"Pacem in Terris" (John XXIII), 149

Page, Sister Vincent de Paul (Sarah), 312n112

Pan-African Conference (London), 58

pan-Africanism, 58, 234, 235, 240

papal bulls: authorizing invasion of Africa and Americas, 265; Dum Diversas (1452), 26; Inter Caetera (1493), 26

papal encyclicals: Encyclical Mystici Corporis Christi, 105–6; In Supremo Apostolatus, 27

Parks, Mrs. P. B. (parent), 221–22

passing, in early US female religious life, 24, 42–45, 74, 104, 304n5; Belizean candidate, 116; expected of light-skinned Black applicants, 123–24; refusal of by Black sisters, 58–59, 292n211

Paul Laurence Dunbar High School (Washington, DC), 143

Paul VI, 201; Decree on Bishops' Pastoral Office, 223–24; Perfectae caritatis, 160

Pax Christi Institute, 158

Pax Christi USA, 254

Pellegrino, Sister Mary, 266, 268

Pellerin, Sister Melinda, 298n82

Perché, Napoléon-Joseph (archbishop, New Orleans), 47, 48

Perfectae caritatis (Paul VI), 160

Perry, Sister Theresa, 198, 226

Phelps, Sister Constance, 254

Phelps, Sister Jamie, 241

Philadelphia's white opposition to OSP, 47

physicians, Black, 112

Pierce v. Society of Sisters of the Holy Names of Jesus and Mary (1925), 76

Pintado family, 57, 284n66

Pittsburgh Courier, xv, xvii, 109, 167, 237

Pius IX, 284n50

Pius XI, 96, 111

Pius XII, 111, 112, 121

plaçage (concubinage system), 34–35

Plantevigne, Albert LeForest, 75

Plantevigne, Father John Joseph (priest), 66–67, 75

Plummer, Sister Phillis Marie (Deborah), 244

police violence, 189–90, 254, 255, 260, 340n104

Polk, Prentice Herman, 14

Polk, Sister Mary Reginalda (Barbara), 14, 162–63

Pollard, Sister Ella, 56

Poor Clare Nuns (England), 54

Poor Clare Sisters (Bordentown, New Jersey), 105

popes: Alexander VI, 26; Gregory XVI, 27, 33; John XXIII, 149; Nicholas V, 26; Paul VI, 160, 201, 223–24; Pius IX, 284n50; Pius XI, 96, 111; Pius XII, 111, 112, 121

Porres, Martin de, Saint, 122, 328n152

Porter, Father Herman (priest), 174, 175

Portuguese Catholics, 26–27

Rosati Kain High School (St. Louis, Missouri), 123
Rousselon, Father Etienne (priest), 37–38
Rudd, Daniel Arthur, 10, 64, 305n20
Rummel, Joseph (archbishop, New Orleans), 146, 147
Russell, William (bishop, Charleston), 66
Ryan, James Hugh (bishop), 96
Ryan, Mary Perkins, 205

Sacred Heart Catholic School (Lake Charles, Louisiana), 65, 293n17
Sacred Heart Novitiate (Nigeria), 239
Sacred Heart School (Ames, Texas), 70–71
Saint Anthony's Mission House, 75
Saint Domingue (now Haiti), 24, 27, 32, 35
Saint Francis Center (Greenwood, Mississippi), 158
Saint Gall Church (Milwaukee, Wisconsin), 163
Saint Louis University, 93, 95, 98, 106, 108–11, 162; secret admission of Oblate Sisters of Providence (1927), 93, 95, 98; admission of Black students (1944), 111; School of Medicine, 108, 111
Saint Mary's College (Winona, Minnesota), 240
Saint Rose Convent (Wisconsin), 144
saints, 5; African and other Black, 122; Augustine, 122; Bakhita, Josephine, 257; Barat, Sophie, 25, 281n8; Bowman as candidate, 248, 263–64; Delille as candidate, 264; Duchesne, Rose Philippine, 24–25, 279n72, 281n8; Iphigenia, 281n17; Lange as candidate, 264; Monica, 122; Porres, Martin de, 122; sainthood candidates, 16–17, 248, 263–64; Seton, Elizabeth, 31, 33, 275n19, 279n72, 282n30, 283–84n50; Tolton as candidate, 264. See also Drexel, Sister Katharine (later Saint)
San Alberto, Juana Esperanza de, 287n105
Sarpong, Father Peter (archbishop, Kumasi, Ghana), 240
Savannah, Georgia, xvi, 53–56, 72–76, 297n69
Savannah Morning News, 56
Savannah Tribune, 56
Schaaf, Sister Charlotte (Anne Constance), 43, 44

School Sisters of Notre Dame (SSND, Baltimore), 42, 44, 78, 80–82, 87, 110, 129; callous response to King's assassination, 172–73
School Sisters of St. Francis, 124, 127, 150, 207, 330n29
Schultz, Sister Mary, 166
Schuman, Mother M. Hildegarde, 119
Schwitalla, Father Alphonse (priest), 111
Seabrook, Sister Jennie Ellen, 114
Second Plenary Council (1866, Baltimore), 48, 49
Second Vatican Council (Vatican II), 20; call to social justice, 157–58; and civil rights movement, 135, 136; Decree on Bishops' Pastoral Office, 223–24; equal membership for Africans formalized, 27; mandate to fight white supremacy, 169; Perfectae Caritatis, 160
segregation, 274n13; of Catholic education, 4–5, 19, 31; of churches in twenty-first century, 266–67; mandated by New Orleans archbishop, 46; during Mass, 46, 78–80; of profession ceremonies, 4, 6, 7; secular state laws, 16, 73, 87, 114, 316n60; segregated menial positions for Blacks in Church, 146–48, 147, 317n62; World War II's effect on, 104–5. See also desegregation; desegregation of schools; desegregation of white sisterhoods; white sisterhoods
Selma, Alabama, 2, 260; and Black sisters, 151–59; Bloody Sunday, 2, 8, 134–35; Kansas City delegation, 153, 153; Protestant involvement in, 206; sympathy marches, 154, 179
Selma, Alabama, voting rights struggle, 133–34
seminarians, Black, 199, 211–13, 229, 233, 277n43
Senegal, 27
Senegal, Sister Mary Letitia (Florence), 138, 193, 314n22
Seton, Elizabeth (Saint), 31, 33, 275n19, 279n72, 282n30, 283–84n50
Seton Hill College for Women (Pennsylvania), 91
sexual abuse in Church, 78, 251, 298n77, 323n42, 338n66
sexual terrorism, 8, 11–121, 78, 298n77; plaçage system, 34–35

Shaw, John (archbishop, New Orleans), 89
Shealey, Sister Nativa (Juanita), 312n113, 339n79
Shehan, Cardinal Lawrence (Baltimore), *163*, 214
Short, Sister Mary Laurentia (Catherine), 94–95, *95*
Signs of Soul (NBSC newsletter), 239
Simon, Sister Jayne Marie, 192, 239
Sinsinawa Dominican Sisters (Wisconsin), 14, 59, 162–63
sister, as term, xiii
Sister Act film franchise, xv, xvii, 17, 248
Sister Formation Institute, 225
Sisters, Servants of the Immaculate Heart of Mary (IHM, Detroit), 14–16, 43, 43–44, 60, 87, 213
Sisters of the Blessed Sacrament (SBS), 16, 54–55, 68, 74, 86, 91, 99, 100, *110*, 136, 146, 241, 279n72; Haynes as first Black president, 252; at NBSC conference, 184; resistance to NBSC, 181
Sisters of Charity of Nazareth (Kentucky), 65, 66, 68, 150; Colored Industrial Institute (Arkansas), 68
Sisters of Charity (SC), 184, 282n30, 283–84n50; as slaveholders, 33, 275n19
Sisters of Charity of Cincinnati (SC, Ohio), 15, 143
Sisters of Charity (SC, Emmitsburg, Maryland), 31, 33, 178, 275n19
Sisters of Charity (SC, Leavenworth, Kansas), 65, 302n145
Sisters of Charity (SC, Mobile, Alabama), 65, 294n19
Sisters of Charity of New York (SC, Bronx, New York), 44–45, 154, *155*, 310n91
Sisters of Charity of Our Lady of Mercy (Charleston, South Carolina), 62, 65–66
Sisters of Charity of Seton Hill (SCSH), 87, 89–91, *90*, 161, 301n132
Sisters of Charity of St. Augustine (Cleveland, Ohio), 128–29
Sisters of Charity of the Blessed Virgin Mary (BVM), 80, 310n95
Sisters' Conference on Negro Welfare, 109, *110*, 111
Sisters of Divine Providence, 173, 176–77

Sisters for Christian Community (SFCC), 252
Sisters of the Holy Child of Jesus (SHCJ), 178, 279n72
Sisters of the Holy Family (SSF), 23, 34–41, 36, 56–58, 64, 85, 284n64, 285n75; African ministries, 236, 237; as Afro-Creole, 25–26, 29, 35, 37, 39–41, 81; after emancipation, 51–53; on archbishop's domestic and cooking staff, 146–48, *147*; and Chicago, 99–100; and civil rights–related efforts, 155, 161–62; decline in membership, 334n111; desegregation efforts by, 137–38; desegregation politics, response to, 146–48, *147*; and education in 1970s, 210, 222–23; and FCC conferences, 94; former students, 65, 138, 176; habits denied to, 38; and higher education, 88–91; at Holy Redeemer School (San Antonio, Texas), 81; King's assassination, response to, 171; Lafon Home for Boys, 58; militancy of sisters, 145–46; at NBSC conference, 184, 193; Old Folks Home, 58, 286n91; post-emancipation experience, 46–47; restrictive admissions policy, 40–41; Sacred Heart School (Ames, Texas), 70–71; School for Boys, 58; public silence about white violence, 146; slaveholding elites in, 39, 285n78, 286n95; St. Mary's Academy for (Colored) Girls, 35, 40, 46, 56, 68, 83; summer normal school attendance, 88–91, *90*, 301n132
Sisters of the Holy Family of Nazareth (CSFN), 131–32
Sisters of the Holy Ghost (later Spirit) and Mary Immaculate (San Antonio, Texas), 59, 81; (Pascagoula, Mississippi), 82–83
Sisters of the Holy Names of Jesus and Mary (SNJM), 69, 123, 143
Sisters of the Holy Spirit (SSpS), 238, 336n22; *See also* Missionary Sisters, Servants of the Holy Spirit (Techny, Illinois)
Sisters of the Humility of Mary, 189
Sisters of Loretto at the Foot of the Cross (SL) (Kentucky), 28–29, 65, 109, 282–83n38, 282n31
Sisters of Notre Dame (SND), 243–45; sisters prevented from joining NBSC, 243, 244
Sisters of Notre Dame de Namur (SNDdeN), 14, 123, 128, 165, 178, 224; African candi-

CPSIA information can be obtained
at www.ICGtesting.com
Printed in the USA
LVHW081943020722
722646LV00013B/405